W9-CLI-947

poodle clipping and grooming

and grooming

THE INTERNATIONAL REFERENCE

by

Shirlee Kalstone

Photographs by Larry Kalstone

Illustrations in the American chapters by Clinton Tingler
Illustrations in the International chapter by Maud Nilsson

THIRD EDITION

HOWELL
BOOK
HOUSE

Howell Book House

Hungry Minds, Inc.
909 Third Avenue
New York, NY 10022

For general information on Hungry Minds' books in the U.S., please call our Consumer Customer Service department at 800-762-2974. For reseller information, including discounts and premium sales, please call our Reseller Customer Service department at 800-434-3422.

Photographs by Larry Kalstone

Illustrations in the American chapters: Clinton Tingler

Illustrations in the International chapter: Maud Nilsson

Charts in the International chapter: Kitty Dekeersgieter

Library of Congress Cataloging-in-Publication Data

Kalstone, Shirlee.
   Poodle clipping and grooming : the international reference / Shirlee Kalstone.
     p. cm.
   Includes bibliographical reference (p.).
   ISBN 0-87605-265-0
   1. Poodles. 2. Dogs--Grooming. I. Title.

SF429.P85 K325 2000
636.72'83--dc21   00-058195

Manufactured in the United States of America

10 9 8 7 6 5 4 3 2

Third Edition

Book and cover design by pink design, inc. (www.pinkdesigninc.com)

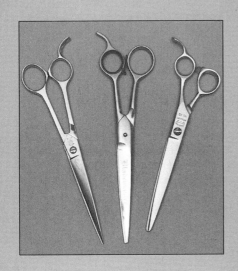

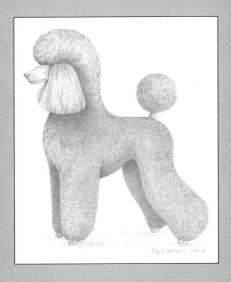

ACKNOWLEDGMENTS

As the founder of Intergroom and organizer of the show for 18 years and as an international competition judge, I have had the opportunity to meet and get to know some of the most talented professional groomers and dog show handlers in the world. Many of them and their outstanding work are pictured in this book.

People from many different countries were consulted during the writing of this book, and I am especially grateful to the following for their participation, information, advice or for supplying photographs.

Thank you to everyone . . . *merci beaucoup . . . grazie . . . gracias . . . danke schön . . . arigato . . . spasibo.* I apologize if I neglected to mention anyone.

FROM THE UNITED STATES

Mike Robertson, of Fine Edge II (who not only supplied important technical information about shears, but also supplied the shears for us to photograph); Christina Pawlosky (and her Standard Poodle Ch. Kaylen's Lamarka Cuervo Time); Loretta Marchese (and her Standard Poodle Dassin Divine Miss Em); Elizabeth Paul; Susan Zecco; Ann Martin; Kathleen Putman; Pam Lauritzen (whose information in *Pet Stylist* magazine emphasizing scissoring techniques and the art of geometrics in canine design were most helpful); Diane Betelak; Carol Kokkeler; Jerry Schinberg; Kathy Rose; Teri DiMarino; Christine DeFilippo; John Stazko; Joseph Villani (and the Nash Academy of Animal Arts in Edgewater, New Jersey, where some of the photographs were taken); Mary Bloom; Clint Tingler; Susan Pratt; Karen Long MacLeod and *Groom and Board* magazine; Sally Liddick and *Groomer-to-Groomer* magazine; Dina Perry; Ianthe Bloomquist; Jean Hitchins; Scott Wasserman; Marea Tully; Linda Kay O'Neill; Racille Karelitz; Susan Tufari (and her Standard Poodle Quay); Danielle Inzinna (and her Standard Poodle Balzac); Wendell Sammet; *Poodle Variety* magazine; Del Dahl; Anne Rogers Clark and The Poodle Club of America; Nancy and Steve Apatow; all the manufacturers of grooming products and equipment who supplied information and photographs; and, most especially, my husband, Larry Kalstone.

FROM BELGIUM

Kitty Dekeersgieter, Jean-Francois Vanaken, Carinne Lewi and Monique Janssens

FROM CANADA

Shaunna Bernardin

FROM THE CZECH REPUBLIC

Vera Buckova, Miroslav Bucek and Romana Divisova

FROM ENGLAND

Peter Young and Anita Bax

FROM FRANCE

Denys Lorrain, Martial Carre, Vincent Pastor, Mijo Klein and Sylvie Guinchard

FROM GERMANY

Christina Gregor (Oster Professional Products) and Thomas Hartkopf (EHASO)

FROM HOLLAND

Jetty van der Hulst and Mirjam van den Bosch

FROM ITALY

Umberto Lehmann, Lorena Merati, Paola Acco and Ferruccio Soave

FROM JAPAN

Masahiro and Naoko Tsujihara

FROM NEW ZEALAND

Sheila Morris

FROM NORWAY

Maud Nilsson (especially for her magnificent illustrations for Chapter 24, "The International Scene")

FROM RUSSIA

David Levin, Vladimir Soloyviev and Roman Fomine

FROM SPAIN

Javier Blanco, David Allan and Alex Artero

FROM SWEDEN

Anders Rosell

introduction

This book is written for Poodle owners who would like to clip and care for their own pets, for prospective show exhibitors and for professional groomers. Anyone who is generally interested can learn how to set patterns and to scissor by careful study of the step-by-step, illustrated instructions provided.

Getting Acquainted

The fact that the Poodle is and has been one of the most popular breeds in the United States and many other countries is unquestionably true because Poodles are splendid animals. They come in a variety of sizes and colors, they are intelligent, they are wonderful companions, they are elegant looking and they can be trimmed in a variety of styles to suit their owners' lifestyle and personal preferences, as well as the dog's own comfort.

For hundreds of years the Poodle has existed very much as we know the breed today. The Poodle undoubtedly originated as a water retriever, and it has been speculated that he might have been the original Water Spaniel. The Standard Poodle is the oldest of the three varieties; the smaller varieties (Miniature and Toy) became well known as trick dogs in circuses, as truffle dogs and as noble companions.

The show trims that we see in the ring today, the Continental and English Saddle, are not just modern-day fads—they are part of the Poodle's history. The age-old tradition of trimming the Poodle to resemble a lion stemmed from making his retrieving work more functional. When the long coat got wet, it became heavy; the area behind the ribs was trimmed to make movement easier, but small tufts of hair were left to cover the joints and keep them warm. The hair was left long over the rib cage to protect the heart and chest from the cold.

As time passed, grooming styles have come and gone. The old lion trim became the predecessor of the traditional show trims of today. Through the years, the dog fancy has seen some smart pet styles that emphasized the elegance of the Poodle become fashionable; some other pet clips were so bizarre that they swiftly lost favor, thank heavens!

Whatever variety you own, Poodles require much more attention than most other breeds. They must be brushed, bathed and clipped regularly because if they are not cared for, they become shaggy. Regular grooming is important not only to make a Poodle look better, but also for his good health and mental fitness. Most professionals will agree that when a dog is groomed regularly, he is less likely to suffer from mats, tangles, skin problems, ear infections, overgrown toenails or infestation by external parasites. In addition, Poodles are proud animals. They know when they look their best, and they really enjoy the attention and praise people give them when they appear perfectly groomed.

This book concentrates on the art of clipping, setting patterns and scissoring. If you intend to show your Poodle in the conformation ring, there are instructions for the four recognized show clips. The first is the Puppy Clip, which is acceptable only for dogs under 12 months of age. Once a Poodle is one year old, he must be shown only in the English Saddle or Continental clip. Neither clip is practical for pets, as they require a great deal of expert and time-consuming coat care. In the Stud Dog and Brood Bitch classes and in a noncompetitive Parade of Champions, a Poodle may be shown in the Sporting Clip.

Pet Poodles can be trimmed into hundreds of different styles or variations. Those that are chic and smart and emphasize the beauty of the Poodle are included in this

book; those that are grotesque and attempt to make the elegant Poodle look like a monkey or other farcical object *are not included!* Among the currently popular pet styles are the Sporting, Lamb, Retriever, Miami (or Summer), Dutch (and some of its variations), Desi, Sweetheart, Swirl and Panda. Throughout the book, the focus is placed on giving a professional finish. This is done by good scissoring, a task that requires a great deal of practice and, when perfected, makes the difference between an unexceptional job and a really artistic finish. If you can scissor well and are familiar with the Poodle Standard, you can make a structurally sound Poodle look like perfection and minimize faults on a Poodle that is not so sound.

To be an excellent groomer, you must first know what a good Poodle looks like.

Before you trim a Poodle, always evaluate it. If the dog is structurally sound, wonderful! Your job is to trim it attractively. A structurally sound Poodle will look good in any style clip if it is done correctly. But can you tell if your Poodle is sound? Can you determine if your dog has major or minor faults? If he does, there are ways to camouflage many imperfections so that they don't stand out like a sore thumb. A talented groomer probably can make an average Poodle look much finer than a near-perfect Poodle trimmed by an amateurish groomer.

Whether you use this book to learn to clip your own dog or to eventually become a professional groomer, first familiarize yourself with the description of the ideal of the breed. This book contains the Poodle Club of America's Illustrated Breed Standard in its entirety. Following the breed standard is a chapter containing some photographs, additional illustrations and grooming tips that will help you to disguise faults and produce a more balanced trim.

If you study these suggestions well, you should eventually be able to determine what must be done to make each dog look his or her best.

Remember, nothing will help you to become an expert groomer more than practice. If you are a beginner, spend at least a few minutes each day working on your dog, even if it means only brushing and combing. Dogs can sense inexperience by the way they are handled, and your dog may try every trick to discourage you when you first begin clipping. By working on your dog a few minutes each day, you will pick up speed in your scissoring and find that you are beginning to handle your clipper like a professional. Eventually, your Poodle will develop confidence in you and stop fussing. He'll realize that the more he cooperates with you, the faster the clipping goes.

Good luck to all you prospective groomers. When your Poodle walks beside you impeccably groomed and someone asks who clipped him, what more satisfying answer can you give than, *"I did it myself!"*

How To Use This Book

A STEP-BY-STEP GUIDE FOR BEGINNERS

If you are a beginner, study the following suggestions before you attempt to do any clipping or scissoring.

1) Read and re-read the section titled "15 Tips for Successful Grooming," in this introduction. It sets the foundation to begin grooming your own Poodle and gives general information to help you understand how to handle and control your dog.

2) Study Chapter 2, "Selecting the Right Equipment," carefully. All the tools necessary for Poodle grooming are described at length. Using the correct tools can make grooming even more enjoyable for both you and your dog. Most beginners tend to overbuy equipment; before you purchase haphazardly, you must think about the kind of grooming you want to do. Do you want only to clip your pet Poodle at home, do you eventually want to groom and show your dog or do you want to become a professional groomer? Today there is such a dazzling array of equipment to choose from that it can be confusing when you set out to buy, and this chapter will help you understand why and how the various tools are used.

While it will be more economical to groom your Poodle at home than to have him groomed professionally, do not try to save money when you are purchasing your grooming tools. Your decision to groom your own dog or go on to become a professional is simply a matter of quality and quantity. Even for home grooming, *quality* should be the most important consideration in deciding what to buy. Basically, you need an electric clipper, some extra blades that clip the hair to various lengths, a few brushes and combs, several types of shears and a hair dryer. Purchase the finest equipment you can afford. Inexpensive tools are not a real savings; they don't last as long as their superior and more expensive counterparts. *Quantity* comes into play as you go on to become a professional. Then you can add the things that make your job easier: spare clippers, blades, shears, brushes and combs; heavy-duty hair dryers; hydraulic or electric tables; professional bath tubs; and the like.

3) Study Chapter 9, "The Official AKC Standard for the Poodle." A breed Standard describes the ideal specimen, point by point, and is composed of sections defining general appearance, head, neck, shoulder placement, body, hindquarters, legs and feet, tail, coat color and texture, size and how the dog should gait. After studying this verbal image of the breed, examine the illustrations and learn Poodle rights and wrongs. Poodle patterns are set by the bone structure of each dog. For this reason, not all Poodles are clipped in the same manner. Expert groomers evaluate every dog they groom, first deciding what the dog's faults are and what must be done to minimize these imperfections and make him look his best. Some clips are more flattering for dogs with major faults, while structurally sound dogs can be trimmed into any pattern.

4) Study Chapter 3, "Coat Care for the Pet Poodle." Learning how to brush and comb your Poodle's coat correctly should be the first actions you attempt. Your dog must be thoroughly brushed out and combed before bathing, fluff drying, clipping and scissoring.

5) Study Chapters 4 and 5, "Bathing the Pet Poodle" and "Fluff Drying the Pet Poodle," respectively. Along with thorough brushing and combing, a correct shampoo, rinse and fluff dry set the stage for final clipping and scissoring.

6) Begin clipping the feet first since this will be the most troublesome area. Before you begin, study the correct way to clip the feet (see chapter 12). Look at the photographs and illustrations in the clipping sections (chapters 18 through 24). To get the feel of your clipper, practice going over the feet once or twice without turning the motor on. Then, with your Poodle in the proper position on a sturdy grooming table (with nonslip top), under good light, begin slowly. If you are using clippers for the first time, remember to hold the blade flat against the area you are clipping. Never point the blade into the skin. Don't be too concerned with getting a perfect job the first few times. Practice several minutes a day on the feet, and your work will gradually improve as you go along. Clipping the feet may be difficult at first because the dog senses your inexperience in handling this ticklish part of his body.

7) Trim the tail next. If you read the instructions in chapter 14 carefully, clipping the tail should be no problem. Remember that the underside of the tail is a sensitive spot and subject to clipper burn. Don't use a fine blade on this area. When scissoring the pompon at the end of the tail, think of circles and balls, and try to trim a round rather than a pine-tree shape.

8) Clip the Poodle's face next. Study the instructions and photographs in chapter 13 carefully. Then, with your Poodle in a sitting position on the grooming table, begin clipping. Don't be concerned with getting an artistic finish the first few times you clip the face. This can be a very sensitive area for beginners, so don't try to progress too rapidly. Take your time. Try to gain the dog's confidence by being firm, *never cross*, and practice the control tips when the dog begins to fuss.

9) Clip the neck according to the directions in chapter 13. The underside of the neck and throat also are tender spots, subject to clipper burn. Never use a very fine blade on these areas.

10) Clip the stomach according to the directions in chapter 15.

11) The next major step is learning how to scissor. Review the information about shears and the scissoring process in chapter 2. If you are scissoring your Poodle for the first time, choose a good-looking, easy-to-maintain style like the Puppy (pet), Sporting or Kennel to begin with. Basically, these are trims in which the feet, face and tail are clipped, and the rest of the dog is clipped or scissored to follow the outline of the dog; this leaves an even amount of hair on the body, with slightly longer hair on the legs. Follow instructions for the clip you select, and always work with the finest-quality scissors you can afford. The real difference between amateur and professional grooming is in the scissoring. Actually, no matter what pattern you choose for your Poodle—one of the easy-to-maintain styles previously mentioned or a more creative pattern—your goal is to produce a balanced and symmetrical finished trim. Balance and symmetry, from a scissoring standpoint, means that all proportions of a dog are in dynamic harmony: the head with the body and tail, the front to the back, side to side, top to bottom. A balanced dog presents a well-proportioned appearance. One feature is never so outstanding that it overshadows another. In other words, *every part of the dog is in harmonious relationship, each one fitting together and looking aesthetically pleasing.* (If scissoring is difficult, you can still produce a lovely and uniform finish by using snap-on combs; see page 19.)

12) Now, if you desire a more artistic look, you are ready to try pattern setting. Begin with one of the easy patterns, such as the Miami (or Summer), Town and Country, or Banded Dutch. Take your time! When you have gained confidence in your clipping ability and have mastered the easy patterns, then and only then should you progress to the more difficult ones if those are what you ultimately envision for your Poodle. Before selecting a pattern, consider your Poodle's size, conformation and coat texture. Dogs with excellent coat texture and no glaring structural faults look good in any clip, but fancy patterns are not a good choice for puppies or for adult Poodles with soft coats or major faults. Remember balance and symmetry when you scissor!

13) Each time you groom your Poodle, follow this sequence:

a) Thoroughly brush and comb your dog to remove all tangles. Check behind the ears, in the "armpits" under the front legs and all the other hard-to-reach places where mats form. Check the skin thoroughly for traces of external parasites or other problems. Feel the skin and coat. Is the skin supple or dry? Is the hair soft and shiny or brittle? Are there any inflamed areas or lumps under the skin? Your hands-on regular brushing sessions gives you the opportunity to inspect your dog for early warnings of health problems and to report them to your veterinarian.

b) Trim and file the nails.

c) Check the ears. Remove any excess hair that is growing in the ear canal, and clean the ears.

d) Check the anal glands and express them if necessary.

e) Shampoo and rinse your Poodle. If necessary, after the bath, apply creme rinse, skin conditioner or moisturizer. *Clean hair is the foundation for the finished trim!*

f) Fluff dry the hair.

g) When your Poodle is dry, comb once again to fluff out the coat.

h) Clip the feet, face and tail.

i) Do all body clipping (neck, stomach and pattern).

j) Do body scissoring work. Start at the back legs, then work forward, scissoring the hindquarters, back, over the rib cage and under the chest, shoulders and front legs.

k) Scissor the topknot, and finish the ears.

Professional groomers generally follow this step-by-step routine, although most prefer to clip the feet, face, tail and sometimes the body pattern in the "rough" before brushing and shampooing the dog. Clipping these areas beforehand saves time and helps the Poodle to dry faster, but they must be reclipped after the dog is dry. Professional groomers always use old shears and clipper blades for rough work; newly sharpened blades and expensive "finishing" shears will be quickly dulled on dirty, matted hair. The sequence you select for home grooming is a matter of personal preference, but remember that you must never do any major pattern clipping or scissoring on a dirty Poodle. Professionals achieve those velvety-looking results by working on clean, well-rinsed, fluff-dried hair.

14) Study the photographs and scissoring instructions in Chapter 16, "Shaping the Topknot," before you scissor your Poodle's head. The topknot should be shaped round and usually is left as full as possible. The front of the topknot always should be even with the eyes. To achieve this rounded look, no hair should be taken off above the level of the eyes when the face is clipped. The mistake most beginners make is clipping or scissoring off the hair directly above the eyes to keep it from falling forward. Doing so destroys the Poodle's expression, and the hair will take *months* to grow back.

15) If you are planning to show your Poodle, concentrate on the following chapters: Chapter 18, "The Changing Fashions of Show Trims"; Chapter 19, "Care of the Poodle in Show Coat"; and Chapter 20, "The Three AKC-Recognized Show Clips."

15 Tips for Successful Grooming

FROM BEGINNER TO EXPERT

1) Use the proper equipment. Chapter 2, "Selecting the Right Equipment," will familiarize you with Poodle grooming tools, what each will do and how to use it correctly.

2) Good grooming behavior should be taught at an early age—and can be—if you remember two basic rules:

- Dogs learn by repetition, correction and praise.
- Dogs should know grooming as a pleasant experience, not something to dread.

This is a fine time to read obedience training books and learn the difference between positive and negative reinforcement.

3) A dog's attitude toward grooming depends on how you handle it and what happens during the first few sessions. It is imperative to establish a regular grooming routine as early as possible, ideally when your Poodle is a puppy. Puppies are like sponges in that they will quickly absorb any lessons given to them. Proceed with patience and gentleness. The lessons you give should all be positive ones, because the bond that you establish with your Poodle in the first few months is the one that will continue throughout your dog's lifetime with you.

4) The sooner you start brushing, looking inside the ears, touching the feet and so forth, the easier it will be to get your dog accustomed to the grooming process. And a dog that enjoys being groomed is much easier to control. The "hands on" during the regular grooming sessions will also accustom your dog to the kind of handling he'll receive by a veterinarian, professional handler or groomer. More importantly, it gives you the opportunity to inspect your dog for early warnings of health problems and to report them to your veterinarian.

5) A firm grooming table with a nonslip rubber top is an essential aid for establishing good habits. Because dogs learn by repetition, each time you brush or comb your dog or perform any phase of grooming, do it on the grooming table. Eventually your dog will learn that he has to behave when he is being groomed. Never use an unsteady table; your dog will be frightened and try to jump off. If you own a Toy or Standard Poodle, invest in an adjustable grooming table for your own comfort so that you won't have to bend over or stand on tip-toe.

6) Never put your Poodle on a grooming table and leave him there unattended. Ideally, your table should be equipped with a grooming post and loop (see chapter 2); basically the post is an **L**-shaped metal rod that can be clamped or bolted to your table. At the end of the rod, there is a loop (made of nylon or leather) which adjusts to fit the dog's neck, holds his head up and keeps him from moving about. This gives your dog more confidence, and it also frees both of your hands to do other work. More importantly, it prevents a dog (especially a young puppy) from walking or jumping off the edge of the table and becoming seriously injured.

7) Groom in a room with adequate lighting. Have light coming from above and behind you. This is especially important when clipping dark-colored Poodles.

8) Your grooming area should be quiet. Don't allow your Poodle to be distracted by other pets, children or loud noises.

9) Teach your Poodle to lie on his side while he is being brushed. This is important if the dog will be shown in the breed ring.

10) Don't expect your Poodle to stand perfectly still for hours on the grooming table when you first begin grooming him. Young puppies have short attention spans and will not stand still very long. If your Poodle is young, spend no more than 15 minutes at a time grooming him. A good way to begin table training is to stand the puppy on the table for brushing. Place your free hand under his stomach for support (and to give him confidence), then quickly run a brush through his coat. Speak quietly and reassuringly to the puppy; raising your voice will only stress both you and the puppy. Praise him often, and let him experience brushing as something pleasant. At first, he may squirm about, but if you repeat this procedure every day for several weeks, he will learn to stand quietly and behave. As the dog matures and his grooming takes more time, he will enjoy the attention.

11) Start getting your puppy accustomed to having other parts of his body handled too. Hold the paws gently in your hands and run your fingers over and between the toes. Tickle him behind the ears, then take hold of each ear and look inside. Touch his face softly, then try to open his mouth and examine the teeth. Later, when it's time to shorten the nails, clean the ears and check the eyes and the teeth, your dog will be much more cooperative.

12) Learn to be firm during the grooming session. *Being firm does not mean being rough.* Never slap, yell at, or inhumanely treat your Poodle to make him behave on the grooming table. If he disobeys, correct him, and as soon as he does what you want, *praise him lavishly!* Use a firm (not angry) tone of voice when making corrections and use a word such as *No* or *Stop,* but always use the same word so that your dog understands what you want him to do. Be consistent. Don't let the dog get away with something one day and then reprimand him for doing the same thing the next day. If a frightening mistake is accidentally made, comfort your dog *immediately.* Never let your Poodle think you intended to cause harm. Immediate comfort and sympathy will help make the dog trust you again.

13) Poodles are sensitive to voice inflections. If you lose patience, immediately stop what you are doing and let the dog off the table. *Never let your dog experience grooming as an unpleasant experience.* Postpone the session until another time if you think you're losing control.

14) Don't talk "baby talk" or play with your Poodle while he is on the grooming table. He's there to be groomed, not to play games. Reward him with lavish praise or a favorite treat after a successful grooming session.

15) If your Poodle is frightened by the sound of clippers at first, hold him in your lap, rest the clippers near his back (with the motor running) and speak quietly and reassuringly, and he should soon become accustomed to the noise.

Figure 1-1. Mr. R. W. Brown, premier groomer at the Dog's Toilet Club, London, England, 1896.

The Poodle is a very ancient breed. There is some controversy over its origins, although most cynologists believe that it originated in Eastern Germany or Russia. Whatever its native land, the Poodle was known in many European countries and, as far back as the breed can be traced, trimming has been a continued practice. Poodle-like dogs with large lion manes and closely trimmed hindquarters appear on ancient Greek and Roman coins, and in the time of Emperor Augustus, around 30 A.D., they were carved on monuments and tombs, resembling, in a primitive way, their modern-day counterparts.

Clipped Poodles are conspicuous in Medieval illuminated manuscripts, fifteenth-century engravings by Albrecht Durer and paintings from the fifteenth, sixteenth and seventeenth centuries, most notably, two scenes of *The Story of Patient Griselda* by Pintoricchio (1454–1513), *Tobit and His Dog* by Martin de Vos (1531–1603), and *The Dancing Dog* by Jan Steen (1629–79). Steen, who delighted in painting animated scenes of merrymaking, has given us one of the most charming representations of a Miniature Poodle. As a young boy plays a flute, the Poodle dances on his hind legs in a tavern courtyard while smiling guests and servants enjoy the scene. The dog's hindquarters are clipped, and he sports a ring of hair and a pompon on his tail.

Numerous authorities believe that the Poodle is closely related to or was the old Water Dog or *Canis familiaris aquaticus*. Early canine historians such as Dr. Caius (1570), Conrad Gessner (1553), Edward Topsell (1607), Gervaise Markham (1621), Aldrovandus (published posthumously in 1637) and Cirino (1653), wrote about and showed crude woodcuts of a water dog with clipped hindquarters and a tuft of hair at the end of the tail. The Standard Poodle is the oldest of the three varieties; the smaller types became well known as trick and stunt dogs in circuses, as truffle dogs and as noble companions. Authorities agree that large Poodles were used in Europe for centuries to retrieve game from water. Stonehenge, the great nineteenth-century British cynologist, describes the Poodle as the favorite water dog of continental fowlers in France, Belgium, Holland, Denmark, Germany and Russia. There can be no doubt that the Poodle's name in different languages suggests a water dog: *Pudel* (his German name) comes from the verb *pudelin*, meaning to splash in water, and *Caniche* (his French name) is a derivation of *Canard Chien*, or duck dog.

The long-practiced custom of shaving the hindquarters undoubtedly evolved because the Poodle's coat was somewhat of a hindrance in the water. The area behind the ribs was trimmed smooth to facilitate efficient swimming. On the shaved hindquarters, small tufts of hair were left to cover the joints and keep them warm. The long hair over the neck, shoulders, ribs and chest protected the heart and added buoyancy while swimming. When the dog emerged from the water with his quarry, the thick, woolly mane coat provided warmth. The later fashion of tying up the topknot was also related to the Poodle's retrieving work. The dog could see his quarry better when his forelocks were fastened above the head instead of falling into his eyes, so owners began to use pieces of brightly colored ribbon to tie back the long hair. This custom also permitted an owner to locate or follow a particular dog as it worked in the water.

An Early Printed Reference to Poodle Trimming

One of the earliest printed references to trimming was in 1621, in *Hunger's Prevention or the Arte of Fowling by Water and Lande* by Gervaise Markham, a book describing the use and training of Water Dogges. Markham tells us:

> *Now for the cutting and shaving him from the Navill downward, or backward, it is two wayes well to be allowed of, that is, for Sommer hunting or for the water; because these Water Dogges naturally are ever most laden with haires on the hinder parts, nature as it were labouring to defend that part most which*

is continually to bee employed in the most extremity, and because the hinder parts are even deeper in the water than the fore parts, therefore nature hath given them the greatest armour of haire to defend the wette and coldness; yet this defence in Sommer time by the violence of the heat of the Sunne, and the greatnesse of the Dogges labor is very noysome and troublesome . . . And so likewise in the matter of water, it is a very heavy burthen to the Dogge and makes him to swimme lesse nimbly and slower . . . But for the cutting or shaving of a Dogge all quite over from the Foote to the Nostrill, that I utterly dislike, for it not only takes from the generall benefits which Nature hath lent him, but also brings such tendernesse and chilnesse all over his body, that the water in the end will grow Yrksome unto him . . .

Markham includes a woodcut of such a trimmed dog (see Figure 1-2) with bird in mouth, and he describes it as "the perfect Water Dogge."

Figure 1-2. "The perfect Water Dogge," woodcut engraving from Gervaise Markham's book *Hungers Prevention*, London, 1621. Notice the bird in the dog's mouth.

Prince Rupert and Boye

One of the first printed references to a Poodle appeared in 1635 in England, when Prince Rupert of the Palatinate helped Charles I in fighting the Roundheads. Rupert brought along his white Standard Poodle named Boye. The dog was described as having "eyes large and almond shaped like genuine black diamonds; nose, shiny, anthracite black; coat bursting with whiteness." Many pamphlets were written about Boye's exploits and extrasensory abilities. He was reported to speak many languages and to put a hex on the enemy. One historical record, preserved in the Bodleian Library at Oxford, entitled *Observations on Prince Rupert's White Dog Called Boye*, describes the Prince in council chambers with Boye sitting on a

table by his side, and how, during debate, Rupert would turn frequently and kiss the dog. This gallant dog was killed in the Battle of Marston Moor in 1644, and it is written that all witches, sorcerers, the Pope and the Devil were invited to mourn at his funeral.

The French Influence

Although Poodles originally were trimmed for occupational and hygienic reasons, when it became the custom to trim them into more outlandish styles, the flair of the French emerged. In eighteenth-century France, the ability to extravagantly transform a dog's appearance by styling and arranging his hair made the Poodle especially fashionable with the aristocracy. During the reign of Louis XVI (1774–92), the art of Poodle trimming became extremely decorative. Professional canine stylists called *demoiselles* practiced their trade along the banks of the Seine and in the streets of Paris, and no clip was too outrageous or difficult for them to perfect. They cut out coats of arms, lovers' knots, monograms and fleurs-de-lis in the Poodles' hair and ornamented them with rakish moustaches and imperiales (small pointed beards on the underjaw, as shown in Figure 1-3) or high pompadours similar to those worn by the ladies

of the royal court. Grooming a Poodle became as time-consuming as coiffeuring a human. Dogs had to sit for hours while their coats were fashioned into intricate patterns and their topknots teased to extravagant heights. As a dramatic final touch, they were powdered and sprinkled with colored confetti, then ornamented with collars and anklets encrusted with semi-precious stones.

Wearing long aprons with pockets, in which they stashed their combs, scissors and hand clippers, the

Figure 1-3. Poodle with moustache and imperiale. From *The Illustrated Sporting and Dramatic News*, July 1880.

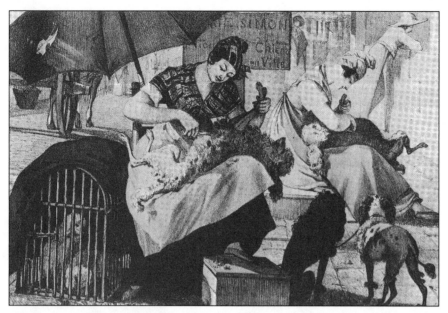

Figure 1-4. *"Les Tondeuses de Chien,"* an 1820 engraving by J. Chalon showing French women scissoring Poodles. From BBC Hulton Picture Library

Barbou tells us in *Le Chien: Son Histoire, Ses Exploits, Ses Aventures* about a Parisian whose business of dog grooming and bathing was conducted along the banks of the Seine under the Pont des Arts, a bridge linking the left and right banks. On Sundays, many working-class Parisians brought their Poodles to be groomed there (Figure 1-5). The dogs were brushed, dunked in sulfur water to kill any fleas and then soaped. For the final rinse, they were sent to retrieve a stick tossed into the Seine, after which they were trimmed (Figure 1-6). Other *coiffeurs pour chiens* made house calls to bathe, clip, powder and perfume the Poodles owned by more sophisticated clients.

Some of the most popular nineteenth-century grooming styles for Poodles were the Lion Cut, the English Cut and the Tonte à la Zoave (a trim where the body was completely shaved, the legs shaped like bouffant pantaloons and the face ornamented with a very large mustache). For warm weather, there was also a Seaside clip, where the body and leg hair were shaved close except for the topknot and tail. For corded Poodles, the Tonte en Macaroms cascades of coiled hair, inspired by a coiffure first worn by Princess Eugenie, the wife of Emperor Napoleon III, became fashionable.

Figure 1-5. *Tondeur de Chiens.* Poodle grooming was often conducted on Sundays along the banks of the Seine River in Paris.

Figure 1-6. *Toilette d'ete.* For the final rinse, poodles were often sent to retrieve a stick tossed into the Seine, after which they were trimmed.

Poodle Trimming in Nineteenth-Century England

Clipped Poodles appear in eighteenth- and nineteenth-century English engravings and paintings resembling their French cousins. Poodle trimming became more popular in England as the years passed and, by Victorian times, it was a full-time occupation for many individuals. In 1870, Hugh Dalziel, one of England's most famous authors and dog historians, begged for an end of the "vulgar fancies of the dog barber" by which

demoiselles provided their services to an abundance of aristocratic clients (Figures 1-4 and 1-5). Solange Belin writes in *Vie de Chien* about the demoiselles Demoncy and Varechon who lived on the *quai Pelletier*. In 1774, they charged clients *1 livre, 4 sous* (at the time, the equivalent of a common laborer's entire day's wages) for various services including

therapeutic bleeding, bathing, clipping and trimming the coat.

After the French Revolution, when the number of upper-class pet owners had greatly decreased, the call for professional Poodle stylists tapered off a bit. But by 1850, the stylists were back in force and enjoying an unprecedented popularity with both upper- and middle-class consumers. In 1888, Alfred

Poodles were clipped in a variety of outrageous fashions. Dr. Gordon Stables, another prominent English dog historian, commented in 1890 about Poodle grooming: "The face is clipped bare with the exception of a daft pantaloon-like pair of eyebrows and a pair of moustachios and a small goatee. Then the body abaft the ribs is clipped completely bare, as well as the belly and the thighs and legs, with the following exceptions: a pair of epaulettes are left on the top of the rump and a fringe of hair around the hocks. The forelegs are clipped with the exception of a fringe of hair around the knees, Zulu fashion."

At the end of the nineteenth century, Paris and London were the focal points of the Western world. "Europe was like one vast kingdom," writes Hebe Dorsey in *The Age of Opulence*, "with emperors, kings and princes galore. Courts were magnificent stages for tiaraed women and dashing officers in bright costumes. The court in London . . . was the most elegant and exotic, with foreign princes and maharajahs reflecting the strength of the British Empire."

The luxury of this era was mind-boggling, and one extraordinary aspect of the lifestyle was the amount of attention given to the subject of dogs. Everybody who was anybody had a luxury dog. The *Paris Herald* published a regular "Kennel" column to keep readers informed about dog shows and doggy gossip, including the fact that Lillie Langtry, the mistress of the Prince of Wales (later Edward VII) had all her Poodles clipped with the initials L.L. And during a dinner party in London, a Poodle devoured a square yard of a guest's dress. "The dress had cost between 40 and 50 pounds," the *Herald* noted, and "The dog is still living!"

A 14-page article entitled "Dandy Dogs," which appeared in *The Strand Magazine*, published in London 1896, describes some of the services and accessories available at a posh grooming salon called the Dogs' Toilet Club, in New Bond Street.

Operated by a cultivated (and obviously enterprising) lady, everything about the salon was luxurious. The business cards were blue and gold with a delicate green ribbon bow at one corner. The sumptuous reception room was furnished with antiques, Queen Anne furniture, canine art and a collection of fashionable requisites for well-bred pets in Victorian London. Money was evidently no object where aristocratic Poodles were concerned. They wore collars and harnesses made of gold or silver, often studded with precious stones. They were works of art. Some of these, including a collar made of 18-carat gold fastened with a diamond brooch, gold and silver muzzles, gold couples for promenading pairs of dogs, gold bracelets with semiprecious stones that locked onto the dogs' ankles, and long chains of gold were pictured. The wardrobe of an elegant Poodle in fin-de-siecle Paris and London might include shirts, handkerchiefs, dressing gowns, traveling cloaks, tea gowns, evening outfits, beach outfits and rubber boots, many of which were monogrammed and color coordinated with their mistresses' clothing.

Owners could bring their Poodles to the Dogs' Toilet Club to be brushed, combed (with silver, buffalo-horn and tortoiseshell combs), shampooed (with the yolks of eggs), clipped, perfumed and attended by a professional canine chiropodist. The foot specialists not only manicured the nails but treated numerous foot complaints caused by the metallic grit on London roads. The Club employed London's premier groomer, Mr. R. W. Brown of Regent Street, who groomed the most outrageous designs on the backs of Poodles, using his "battery of clippers, razors and scissors." His clippers, mind you, were not the electric kind that groomers so deftly use today, but hand clippers that were time-consuming and sometimes difficult to manipulate. The cutting action of the hand models worked on the same principle as a hedge-clipper in which the opening and closing of a groomer's hand controlled a small blade that cut the hair. According to the article, Brown also used many different kinds of barber shears, some of them curved in strange ways, so that he could get into small corners to reproduce fine lace work on a Poodle's back.

Mr. Brown would trim any pattern on a Poodle: elaborate crests for titled owners, monograms, coronets and even pastoral scenes. The charge for setting a different pattern or "set scene" started at about two Pounds sterling (about $12 in those days). Clients could send personal articles with crests or monograms, and Brown would copy the patterns on the Poodles' backs. Some of his more intricate patterns took two settings to complete, and once the design was traced, the dog had to return every month for a touch-up.

In the photograph reproduced from the 1896 article (see Figure 1-1 on page 6), Mr. Brown appears with Mouton, a Poodle he has just trimmed. Poor Mouton probably never knew of the desperate struggle that took place on his back: His pattern depicted a scene from the Corbett-Mitchell boxing match that took place in New Orleans, and the English Champion has apparently just received the knockout punch.

Brown had one Irish client who would have nothing but a huge shamrock shaved on his Poodle's back; another client insisted that his Poodle sport a quaint-looking thistle, the prickly part being cunningly fashioned from the dog's own stubbly bristles. Another photograph in the article showed a black standard Poodle named Zulu, who bore the crest of his master and mistress: a pelican feeding its nest of young with blood from its own breast, accompanied by the motto *Rein sand peine* (nothing without pain)!

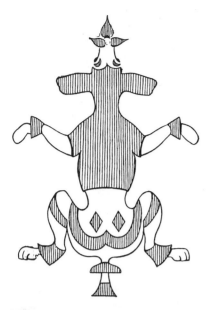

Figure 1-7. Early diagram for clipping the Poodle, from *The American Book of the Dog* by G. O. Shields, 1891.

Figure 1-8. A typical corded coat Poodle, reproduced from *The English Stockkeeper*. Corded Poodles occupied a commanding position at the dog shows in England and in Europe in the late 1800s.

Figure 1-9. "Nero," a famous German Poodle, as he appeared at the Berlin International Dog Show in 1880.

Corded Coats

Poodles were once divided into two coat types: corded and curly. The corded Poodle's coat hung in long, ropelike cords from the body, ears and tail (see Figure 1-8). The cords, often more than 20 inches long, covered the front legs like a skirt when they hung naturally to the ground. To keep them from dragging along and attracting dirt, the cords were often tied up in cloth bundles with leather straps or ribbons over the dog's back. Regardless of the Poodle's sex, the cords above the eyes were pulled upwards on the top of the head and knotted or tied with a velvet or satin bow, which author Ernest Baines described as "looking like a little girl going to a party." A great deal of time was devoted to maintaining the cords. They were never combed out and were seldom bathed, although they had to be oiled frequently to keep the long ends from becoming brittle and snapping off. Writers of the times sometimes described corded Poodles as "offending the nostrils" and mentioned how difficult it was to make pets of them or to keep them in the house.

Corded Poodles made their debut in the British show ring in 1876 and occupied a commanding position at dog shows in England and on the European continent for years (see Figure 1-9). They must have been the "darlings" of newsmen of the day, as they are described and portrayed frequently in popular magazines, newspapers and books. Rawdon Lee describes a Poodle in 1899 named Fairy Queen, shown by an Englishwoman from Leeds, that caused a great distraction at the shows: "This was a white dog and its cords were of such length that they were many inches longer than the

Figure 1-10. Two corded Poodles from a nineteenth-century painting by Arthur Wardle. To protect the cords from damage, they were often tied up in linen bundles with leather straps or ribbons over the dog's back. Modern Poodle groomers can only imagine how difficult it must have been to maintain a corded coat.

height of the animal. When lying at rest, a close examination had to be made to discern which was the head and which the stern of this curious creature."

Lee mentions another large Poodle of the day, named Lyris, 21½ inches high at the shoulders, whose cords measured 37 inches from tip to tip; he also mentions Lyris's son, Achilles, standing 23 inches high at the shoulders with cords 30 inches long, falling 6 inches below his feet. A reporter commented in 1890 in *The Canine World* (a weekly dog show gazette) that Achilles was the only entry in the Challenge Dog Class at the Holborn Championship Show in London, and he "was in very grand fettle and coat, and frightened away other exhibitors because of his magnificence."

The first diagram for trimming Poodles "in the style generally adopted in England and which is best adapted to showing off the dog to the greatest advantage," to be published in the United States appeared in 1891 in *The American Book of the Dog*, edited by G. O. Shields (see Figure 1-7). The book describes the Poodle's cords as being about the thickness of a crow quill. "The entire coat," it said, "from the base of the skull to the root of the tail should divide evenly down the back, showing a clearly defined parting, and should touch the ground completely, hiding the forelegs and feet. Thus, combining with the cords from the throat and chest, give the dog the appearance of being in petticoats. The coat should cord all over the body, except in the eyebrows, moustache and imperiale, which should be straight, even without wave, and of a glossier texture than the rest of the cost. The cords on the ears should reach far down on the shoulders, and so mingle with those of the neck as to render the ears nearly undistinguishable. On the head, the cords should fall away from the center, leaving a well-defined brown, and should have no tendency to stand erect, like those of a Water Spaniel."

The popularity of the corded Poodle has diminished, but every now and then, one will appear in a show ring somewhere in the world. The corded variety will long be remembered and has given us a precious legacy (see Figure 1-10). Some of today's finest Poodles descend from the distinguished British corded bloodlines, from whom they undoubtedly inherit their lush coat textures.

Nineteenth-Century Grooming Tips

Nineteenth-century books offer some intriguing grooming advice. In *House Dogs and Sporting Dogs* (1861), John Meyrick writes that "a dog who is well brushed regularly seldom requires washing and is never infested with vermin. If the dog is to be washed, he said, let it be done with the yolks of eggs, and not with soap, which irritates the skin, inflames the eyes, and by temporarily depriving the skin of its natural oily secretion, makes the dog extremely liable to become chilled afterwards. The washing with the yolks of eggs may be managed as follows: Let the dog stand in an empty tub, rub the yolks of two, four or more eggs by degrees into his coat, adding a little lukewarm water at a time, until the dog is covered with a thick lather. When it is well rubbed in over the whole coat, pour clean warm water over the dog till the egg is entirely washed out."

Rawdon Lee advises in *Modern Dogs: Non-Sporting Division* (1899) that "the coat of a black Poodle has to be dressed with some emollient, and nothing is better for this purpose than a mixture composed of a quarter pound of Vaseline to a half-pint of paraffin. This should be put into a suitable receptacle, which is to be placed into a heated oven and kept there until the concoction is thoroughly blended. It may be scented with any perfume fancy suggests and

must then be placed in a jar, kept covered, and applied when cold."

Modern Poodle Trimming

Today, although most Poodles no longer retrieve for a living, two variations of the old Lion trim, the English Saddle clip and the Continental clip (with long mane coats over the shoulders, ribs and chest, and short hair or rosettes on the hindquarters) remain the only acceptable adult trims for the show ring in the United States. A Poodle under 12 months of age may be shown in the Puppy clip, but Poodles 12 months of age or over must be trimmed into either of the two other recognized styles. In the Stud Dog and Brood Bitch classes and in a noncompetitive Parade of Champions, Poodles may be shown in the Sporting clip.

The art of Poodle trimming has blossomed into a sophisticated profession throughout the world, especially in the United States. In addition to the acceptable show clips, there are hundreds of pet trims in which a Poodle's coat can be clipped and scissored into various body patterns and leg styles. These are called "pet" trims because they are unacceptable in the conformation show ring.

Along with the many different clip styles, great advances in equipment and products have been made in the last few decades. The introduction of electric clippers for small animals, especially those with a variety of detachable blades that can cut a Poodle's hair to various lengths, have greatly simplified trimming for the breeder, exhibitor, handler and groomer. Today's Poodle groomers can also choose from different types of brushes, combs, shears, nail trimmers, dematting tools and hair dryers, making it possible to match grooming tools to each dog's coat type for more efficient grooming. These items are explained at length in Chapter 2, "Selecting the Right Equipment."

The Poodle owners of yesteryear had to mix grooming preparations by trial and error when they needed them. In some cases, the formulations they used to combat skin diseases or to kill external parasites were quite likely to destroy their dogs as well. While today's owners might want to whip up certain formulations from ready-at-hand natural ingredients, they certainly don't have to. The extensive array of shampoos, coat conditioners, tangle removers, rinses, products to moisturize the skin or to restructure the hair, grooming powders, ear cleaning products, insecticidal products, lotions and creams for skin diseases, and other cosmetic preparations not only make grooming and care more efficient and comfortable for the groomer, but also—and more importantly—safer and more humane for the dog.

Further Reading

If you're interested in more information about the history of the Poodle or Poodle grooming, the following are excellent resources:

Barbou, Alfred. *Le Chien: Son Histoire, Ses Exploits, Ses Aventures.* Paris, 1883.

Dorsey, Hebe. *The Age of Opulence.* New York: Harry N. Abrams, Inc., 1986.

Kete, Kathleen. *The Beast in the Boudoir: Petkeeping in Nineteenth-Century Paris.* Berkeley: University of California Press, 1994.

Macdonogh, Katharine. *Reigning Cats and Dogs.* New York: St. Martin's Press, 1999.

Shields, G. O., ed. *The American Book of the Dog.* Chicago: Rand McNally, 1891.

Thurston, Mary Elizabeth. *The Lost History of the Canine Race.* Kansas City: Andrews and McMeel, 1996.

Tracy, T. H. *The Book of the Poodle.* New York: Bonanza Books, 1960.

chapter 2

Now that you have decided to learn how to groom your own Poodle (whether the dog is a pet or is to be a show dog) or to eventually become a professional pet stylist, the next step is to assemble the proper equipment to do the job correctly.

There is such an imposing array of grooming equipment to choose from that it can be confusing when one is trying to determine what tools are correct—even for a single breed. More importantly, while it is necessary to select the right grooming tools, you must know how to use them properly. Even the most basic tools, incorrectly used, can damage a dog's skin and hair. When used correctly, however, they can contribute significantly to the health of the skin and hair as well as to enhance the dog's general appearance.

If you were to query professionals about buying grooming equipment, one point on which they unanimously would agree is to invest in the finest equipment that you can afford. Don't compromise on quality. It cannot be overstressed that one gets what one pays for. Considering how much it costs to have a Poodle groomed professionally once a month, you will see that your equipment will pay for itself in a year or less. Moreover, the best equipment lasts longer, saves time and, in the hands of someone knowledgeable, produces expert results.

All the tools and equipment that are used for Poodle grooming are listed in this chapter. Each one is described and, when appropriate, comments are added about its use and maintenance. If you're a beginner, don't panic and think that it's necessary to run out and buy everything mentioned in this chapter. Because so many grooming schools will use this book as a text, I've tried to make it as comprehensive as possible for those intending to become professional pet stylists.

To groom your dog at home, you need an electric clipper, a few pairs of shears, a brush and comb, nail trimmer and hair dryer. If you like grooming and are planning eventually to become a professional, all the information you need is here; the additional equipment can be added gradually as your skills develop. Where do you purchase equipment? You can find many of the clippers, shears, brushes, combs and nail trimmers you need for home grooming at pet stores; on the other hand, professional-quality tools and equipment (premium scissors and shears, high-velocity hair dryers and hydraulic grooming tables, for instance) may be harder to find. Look through dog magazines for mail-order pet supply companies and send for their catalogs. Go to dog shows and grooming competitions and visit the concessionaires. This will give you the advantage of handling clippers, shears, and other tools to see that their weight and balance are comfortable.

Electric Clippers

You need an electric clipper to clip your Poodle's hair. Finding the right clipper can be confusing for beginners because today there are so many different models to choose from: single speed, two-speed and cordless. But don't be perplexed about choosing a clipper: To groom your dog at home, you need only a single-speed clipper. You can add other types if you decide to become a professional pet stylist or to show your Poodle in the breed ring.

Some clippers are designed for "pet" grooming while others are constructed for heavy-duty use. Pet groomer clippers are recommended for the economy-minded owner who wants to keep his or her pet well-groomed at home. Although they are serviceable, they are not recommended for the serious dog show exhibitor or handler, or for the aspiring professional pet stylist.

The price difference between the pet and professional animal clippers is negligible, especially when you consider that the professional models will last a lifetime with regular maintenance. When you are purchasing a clipper that will be used on show dogs, in breeding kennels or in grooming salons, the machine must be powerful and built to last through continuous use.

Moreover, for the professional models, a full range of blades is available that cut dog hair to various lengths and that detach and change easily, usually by pressing a small hinge at the base of the blade. This is an enormous benefit because, during the clipping process, you will be trimming the hair on various parts of the dog's body to different lengths.

A considerable number of electric clippers are manufactured by American and foreign companies, most notably Oster™, Andis™, Laube™, Wahl™ and Aesculap™. Aesculap may be hard to find in the United States, but it is extremely popular in Europe. You will notice that the manufacturers listed in this chapter offer a variety of models: single-speed, two-speed, cordless and trimmers. *A single-speed clipper is the best choice if you intend to groom only your own Poodle.* Two-speed clippers offer the versatility of regular or high-speed clipping, but they are recommended for

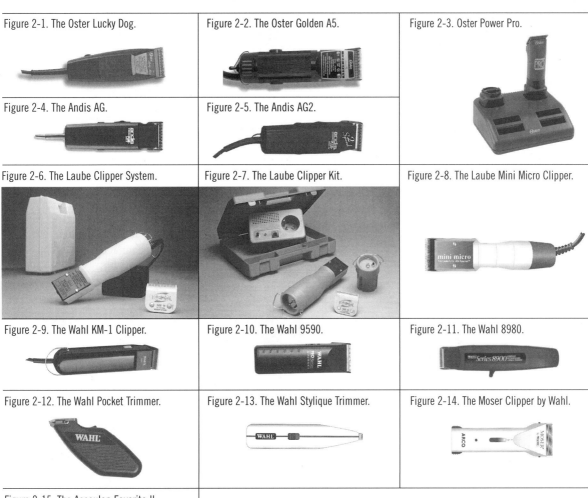

Figure 2-1. The Oster Lucky Dog.

Figure 2-2. The Oster Golden A5.

Figure 2-3. Oster Power Pro.

Figure 2-4. The Andis AG.

Figure 2-5. The Andis AG2.

Figure 2-6. The Laube Clipper System.

Figure 2-7. The Laube Clipper Kit.

Figure 2-8. The Laube Mini Micro Clipper.

Figure 2-9. The Wahl KM-1 Clipper.

Figure 2-10. The Wahl 9590.

Figure 2-11. The Wahl 8980.

Figure 2-12. The Wahl Pocket Trimmer.

Figure 2-13. The Wahl Stylique Trimmer.

Figure 2-14. The Moser Clipper by Wahl.

Figure 2-15. The Aesculap Favorita II.

professional salons where groomers must deal with dirty, matted or heavy coats on a daily basis. Cordless clippers are especially useful if you are exhibiting at dog shows or competing at grooming contests where electrical power is not easily accessible. Trimmers are smaller clippers that are used for last-minute touch-ups at shows or in shops for clipping delicate areas like between the toes and pads of the feet, the face or the ears, and for detailed precision work. Some trimmers are cordless, others plug in. Almost all models have removable filter screens to prevent hair and debris from passing into the clipper.

OSTER CLIPPERS

Clippers made by Oster Professional Products are popular and widely used around the world for clipping dogs.

For at-home pet grooming, Oster makes the Lucky Dog clipper which comes with five detachable snap-on/off blades (Figure 2-1). For heavy-duty professional work, the Oster Golden A5 (the brand's flagship product, shown in Figure 2-2) with 18 detachable snap-on/off blades, is available in two models: single-speed or two-speed. In the two-speed model, the low speed is designed for normal cutting; the high-speed motor runs 30 percent faster and is designed to penetrate through dense, heavy or matted hair. The newest A5 clippers have been designed to run smoother and cooler than ever before. The 18 detachable blades are available in both standard or Elite form (the Elite blades being coated with titanium to make them last longer and cut smoother than conventional blades).

Oster also makes a rechargeable clipper, the Power Pro Cordless Clipper (Figure 2-3), which can be a valuable companion piece to the A5 clipper on special occasions, particularly when electrical outlets may not be available. This clipper will operate approximately 30 minutes on a single charge and require about 20 minutes to recharge (with two batteries the Power Pro can be used continuously). The Power Pro Cordless is ergonomically designed for a comfortable and well-balanced grip. It is an excellent choice for last minute touch-ups before entering the show ring.

Figure 2-16. Oster clipper blades.

Oster also manufactures several other trimmers: the Groom-Master, an all around heavy-duty clipper with wide blades; the Adjusta Groom Clipper with a side lever to adjust the blade from coarse to fine (this model also comes with four snap-on comb attachments for additional lengths); the Sculptor Trimmer, a lightweight, ergonomically designed cordless trimmer; and the Finisher Trimmer with narrow blade for precision edging and finishing work, especially on the face and ears and between the toes.

ANDIS CLIPPERS

The Andis company makes several excellent professional clippers.

For heavy-duty shop or professional work, the Andis AG clipper, with 16 detachable snap-on/off blades, is available in three models: single speed (Model AG, Figure 2-4), two-speed (Model AG2, Figure 2-5) and super two-speed (Model AG2 Super). The two-speed and super two-speed models run 50 percent faster than the single-speed AG clipper and are ideal for continuous use in a busy grooming salon.

All Andis clippers are contoured to fit the groomer's hand. All models are maintenance free; they require no oiling and greasing of internal parts. The only oiling that is required is to the blades. Andis also makes the AGR rechargeable model which provides heavy-duty cutting with complete freedom from an electrical cord. With a full-charged battery pack, the clipper will run continuously for one hour. The clipper can be recharged with battery intact, or the battery pack can be recharged separately. In the trimmer category, the Andis TrendSetter Cordless rechargeable narrow clipper (with four snap-on comb attachments) is designed for trimming delicate areas or to take to shows for quick touch-ups.

LAUBE CLIPPERS

The Laube Clipper System is quite unique and versatile (Figure 2-6). With a variety of clipper handpieces, battery packs/chargers and cord packs that are sold separately, professionals can create the system most suitable to their needs. All Laube clipper handpieces are interchangeable with all Laube battery packs and cord packs, and obtainable in different colors including black, neon pink, blue and purple. There are 22 detachable snap-on/off blades available for the handpiece which clip the hair to various lengths. Laube blades are made of stainless steel; they will not rust, pit or deteriorate.The most basic item is an impact-resistant, easy-to-grip clipper handpiece that can be used with various batteries, chargers and cord packs. The handpiece has a high-tech sealed ball-bearing motor that keeps it cool to the touch and running quietly from 1,100 to 4,000 rpm, depending on the battery or cord pack you use. The motor is sealed so that hair and debris cannot get inside the clipper or doesn't blow in the groomer's face. The battery packs charge quickly and require no tools. The cord packs (with an 18-foot cord) snap into the handpiece and plug into any wall outlet.

You can also purchase a pre-assembled Laube Clipper Kit, packaged in its own color-coordinated case (Figure 2-7). There are many different sets available, each with different features, ranging from the #503 kit, which includes a clipper handpiece, two-speed cord pack and transformer to the #513 kit which includes a clipper handpiece, a variable-speed cord pack and transformer. There is also the #514 kit, which includes a clipper handpiece, variable-speed battery pack and velocity charger. Another recently introduced clipper is the Laube Mini Micro (Figure 2-8).

WAHL CLIPPERS

Wahl clippers are popular worldwide. The company makes several excellent professional clippers.

For heavy-duty work, the powerful Wahl Single-Speed KM-1 (Figure 2-9), with nine detachable snap-on/off blades, is ergonomically designed for a groomer's comfort and ease of use. The sturdy KM-1 is a smooth-running, quiet machine. Precision-designed with all wearing parts constructed of metal, it is maintenance free. No oiling or greasing of internal parts is needed. The only oiling that is required is to the clipper blades.

Wahl's cordless clipper, the Platinum Pro, actually operates with or without a cord. The battery is rechargeable and the set comes with a #10 high-carbon steel detachable blade with blade guard, a recharging unit, and a cord to plug into the clipper.

The 9590 (Figure 2-10) and 8980 (Figure 2-11) are also available, and Wahl makes three innovative clippers designed to ease hand fatigue:

- The compact Palm Size/Pocket Trimmer (Figure 2-12) operates on one AA battery and is great for quick touch-ups at home or at shows.

- The Stylique Trimmer (Figure 2-13) comes with a narrow blade for detailing, edging and sculpting.

- The sleek, easy-to-handle Moser designer-series cordless adjustable trimmer is a powerful, ergonomically designed machine that weighs less than half a pound (Figure 2-14).

AESCULAP CLIPPERS

Clippers made by Aesculap are precision-engineered in Germany and are better known in Europe than in the United States. The most popular model for dog grooming is the powerful and cool-running Favorita II (Figure 2-15), with 12 detachable snap-on/off blades or cutter heads. The Favorita II is designed for heavy duty continuous use in grooming salons with nearly vibration-free running. Ergonomically designed

for optimal comfort, the clipper has a grained casing that lets the groomer grip the machine comfortably. The front design of the clipper casing eliminates clogging from cut hair.

CLIPPER MAINTENANCE

Like any other electric tool or appliance, systematic maintenance will help keep your clipper in good working condition. Whichever model you choose, do remember to study the operating instructions that come with the clipper. Like a new car, a new clipper needs a few weeks to become broken in. It will tend to run hotter and slower until the break-in period is over. Just remember to follow the manufacturer's instructions for oiling and greasing (some clippers need no oiling/greasing) and periodic maintenance. When your clipper is maintained according to instructions, it will deliver power and speed ample for professional grooming requirements.

In everyday heavy-duty use in a salon or kennel, however, clippers do heat up occasionally. You may be able to avoid overheating by checking if you are plugging into the proper voltage supply. If you are not (perhaps because of a faulty wiring system or because you are operating different items on double sockets), your clipper will be under-voltaged. In this situation, a clipper runs slowly, heats up, has slower blade strokes and does not cut as efficiently.

For best results, hold your clipper as you would a pencil. When in use, the clipper is held lightly but firmly with the blade resting flat against the skin as it clips. For smooth and even results, move the clippers in a slow, steady motion. Where the dog's skin is loose, around the lips, for instance, you will need to stretch the skin to prevent nicking. Refer to Chapter 13, "Clipping the Poodle's Face and Neck," for illustrations on how to do this.

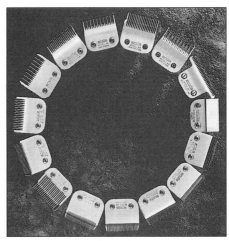

Figure 2-17. Andis clipper blades.

When not in use, protect the tips of the clipper blades with a plastic snap-on blade guard.

CLIPPER BLADES

A full range of snap-on/off blades that cut dog hair to various lengths is available for the Oster (Figure 2-16), Andis (Figure 2-17), Laube, Wahl and Aesculap clippers. These blades, made of high-carbon or stainless-steel or titanium, come in many different cutting lengths that are named and described in the table on pages 16–17. An added bonus is that, with the exception of Aesculap, each manufacturer's blades are fully compatible with all other major clipper brands. In other words, Oster blades not only fit Oster clippers, but also Andis, Laube and Wahl clippers, and the other way around. Aesculap blades, however, are not interchangeable with other machines.

As you can see in the table, the higher the blade number, the closer the clip. The hair lengths suggested are those produced by clipping *with* the growth of the hair (from the head towards the tail). When clipping *against* the growth (from the tail towards the head), each blade will cut closer. The suggested hair lengths will also vary slightly because of coat texture.

CLIPPERS

Clipper Blade Function	OSTER CLIPPERS	ANDIS CLIPPERS	LAUBE CLIPPER SYSTEM†	WAHL CLIPPERS	AESCULAP CLIPPERS
	Golden A-5 (Single- and 2-Speed) and Power Pro Cordless	Models AG (Single- and 2-Speed) and AG AG2 Super Speed and AGR+ Rechargeable	All Laube System Clippers and Laube Mini Micro and Laube Mini Lazor	Models KM-1 and Platinum Pro Cord and Cordless	Favorita II
Longest cutting blade available; leaves hair about 1" long.			#2		
Leaves hair about 1" long (same as #2) but produces a smoother, more velvety finish resembling scissoring. *Use on clean hair only.*			#2FC		
Skip-tooth blade that leaves hair from ½" to ¾" long to produce a short but not shaved look.	#3	#3-3/4	#3-3/4		GT-782
Leaves hair from ½" to ¾" long (same as the 3-3/4) but produces a more velvety finish. *Use on clean hair only.*	#3F	#3-3/4FC	#3-3/4F		
Plucking blade that leaves hair about ⅜" long. Primarily used for general body clipping and blending. Does not always leave a smooth coat texture, particularly on soft coats.	#4 SKIP TOOTH	#4 SKIP TOOTH	#4		GT-779
Leaves hair the same length as #4 but produces a smoother, more velvety finish, closely resembling hand scissoring. Leaves a beautiful finish on the body of a Sporting or Retriever clip. *Use on clean hair only.*	#4F	#4FC	#4F	#4F	
Plucking blade that leaves the hair about ¼" long. Primarily used for general body clipping and blending.	#5 SKIP TOOTH	#5 SKIP TOOTH	#5		GT-758
Cuts hair the same length as #5 but produces a smoother, more velvety finish, resembling hand scissoring. Leaves a beautiful finish on the body of a Sporting or Retriever clip. *Use on clean hair only.*	#5F	#5FC	#5F	#5F	
Closest cutting of the skip-tooth blades. Leaves hair about ⅛" long. Most often used when it is necessary to strip down the coat. Also effective when used at those areas of the body where the groomer wants to skim, or clip over the top level of the coat, gradually blending it from close work into longer hair.	#7 SKIP TOOTH	#7 SKIP TOOTH	#7		GT-748
Cuts hair the same length as #7 but produces a smoother, more velvety finish. Leaves a beautiful smooth finish on the body and legs of a Summer Miami and the Retriever clip. Also good for skimming (clipping over the top level of the coat and gradually blending it from short into long hair). *Use on clean hair only.*	#7F	#7FC	#7F	#7F	GH-754 FINE
Skip-tooth blade, wider than the standard #7 blade. Leaves hair about ⅛" long. Good choice for stripping down matted coats. Because of added width, the hair comes off quickly and easily.			#7W		
Medium-cutting all-purpose blade. Leaves hair about 7/64" long. Cuts close without denuding the dog. Excellent choice for stripping extremely matted coats.	#8-1/2	#8-1/2	#8-1/2	#8-1/2	GH-715
Medium-cutting all-purpose blade. Cuts off slightly more hair than #8-1/2. Good choice for clipping *very sensitive* Poodles, especially the cheeks, front of the neck and underside of the tail.	#9	#9	#9		GH-736 COARSE
Medium-cutting all-purpose blade, wider than the standard #9 blade. Leaves hair about 1/16" long.			#9W		

CLIPPERS

Clipper Blade Function	OSTER CLIPPERS	ANDIS CLIPPERS	LAUBE CLIPPER SYSTEM†	WAHL CLIPPERS	AESCULAP CLIPPERS
	Golden A-5 (Single- and 2-Speed) and Power Pro Cordless	Models AG (Single- and 2-Speed) and AG AG2 Super Speed and AGR+ Rechargeable	All Laube System Clippers and Laube Mini Micro and Laube Mini Lazor	Models KM-1 and Platinum Pro Cord and Cordless	Favorita II
Medium-cutting all-purpose blade most often used for general and underbelly clipping. Produces a smooth finish, shows the natural color of the coat. Excellent choice for clipping with or against the hair growth on the face, feet and tail of white and light-colored Poodles whose skins may easily become infected.	#10	#10	#10	#10	GH-712 FINE TOOTH
Medium-cutting blade, wider than standard #10 blade, for general and underbelly clipping. Because of added width, the hair comes off quickly and easily. Can be used to strip the coat when mats are too close to the skin to permit the use of any other blade.	#10 WIDE	#T-84 EXTRA WIDE	#10W	#10 WIDE	
Medium/close cutting. Produces a smooth finish, showing more skin than #10 blade. Most often used to clip a Poodle's feet, face and tail. The blade of choice for most grooming contest competitors in the United States.	#15	#15	#15	#15	GH-730
Close cutting. Often used to clip face and feet of dark-colored dogs (if they can take a close clip). The blade of choice for show clipping. Can be used under a snap-on comb attachment to give a nice finish on longer coats.	#30	#30	#30	#30	
Extra-close cutting. Used by veterinarians for surgical prep. In the hands of an experienced groomer, it produces a very close show-quality finish on skin that is not sensitive and with coat texture that is hard and profuse. Excellent for clipping the underbelly of pregnant bitches before delivery. Can be used under a snap-on comb attachment to remove excess body coat.	#40	#40 SURGICAL	#40	#40	GH-703
Micro-close cutting. Primarily used by veterinarians for surgical prep. In the hand of an experienced groomer, this blade produces an extremely close show-quality finish on the face or feet of Poodles with skin that is not sensitive and with coat texture that is hard and profuse. Excellent for preparing the underbelly of a pregnant bitch before delivery. Can be used underneath a snap-on comb attachment when attempting to remove excess body coat.	#50	#50	#50	#50	GH-700
Extremely close cutting. Primarily used by veterinarians for surgical prep. Clips closer than a #40 and a #50 and removes the hair all the way to the skin.			#45		
Close-cutting blade ⅝" wide. When used with the growth of hair, removes the same amount as a #15 blade; when used against, cuts equivalent to a #30. Most often used to clip the feet, around the muzzle, and for clipping pattern designs on small Poodles (when a standard-size blade might be too wide and too cumbersome).	#5/8		#5/8		GT-772
Close-cutting blade, ⅞" wide. When used with the growth of hair, takes off the same amount as a #15; when used against, cuts equivalent to a #30. Primarily used to clip the feet, around the muzzle, and for clipping pattern designs on small and medium-sized Poodles.	#7/8				

†At publication time, several new coarse-cutting blades were available for Laube Clippers: #2C, #3-3/4C, #4C, #5C and #7C. The C or "coarse" blades cut the same as their numbered counterparts in this table, but the configuration of the teeth produces a coarser, more textured finish.

Figure 2-18. Laube snap-on combs.

Figure 2-19. M.D.C. Romani snap-on combs.

New clipper blades are coated with a factory preservative to prevent rusting and for storage purposes. Before use, this coating should be removed with a solution of either Oster Blade Wash or Wahl H-42, otherwise the blades can clog with hair and stop working properly. To remove the factory coating: fill a shallow dish with just enough Blade Wash to cover the blade. Attach the blade to the clipper and turn on the motor. You will hear it begin to run faster and faster. After about a minute, turn off the switch and remove the blade from the clipper. Use a paper towel to absorb the excess solution, then wipe the blade dry with a soft cloth.

Before you begin clipping hair, if your clipper requires oil, apply a thin film of lubricating oil (this is usually packed in the box with a new clipper) on the mating faces of the blade and the tension spring guide. It is important to always keep your blades lubricated. Good lubrication will reduce wear on the metal surfaces of the cutting blade

which enables you to retain that sharp edge longer and prolong the life of your clippers and blades.

During the clipping process, professionals use the cleaning solutions previously mentioned or an aerosol coolant or lubricant (such as Oster Kool Lube, Laube Mr. Lube 'N Cool or Wahl H-42 Clean Clippers). These aerosol products are sprayed directly onto the clipper blade. They cool the blade, flush accumulated hair away from the cutting surfaces and provide some lubrication without leaving a heavy oil residue.

SNAP-ON COMBS

In addition to the high-carbon steel clipper blades previously described, you can also buy numerous inexpensive snap-on clipper combs made by Oster, Laube (Figure 2-18) and M.D.C. Romani (Figure 2-19) that will reduce the hair to a workable length but minimize the "stripped-down" look. These self-adjusting combs, made of tough impact- and heat-resistant plastic, are named and described in the sidebar on page 19. They fit almost all clippers by attaching onto the bottom of a regular clipper blade (most professionals say that best results are obtained by using a #40 or #30 blade as a base). You simply snap the comb onto the base of the clipper blade, then pull it up to lock it in place. Once securely attached and in use, the tapered ends penetrate the coat quickly and evenly, but without the risk of gouging the dog's skin.

Snap-on combs can be used on both the body and the legs. They are true time-savers, literally cutting scissoring work in half, especially if you want to trim your Poodle in an easy-to-maintain style, such as the Sporting, Lamb, Miami or Panda clip, where a short, velvety covering of hair is left all over the body. You can snap on a comb and end up with hair anywhere from ⅟₁₆ inch to 2 inches long, depending on the

size you choose. Professional pet stylists also use snap-on combs in three ways:

- To quickly shorten excess body coat
- To block a pattern in the rough
- To outline the hair to an overall even length, and then finish by hand-scissoring

Snap-on combs are easy to clean: wash them in warm, sudsy water, rinse well, then dry the metal parts with a clean cloth.

Scissors/Shears

When the first edition of this book was published, there were only a few kinds of shears available to groomers. The majority of them were not only poorly designed but were also made from inferior materials. Groomers suffered from hand and wrist fatigue and strain, and the low-quality scissors didn't last very long.

With the tremendous increase in the number of pet grooming salons and boarding kennels that offer grooming services, as well as the number of dog shows throughout the United States—indeed, the world—manufacturers have provided us with a multitude of innovative grooming shears of outstanding quality that are balanced, super smooth and extremely durable.

There are so many different styles and shapes of scissors on the market today that it would take a small book just to adequately describe them. Here is some basic information about the different types of scissors you need for Poodle grooming, how to choose the correct shears for the type and structure of your hand, how to hold your shears correctly, how to develop the correct scissoring technique and how to keep shears in good working order.

Throughout this section (and certainly in other grooming articles and books you may read), you may be confused when you see the words *scissors* and *shears* used interchangeably. Technically, the difference depends on the length of the implement: *Scissors* is used to describe implements under 6 inches long, while *shears* refers to anything longer than 6 inches.

Many scissor specialists provided information on shears for this chapter, but I am most indebted to Mike Robertson of Fine Edge and Pam Lauritzen, Executive Director of The International Society of Canine Cosmetologists and Editor of *Pet Stylist* magazine, for their contributions on scissoring.

THE DIFFERENT TYPES OF SCISSORS/SHEARS

While there are many sizes and shapes of scissors/ shears available today, basically there are two main styles: straight blades and curved blades. Both styles come in a variety of blade widths (narrow, average and wide) and lengths for right-handed and left-handed groomers: 4½-inch, 5-inch, 6-inch, 6½-inch, 7-inch, 7½-inch, 8-inch, 8¼-inch, 8½-inch, 10-inch and 12-inch. As if that weren't confusing enough, all of these are available with a variety of handle styles: straight shank, bent shank, long or short shank, and offset handles, all with or without finger rests. These are described fully in the sidebar "Scissors/ Shears: Glossary of Important Terms" on page 24.

The type of shears that you select depends on the size of the Poodle or Poodles you will be grooming and the size and shape of your hand. If you really want to give your Poodle a professional finish, it will be necessary to purchase several different shears, but whatever kind you require, always buy the finest quality you can afford. Finely crafted shears hold an edge longer than inexpensive ones, so don't skimp at the beginning. Shears of lesser quality will require sharpening more often and will prove more costly in the long run! Shears are available in every price

range from inexpensive to very expensive. Mario DiFante, a former Intergroom international scissoring champion who conducts scissoring clinics throughout the country, says that comparing inexpensive to expensive shears is almost on a par with comparing a Ford to a Rolls Royce. Both have the same objective, but the expensive one will outlast and outperform the other through advanced technology and expertise in quality craftsmanship.

THE SHEARS YOU NEED FOR POODLE GROOMING

To groom Poodles, you will need shears with medium or long straight blades and shears with medium or long curved blades. The straight-bladed shears (Figure 2-22) are used for overall scissoring (the body and legs) and finishing, while the curved-bladed shears (Figure 2-23) are used principally to trim curved and rounded areas (such as the topknot, tail, puffs,

---

Snap-On Combs by Oster, Laube and M.D.C. Romani

Snap-on comb attachments are designed to fit almost all clippers. Simply clamp the comb to the base of a regular clipper blade (preferably a #30 or #40), then pull up to snap it firmly into place. Always use any snap-on comb on hair that is thoroughly brushed. The hair may be dirty or clean but it must be tangle-free. The hair lengths suggested here will vary slightly because of coat texture.

OSTER UNIVERSAL SNAP-ON COMBS

Hair Length	Comb Size
¹⁄₁₆ "	¹⁄₁₆ "
⅛ "	⅛ "
¼ "	¼ "
½ "	½ "
¾ "	¾ "
1 "	1 "
1¼ "	1¼ "

LAUBE SNAP-ON COMBS

Hair Length	Comb Size
⅞ "	0
¾ "	½
⅝ "	1
½ "	1½
⅜ "	2
⅝ "	3
³⁄₁₆ "	4
¹⁄₁₆ "	5
1 "	A
1¼ "	B
1½ "	C
1¾ "	D
1⅝ "	S
2 "	E

M.D.C. ROMANI SNAP-ON COMBS

Hair Length	Comb Size
¾ "	A
¹³⁄₁₆ "	B
⅞ "	C
¹⁵⁄₁₆ "	D
1 "	E
1¼ "	F
⅝ "	0
⁹⁄₁₆ "	½
½ "	1
⁷⁄₁₆ "	1½
⅜ "	2
⁵⁄₁₆ "	3
¼ "	4
³⁄₁₆ "	5

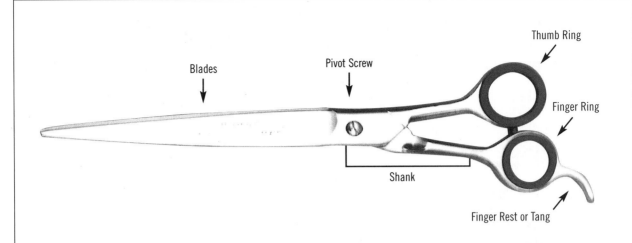

Blades   Pivot Screw   Thumb Ring

Finger Ring

Shank

Finger Rest or Tang

Figure 2-20. The basic components of a shear.

Keep Your Shears in Top Condition

Dog grooming shears should be used exclusively for that purpose and never for cutting paper, string or ribbon, or for dressmaking.

Keep your scissors sharp. Dull shears chop (rather than glide) through the coat and leave an uneven finish. Scissoring dirty hair dulls sharp blades quickly. Always shampoo and dry a Poodle's hair before you use your best and sharpest shears. If you do any rough-cutting before shampooing, use shears that are nearly ready for sharpening.

During the scissoring process, when the blades are sharp, the hair should drop off immediately as the shear closes. As the blades begin to dull, however, you will notice that the hair does not drop off immediately, but slips forward toward the tips of the shears. When this happens your shears need to be sharpened by a professional.

Never leave your shears lying on the grooming table where they can be easily knocked off. The tension will be destroyed and the blades may develop nicks.

The most annoying aspect of keeping and using shears is rust. Any shears made from steel, even stainless, will rust if given the chance. Rust is the reddish brittle coating that forms on metal when chemically attacked by moist air or a liquid. This process is called oxidation. To prevent oxidation, some type of protective coating must stay between the steel and the moisture. This is usually accomplished with oil. Here are some simple remedies to prevent rusting:

1) At the end of each day's use, always wipe your shears before you put them away. Put several drops of lubricating oil on a tissue and wipe over the blades and edges and around the pivot screw (you can purchase special oils/cleaners from your sharpening/clipper blade service center or from grooming supplies mail-order catalogs). Try not to leave finger marks on the blades because the moisture and salt from your hand perspiration will mark the steel. Once the shears are cleaned, store them in their protective sheath or zippered pouch with protective foam lining.

2) Keep your shears in a dry place. It's not a good idea to store them in a drawer, especially if you live in a humid climate since moisture can

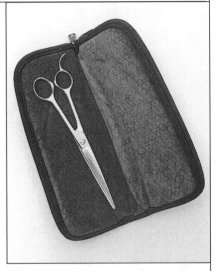

Figure 2-21. Always store clean shears in their protective sheaths or, as shown here, in a zippered pouch.

accumulate inside the sheath or pouch. However, if you must store your tools in a drawer, cabinet or tack box, add some plain white blackboard chalk. It will help to absorb moisture out of the air. Small packets of Silica gel also help to absorb moisture. You can buy these at most electronic supply stores. If you live or work where humidity is a constant problem, consider purchasing a dehumidifier.

Unless rust has heavily pitted the surface of scissors, it can usually be polished off without too much difficulty.

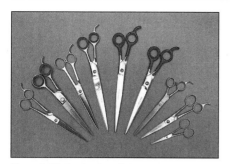

Figure 2-22. A selection of shears with straight blades.

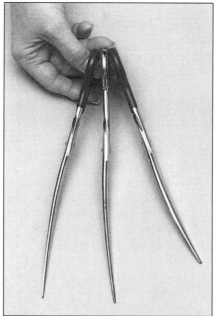

Figure 2-23. A selection of shears with curved blades.

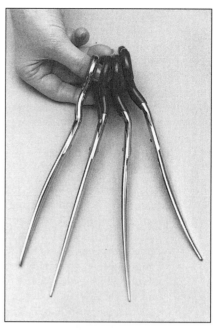

Figure 2-24. A selection shears with bent shanks.

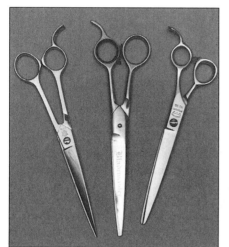

Figure 2-25. The most important consideration in choosing shears is that they fit your hand comfortably and perform efficiently without causing fatigue or straining the nerves and muscles. Handle style is of great importance. Here you see shears with three different handle styles: short-shanked, medium-shanked and long-shanked.

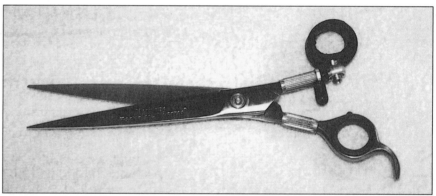

Figure 2-26. Ball-bearing therapeutic grooming shear designed to reduce hand fatigue and Carpal Tunnel Syndrome. (Courtesy Scissorman International)

bracelets and around pattern lines) more efficiently than a straight-bladed implement could.

You also need scissors with short blades and ball-tips for trimming around the face, under the tail, between the pads of the feet and other sensitive areas, and scissors with sharp-tipped short blades for delicate work around the toenails and to finish more detailed designs. If you are only planning to groom your own Poodle, one pair of each type will be sufficient. Professional pet stylists, of course, will need additional shears of various styles and lengths, particularly to use as backup equipment during routine maintenance and repairs. These can be added as you become more proficient.

Your shears can be made of either carbon steel (these "hold" a very sharp edge but have the tendency to rust when not properly maintained) or of ice-tempered stainless steel. It has been said that stainless shears do not hold an edge as long as those made of carbon steel, but this is not true if you purchase a fine grade of stainless.

Short-shanked handles are the best choices for individuals with small to medium hands, short-to-medium fingers and thumbs. The index finger can comfortably reach the pivot screw to hold the shear in place. Medium-shanked handles are suggested for average-sized hands, fingers and thumbs. Long-shanked handles are excellent choices for individuals with large or long hands, and long fingers or thumbs. Bent-shanked shears are also available (Figure 2-24).

Once you have determined the handle style that best suits your hand, then you can choose blade lengths (short, medium and long) and shapes (straight or curved). You will need a variety of blade types and lengths to groom the various sizes of Poodles.

CHOOSING THE CORRECT SHEARS FOR YOUR HAND

It is important to choose shears that not only accommodate your needs but also, and more importantly, your hand type. First and foremost, your shears must feel comfortable in your hand. Look at your hand: Consider its size and shape. Is it small, average-sized, large and broad, delicate and refined? Study your fingers, especially the little one, and your thumb. Are they short, average or long? Do they appear slender, average or muscular? All these physical attributes play an important role in determining which shears will work best in your hand. Using shears that are the right size and length for your hand keeps you from having to "adjust" by using awkward positions to hold them.

Ordinarily, short-shanked shears are more comfortable for groomers with small hands because the index finger can comfortably touch the pivot screw. Short- and medium-shanked shears are more comfortable for average hands, and long-shanked shears are best for large or long hands (Figure 2-25).

Your shears also should be the proper weight for the size and structure of your hand. As an example, if your hand is small and dainty, you would *not* want to choose heavy long-shanked shears. Lifting, gripping and using them can cause too much pressure on the median nerve than runs through your wrist, and you could be setting yourself up for repetitive motion injuries. Conversely, if your hand is long and muscular, you *would* want to choose heavy long-shanked shears so you won't

put too much force on the wrong part of your hand.

After determining the style and weight of the shears that best suits your hand, the next detail to consider is the length and type of the blades. It was previously mentioned that you will need several different shears to properly groom a Poodle. The different blade lengths (short, medium and long) and shapes (straight and curved) are designed to save you time and energy for the specific variety, anatomy and coat type of dogs you will groom. Using the right shears will enhance the quality of your scissoring and make it faster and easier to accomplish. Consider these two examples:

- You could use lightweight, short-bladed 7-inch shears to trim a Standard Poodle with a long, thick coat, but it would take you hours longer to finish than if you used an 8½- or 10-inch shears.

- You could use an 8½-inch shears with straight blades on a skittish Toy Poodle, but a shorter one with curved blades might be a better and safer choice.

HOLDING YOUR SHEARS CORRECTLY

Scissoring will be easier and less fatiguing when you hold your shears correctly, as shown in Figures 2-27 and 2-28.

To hold your shears correctly, follow these steps. The numbers shown in Figure 2-27 correspond to the step numbers.

1) Slip your thumb through the thumb ring. (You will use the pad of your thumb, *not the rest of your hand*, to move up and down to open and close the blades.) Do not allow your thumb to extend through the ring (Figure 2-29).

2) Place your third finger (*not the index or middle finger*) through the finger ring.

3) Rest your little finger in the finger rest letting it support the

third finger at the ring. If it cannot reach the finger rest, hold it comfortably next to your third finger.

4) To support the blades, rest your index finger under the shank directly behind the pivot screw.

5) Allow the shear to lay comfortably across your fingers without strain on your hand or without pressure against your fingers.

DEVELOPING THE CORRECT SCISSORING TECHNIQUE

Here are some suggestions to help you produce a smooth and balanced scissors finish in the least amount of time and without wasted motion. Certain hand and wrist movements may increase your chances of developing repetitive motion problems such as tendonitis and Carpal Tunnel Syndrome. This is nothing to worry about if you only intend to groom your Poodle at home. However, it is another matter, and a serious one, for professional pet stylists. Groomers who repeat the same motions, the same way, for long periods of time, are likely to overuse and stress their muscles.

On the palm side of the wrist, a large nerve passes through a tunnel of tissues on its way to the fingers. Stress on that tissue tunnel squeezes the nerve. The result is numbness of the thumb and index, middle and part of the ring fingers, accompanied by pain. If steps are not taken to relieve pressure on the nerve, tendonitis or Carpal Tunnel Syndrome can develop. A wrist splint may be necessary to diminish inflammation in the tunnel. The way to avoid such problems is to work with well-designed tools (see Figure 2-26), know how to hold and use them, and learn how to use your wrist and hand to avoid causing harm to your muscles, nerves and joints.

Your goal in scissoring your Poodle, whether you are shaping the body, the legs, the topknot or the tail, is to produce an even,

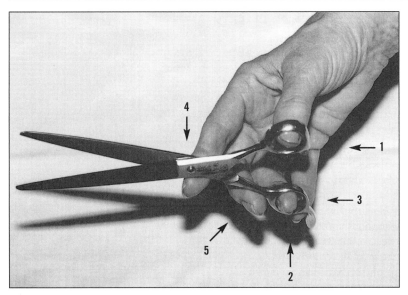

Figure 2-27. Learning to hold the shears correctly is important for all grooomers.

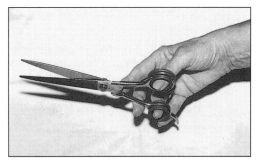

Figure 2-28. Maintaining a straight line between your hand and wrist is important to your comfort and the finished product.

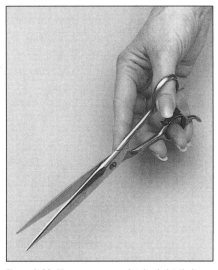

Figure 2-29. Many groomers mistakenly let their thumb project through the thumb ring and open shears by lifting the blades. This not only causes strain, but also produces excessive motion on the blades. If your thumb is narrow and keeps slipping through the thumb ring, add a rubber thumb guard to help correct this problem.

balanced finish that is plush and velvety looking and free of scissors marks. Before you begin, see that the tension on your shears is adjusted properly.

Professionals like their scissors to open and close easily and smoothly with no wasted blade motion. When you open properly adjusted shears and let them fall to close, they should close completely by themselves. If the tension is too tight, the blades will grind against each other, you will use too much force to open and close your shears (increasing the odds of strain), your hand will cramp and your work will look choppy.

Pick up your shears and grip them in the manner previously described. When being held in the scissoring position, a correctly balanced pair of shears should remain level and not dip downwards or raise upwards. Now open and close your shears by moving only your thumb, *not the rest of your hand* (if you move both thumb and fingers, the result will be a very uneven cut). Remember, if the tension is properly adjusted, just the slightest pressure by your thumb pad (not the whole thumb) should be all that is necessary to open

and close the shears. As the blade closes, your thumb should return to a natural position, resting between the index and middle fingers. Practice opening and closing your shears by only moving your thumb, not the rest of your hand; the process may seem a little difficult at first, but it soon should become spontaneous.

When you do start scissoring your Poodle, always hold the shears flat against the hair you are working on and trim a little hair off at a time. By holding your shears parallel with the ends of the hair, each shaft is cut as wide as the root and creates a thick, profuse look. Hold your shears steady against the hair. Don't gouge! And don't point the tips of the blade into the coat; this will create indentations in the hair, and you will never achieve that "plush velvet" finish that is your goal. While scissoring, try to maintain a straight line between your hand and wrist (Figure 2-28). Avoiding bent, extended or twisted positions for long periods of time keeps extra pressure off your wrist and hand.

More information about shaping the various areas—the legs, the body, the topknot, the tail and so

forth—are provided in the grooming instructions in Chapter 20, "The Three AKC-Recognized Show Clips," and Chapter 23, "Pet Clips." No matter what part you are shaping, however, to achieve the desired smooth, even finish, as you are scissoring, you must fluff the hair upward and outward with your comb several times to ease out any straggly hairs and make every hair stand out straight. Do not pick out the coat with your fingers. Fluff the hair out with the comb, and rescissor any uneven sections of the coat

Scissors/Shears: Glossary of Important Terms

Anodized: A protective coating or oxide film, often colored (usually black or gold), on scissors. The finish covers only the sides, not the cutting edges of the blades.

Ball-tipped/Blunt-tipped shears: Shears with rounded tips at the end of each blade. Designed primarily for safety, these help prevent accidental puncturing (especially when grooming nervous dogs) and are useful for trimming sensitive areas, such as around the eyes and the toes or the undersides of the feet.

Bent-shank shear: A shear in which the shank (the part between the blade and finger holes) is bent to reduce finger tracks through the coat, and to make it easier to trim around the bottoms of the legs, the feet, the underbody and other hard-to-reach areas. See Figure 2-24.

Carbon steel: The steel most often used to make shears. Heated to extremely high temperatures, it is then forged to hold a very sharp edge and to maintain the longest life. Shears made of carbon steel have a tendency to rust if they are not kept in good condition. Consequently, they always should be well-oiled and, when not in use, stored in a protective sheath or case.

Coated/Dipped handles: Handles coated with soft plastic or a rubber compound, often in a variety of colors. Coated handles help to reduce shock and also act as permanent finger and thumb guards for better comfort and control.

Corrugated/Serrated blades: During the scissoring process, hair sometimes has a tendency to be pushed forward rather than cut off. Corrugating or serrating is a process in which micro-grooves are notched into the edge of the blade to hold the hair shafts more securely and to provide nonslip cutting. Shears with both blades serrated will not cut as smoothly

as those that are plain ground. Thus, many professionals prefer a combination of one blade finely serrated to hold the hair and the other razor-sharp to cut smoothly and efficiently.

Curved shear: A shear in which the blades are curved to make it easier to shape rounded and/or curved areas (topknot, tail, bracelets, puffs), to bevel around pattern lines and for all contouring. Professionals also use a curved shear in reverse above the hock joint on the back legs to cut in more angulation. See Figure 2-23.

Ergonomic shears: Arthritis, Carpal Tunnel Syndrome and other repetitive-motion injuries are common in grooming. Ergonomic shears are designed to cause less fatigue and strain for groomers who suffer from these conditions. See Figure 2-26.

Filipino style: A type of sturdy shear with a wide 8¼-inch-long blade for general-purpose and heavy-duty use. Excellent for scissoring thick coats.

Finger guards: Rubber rings (available for thumb or finger) that can be inserted into the shear handles. Guards are used for different reasons:

- Comfort and protection. When shears are used for a long time, guards can help to reduce or prevent uncomfortable blisters, especially in new groomers.

- For groomers with small hands, guards make shears easier to control by decreasing the size of the thumb or finger ring.

- Guards also help to prevent "scissors shock," the reaction that occurs when the handles of the shears close and strike against each other. This mild shock is transmitted to and absorbed by the hand, wrist and lower arm, and is a major contributor to Carpal Tunnel

Syndrome and other groomer hand problems.

Hollow ground: A process in which the inside of a blade is ground down to give a sharper edge and smoother cut.

Honed/Razor edge: Edges on a cutting implement that are honed to razor sharpness.

Ice-tempered: A process, most beneficial to stainless shears, in which the steel is hardened by heat-treating and then cooled to frigid temperatures, culminating in a longer-lasting cutting edge.

Nasal scissors: Short, straight-blade scissors with ball-tip end, generally 4½ or 5 inches long, frequently used to scissor around the eyes and ears, under the tail and between the toes, especially on toy Poodles.

Offset handles: When the finger hole is slightly longer than the thumb hole, the handles are called offset. This provides a more comfortable hold on the handles for highly accurate and detailed cutting. Usually found on shears of the finest quality.

Scissor guards: See Finger guards.

Serrated blades: See Corrugated/Serrated blades.

Silencer: A piece of rubber or plastic placed between the handles to absorb the shock and sound made when shears close. A silencer is not necessary if shears have coated, plastic or molded handles.

Stainless steel: A high-quality steel combined with chromium and other alloys and highly polished to resist corrosion.

Straight-edge shears: Shears with straight blades that taper to a point, mostly used for general-purpose cutting. See Figure 2-22.

Teflon-coated: A protective coating on scissors, often colored, that helps to prevent surface rust.

Figure 2-30. Flat-backed slicker brushes.

Figure 2-31. Curved-back slicker brushes.

Figure 2-32. Pin brushes.

until the finish is completely even and velvety looking. You'll probably have to repeat this several times until no more straggly hairs come out of the coat.

If you wish to learn more about the art of scissoring and geometrics in canine design, Pam Lauritzen, the founder and Executive Director of the International Society of Canine Cosmetologists (ISCC) has produced an informative guidebook and video on the subject. Contact the ISCC at 2702 Covington Drive, Garland, TX 75040, USA.

SCISSOR PLIERS

This tool is used to adjust the tension of all manufacturers' scissors and shears. Before beginning to use new shears, the tension often needs to be adjusted. The correct tool to use is a scissors pliers, not a screwdriver. Scissors pliers help to adjust a shear's tension by either loosening or tightening the holding screw without impairing the performance of the scissors.

Brushes

There are several types and styles of brushes for Poodle coats, and each is meant to do a specific job. The various brush types and styles also are available in different sizes and shapes to fit the groomer's hand because, like choosing shears, what is comfortable for one person may feel cumbersome to another.

The most popular brush for Poodles in pet trim is the slicker brush. An oblong-shaped, flat-backed (Figure 2-30) or curved-backed (Figure 2-31) brush with a wooden or plastic handle, the slicker has bent-wire teeth set close together in a foam rubber pad. This is an excellent brush for penetrating the coat and for removing mats and dead hair. Slickers come in many sizes: mini and small (for Toy Poodles and puppies), medium (for Miniatures) and large (for Standards). The bent-wire teeth are available in different gauges: soft and flexible, average and extra stiff.

For Poodles in show coat, a slicker can be used to brush out the bracelets, puffs or pack, but not the mane, as it would pull out the long hair. Instead, use a brush with long pliable pins or bristles set in a cushioned rubber base for "down-to-the-skin" brushing of a show coat (Figure 2-32). The finest pin brushes have long, polished stainless-steel or chrome-plated pins with rounded tips to prevent scratching or irritating the skin. When passing through the long hair, the pins should be flexible enough not to pull out coat. (**Note:** Pins that have bent or have sunk into the rubber cushion tend to damage the coat. When either condition is present, the brush should be replaced immediately.) The pin brush preferred by most professional groomers and dog show handlers is the No. 1 All-Systems™ brush. The best bristle brushes are those with tufts of natural bristle; the bristles in each tuft should be graduated in length to give even, deep penetration through the long hair.

Combs

Poodle combs are made in many styles and sizes, and today it is possible to match the tooth length and spacing to your Poodle's size, coat texture and coat length. Quality is important. The best combs are made of chrome-plated sold brass or of stainless steel and have spring-tempered teeth with rounded tips to prevent scratching and skin irritation. Some are coated with Teflon™ to reduce static electricity. Many of the most popular styles are shown in Figure 2-33. Generally speaking, fine-tooth combs are used for soft or sparse hair; medium-tooth combs are used for average coat textures, and coarse-tooth combs work best on dense or heavy coats. The tooth length of most of these combs ranges from ⅞ inch to 1¼ inches long, making it possible to get down to the skin of even the longest coats for an effective comb-out.

Figure 2-33. The popular Greyhound comb and some similar models.

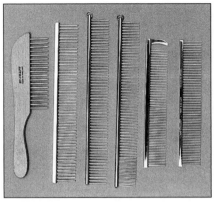

Figure 2-34. A selection of combs normally used with Poodles.

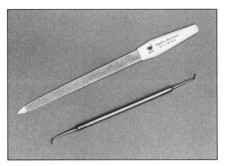

Figure 2-35. A dental scaler (bottom) and a nail file (top).

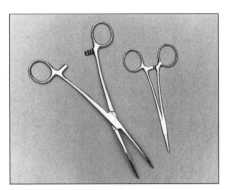

Figure 2-36. A pair of hemostats: Curved (left) and straight (right).

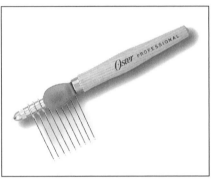

Figure 2-37. The Oster Professional Mat Comb.

Figure 2-38. The Wahl Electric Detangling Comb.

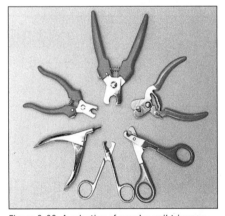

Figure 2-39. A selection of popular nail trimmers.

The comb preferred by most professional groomers and handlers is the "Greyhound" or Greyhound type (the style originated in Belgium; many manufacturers from various countries have produced their own versions of it) shown in Figure 2-33. It is 7½ inches long, and comes with long, polished teeth spaced in a combination of either half-fine/half-medium or half-medium/half-coarse. It is an excellent choice for use on both show and pet coats.

There is another type of metal comb that is used by dog show handlers, exhibitors and professional groomers, especially for Standard and Miniature Poodles. It has a long back (about 10 inches) with many extra-long, widely-spaced teeth. Because the teeth are so long (about 1¼ inches) and so wide, it is especially effective for slipping into the long coat to lift and fluff the hair. Two examples are illustrated in Figure 2-34: the Ultimate Poodle Comb with 48 teeth (#1 All Systems) and the Ultra Lift (Liz Paul) with 59 teeth.

Other Tools and Equipment

There is a lot more to grooming a Poodle than clipping, brushing, combing, and scissoring. Here are the additional tools and equipment you should have in your grooming toolbox.

DENTAL SCALER

To remove tartar from the teeth, select a right- and left-angled dental scaler (Figure 2-35) with a flat, not pointed surface (see the section titled "Care of the Teeth and Mouth" in chapter 7).

FORCEPS/HEMOSTAT

Poodles and other "hairy" breeds with long, hanging ears often experience problems because of the hair growing in their ears and the fact that the ear flap covers the

Figure 2-40. The Oster Pet Nail Groomer.

Figure 2-41. The Rapid Electric Stand Dryer.

Figure 2-42. The Edemco Stand Dryer.

opening. A forceps or hemostat is a two-pronged instrument with straight or curved tips and is used for grasping or seizing (Figure 2-36). In grooming, it is used to pluck out excessive hair that normally grows inside the ears. When the ears are long and heavy or when the opening into the canal is comparatively small, if the superfluous hair is not removed periodically, the air circulation will be shut off, leading to excessive wax formation and infection inside the ear canal. (See the section titled "Cleaning the Ears" in chapter 7).

DEMATTING TOOLS

These are special combs, splitters and rakes designed to help break apart tangled and matted hair. Because of the angle of the teeth, they are more efficient than regular combs for difficult jobs. When used correctly, they can make the unpleasant task of removing tangles easier and often more bearable for the dog.

One of the more popular tools of this type are the Oster Professional Mat Comb (Figure 2-37), with long tapered metal teeth, a metal

thumb rest and wooden handle. The teeth are reversible and can be used by a right- or left-handed person. Other tools include the Matbreaker dematter, with stainless steel "tease point blades" which can be reversed for left-handed use, and a variety of tangle combs and rakes, implements that resemble tiny garden rakes, with rows of straight or diagonally set teeth (of various lengths) with rounded tips that will not scratch the skin.

Dry coats are difficult to detangle. In conjunction with any mat-removing tool, consider using a liquid detangling product to help break the static lock of the mats and make the process easier for the groomer and more comfortable for the dog. (See the section titled "Untangling Matted Hair" in chapter 3).

A new innovation in detangling hair is the Wahl Electric Detangling Comb (Figure 2-38) with eight alternating teeth that oscillate back and forth at the rate of 3,000 times per minute to remove mats quickly. It should be used on dry hair only.

NAIL TRIMMER

Nails should be trimmed each time the Poodle is groomed; if they are neglected and allowed to grow long, the feet will spread and the dog could eventually become lame. There are several manual and electric tools that will shorten a Poodle's nails. The type you choose depends on personal preference.

Manual trimmers are available in different sizes to accommodate Toy, Miniature or Standard Poodles. The most popular ones are the following types, which are illustrated in Figure 2-39:

- The guillotine type, where the nail is inserted into an opening above the cutting blade. As the handles are squeezed together, a blade passes over the opening and cuts off part of the nail, hence the name guillotine.

- The scissors type, where the nail is inserted into an opening and the scissor-type handles are pressed together.

- The "safety guard" trimmer, a tool, resembling a pliers, that is equipped with a safety stop near the cutting blade. The safety can be moved into place

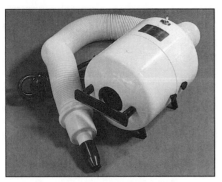

Figure 2-43. The Edemco High-Velocity Dryer.

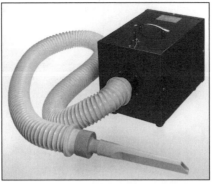

Figure 2-44. The Rapid Electric High-Velocity Dryer.

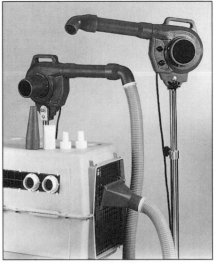

Figure 2-45. The Double K Challengair 900 Drying System.

to limit the amount of nail to be trimmed, or can be pushed aside when not needed.

An electric nail groomer is a small, lightweight two-speed grinding tool with a drum and sanding band at one end. It shortens the nails by high rotating speeds. The most popular electric nail groomers are made by Oster Professional Products (Figure 2-40). Replacement drums, bands and abrasive wheels can be purchased separately. (See the section titled "Trimming the Nails" in chapter 7.)

NAIL FILE

A nail file should be used to shorten the nails completely or to smooth sharp edges left after cutting them with a manual trimmer. (See the section titled "Trimming the Nails" in chapter 7.)

HAIR DRYER

Electric hair dryers speed drying time considerably and help add a more "finished" look to the Poodle's final grooming. For home grooming, use any good-quality handheld dryer to dry your dog quickly. You can build body and fullness into the hair by directing the airflow against the natural

growth of the hair while brushing the area at the same time.

Pet grooming stylists and dog show handlers and exhibitors prefer either heavy-duty heat or high-velocity professional dryers. A professional heat dryer is one supported by a sturdy, adjustable-height stand (Figures 2-41 and 2-42). The non-tippable legs are equipped with ball casters so the dryer can be moved about without difficulty. Most heat dryers have long rigid arms with rubber-insulated nozzles that rotate a full 360 degrees to direct the heat and air flow where it is needed. Heat and air output vary depending on the model chosen, but most will dry the heaviest coats in a very short time. Some dryers have three-position switches (cool, warm and hot), while others have infinite-range heat control, allowing you to select any temperature between cool and hot.

The other type of professional dryer is called a high-velocity dryer (Figures 2-43, 2-44 and 2-45). On most models, no heating element is used. Rather than a rigid arm with a rotating rubber nozzle, these dryers have one or more flexible hoses with nozzles attached. How is warm air

generated without a heating element? The high-velocity air flow cools the motors which themselves generate considerable heat; the heat is carried away through the flexible hose to the nozzle outlet.

High-velocity dryers, such as the Edemco™ Force, the Rapid Electric™ Drying Saucer, the Romani™ Quiet Force Dryer, the Double K™ ChallengeAir 850 XL and three models from Metro— the Air Force Commander, the Air Force Blaster and the Air Force Master Blaster—are capable of extremely high speeds, providing a higher airflow than regular stand dryers to cut drying time (and the use of electrical energy) almost in half. As the nozzle is directed at the coat, the powerful flow of warm air blasts beads of water down the hair shafts and off the dog. As this happens, the hair dries faster and straighter from the skin out (heat dryers, conversely, dry hair from the tips in), often without the use of a brush, making them excellent choices for use on Poodles in show coat and other longhaired breeds (especially those with difficult-to-dry heavy undercoats). One caution: Some high-velocity dryers are so powerful that they can frighten small dogs

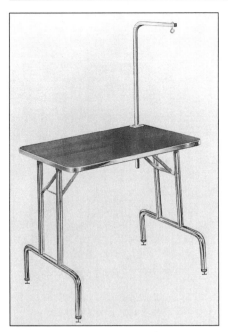

Figure 2-46. The basic portable professional grooming table is universally popular.

Figure 2-47. The hydraulic grooming table by PetLift, Ltd.

Figure 2-48. The hydraulic grooming table by Rapid Electric.

and almost blow them off the grooming table.

In a busy all-breed grooming salon, most professionals use both types of dryers: a high-velocity dryer to quickly remove the excess moisture after a bath, and a stand dryer with a heating element to fluff and finish the coat.

GROOMING TABLE

Choosing a grooming table is important because it is an important aid for establishing habit patterns of good grooming behavior in any dog. Your grooming table must be sturdy and not tip over, especially if you intend to groom a large, strong Poodle that likes to move around.

For home grooming, use any rigid table that is comfortable to work on. One that is about 30 inches high, or halfway between your hip or knee will be less tiring. Your own height and the size of your dog are important in determining how high your table should be. If your table has a smooth top, buy a "table topper" mat through

any of the pet supply catalogs or grooved rubber matting at any hardware store to keep your Poodle from slipping.

The most basic professional grooming tables feature a rectangular-shaped thick plywood top covered with slip-resistant, heavy-duty rubber matting (Figure 2-46). They are available in several different sizes: 24 × 36 inches (the size most widely used), 18 × 30 inches and 24 × 48 inches. These tables are portable and many are fitted with carrying handles. They fold up and may be stored away when not in use and conveniently transported to and from dog shows or grooming contests and by groomers who make house calls.

Most portable tables are about 30 inches high with chrome-plated non-adjustable tubular steel legs. It is possible, however, to buy a set of leg extenders in either a 6-inch fixed height or adjustable to 7½ inches. You can also purchase a special set of four swivel casters or wheels, complete with a pulling

rope, which can be fitted to the underside of the grooming table top. These are especially beneficial for dog show exhibitors/handlers and grooming contest competitors; once the wheels are attached, the folded table converts into a "dolly" or carrier base for moving crates and tack boxes at shows.

For the professional pet stylist, the ultimate in grooming tables are equipped with hydraulic or electric mechanisms (Figures 2-47 and 2-49). These greatly reduce fatigue and strain on the neck, shoulders and back as they offer a greater range of variable heights, so that groomers do not have to stoop over or stand on tiptoe when they are working. The finest models are manufactured by PetLift™ (Figures 2-47 and 2-49), Edemco (Figure 2-50) and Rapid Electric (Figures 2-48 and 2-51).

The hydraulic models are available with sturdy rectangular, oval or round tops that are situated on heavy, tip-proof bases. The tables adjust, with the pump of a foot pedal, from a low of about

Figure 2-49. The electric grooming table by PetLift, Ltd.

Figure 2-50. The electric grooming table by Edemco.

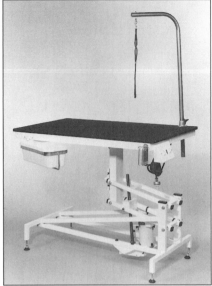

Figure 2-51. The electric grooming table by Rapid Electric.

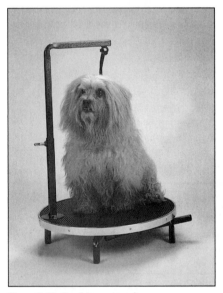

Figure 2-52. The Edemco Lazy Susan.

19 inches to a high of about 41 inches. On the best hydraulic models, the tops swivel, allowing a groomer to work from several locking positions without having to continuously walk around the table. Some hydraulic tables are available with Formica™ cabinets (beneath the table top and above the hydraulic mechanism) for tool storage.

Electric grooming tables are available with both stationary and rotating nonskid rectangular tops, generally in sizes 24 × 42 inches and 24 × 36 inches. They glide smoothly up and down, by pressing an electrically operated foot control, from 19 inches to about 40 inches, and their powerful motor-driven gears can lift up to 400 pounds. Some electric tables have illuminated tops which diffuse light through opaque Lucite™. The soft light helps to reduce eye strain by giving a clear view of the dog's coat—underbody and insides of the legs, as well as the back and sides—at all times. Most also have built-in outlets for clippers. The best hydraulic and electric tables are extremely solid and do not wobble or tip over at any height. They are rather expensive, however, and before purchasing such a table, it is a good idea to determine that it is solid by leaning on it or resting against it.

An excellent innovation that should be mentioned here is the Edemco Lazy Susan (Figure 2-52), an 18-inch round grooming platform with its own post, designed to rest on the top of any regular grooming table, which turns smoothly and locks with the touch of a finger. Its smaller surface is ideal for controlling small Poodles and keeping them from moving about. The groomer has much less stretching to do to reach the dog.

GROOMING POST AND LOOP

A grooming post is a round or square post constructed of heavy gauge chrome-plated steel that can be either bolted to a grooming table top or clamped onto its side (Figures 2-53 and 2-54). Both types are adjustable and are available in regular or heavy duty strengths. At the shorter end of the post is an adjustable loop (usually made of nylon or supple leather) that fits around the dog's neck to hold his head up when in a standing position. It also prevents the dog from falling or jumping off the table. Using a grooming post and loop should be mandatory since it frees both hands for the groomer to do other work. Choose a heavy-duty post for large or strong Poodles; their size or strength can cause a regular post to bend.

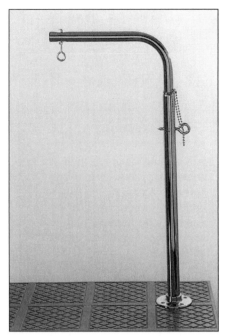

Figure 2-53. A grooming post that is bolted to the table by PetLift, Ltd.

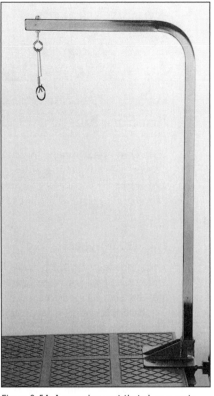

Figure 2-54. A grooming post that clamps on to the table by PetLift, Ltd.

Figure 2-55. A selection of tack boxes suitable for dog shows or many other grooming applications.

EQUIPMENT ORGANIZER

No matter what your goal is—to groom your own Poodle at home, to show your Poodle in the breed ring, to become a professional groomer (operating out of a salon or mobile grooming van) or to compete in grooming contests—you need some type of container to organize your tools and keep them at your fingertips.

If you only intend to groom your pet Poodle at home, a plastic carry-all or basket makes an ideal container for storing all your tools and supplies without having to stop and search for a particular item while you are grooming.

If you're planning to exhibit your Poodle at dog shows or to compete in grooming contests throughout the country, you will need to carry certain tools and supplies with you. You may want to consider purchasing a grooming case or *tack box*. Tack boxes are metal or wooden containers, available in various sizes, with a number of compartments and trays to hold smaller grooming tools as well as deeper areas for storing bottles and sprays (Figure 2-55). Most have recessed areas in the lid to hold leads and collars. For convenience, the carrying handle on the top of the box is usually bolted for added strength.

For those who will be grooming in salons or vans, there are many professional organizers to choose from that will not only save space and effort but also protect expensive equipment from damage:

- Wall-mounted sturdy holders to keep clippers secure

- Clear acrylic racks, magnetic holders or blade caddies/cases to protect and store clipper blades

- Specially designed Lucite holders that align and protect shears

- Heavy-duty plastic countertop containers to sort brushes, combs, shears and other small implements

- Leather roll-up cases or holsters to protect shears

- Acrylic ribbon and nail-polish dispensers

Another option is a portable polystyrene grooming cart (with drawers and compartments) on rolling casters. These furnishings are available from most mail-order pet supply companies, especially those that specialize in materials for groomers. Just remember that in a grooming salon or mobile van, expensive shears, clippers and other tools should never be left lying on a grooming table; they can be accidentally knocked off by a dog, resulting in some very expensive, very avoidable repairs.

As soon as you acquire a poodle, you must set up a regular brushing and combing schedule, for these are the most essential of all grooming tasks. The easiest way to keep your poodle's coat in good condition is to brush and comb it regularly. A thorough brushing is a prerequisite for a beautiful finished trim. Right away, get your poodle accustomed to being placed on a steady grooming table. If the poodle is a puppy, place your hand under the stomach for support and confidence as you gently brush through the coat. Doing this several times a week is all that is necessary to make your dog behave and think of brushing as a pleasant experience.

Brushing and Combing

Regularly brushing the coat achieves the following results:

- Massages the skin, stimulating new hair growth.

- Removes dirt, dust and dead hair.

- Helps prevent tangles and mats from forming.

- Keeps the skin clean and healthy and makes the dog less susceptible to disease and external parasites.

- Spreads the natural oils evenly through the coat.

- Keeps hair looking healthy and more glossy.

Brushing the hair three times a week is sufficient, provided that you do it correctly. Every hair must be brushed, not just the ones that are easy to reach. The mistake most pet owners make

---

Brushing Aids

Both coat conditioners and coat dressings are brushing aids. The basic difference is that one product contains oil while the other does not.

COAT CONDITIONERS

These products (in both aerosol and nonaerosol form) are generally applied during brushing or combing to condition the hair. They make hair easier to brush or comb, minimize dryness and help to reduce tangling. Most of the better brands contain an anti-static compound to keep hair from becoming flyaway, plus conditioners and oils (e.g., mink oil) to condition and add a gloss or luster which deepens and enriches the natural coat color. Some also contain a PABA ultraviolet sunscreen to protect the hair and skin from excessive ultraviolet radiation when a dog

is in an outdoor run. Conditioners containing protein help to rebuild and restructure the hair by bonding to the shaft. They help add body to thin hair and improve its appearance and manageability.

FINISHING SPRAY OR COAT DRESSING

These products contain a number of ingredients to make the hair shine, plus anti-static compounds to control flyaway hair (caused by the build-up of static electricity) and nonoily conditioners. They also help to repel dirt. Many contain an ultraviolet sunscreen to protect the hair from the sun's rays when the dog is outdoors. They are used during brushing and combing when no oil is desired on the coat.

---

is not brushing the hair close to the skin. This means parting the coat and holding down the unbrushed hair with your free hand to separate it from the hair that is being brushed. If you can learn to do this correctly, your dog will never become matted.

Selecting and correctly using the right brush and comb plays an important part in the health of your Poodle's skin and coat. Using the wrong tools or the wrong techniques can cause the hair ends to break off.

Along with the correct brush and comb, use a protein-added coat conditioner, light oil or nonoily

coat dressing (see the sidebar titled "Brushing Aids" above). These are specially formulated products that are sprayed lightly onto the hair to moisten it before brushing. Brushing dry hair causes static electricity; the hair will be brittle and flyaway, and often the brush bristles or teeth of the comb will snap the hair ends and cause them to break off. A little moisture helps the brush and comb pass more easily through the dog's coat. Before you begin brushing, spray a little conditioner or coat dressing on the hair; don't saturate it.

Follow this illustrated step-by-step procedure for brushing and combing your poodle.

Figure 3-1. **Step 1:** Start with an unbrushed pet Poodle.

Figure 3-2. **Step 2:** While there is no special way to brush a pet Poodle, it seems easier to start at the dog's tail and hindquarters and work forward. Using the slicker brush described in chapter 5, brush the back legs first, using a downward stroke. Notice that the hair is parted to the skin and that the palm of your free hand should be holding down the unbrushed hair to separate it from the section that is being brushed. With each new brush stroke . . .

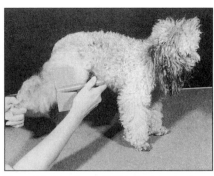

Figure 3-3. **Step 3:** . . . Pull the back leg backward carefully, and brush the hair upward, using brisk strokes that lift the hair rather than flatten it.

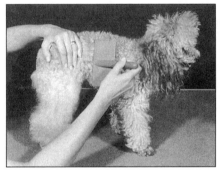

Figure 3-4. **Step 4:** Continue working forward and brush the tail, hindquarters, back, ribs and chest, parting the hair and brushing from the roots outward.

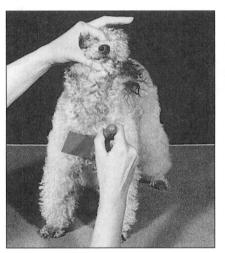

Figure 3-5. **Step 5:** Turn the dog around to stand facing you, and brush the front of the chest.

Figure 3-6. **Step 6:** Gently pull each front leg forward as you brush the hair upward. Be sure to brush the area under the front legs (the armpits) and on the neck behind the ears, as most owners forget these spots and tangles often form there as a result.

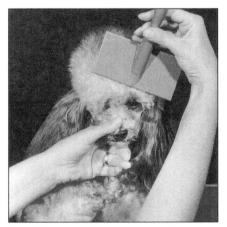

Figure 3-7. **Step 7:** Place the dog in a sitting position facing you. Brush the topknot upward and backward. Brush the ear feathering downward.

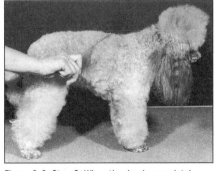

Figure 3-8. **Step 8:** When the dog is completely brushed, comb through the coat to be sure all tangles are removed.

Figure 3-9. **Step 9:** The Poodle after brushing and combing is a handsome dog, indeed.

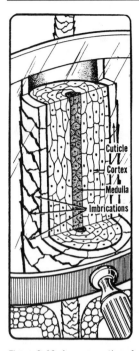

Figure 3-10. A cross-section of the hair shaft: how tangles form.

Figure 3-11. In severe cases of tangling, it may be necessary to clip off most of the body and leg hair. On this black Miniature Poodle, the matted areas were almost one solid mass close to the skin. As the dog had a lot of coat (the mats were so tight that the true hair length is not evident in this photograph), it was decided to trim him in the Miami clip. The coat on the body and three-quarters of the legs was clipped with a #7 blade. The remaining matted hair on the topknot, ears, tail and bottoms of the legs were soaked in a liquid detangler, then brushed out.

Tangled and Matted Hair

The most common reasons for mats and tangles are neglect in brushing or incorrect brushing. While a pet owner may select the correct brush and comb for his or her Poodle, they are often used incorrectly, perhaps only whisking through the topcoat, instead of going through to the skin. The dead hair becomes tangled with the live portion of the hair, and within a short time a solid block of matted hair forms near the skin.

Even when one knows how to properly brush a Poodle's coat, there are critical "coat matting" periods to face. Long spells of damp weather and humidity make the hair mat easily. Heavy snow is harsh on Poodle hair. Dogs that go outdoors and become soaked tend to mat quickly if the hair is not brushed and dried properly afterwards. The most critical coat period for a Poodle, however, is when the puppy coat is *blowing*

or changing to adult texture. At this time, the ends of the hair are rather sparse while the coat at the skin is much thicker: The fine puppy hair is being replaced by a coarser hair in the same follicle. As the new, harder coat grows in, it becomes tangled with the soft puppy coat. During this changeover period, if the Poodle is not brushed daily, the hair mats almost overnight and forms large clumps near the skin. The most troublesome spots are the neck and shoulders, behind the ears, in the "armpits" under the front legs and between the back legs. The change of coat texture can be exasperating to owners of show prospects; in fact this interval often separates the true exhibitor from the amateur, because it's usually the time that many owners decide they are not up to growing and maintaining a show coat.

Before you can cope with matted hair, it is necessary to understand how tangles form. All types of

hair (human and canine) have two basic parts: the root and the shaft. The root is implanted in the skin, and the shaft is the part that projects from the surface. As you can see in Figure 3-10, the hair shaft is composed of three separate layers: *the cuticle*, or outer layer; *the cortex,* or middle layer, and *the medulla*, or inner layer.

The cuticle is formed by overlapping, hard and flat scales (similar to roof shingles or fish scales). These scales project upward and outward like barbs in the direction of the hair growth. On healthy hair, especially hair that is brushed regularly and correctly, these scales lie flat and reflect light. However, they tend to attract much dirt, debris and foreign matter. If the hair is neglected or subjected to harsh brushing techniques, the scales become uneven, raised and very dry. Subsequently, when there is a lack of oil on the hair shaft, the ragged edges of the barbs interlock with those of other hairs like strips of Velcro™, and form tangles. The longer the coat is ignored, the more extensive the tangled area becomes. If the coat is continuously neglected, one solid mat will eventually result. Hair is also charged negatively by static electricity accumulating on the cuticle. Excess electricity causes flyaway ends, and it also can cause matting and tangling. Also, fine hair tends to tangle more easily than coarse hair.

Untangling Matted Hair

If the hair is badly matted, you may have to decide whether to clip off the dog's entire coat and start from scratch or to try and remove the tangles. With enough patience and practice, though, even the largest mat can be removed with little hair loss. You must, however, consider the comfort of the dog, for no Poodle can be expected to sit quietly while you rip through the coat trying to detangle it! Probably the easiest and fastest way to save as much coat as possible and to restore the hair to optimum condition is to use a tangle removing product in conjunction with a slicker brush or mat-removing tool. Products such as Ring 5™ Untangle or Outrage, Oster's Pawformance Spray-On Detangler, Lambert Kay's™ No Tangle, or The Stuff™ and others contain untangling components that help break the static lock that makes mats and tangles so difficult to remove. They also contain special conditioning oils to add body, help repair damage caused by the tangling and help to reduce further tangling. One thing you must remember: Such products are not "magic" in a bottle; they help tremendously, but removing mats is often a very tedious job.

For best results, saturate all the matted hair with the detangling product. Make sure the mats are completely wet; use your fingers to massage the detangler deep into the tangled clumps. This is important because the combination of

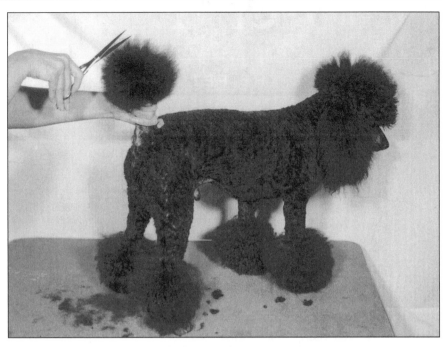

Figure 3-12. After bathing, the hair on the tail, leg puffs, topknot and ears was fluff dried. The body and legs were clipped with a #7F for a smoother finish. Here, the groomer is ready to begin scissor finishing.

lubricants, detanglers and conditioning oils work by lubricating the locked barbs so that one hair slides over the other and breaks the friction of the static lock. Allow the product to remain on the coat until the hair is damp or almost dry. Use your fingers or favorite mat-removing tool (these are described in chapter 2) to pull apart large clumps of mats, separating them into smaller sections. Then brush out each small section. Keep breaking the mats into smaller and smaller sections and brushing the hair until the dog is completely tangle-free. Always remove tangles from the tips of the hair first then gradually work down the hair shafts towards the skin. Some grooming guides advise using scissors (with one blade pointed downwards) to split through densely matted areas; be *very* careful if you try this as it is easy to accidentally cut the skin. If your Poodle is badly matted, don't even try to finish the entire job in one sitting. Stop when you feel tired or impatient, or if your dog becomes restless.

To save time in a busy salon, some professional groomers, would

sooner deal with tangles while the dog is in the bathtub. In this process, the dog is shampooed and rinsed well. The coat is squeezed to remove as much dripping water as possible, then plenty of creme rinse, conditioner or liquid detangler is applied to the damp hair and worked into the matted parts. The groomer then gently begins to break up the tangles, *before* rinsing out the product, starting at the hair ends and gradually working down to the roots. Once the tangles are removed, the coat is thoroughly rinsed one last time.

In severe cases of matting, as previously mentioned, it may be necessary to clip off the body and leg hair with a #5 or #7 blade (Figure 3-11). If these won't go through the mats easily, it will probably be necessary to switch to an #8-1/2, #9 or #10 blade. Try to save some topknot hair and the tail pompon. Once the mats are off, the new coat can start growing in. However, neglecting the new coat will result in matting just as before. The groomer or owner who lets a coat fall into neglect must resolve to be more conscientious to totally avoid the problem.

Bathing stimulates the skin; removes excess oil, dirt and bacteria; washes away dead hair, dander and external parasites and their droppings; and keeps a dog looking good and smelling clean. You might think that bathing a dog is straightforward and simple, but there are many diverse opinions on the subject. Some people say that much of the natural oil in the skin and coat is lost during bathing, and that excessive shampooing leads to dry skin and hair. Others insist that a dog can be bathed as often as one chooses. Excessive bathing should be avoided, of course, but providing you observe the proper precautions and use the right products and techniques, frequent shampooing will not harm a dog's skin and coat and will actually remoisturize it.

Actually, how often you should shampoo your Poodle depends on his coat texture, color (how quickly he gets dirty), and the temperature and humidity in your area. For the average Poodle, a bath every two weeks or so will keep him looking good, but if you use a correctly pH balanced shampoo, you can bathe as often as necessary. Since no one wants a smelly pet around the house, the answer to the question "How often should I bathe my dog?" is "Whenever he needs it."

Don't underestimate the importance of a bath. Clean, bouncy, tangle-free hair that has been thoroughly shampooed and rinsed (with no soap residues left behind) and properly dried is *the foundation* for final grooming.

Choosing the Right Shampoo

Choosing the right shampoo can bewilder even the most knowledgeable professional groomer. With dozens of products available, it is often difficult to know which ones to use. The first consideration is that the shampoo should be pH balanced for dogs, not humans.

The determination of pH is an important factor in human as well as animal hair and skin care. To explain briefly, all chemicals are acid, alkali, or neutral. The degree of acidity or alkalinity in a product is measured by a pH scale which runs from 0 to 14, with 7—the mid-point—being neutral. Anything between 0 and 7 is acid; anything between 7 and 14 is alkaline.

Human hair and skin are slightly acidic. On the other hand, the pH range for the dog's skin and hair is slightly more alkaline and not the same as that of humans. Therefore, try to avoid using your own personal shampoos to wash your Poodle. Dogs need an alkaline-based shampoo to keep their coat and skin at the healthiest, strongest state.

All shampoos have the same basic purpose: to clean the hair and leave it in a normal, healthy condition. While most do a good job, their various formulations can make significant differences in the coat. Within the grouping of correctly pH balanced shampoos for dogs, you can find many excellent products designed for general or special use from such top manufacturers as Ring 5, #1 All Systems, Oster, Lambert Kay, BioGroom™,

Tomlyn™, Tropiclean™, Nature's Choice™ and many, many others. From this available array, you can choose an effective shampoo to suit your particular needs.

ALL-PURPOSE SHAMPOOS

These are formulated for all coat textures and all colors. Some contain special ingredients and conditioning agents—protein, jojoba, aloe vera or other herbal extracts, mink oil, coconut oil— for example. All-purpose shampoos clean thoroughly and condition the skin and coat, add just the right amount of body, leave the hair shiny and keep the coat in optimum condition. Those with special conditioning ingredients help to restore luster to dull hair and, depending on the added conditioner, to rebuild damaged hair.

TEARLESS SHAMPOOS

These are mild formulations and are especially recommended for puppies and for adult Poodles with sensitive skins. Tearless formulations are best for washing the head without irritating the Poodle's eyes.

MEDICATED SHAMPOOS

These shampoos, containing antifungal, antibacterial or antipruritic ingredients, are formulated to help relieve itching, scaling, bacterial fungus, dry skin caused by allergies and nonspecific types of dermatitis and to soothe irritated skin.

HYPO-ALLERGENIC SHAMPOOS

These are extremely mild formulations that contain no fragrances or dyes and are specially designed for dogs with extra-sensitive skins or skin allergies.

COLOR-ENHANCING SHAMPOOS

These are formulated for specific coat colors. They are not permanent dyes or color changers, but products that intensify the natural coat color through the use of optical brighteners by highlighting rather than changing. For example, shampoos for white and light-colored Poodles help to remove yellow or grayish discolorations from the hair. Shampoos for black or brown Poodles help to remove oxidation (or more simply, the reddish/orange tipping) and make the coat a more normal color.

TEXTURIZING OR BODY-BUILDING SHAMPOOS

These are formulated to add body to the hair and are recommended for soft coats when more texture is desired. Such products only give temporary results, however, as nothing will permanently change the natural texture of hair.

INSECTICIDAL (FLEA/TICK) SHAMPOOS

These are formulated to safely kill fleas and ticks. Pyrethrin is the most widely used shampoo insecticide. They clean and condition the coat at the same time and, when used according to directions, are safe for puppies. Always read and follow label directions when using any flea/tick shampoo.

CONCENTRATED SHAMPOOS

These generally are all-purpose shampoos, available in two types: a gel or creme form (at a slightly more-than-average concentration) and a highly concentrated form, diluted at the rate of from 12 to 16 parts water to 1 part shampoo. Because of its low cost/high yield, the latter is popular for salon use.

Grooming contest and dog show concessionaires, mail-order supply catalogs for pet care professionals and most pet stores sell the shampoos described above. They also stock many other kinds of effective specialty shampoos, some of which contain oatmeal, seal kelp, citrus, cedar, Australian tea tree oil, nova pearls and a variety of herbs, florals and botanicals. The wide variety of available shampoos is overwhelming!

The Five Phases of Bathing

Correct shampooing is a fine skill that you accomplish in five phases.

1. Prepare the dog.
2. Prepare the facilities.
3. Shampoo the dog.
4. Rinse the dog.
5. Apply a creme rinse or hair conditioner.

I. PREPARE THE DOG

Preparing a Poodle for a bath is as important as the actual shampooing. All the dead hair and tangles must be carefully brushed and combed from the coat beforehand. Brushing also helps to loosen dirt and grime. Your goal is to give a thorough brushing from the skin outward to be sure the dog is free of mats before you put him in the tub. Bathing matted hair only complicates matters. The mats tend to clump together when the hair is wet, making them even more difficult to remove after shampooing. And when the shampoo is applied to wet, matted hair, it becomes trapped inside the mats and is then nearly impossible to completely rinse out.

The brushing and combing session before the bath is an ideal time to check for the presence of fleas or ticks.

2. PREPARE THE FACILITIES

After your Poodle is thoroughly brushed and combed, give him the opportunity to relieve himself. Clean any dirty hairs off your grooming table and spread a large, thick bath towel on top. Place a clean brush and comb on the tabletop, and have a hair dryer ready to switch on as soon as you bring your wet dog back to the table.

Gather all the equipment and supplies you need for the bath beforehand:

- A rubber mat for the tub bottom
- A hand-held hose (preferably equipped with a pressure spray nozzle) or large plastic container for wetting and rinsing
- Shampoo brush
- Sponge or washcloth
- Cotton
- Mineral oil
- Shampoo
- Creme rinse or hair conditioner
- Several large bath towels

Never leave a wet dog alone in the tub while you scramble about searching for shampoo or other supplies. Wearing a waterproof apron is always wise when bathing a dog. If you have never bathed your Poodle before, or if you know he's difficult to control in the tub, using the apron becomes imperative.

Where you bathe your Poodle depends on his size and your grooming area. At home it can be in the kitchen sink, a laundry tub, or bathtub. If you are a breeder and exhibitor or plan to do any professional grooming, then your facilities must be designed for comfort and efficiency. It will be less tiring for you to install a waist-high stainless-steel tub designed for groomers or animal handlers, or to buy a small porcelain bathtub and have it raised waist-high to eliminate unnecessary bending. Placing a rubber mat (or nonskid strips) on the tub bottom will give your dog better footing.

Plug the dog's ears with cotton before putting him into the tub to prevent water from reaching the ear canal. Put a little Vaseline™ on the end of the cotton if your Poodle has chronic ear trouble to

Figure 4-1.

make certain that no water gets inside to further irritate them. Use a tearless shampoo to wash the head area. If you do not use tearless shampoo, place a drop or two of mineral oil into each eye to protect them from stinging. Once your dog learns to enjoy his bath, these steps can be skipped; but if he resists or is in any way hard to handle, his eyes and ears should be protected.

3. SHAMPOO THE DOG

There are two ways to wash your Poodle. Whichever method you choose is a matter of personal preference; either way will get the dog clean.

The first method is to fill the tub with about 3 to 4 inches of warm water, then add about ½ cup of shampoo, swirl it around to make suds, and then stand the dog in the water. Some dogs seem soothed by soaking in warm water, but never make the water level so high that it stresses the animal. This method works well if you don't have a spray hose and intend to use a plastic container to wet the dog.

Tip: Incidentally, you can make a very efficient scoop out of a gallon-sized plastic bottle. With the cap on the empty bottle, cut off the bottom on a slant, making sure that the short side of the scoop is on the same side as the bottle handle.

The second method and the one preferred by most professionals, is to stand your dog in the tub. Using warm water, wet the hair thoroughly with the spray hose or with water scooped from the bottom of the sink. At this point avoid wetting the head and ears. Use lots of water; make sure the hair is thoroughly wet before you apply shampoo. By working from back to front and wetting the head and ears last, your Poodle will be less frightened in the water. If fleas are a problem, however, start at the head and neck and work backward. This helps to cut off the fleas' favorite avenue of escape: into the eyes and ears. Speak quietly and reassuringly as you wet your dog. If you are using a hand-held spray, hold the nozzle as close as possible to the dog's body; this will force the water to the skin and flush out dirt and debris. More important, the water won't splash off the coat and startle the dog.

After you wet your Poodle, squeeze some shampoo onto the hair and gently massage it in with your fingertips or the sponge until it reaches the skin. Shampoo the tail, back legs, body, underbody, front legs, shoulders and chest, as shown in Figure 4-1, massaging the skin with your fingertips in a gentle, kneading motion. If your Poodle's coat is rather long, don't rub the soap in to form a lather, but rather squeeze it into the hair as if you were washing a delicate sweater. Pay attention to the hard-to-reach areas between the front and back legs, and any stubborn spots at the hock joints by using extra shampoo and the brush or sponge. Many groomers like to check the anal glands at this

point. Once any fluid in the glands is expressed onto cotton, the unpleasant odor is easy to wash away with the soapy water.

By now, the only part that has not been shampooed is the head and ears, which has been purposely left dry to avoid unnecessarily frightening the dog. Place your hand under the dog's chin and lift the head slightly to make the water run away from the nose; wet the head and ears, and wash these parts taking care not to get shampoo into the eyes or excess water into the ears. Take extreme care not to spray water up the nose. If you worry about getting suds into your Poodle's eyes, use a washcloth to clean the face. As previously mentioned, it is best to wash the dog's head with a tearless shampoo to avoid irritating the eyes.

4. RINSE THE DOG

Rinse the hair lightly and shampoo your Poodle a second time. It really takes two shampoos to thoroughly clean the hair.

After the second sudsing, you must rinse every trace of shampoo out of the coat. Begin the final rinse at the head. Cover the Poodle's eyes with your hand, holding the ear flaps down at the same time to keep water out. Using warm water and the spray nozzle, work methodically down the neck and back toward the tail, over the sides of the body, under the stomach, and down and under the legs to the feet, rinsing thoroughly until clear water comes off the dog. If your dog is standing in water, be sure to pull the plug and let all the suds drain out before beginning the final rinse. Thorough rinsing is important; you must rinse and rinse until all the suds are out of the coat. When traces of shampoo are left in the coat, it can irritate the skin and cause the dog to scratch. Hair that is not thoroughly rinsed will feel gritty and look dull, and it also will be difficult to scissor into a plush-looking finish. It is much wiser, therefore, to be on the safe side and make sure all excess shampoo is completely rinsed from the hair. Remember: *Even when you think you have rinsed sufficiently, rinse again!*

For information about bathing a Poodle in show coat, see Chapter 6, "Bathing and Drying a Poodle in Show Coat."

5. APPLY A CREME RINSE OR HAIR CONDITIONER

You may wish to use a creme rinse, finishing rinse, hair conditioner or moisturizer on your Poodle's coat after the shampoo. Shampooing cleans but at the same time often tangles the hair. A creme rinse or finishing rinse helps to reduce static electricity, making the hair more manageable and less inclined to mat after bathing. Deep conditioners like Hair Care™ work magic on damaged hair. They moisturize the hair and skin, smooth the cuticle, restructure the hair shaft, restore elasticity and add depth of color. Instructions for applying a rinse or conditioner will vary depending on the brand you select. Generally, these products are applied after the final rinse. The excess moisture is squeezed out of the hair, the rinse or conditioner is applied and gently worked into the hair using the pads of your fingertips, left on the coat for a few minutes, and then rinsed out. (However, some newer conditioners can be left in the hair for added body and protection.) After thoroughly rinsing, rinse again!

Note: It is very important to remove the dead hair from your brushes and combs regularly and to wash them periodically; otherwise, you will be brushing and combing dirt and oils back into your dog's clean hair.

Glossary of Shampoo/Conditioning Ingredients and Terms

Aloe Vera: A compound expressed from the leaf of the aloe plant (the lily family) used for its softening and soothing benefits. Used for more than three thousand years, it is referred to in *The Bible*.

Antioxidants: Preservatives that inhibit oxidation which causes color changes and rancidity in products.

Antistatics: Substances that reduce, remove or prevent the buildup of static electricity by neutralizing electrical charges that hair attracts from various environmental or product sources.

Biodegradable: Capable of being broken down, especially into innocuous substances.

"Blow-dry" creme rinses: Conditioners that are not rinsed out after application. During the drying process, they help to protect hair from excessive heat, as too much heat can strip much of the hair's natural oils and moisture.

Botanicals: Organic substances that are derived from plants through various processes.

Buffers: Chemicals added to products that maintain the degree of acidity or alkalinity of a product (pH balance).

Coconut oil: Oil which is expressed from the kernel of the coconut palm tree.

Conditioners/Conditioning agents: Agents that improve manageability, reverse the negative charge found on hair after it is washed, and add shine and softness. The agents used depend on what the conditioner is formulated to do (build body, remoisturize, detangle) and on the degree of strength required.

Creme rinse: Products formulated to control static charges that make antistatic compound as a basic ingredient to give hair a soft feeling, making it more manageable and improving its gloss. See also **Finishing rinse**.

D-Limonene: Botanical insecticide derived from citrus fruit.

Dry or foam shampoos: Products (powders, aerosol foams or liquids) that are formulated to supplement regular bathtub bathing. While they do not clean as thoroughly as wet shampoos, they do remove some surface oils, dirt and odors, and are helpful when illness or other factors preclude shampooing. The method of application varies according to the product, but the principle is the same: The product is applied to the hair, left on a few minutes, then brushed out or toweled off, carrying with it dirt and oils.

Emollients: As a rule, emollients are used to soften, smooth and soothe, especially the skin. Shampoos with emollients are formulated to condition the hair and soften the skin.

Finishing rinse: Antistatic products that coat the surface fibers of the hair and add a gloss. They make the hair easier to brush when it is wet, so there is less tearing and pulling during the drying process. Like creme rinses, these products help to control long hair and make it more manageable between groomings. Some are added to wet hair after shampooing and then rinsed off; others are sprayed directly onto the wet hair and not rinsed off.

(continues)

Fixatives: Substances added to fragrances or flavors that reduce the tendency to evaporate and make the scent or flavor last longer.

Foaming Agents/Boosters/ Stabilizers: Shampoos are expected to foam because most users identify foaming ability with cleansing performance. Foam, however, does not necessarily add to the cleansing effect, as some top-quality shampoos produce little lather. Foaming agents produce foam; boosters enhance the quality and quantity of lather; and stabilizers delay the tendency of the lather to disappear.

Fragrance: Any natural or synthetic substance used to impart an odor to a product.

Hair moisturizers: Reconditioning, deep-penetrating treatments for damaged hair. These products contain additives that restructure the hair shaft, restore moisture to the hair and skin, and restore elasticity.

Humectants: Substances that preserve retention of moisture.

Hypoallergenic: A term for products supposedly devoid of common substances that frequently cause allergic reactions.

Opacifiers/Pearling agents: Products can be clear or opaque. Opacifiers and pearling agents are often added for aesthetic reasons— to make a product look more attractive by appearing to be thicker or richer—or for practical reasons, such as to make tinting of the product easier.

pH: A measurement to determine the acidity or alkalinity of a product.

Preservatives: Found in all hair preparations and cosmetics, preservatives control the growth of germs and prevent the decomposition of a product.

Proteins: Contained in one form or another in various hair care products. They are particularly recommended for damaged hair; when applied externally, proteins coat the hair shafts to strengthen them, make them less porous and add body.

Pyrethrins/Pyrethrum: A natural insecticide extracted from dried blossoms of pyrethrum flowers *(Chrysanthemum cinerariaefolium)* grown in Africa. Pyrethrins are highly effective in killing fleas and are considered the least toxic of insecticides used on mammals. Combined with a synergist, natural pyrethrum is one of the fastest-acting insecticides known.

Pyrethroids: Synthetic forms of pyrethrins.

Quaterniums: An extensive group of compounds whose properties are mainly conditioning or anti-microbial. Usually identified on product labels as *Quaternium (followed by a number)*.

Self-rinse shampoos: See **Dry or foam shampoos.**

Surfactants: A contraction of the expression "surface-active agent," surfactants supply foaming power and cleansing action. They also perform certain other specialized tasks, including conditioning and reducing irritation.

Synergism: The joint action of two or more agents that is greater than the sum of their activity when used alone.

Tea-Tree Oil: Essential oil obtained from the *Melaleuca Alternifolia* tree found only in Australia. Penetrates the skin quickly to soothe and heal.

chapter 5

While your Poodle is still standing in the tub, gently squeeze the hair on the topknot and ears, the body, the legs and feet, and the tail to coax out as much water as you can. Wrap the dog in a large, absorbent towel to soak up the additional moisture, take him out of the tub, and carry him to the grooming table. Remove the wet cotton from his ears, and use fresh cotton to dry any damp areas inside the canal or underside of the flaps. Continue blotting the coat—don't rub, you'll only tangle or break the hair—with dry towels to absorb as much of the excess moisture as possible. If you plan to use a volumizing gel or mousse, apply it now, and squeeze the product into the damp hair with your fingertips.

Poodle hair should always be dried with a hair dryer, not only to speed up the drying process but, more importantly, to lift and aerate the hair and make it as straight as possible. (The higher the velocity of the dryer, the smoother the hair will be when the dog is dry.) If the coat is left to dry naturally, it will be curly, kinky and rather difficult to finish with scissors.

Set your hair dryer on warm, never hot, as too much heat at too close a range can strip much of the natural oils and moisture from the hair.

If you brush a Poodle's coat in small sections as the dryer blows on each section, the hair will dry faster, look straight and plush and be easier to scissor finish. In professional grooming salons, this process is called fluff drying. Fluff drying is very important because it prepares the hair for proper finishing.

Figures 5-1 and 5-2 show a Poodle being fluff dried with a slicker brush. A fine-wire slicker is a good choice to dry a pet Poodle's

hair that will be clipper- or scissor-finished (see chapter 2). A slicker brush should *not* be used, however, on the long mane coat of Poodles in show condition (see chapter 6).

Speak to your dog in soothing tones, hold the dryer about 6 inches away and direct the nozzle at the area to be brushed. As a stream of warm air blows on a section of the hair, brush it from the skin outward, using a sweeping upward stroke to lift the hair. This will help to separate each hair and eliminate any tendency to curl. The ideal brushing motion is a light, gentle stroke that does not pull out or break off the hair. Always remember that during the drying process, wet hair is pulled and stretched. While healthy hair has considerable elasticity, there are limits. When it is wet and brushed improperly, especially when warm air is blowing on it, the hair can be over-stretched and weakened.

Just as with the brushing process, the drying process can be made more efficient by establishing a routine—for instance starting at the back and working forward, drying the head and ears last. As soon as the section you are fluffing is completely dry, move on to another section, and brush and thoroughly dry it in the same manner. If you don't dry thoroughly as you go along, the curl will return immediately, and mats can set in the damp hair. Continue until the Poodle is completely brushed and dried down to the skin. Use gentle strokes when drying the hair under the chest to avoid scratching the nipples with the wire brush.

Speed is paramount during the drying process. You want to reach every part of the coat *before* it dries by itself. It's a good idea to keep a trigger-spray bottle close at hand filled with either of the following:

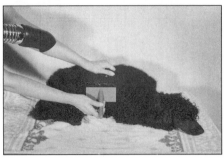

Figure 5-1.

Figure 5-2.

- A nonoily coat dressing or finishing spray.
- One to 2 tablespoons of creme rinse diluted with water.

Spray this on the hair to dampen any areas that are drying too quickly to keep them from becoming curly or frizzy.

After the hair is dry, stand the Poodle on the grooming table and go through the coat with your hands to check for dampness, especially behind the ears or in the hard-to-reach areas under the legs. Carefully brush or comb the coat once more to see that all small mats near the skin have been removed. Everything should be completely dry. When it is, comb your Poodle to lift and separate the individual hairs and prepare the coat for scissors finishing. The best time to finish grooming the coat is immediately after the bath when the hair is clean and straight.

chapter 6

Bathing is very important to Poodles in show coat. It is part of the weekly regimen of dogs that are being campaigned as well as for dogs that are growing coat before the start of their show careers. A shampoo maintenance routine is as important as regular brushing because clean hair is healthier and grows faster than dirty hair.

Basically, you will follow the five phases of bathing as outlined in Chapter 4, "Bathing the Pet Poodle," with a few variations since the show coat is longer and more susceptible to damage if the improper techniques are used.

As mentioned in chapter 4, preparing the dog for a shampoo is as important as the actual shampoo. Trim the Poodle's toenails before the bath, and clean any debris out of the ears. Brush the hair thoroughly following the instructions outlined in Chapter 19, "Care of the Poodle in Show Coat." Remove all topknot and ear wrappers and bands. Plug the ears with cotton to prevent water from reaching the ear canals. Put a little Vaseline™ on the end of the cotton if your dog has chronic ear trouble to assure that no water gets inside to further irritate them. Use a tearless shampoo to wash the head area. If you don't use a tearless shampoo, place a drop or two of mineral oil into each eye to protect them from stinging.

Before putting the dog in the tub, some exhibitors like to part the long mane down the center of the back with a pin brush, letting the long hair fall to either side of the body. It is not mandatory to do this; just keep in mind that your goal is to wash the long hair carefully to keep it from tangling.

When bathing a Poodle in show coat, you don't want to rub the long hair with your fingers or a sponge, but rather gently squeeze the suds through the coat, as if you were washing a delicate sweater (you can, however, scrub the shorter hair on bracelets, rosettes or pack).

There are two ways to shampoo a Poodle in show coat. The first method is to fill the tub with 3 or 4 inches of warm water, add shampoo, then swirl it around to create suds. Stand the dog in the tub (a rubber mat in the bottom will prevent him from slipping). Use a plastic bowl to scoop up the sudsy water and pour it all over the dog. The second method, and the one preferred by most professionals, is to stand the dog in the tub, wet him thoroughly with a powerful spray hose, as shown in Figure 6-1, and let the water run free during the shampoo. Before you do this, fill a large container (a plastic bucket, for instance) with water, add shampoo (swirling it around to make suds), and keep it nearby to pour over the dog. Whichever method you choose is a matter of personal preference, either will get the dog clean.

Wetting a Poodle in show coat, especially hair that is very dense in texture, can take quite a long time. If you are using a spray hose, hold the nozzle close to the body; this will force the water to the skin and flush out any dirt and debris more efficiently. Before you apply shampoo, be sure that all the hair is thoroughly wet down to the skin.

Once the dog is wet to the skin, scoop up the sudsy water in a plastic bowl and pour it over and over the dog. Start cleaning the puffs and bracelets on the legs first, then wash the stomach, tail, hindquarters, back and neck, leaving the head and ears until last, as shown in Figure 6-2. Use your fingers to gently work the lather down to the skin.

When the Poodle is thoroughly shampooed all over, rinse carefully and shampoo a second time. If you dilute the shampoo even more for the second wash, it will be easier to rinse out. If you are keeping your Poodle in oil, three shampoos may be necessary to remove all oil traces from the coat. (If your shampoo is not strong enough to remove all the oil from the coat, try using the Lux™ glycerine and vinegar mixture mentioned in chapter 19.)

After the second sudsing, you must rinse every trace of shampoo out of the coat. Begin the final rinse at the head. Cover the Poodle's eyes with your hand. Use warm water. Work methodically with the spray nozzle: down the head and the ears (don't forget to lift them and rinse underneath), down the neck and the back toward the tail, over the sides of the body, under the stomach, and down and under the legs to the feet. Rinse and rinse until clear water comes off the dog. Hold the spray nozzle close to the skin, as shown in Figure 6-3, to flush out all the scurf and dandruff. If the Poodle is standing in water, be sure to pull the plug and let all the suds drain out before beginning the final rinse. Hair that is not thoroughly rinsed will feel gritty and look dull. It also will be difficult to scissor into a plush-looking finish. As previously mentioned, it's much wiser, therefore, to be on the safe side and make sure that all excess shampoo is completely rinsed from the hair.

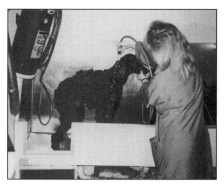

Figure 6-1.

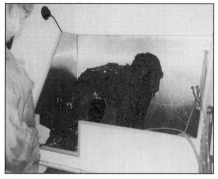

Figure 6-2.

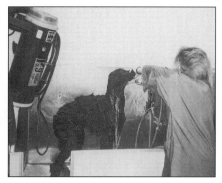

Figure 6-3.

After the final rinse, your next step take depends on your own schedule:

- If you intend to show the dog within a day or so, you will probably want to use a creme rinse or conditioner (such as Hair Care or Bio Groom Super Creme Conditioner) to add moisture to the coat. However, do not use a product so heavy that it causes oil to accumulate on the coat. Mix the conditioner in a plastic bowl, pour it over the long hair and massage it in with your fingers. Leave the conditioner on for the required length of time, then rinse thoroughly once again, carefully squeeze the excess moisture from the coat, blot it with a towel, and dry. This step is also important because it will help to eliminate static electricity.

- If the bath was part of a maintenance or growth/maintenance program and the dog is not going to be shown within a day or so, you must protect the hair from tangling and matting. In this case, you would want to apply a heavier creme rinse or moisturizing conditioner, or to oil the dog after he is shampooed and rinsed. The type of products you might use and how you might apply them are explained at length in chapter 19.

Drying the Show Coat

Drying the show coat takes time and must be done with no short-cuts. While the Poodle is still standing in the tub, gently squeeze the hair to remove as much water as you can. Wrap the dog in a towel to soak up the additional moisture, take him out of the tub and place him on the grooming table, which should already have been covered with a large, thick bath towel to keep the hair from drying too quickly or tangling. If the topknot is long, band the hair to keep it from falling into the mouth. Have on hand a pin brush, slicker brush, wide-tooth comb, trigger-spray bottle filled with water (or water with either a little creme rinse or conditioner added) and nonoily coat dressing or finishing spray.

Always dry a show coat with a hair dryer, not only to speed up the drying process but, more importantly, to lift and aerate the hair and make it as straight as possible. The higher the velocity of the dryer, the smoother the hair will be when the dog is dry. To speed the drying process, many professionals like to use a high-velocity dryer first to blow the water down the hair shaft and off the dog, as shown in Figure 6-4. Once this is done, the drying process is finished with a conventional stand dryer.

If you are drying a Poodle in the Continental or English Saddle trim, start on the short hair first (rosettes or pack, puffs, bracelets) because these sections of the coat tend to dry faster. Brush the hair upward and outward with a slicker to make it as straight as possible. (If you are working for a curly pack on an English Saddle clip, don't fluff dry this area with a slicker brush. Instead, just lift it with the comb to encourage curls to form, then let it dry naturally.) Dry the tail next, using a pin brush.

The long mane hair is dried in layers. While dog show exhibitors and handlers might use slightly different methods to dry the mane coat, their goal is to always brush the hair *straight*, as it is drying, in the direction you want it to be when the dog is in the show ring. If you are getting the dog ready for a show, always brush the judge's side last.

Probably the most preferred method of drying the long hair is to place the dog on his side on the grooming table with feet facing you. Start in the center of the neck and work backward to the end of the mane. Separate the hair into layers, about ½ to 1 inch wide, and as the dryer blows on it, brush it upward and forward. Figure 6-5 shows a Standard Poodle puppy's hindquarters being brushed with a slicker brush.

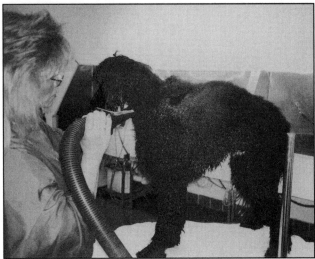

Figure 6-4.

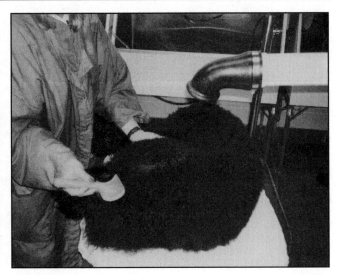

Figure 6-5.

However, when brushing the long mane coat of the Continental or English Saddle clips, be sure to use a pin brush. The brushing strokes should be slow and steady. Start at the ends and work down to the skin. You always want to see the skin at the bottom of each layer. Use gentle, sweeping brush strokes that go beyond the ends of the hair to keep the tips from splitting or breaking. If you find a matted area, use your fingers to separate the mat into small sections, then use the pin brush to work them out. Once each layer is dry, comb through it with the wide-tooth comb to be sure that no tangles remain.

Keep brushing and drying the hair, section by section, working from the backbone down to the chest. Pay special attention to the hair under the elbows and behind

the ears, because mats form very quickly in these areas. To reach the hard-to-get spots under the chest, lift the front leg.

Keep your dryer set on warm, not hot. Keep in mind that during the drying process you are pulling and stretching the wet hair. Hair has a great amount of elasticity, but it can be over-stretched, weakened and damaged by hot air. *Always* keep a spray bottle filled with water (or water with a little creme rinse or Hair Care added), a nonoily coat dressing nearby to remoisturize any areas you are working on that have dried too quickly. Brushing dry hair will cause it to break.

When the first side is completely dry, stand the dog up, remove the wet towel from the top of the table, put down a dry towel, and

turn the dog over. Brush and dry the other side of the mane, using the same layering method. If any areas on the second side are almost dry, mist them with the spray bottle to re-wet them, then continue brushing and combing as usual.

Before turning off the dryer, *feel the hair and skin* to make sure there are no damp areas, especially on or behind the ears, on the neck, the shoulders or chest, or under the elbows. These can become curly, possibly turning into matted clumps overnight, especially when a Poodle's coat is changing from puppy to adult texture. Wrap or band the topknot and ears when the hair is dry.

Always brush your Poodle the day *after* the bath because the hair has a pronounced tendency to mat at this time.

chapter 7

Grooming involves more than caring for and clipping the Poodle's coat. A Poodle's general hygiene is important for his health as well as his good looks.

Trimming the Nails

Trimming the nails is an extremely important part of the Poodle's grooming routine, but one that is frequently neglected. Most dogs detest having their nails clipped or their feet handled for any reason, so it is best to train them during puppyhood—especially prospective show dogs—to allow their nails to be trimmed and their feet to be examined for potential problems. If you don't, a serious clash of wills may ensue each time you attempt to attend to the feet. Such sessions are critical and potentially damaging for show prospects, for they may cause a Poodle to associate the handling of its feet as a negative experience, and later the dog may shy away from a judge's examination of these parts in the ring. And for proper movement, a show dog should have *short* nails.

The nails should *always* be kept short, as shown in Figure 7-1. When they are trimmed regularly, they stay short and neat. But when the nails are neglected, they keep growing long and eventually make the feet spread and cause serious damage to the dog's legs and feet. Walking and running become uncomfortable, even painful, and eventually, in its effort to compensate, the dog may appear lame. Long nails can also get caught between cracks or grates, or be torn off, which is extremely painful for a dog and often requires veterinary attention.

Long nails are not always the result of deliberate neglect. It's surprising how many people believe that dogs naturally wear down their nails. While this may be true of wild animals, things are a little different with their domesticated cousins. Dogs that walk or exercise regularly on city pavements, in concrete-surfaced runs or on hard ground may wear down their nails naturally, but they are in the minority. Indeed, even some of these dogs need periodic attention to their nails. The average dog spends most of his time indoors and when he does go outside, usually it's to a grassy lawn or other surface too soft to shorten the nails.

It's up to you, therefore, to establish a regular schedule for trimming your Poodle's nails. The job can be done by a groomer or veterinarian, or you can learn to trim your Poodle's nails yourself. Actually, for a small fee, most groomers should be willing to instruct you.

Nail growth varies from dog to dog and depends on a number of factors, so it is difficult to say just how often you should shorten your Poodle's nails, but a trimming every two weeks seems advisable. Whether you cut the nails before or after the bath is a matter of personal preference. Novice groomers, however, may find it easier to shorten the nails after the bath because the warm water helps to soften them. Use either of the following methods to shorten the nails. All of the necessary tools, described at length in Chapter 2, "Selecting the Right Equipment," are available at pet stores, from dog show concessionaires or through pet supply catalogs.

METHOD A: MANUAL NAIL TRIMMER AND NAIL FILE

The tools you need are a trimmer to shorten the nails and a file or

Figure 7-1.

emery board to smooth away rough edges. Always use a trimmer designed especially for a dog's nails, never regular scissors. The two popular models, guillotine and scissors, are both described in chapter 2. If you are a new groomer, ask your pet supplies dealer or the dog show concessionaire to show you the different types. Hold each one and simulate the cutting action to see which type seems best for you. At the same time, purchase a small container of nail-clotting powder, such as Kwik Stop™ or MediStyp™ Powder, or silver nitrate sticks. It's important to have a coagulant on hand to stop bleeding if a nail is accidentally cut back too far.

Sit the Poodle facing you on a grooming table or other sturdy surface. It is important to keep the paws from shaking or moving, so if you do need restraint, have someone steady your Poodle's legs. This is done by placing a hand at the elbow as you cut the nails on

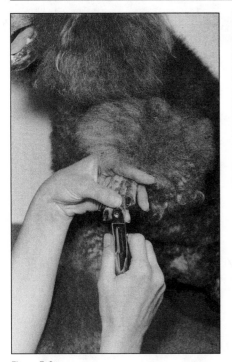

Figure 7-2.

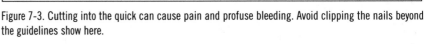

Figure 7-3. Cutting into the quick can cause pain and profuse bleeding. Avoid clipping the nails beyond the guidelines show here.

each front foot, and at the hock joint as you cut the nails on each back foot.

Begin by picking up one of your Poodle's feet in your hand and pulling it slightly forward. Insert the tip of the nail into the trimmer opening, as shown in Figure 7-2, and cut it back a little at a time. The outside of each nail is a hard, protein shell called keratin. Inside the nail is a soft, fleshy area called the quick, which contains the nerves and blood supply (Figure 7-3). Try not to cut into the quick, or you may sever the capillaries and cause bleeding. Unfortunately, when the quick is cut, it bleeds easily and profusely. The quick is easy to locate inside the nails of white and light-colored Poodles, but it is nearly impossible to locate on dark-colored dogs. As the tip of the nail grows downward, a good rule to use in trimming dark nails is to start at the tip and snip off a tiny bit at a time, stopping just at the point where the nails begin to curve downward. If you are unsure, always snip off *a little at a time,*

and you will not seriously injure the nail.

If you do snip into the quick and the nail starts bleeding, don't panic. Even the best professional groomers occasionally nick a nail. You can either press a little nail-clotting powder on the end of the nail and apply pressure for a few seconds to stop the bleeding, or you can apply the silver nitrate stick to the end of the nail. When a dog is hurt during a nail-clipping session, he often becomes very sensitive about the process. Do everything possible to soothe him and to help assure him that the process is not one he should fear.

The best way to avoid cutting into the quick is to trim the nails often. As the outside of the nail grows long, the quick grows along with it. When the nails are cut frequently and regularly, the quick tends to recede naturally. The more often you shorten the nails, the farther back the quick recedes. But when the nails are neglected, the quick grows long too, and it's very difficult to shorten the nails without severing the quicks.

Your Poodle may have an extra toe on the inside of each front leg just above the paw. This is called a dewclaw, and its attached nail should be trimmed like the others. Dewclaw nails are not worn down by exercise so they must be clipped. Neglected dewclaw nails can grow backward in a semicircle, pierce the flesh and become embedded into the front leg! Most Poodles, fortunately, have their dewclaws removed several days after birth.

After all the nails have been trimmed back, smooth away any rough edges with a nail file or emery board. Draw the file in one direction, from the top of each nail downward, in a curved stroke to the end of the nail.

METHOD B: OSTER ELECTRIC NAIL TRIMMER

Oster manufactures two electric nail trimmers (see chapter 2). One, a cordless rechargeable model, is excellent for last-minute touch-ups before going into competition at a dog show or grooming contest. It takes just a little practice to become accustomed to an electric nail trimmer, but once you master the proper technique, sanding is a fast, efficient way to shorten the nails and creates a tighter paw without leaving rough edges.

If your Poodle is fussy, have someone steady him until he becomes familiar with the sound of the motor. Place your dog in either of two positions:

- Sit the dog facing you on a grooming table or other sturdy surface. In this position, you will hold the foot you intend to work on in the palm of your hand, pulling it gently forward, as previously instructed for manual trimming.

- Stand the dog on the grooming table while you work from behind or beside each foot. In this position, the nails on each back foot are sanded with the leg pulled backwards. The nails on each front foot are sanded by gently bending the leg at the carpal joint, as shown in Figure 7-4. This position is recommended for Standard Poodles, and particularly for "fussers," because they can't easily see or interfere with the sander in operation.

Once the dog in is a sitting position, turn on the electric nail trimmer and place the sanding drum against the side of a nail, rolling it gently to the center. Repeat the same procedure on the other side of the nail. Grind it in short, rolling strokes; don't press on one area very long because the trimmer gets *very hot*. One feature of an electric nail trimmer that most people don't recognize is the extreme heat buildup, caused by the friction of the disc on the nail. The extreme heat can cause more pain to a dog than cutting into his quick.

Be careful to hold the sander near the nails and not close to the leg hair while the motor is running; otherwise, the hair on the legs may catch and wind around the disc as it rotates. One way to avoid this is to buy an infant's stretch knee-length stocking. Cut

the toe off the stocking, then slide it up your Poodle's leg, leaving just the foot exposed. This will protect the hair around the ankles and keep it from becoming tangled in the sander. Another caution—and a serious one—is the long ear feathering. Should the dog lower his head to see what you are doing while the motor is running, the long hair could become tangled in the rapidly rotating disc and cause excruciating pain. You can prevent this from happening by temporarily fastening the ear feathering back with a latex band while the sanding is in progress.

Sand each nail back to the quick. By working in short strokes on each side of the nail, you should spot the quick easily before you reach it; it will look like a dot in the center of the nail. It is possible to sand too far back and make the nail bleed. Usually, this kind of bleeding is not the profuse spurt that comes when you sever the quick with a manual trimmer. As with manual trimming, a nail clotting powder or solution will stop the bleeding quickly.

Cleaning the Ears

Cleaning the ears is a very important part of a Poodle's grooming routine. If the long ears become heavily weighted with hair, the ear canal can become blocked and infection can develop inside. When Poodles are trimmed regularly by professional groomers, ear cleaning (and the removal of excess hair on the insides of the earflaps) is always included as part of the complete grooming service. If you trim your dog at home, consequently, it is extremely important to make ear care part of his regular grooming routine. When the ears are attended to every month, they should remain in good condition and the cleaning will take only a short time. If you do not want to clean your Poodle's ears yourself, let your groomer or vet do the job, but do not neglect them.

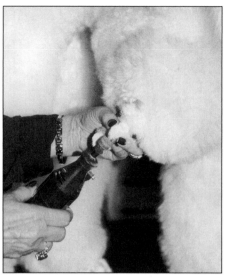

Figure 7-4.

One of the most common reasons for failing to care for the ears is lack of understanding of the ear canal by the novice groomer. It is important, therefore, to know a little about the structure of the ear. As illustrated in Figure 7-5, the dog's ear is divided into three parts:

- The external ear consists of the *pinna* (or earflap) and the ear canal.

- The middle ear consists of the tympanic membrane, the tympanic cavity, and the auditory canal (this connects with the nose and throat).

- The internal ear is composed of the organs of hearing and equilibrium. *The ear canal extends from the opening in the visible part of the external ear, or the pinna, to the tympanic membrane.* It is not a straight canal but forms nearly a right-angle turn in the deeper part of its course.

HOW TO CLEAN THE EARS

Here is the correct procedure for examining and cleaning the ears.

1) Examine the inside of each ear and the entrance to the ear canal carefully about once or twice every month. The skin inside the ears and on the flaps should be

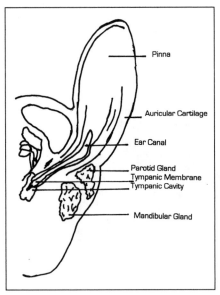

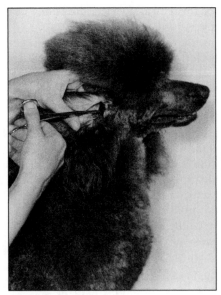

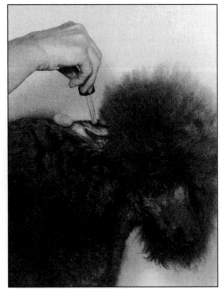

Figure 7-5.

Figure 7-6.

Figure 7-7.

pale pink. Red, brown or black skin may indicate trouble. Smell the ears. Unhealthy ears smell foul. A little wax is normal; excessive amounts are not.

2) The first step in cleaning the ears is to remove the long hair leading into the canal. If this hair is neglected and allowed to grow long, wax will accumulate inside, cut off the air circulation, and eventually cause infection. Always do this job on a sturdy grooming table with adequate lighting. Sit the dog on the table and, if necessary, have someone steady him.

3) Because the ear canal is deep and almost **L**-shaped, the safest position for removing excess hair is to grasp the earflap (or hanging portion) and draw it backwards, or flat to the head. Use your thumb and index finger or, if you are more experienced, a small fine-point forceps (Figure 7-6) to carefully pull out the excess hair leading into the canal. If the hair is hard to grip, sprinkle a little ear powder into the opening to give you a better hold. Do not liberally dump

powder into the ear. Doing so will only plug up the canal and restrict air circulation. It is often wiser to put a little powder into a container and dip your fingers into it before attempting to grasp any hair growing out of the ear canals.

Never probe deeper than you can actually see, and pull out only a few hairs at a time; otherwise, it will be painful to the dog. Remember, though, if you use the position described above, it is almost impossible to reach the delicate inner structures, even if a straight instrument is used. But if you draw the ear outward, or away from its base, you could reach the sensitive tympanic membrane and cause serious damage.

4) Once the hair is removed, moisten a cotton ball or gauze square with a canine ear lotion (formulated to clean ears and to help loosen excess wax accumulation) or a little mineral oil or alcohol to clean away any dirt, wax or remaining ear powder. Wipe around the earflap and the opening into the canal as far as you can see. Do not probe more deeply. A light

swabbing is enough if there is no evidence of wax accumulation.

5) If there is a great deal of wax on the cotton, and especially if the ears smell foul, you will have to flush out the canal with the ear lotion. You do not want to draw the earflap backward and flat to the head (as previously instructed) because this position makes it almost impossible for the lotion to reach the horizontal portion of the canal. Now, you want to grasp the cartilage at the base of the ear (Figure 7-7) and carefully draw it outward and away from the head so that any liquid dropped inside will make its way down the entire portion of the ear canal and insure proper cleaning. Put several drops of ear lotion or mineral oil into the canal.

6) Lower the earflap and temporarily steady the head with your hand to keep your Poodle from shaking. Use your other hand to gently massage the base of the ear to distribute the lotion or oil inside. This will help to dislodge any waxy fragments inside.

7) After a short massage, release your hold on the muzzle. As soon as you let go, your Poodle will shake his head, but don't be alarmed. This is nature's way of protecting the delicate structure of the ear canal, and it also helps to float any deep-seated wax to the surface.

8) Once the wax is brought up, use cotton balls or swabs to wipe the ear until it is clean and dry. There is no need to probe deep into the ear to remove wax. On Poodles with long, thick and hairy earflaps, you can pull up the ears behind the head and hold them in place with a latex band for a few minutes to let them dry completely. Do not apply the band around the earflaps themselves, *only around the hair below them.*

WHEN TO CONSULT YOUR VETERINARIAN

Poodles that are prone to severe and chronic ear infections, or those that accumulate excessive amounts of wax deep inside the ear should be attended to by a veterinarian. Dogs have many ways of letting you know that an ear is causing pain. If you notice your Poodle shaking his head persistently, scratching his ears (especially whimpering while scratching his ears), holding his head to one side, or if the ears have a foul odor and a reddish-brown discharge, seek professional attention immediately. Only a veterinarian is qualified to make a diagnosis and prescribe therapy.

Care of the Eyes

Your Poodle's eyes should be checked daily and cleaned of any mucus and foreign matter that may have collected on the inside corners. It is normal, incidentally, to find a little matter on the inside corners of the eyes from time to time. This can be removed by moistening a cotton ball with warm water and dabbing carefully at the eye corners. Never rub over

Figure 7-8. Poodles occasionally have problems with epiphora, an abnormal overflow of tears down the cheeks, mainly due to the stricture of the lacrimal drainage passages, or tear ducts. This is a problem of Toy and Miniature Poodles; it is rarely seen in Standards. Epiphora causes a chronic clear or mucous discharge that flows under the eyes and down the sides of the face, causing reddish-brown stains. The condition is also known as "wet eye." It is very evident on this unclipped white Toy Poodle.

Figure 7-9. Here is the same Toy Poodle after bathing, fluff drying and face clipping. Because the area is constantly wet, the skin also may become quite inflamed (and possibly infected), and that is evident here. Overproduction of tears can also be caused by distichiasis (an abnormal extra row of eyelashes on the upper or lower lid), trichiasis (ingrown eyelashes), entropion (eyelids that turn inward), conjunctivitis, foreign bodies and allergens.

the eyes with cotton; the fibers could scratch them.

The easiest way to flush out any foreign matter or loose hair is with a canine eye wash, such as Eye Brite™ (Lambert Kay) or Opticlear™ (Tomlyn). Such products also help to clean the eyes and to treat minor irritations or infections. Raise the Poodle's head slightly, gently open the lower lid and drop the fluid into the eye. Then use dry cotton to absorb the excess moisture that floats to the eye corners.

White and light-colored Poodles, especially Toys, sometimes have stained hair under the eyes, which is caused by a discharge from the tear ducts (Figure 7-8). The discharge often makes the hair an unsightly reddish-brown and, when excessive, creates the effect of dark circles under the eyes.

Excessive tearing can be caused by many factors: heredity, allergy, neglect in grooming the face, infection of the tear ducts, improper diet, conjunctivitis or teething. Your veterinarian may be able to determine the cause of excessive tearing and control it (Figure 7-9).

Daily attention to the eyes and the hair under them is the best way to control staining. You (or your professional groomer) should remove the stained hair with clippers. After the hair has been trimmed, a daily program of cleansing the area with water or with a product such as Erase Tear Stain Remover™ (Ring 5), Diamondeye™ (Vitacoat) or Tear-Stain Remover™ (PPP) should help prevent further staining. These products should not be used in the eyes, only on the stained hair.

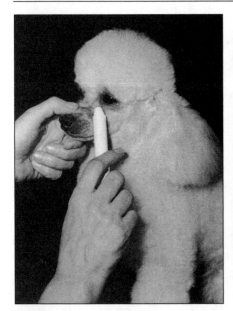

Figure 7-10. Eye stains can be camouflaged cosmetically.

Figure 7-11. The stains are completely covered. Staining is a recurring problem, and cosmetic camouflage is only a temporary solution. If your dog has chronic weepy eyes that cause severe staining, consult your veterinarian, who can determine exactly what is causing the problem and prescribe a course of treatment. Always keep the eyes and the hair around them as clean as possible.

If the area under the eyes is still discolored, after clipping and/or the use of a tear stain remover, you can try blending the stains away with a canine "cover" creme, which can be purchased at pet stores or from dog show concessionaires. You can also use a white concealer cream or lipstick, Clown White theatrical makeup or Desitin™ ointment. Apply the product under the eyes, and blend into the skin with your fingers until a natural look is achieved (Figures 7-10 and 7-11). None of these products should be put into the eyes.

Because the eyes are fragile, sensitive organs, neglect of minor irritations can lead to serious problems. Regular inspection of the eyes can help you notice potentially dangerous conditions at an early stage. Any irritation that does not clear up within 24 hours or other abnormal condition should be reported to your veterinarian immediately.

Care of the Teeth and Mouth

Clean teeth and healthy gums are important to your Poodle's general health. Periodontal disease is one of the most common canine health problems. Veterinary studies have found that periodontal disease is the most widespread disease of any kind in dogs; it is present in approximately 85 percent of all small animals over six years of age. The studies conclude, however, that frequent and correct oral hygiene is the best way to prevent tooth problems. Therefore, by incorporating regular dental care into your grooming routine, you can help keep your Poodle's mouth healthy and his breath fresh.

Like humans and most other animals, during their lifetimes dogs get two sets of teeth: 28 deciduous or temporary teeth and 42 permanent teeth. Puppies are usually born without teeth. The needle-sharp temporary or baby teeth,

which are softer and thinner than the permanent teeth, begin breaking through the gums between two to three weeks of age. By the time a puppy is six weeks old, all 28 deciduous teeth are usually in place.

Between 12 and 14 weeks of age, a puppy's baby teeth begin to loosen and fall out as the permanent teeth start coming in. The first permanent teeth to emerge are generally the incisors, followed by the canines and the premolars. The molars are the last to appear. With the exception of the tusklike canines, the baby teeth are loosened by pressure from the permanent teeth growing underneath. The permanent canines can erupt through the gums alongside the baby canines, not directly underneath. If this happens and nothing is done to loosen the puppy teeth, both sets of canine teeth may remain in the gums for some time.

Become familiar with your Poodle's dentition. When a puppy is teething, his mouth should be inspected regularly to see that the baby teeth are problem-free. This is an excellent time to accustom your Poodle to having his mouth handled and his teeth examined. Check the canines especially for double-teeth (retained baby and permanent teeth in the same spot). This can lead to overcrowding, which can cause the teeth to rotate. When retained baby teeth are present and appear to be causing displacement of the permanent teeth, have your veterinarian pull any baby teeth to avoid later bite problems.

When a puppy is teething, his gums will be swollen and irritated, and he will act much like a teething baby, trying to put anything available into his mouth for relief. Give the puppy safe things to chew on; they will help to loosen the baby teeth, relieve the irritation of sore gums and aid normal jaw development. Rawhide chips, bones and chewy twists; hard-rubber balls and rings; and nylon bones will be welcomed by the puppy at this time, and they will make your

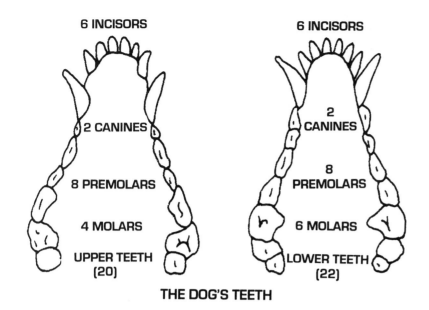

6 INCISORS

2 CANINES

8 PREMOLARS

4 MOLARS

UPPER TEETH
(20)

6 INCISORS

2 CANINES

8 PREMOLARS

6 MOLARS

LOWER TEETH
(22)

THE DOG'S TEETH

Figure 7-12. Canine dental chart.

furniture, rugs and shoes less subject to chewing damage.

The permanent teeth should be in place by the time your Poodle is between six and seven months old. There are 20 teeth in the upper jaw and 22 in the lower jaw (Figure 7-12). As soon as the permanent teeth are in place, preventive home dental care should begin.

Dogs are subject to all the dental ailments that affect human teeth: tartar buildup, loose teeth, tooth root abscess, gum inflammations, cavities and oral tumors. Tartar and secondary gum infection are the most common problems likely to be encountered. The teeth should be examined by a veterinarian semiannually. At home, between professional checkups, you should inspect your Poodle's teeth regularly and clean them when necessary. Dogs are usually not cooperative when it comes to mouth inspections, and owners can easily miss the early stages of periodontal disease.

The object of home care is to control dental plaque (a sticky, invisible film of food particles, saliva and bacteria) which clings to the teeth and is the very same substance your dentist tells you to brush off your teeth. Plaque collects between the teeth and around the gum line. It will build up if it is not removed soon after forming and will eventually mineralize into a hard, brown substance known as tartar or calculus. The longer the plaque remains on the teeth, the more stained they will appear. The high-alkaline pH level of canine saliva stimulates the conversion of dental plaque into tartar faster than in humans. The gums, irritated by the tartar buildup, become swollen and inflamed where they meet the teeth. This is caused by the plaque deposits that build up on the surface of the tooth *beneath* the gum tissue. Aside from the physical presence of tartar accumulation, the most obvious symptom of a developing problem is the dog's foul breath. If the condition is ignored, the irritation will spread to deeper tissues and the bone in which the teeth are embedded. Pockets form around the teeth, and they loosen. If the buildup of plaque and tartar

still remains untreated, a general infection can develop which may result in the loss of several teeth while the dog is still young or may even result in early death. Cavities are almost nonexistent in dogs, but when they do appear, they look like black marks on the tooth or near the gum line.

INSPECTING THE MOUTH AND CLEANING TEETH

Whether your Poodle is still a puppy or already an adult, with a little patience and practice you can get him accustomed to having his mouth opened and teeth examined. At first, just get your Poodle accustomed to your inspection of his mouth and teeth. Establish a routine. Begin by sitting your dog on the grooming table, facing you. Steady his head firmly with one hand, then open the mouth and examine his teeth with the other. Inspect all the teeth—top and bottom. Speak reassuringly to your Poodle as you rub your finger along the gums. At the end of the session, praise your dog lavishly so that, like every other phase of grooming, he associates dental care with a pleasant experience. Once you have accomplished this, you should begin cleaning his teeth on a regular basis.

The easiest way to prevent the buildup of dental plaque is to clean the teeth with one of the following:

- Flavored toothpaste, formulated for dogs, which contains abrasive agents and is totally digestible. Do not use human toothpaste; some contain agents that are harmful to dogs when ingested. Detergent, a foaming agent in human toothpaste, for example, can irritate a dog's digestive system.

- A mixture of equal parts baking soda and salt with a little water added to make a paste. Clean the teeth with a child's soft toothbrush for Toy Poodles or a regular brush

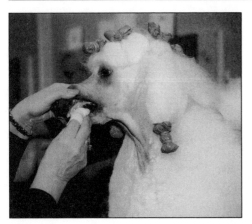

Figure 7-13.

for Miniature and Standard Poodles. Brush the teeth as you do your own. Lift the Poodle's lip and use gentle, circular scrubbing strokes on each side as well as the biting surface of the back teeth.

If your Poodle objects to the toothbrush, wrap a piece of soft gauze bandage around your index finger and squeeze some toothpaste on it (or dip it into the baking soda and salt mixture). Rub gently over the teeth and along the gums (Figure 7-13), just as you did with your finger during the first week. Use the gauze like a toothbrush, making small circles or short back-and-forward rubbing motions over the teeth and the gums. After the teeth are cleaned, put water into a plant mister and spray the dog's mouth to rinse away the cleaning mixture. When the cleaning is finished, don't forget to praise your dog and to reward him with his favorite toy or treat.

If there is a heavy plaque formation around the gum line, this can be scaled off to prevent infection. To do this, you will need a dental scaler with right and left angles, an instrument similar to the one your dentist uses on your teeth (see chapter 2). On the top teeth, place the sharp part of the scaler slightly under the gum line and gently scrape downward, using your free thumb to shield the gums and lip below. Tartar seldom accumulates

on the bottom teeth, but if it is necessary to scrape this area, place the edge of the scaler under the gum line and scrape upward, using your thumb to shield the upper teeth. Scaling the teeth frequently makes the gums bleed. After the tartar is removed, moisten a cotton ball with Chloraseptic™ and swab the gums to prevent infection. If this sounds intimidating or if the tartar buildup is very heavy, have your veterinarian perform the teeth-cleaning procedure. Immediately afterwards, though, begin your preventative procedures.

Always make mouth inspection and teeth cleaning a part of your regular grooming routine. Good oral hygiene will make your dog feel better and, more important, will help to prolong his life. Regular home care can slow down the buildup of plaque, which in turn slows down the progression of periodontal disease. By being a caring, observant owner, you will be able to report any changes in your dog's mouth, especially the beginning of periodontal disease, to your veterinarian in time to reverse its effects.

Care of the Anal Glands

Every dog has a pair of anal glands situated under the skin at each side of the opening to the rectum at about five and seven o'clock positions, as shown in Figure 7-14. Each gland or sac opens into the anal area through a small duct. It's easy to locate these pear-shaped sacs externally (especially if they are filled) by placing your thumb on one side of the anal opening and your index finger on the other side. Unfortunately, the anal sacs can, on occasion, cause a variety of serious and painful problems.

The exact function of the anal glands is often disputed and scientists still do not know why the sacs are there at all or why they sometimes cause problems. Some experts believe that they lubricate

the passage of bowel movements. Others think they are involved in sex determination—that the odor secreted by these glands enables a dog to determine the sex of another dog upon meeting. Dogs usually meet one another by smelling the anal sac area; this has led to the assumption that pheromones (hormones that stimulate the social and sexual behavior of animals of the same species) released from the sacs play an important role in communication. A third theory is that the anal sacs are vestigial scent glands left over from the dog's primitive state and that they once functioned like those of a skunk to frighten away possible attackers. It is true that the skunk's musk glands are located in the same spot as the dog's anal glands and that the secretion from them is similar to that of the dog except for intensity of odor.

Normally, the anal glands secrete a watery, brownish fluid that empties into the rectum during defecation. Occasionally, though, the fluid is not expelled completely; the sacs become clogged and accumulate a foul-smelling mass inside. This leads to an irritation which the dog tries to relieve either by scooting (pulling himself across the carpet or floor by his hindquarters), by chasing his tail or by incessantly licking and biting at the base of his tail. Eventually, an abscess, which is quite painful, may develop. The dog becomes listless when this happens, his eyes appear dull and he often refuses to eat or becomes constipated. Upon examination, the anus appears inflamed and so enlarged that you may notice the skin bulging over the glands.

Veterinarians say that a large number of dogs they examine have impacted anal glands and that the owners are completely unaware of what the problem is. When a dog starts scooting across the floor, the owner often consults a veterinarian, thinking that the animal has worms.

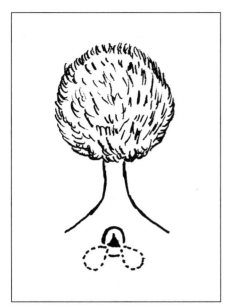

Figure 7-14.

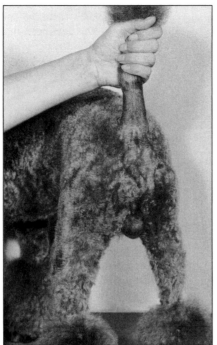

Figure 7-15.

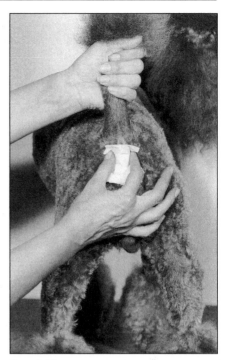

Figure 7-16.

If you are going to do most, if not all, of your Poodle's grooming, it is important that you know about the anal sacs. You must check these sacs periodically—once a month will suffice—for impaction and empty them when necessary. How often they need to be emptied depends on the frequency of accumulation in each dog. Some dogs need monthly attention, while others may go from two to three months without any accumulation; and many dogs never need to have their anal sacs emptied. Impaction seems to be more common in Toy Poodles (and other small breeds), possibly because they are fed softer food than larger dogs, which are normally fed bulkier diets that produce stiffer fecal matter.

When the anal glands become clogged, they must be emptied by squeezing them to discharge the accumulation inside. Expressing the anals is not a pleasant job, but it must be done to prevent further infection and serious medical problems. When you bathe your Poodle, make it a point to check

the glands immediately before putting him into the tub, or do it just after you stand him in the water, since the accumulation is so pungent-smelling.

To properly empty the glands, follow these steps:

1) Stand your Poodle on a firm surface. Have someone restrain your dog if necessary. Hold up the tail in one hand (Figure 7-15).

2) It is necessary to cover the anus with absorbent cotton or antiseptic wipe, as the accumulation will spurt out when the glands are emptied. Hold the cotton or wipe in your free hand and place it over the anal opening. Place your thumb on one side of the anus and your index finger on the other (Figure 7-16). Gently squeeze until the contents of the glands squirt out.

3) If the glands have been clogged for some time, the secretion may come out like toothpaste from a tube instead of spurting. Usually just the slightest pressure will

release the accumulated fluid. If, however, your dog's anal glands are difficult to express, pressure should be exerted in a different manner to release the accumulated matter. Try placing your finger and thumb underneath and slightly behind the glands, then squeeze gently in an upward and outward motion.

If you are not going to bathe your Poodle and there is an pungent odor after you have expressed the anal glands, moisten a washcloth or sponge with warm water and a little shampoo, and then cleanse and rinse the skin and hair; otherwise the odor will remain. The normal anal gland secretion is yellowish-brown in color, ranging in consistency from watery to pastelike, with a fetid odor. The presence of pus or blood indicates that an infection is present and a veterinarian should be consulted as soon as possible.

If you can feel an accumulation and cannot expel it, most likely the anal glands are impacted.

Prompt attention is important, as they can become abscessed and even swell to the size of a golf ball. When the condition reaches this stage, consult your veterinarian immediately. He or she can insert a softening agent into the sacs with a special needle and syringe. The impaction can be cleared within a few minutes. If not treated promptly, an abscess can also rupture spontaneously or, if it has not already opened, surgery may be necessary to drain the sacs. After drainage, treatment usually consists of injecting the sacs with antibiotics. This may be repeated several times until improvement is noted.

Check your Poodle's anal sacs on a regular basis, and accustom him to having them emptied to avoid a buildup. The entire procedure should only take about 30 seconds of your time, and your dog will feel much better afterward. If you don't want to empty the anal glands yourself, however, your groomer or veterinarian can do it for you. Just don't ignore this important check. Abscessed glands are extremely painful.

EXTERNAL IMPACTION

You should be aware that Poodles (and other long-haired breeds) may suffer from outward impaction. If your dog has a soft bowel movement, a portion of the feces might cling to the hair around the anus and form a mass. The mass can harden and seal the anal opening, making it difficult for the dog to have a subsequent bowel movement. To remedy this situation, soak the tangled hair in warm water until the mass softens and can be removed. When the hair dries, apply an antibiotic ointment to the skin.

Depending on the clip, the individual Poodle is in, keeping the hair as short as possible around and under the anus is the best insurance against outward impaction. This is a prime example of prevention being infinitely preferable to cure.

External parasites can be extremely irritating and debilitating. They multiply rapidly and can quickly become a serious health problem. If you are neglectful and don't take steps to destroy external parasites, your dog may be stricken with some other serious illness because of his deteriorated physical condition. To save your Poodle a great deal of discomfort, check periodically for the presence of parasites. Each time you brush or comb, part the hair to the skin and examine your dog from head to tail, especially on the abdomen, around the front and back legs, between the toes, at the base of the tail and near the head and ears.

Fleas

Fleas are the most common external parasite. In some locations, they are a menace in the summer; in other places, especially hot and humid areas, they are a problem 52 weeks a year.

Fleas are tiny, brown blood-sucking parasites with piercing/sucking mouth parts (Figure 8-1). They also have long legs that make it easy for them to hop from dog to dog, dog to cat and even from dog to human searching for a host to feed on.

Fleas are quite difficult to see on Poodles because they bury themselves in the coat and dart quickly about. The first sign may be a glimpse of a small, dark bug scurrying through the coat, or you may see small black specks (that look like pepper) on the skin or in the dog's hair. These specks are flea excrement, made up mostly of blood sucked from the dog, passed through the flea's digestive system and eliminated as dried blood.

A flea bites by sticking its syringe-like mouth into the skin and sucking the dog's blood into its stomach. During this feeding process, the flea deposits saliva under the skin which causes the dog to itch considerably.

Fleas should be eradicated immediately because they transmit several viral and bacterial diseases, and they are the intermediate host for a species of dog tapeworm. Their bloodsucking also causes anemia in young or sick dogs.

HOW TO ERADICATE FLEAS

After years of killing fleas and other external parasites with the use of a combination of products such as shampoos, collars, and foggers, new technology has caused many changes in the parasite control industry. Now pet owners can choose between new and traditional methods of killing fleas, ticks and other pests. Recently, new and effective oral remedies and drop, spot-on or stripe-on treatments have become available. These are applied to the skin between the shoulder blades, from where they spread over the entire pet. The first of these products were and are available through veterinarians (Frontline™, Program™, Advantage™ and Top Spot™). Now, over-the-counter formulations (Bio Spot™, Power Spot™, Flea Halt™) are also widely available. Simple and effective, these pills, drops and spot-ons quickly kill and repel adult fleas, kill flea eggs and larvae, kill and repel ticks and kill and repel mosquitoes (the vectors of heartworm). They offer pet owners a new alternative to traditional approaches, limiting the need for a combination of products to control parasites. Ask your pet supplies dealer for more information.

Figure 8-1. Fleas and ticks are the most common external parasites.

Traditional flea control, to be successful, involves not only treating the animal but also his environment and the use of products such as shampoos, collars and foggers.

1) Begin with the animal (or animals, for you must attend to *every* dog or cat in your house). Carefully go over your Poodle with a fine-tooth flea comb to remove as many adult fleas as possible.

2) Bathe the dog with an insecticidal shampoo or use an insecticidal dip to kill the adult fleas. The killing agent in most of these products is pyrethrins, a natural ingredient extracted from African chrysanthemum flowers, that is safe and highly effective for use on puppies as well as adult dogs. Shampoo your Poodle's head and ears first, squeezing the suds into the coat, and work toward the tail; if you start at the back, all the fleas will scurry forward to the hard-to-reach areas up front.

3) While your Poodle's hair is drying (or being shampooed or dipped at the grooming salon), the next step is to break the flea's life cycle by treating all the areas of your home where the dog spends a great deal of time. Throroughly vacuum the carpets, upholstered furniture (especially tufted areas), floors, baseboards and crevices. Concentrate on all the secluded places where fleas go into hiding: under the furniture and cushions, behind the drapes and in the corners of rooms.

4) After your dog and his environment are clean, the use of flea collars, dips, sprays or powders will help to kill any flea eggs before they hatch and to prevent re-infestation.

Pesticides can interact with each other and cause damaging side effects. Always follow label directions. More is not better, and could be lethal. If you have *any* doubts about using flea control products, contact your veterinarian.

Ticks

Ticks (Figure 8-1), members of the wingless arachnid family, are the hardiest and most dangerous bloodsucking parasites. They belong to an ancient group of ectoparasites whose ancestors probably originated in the Cenozoic era some 65 to 70 million years ago. Several species can infest dogs. The brown dog tick (the most common variety) carries no human disease and rarely bites humans. The American dog tick, Rocky Mountain wood tick, Lone Star tick and others do bite humans. Ticks cause several diseases that vary geographically, including Lyme borreliosis, Rocky Mountain spotted fever, tularemia, relapsing fever, typhus, Q fever and some forms of encephalitis in humans. Lyme borreliosis, or Lyme disease, was first recognized in the mid-1970s in Lyme, Connecticut, and is now considered the most common tick-transmitted disease reported in humans and is also an important disease in dogs.

Dogs pick up ticks from infested premises or by running through woods, fields, high grass, damp areas and sandy beaches. The ticks attach themselves to the dog's skin and feed on his blood. Once mating has occurred, the female remains attached for several days, sucking the dog's blood and enlarging up to 10 times her normal size. The female then drops off her host and moves to a dark, quiet spot to lay her eggs.

Each adult female can lay from 1,000 to 5,000 eggs at one time. They hatch into larvae after an incubation period of from three to eight weeks, depending on temperature and humidity. To complete their life cycle, the larvae molt into nymphs, and they, in turn, molt into adults. The new ticks look for a host to feed on but can live in your house up to two years without attaching themselves to a dog.

When a tick bites a dog, it forces its barbed mouth deep into the dog's skin. The barbs on the mouth prevent the tick from being easily pulled out. Tick bites are painful and extremely irritating to a dog. The irritation leads to intense itching and persistent scratching, which often results in secondary skin infections. Ticks can cause a dog to become anemic quickly because they ingest so much blood. If you live in a tick-infested area, consider using one of the new pill, drop, spot-on or stripe-on products that kill and repel ticks.

HOW TO REMOVE TICKS

If you find ticks present on your dog, follow these steps to remove them.

1) Examine the dog thoroughly to locate all ticks. Check any small lumps on the skin; they may be ticks. Check between the feet, inside the ears and in other hard-to-reach areas where ticks love to hide.

2) Soak all visible ticks in alcohol or petroleum jelly. Doing this will help paralyze and asphyxiate the tick, causing it to loosen its grip.

3) Remove the ticks in a way that will not increase the possibility of spreading disease. All parts of the tick must be pulled out; the tick should not be crushed, and the person removing the tick should not touch it with bare hands since infection is possible through breaks in the skin or through the mucous membranes.

4) Carefully grasp each tick with a pointed tweezers or forceps. Shield your hand with paper if you must use your fingers, or wear rubber gloves. Pull the tick straight outward—do not twist the tick—to remove it. Twisting or jerking may cause part of the mouthpiece to be left behind in the skin; this could result in infection.

5) Swab the skin with hydrogen peroxide, alcohol or an antiseptic after the ticks are removed.

6) As soon as all ticks are pulled from the dog, burn them or flush them down the toilet. Don't crush them.

7) Wash your hands thoroughly after removing the ticks.

8) Shampoo or dip the dog following the instructions previously mentioned.

9) Disinfect the dog's bedding, and spray the baseboards, carpets, floor cracks, etc., with a nontoxic insecticide. If there are ticks throughout your home, use a fogger for general fumigating. Stubborn cases of tick infestation may have to be turned over to a pest control expert who possesses both the professional expertise and the proper insecticides to do the job.

10) For added protection, have the dog wear a flea/tick collar with vaporizing agents designed to kill external parasites for several months. Read the manufacturer's directions carefully before applying the collar.

For your own protection when walking through woodsy or moist areas, high grass or brush, wear long pants and a long-sleeved shirt. Keep the shirttails tucked into the pants and the pants tucked into socks. Spraying yourself with a commercial insect repellant (especially around the ankles) containing the chemical diethyl-meta-toluamide (DEET) will help prevent tick attachment.

chapter 9

Note: The author and the publisher express appreciation to the Poodle Club of America for graciously granting permission to reproduce its "Illustrated Breed Standard" in this book.

The Standard for the Poodle (Toy variety) is the same as for the Standard and the Miniature varieties except as regards height.

General Appearance, Carriage and Condition

That of a very active, intelligent and elegant-appearing dog, squarely built, well proportioned, moving soundly and carrying himself proudly. Properly clipped in the traditional fashion and carefully groomed, the Poodle has about him an air of distinction and dignity peculiar to himself.

Size, Proportion, Substance

Size—The Standard Poodle is over 15 inches at the highest point of the shoulders. Any Poodle which is 15 inches or less in height shall be disqualified from competition as a Standard Poodle.

The Miniature Poodle is 15 inches or under at the highest point of the shoulders, with a minimum height in excess of 10 inches. Any Poodle which is over 15 inches or is 10 inches or less at the highest point of the shoulders shall be disqualified from competition as a Miniature Poodle.

The Toy Poodle is 10 inches or under at the highest point of the shoulders. Any Poodle which is more than 10 inches at the highest point of the shoulders shall be disqualified from competition as a Toy Poodle.

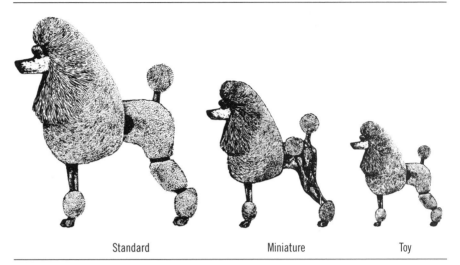

Standard   Miniature   Toy

Figure 9-1. Size variation.

As long as the Toy Poodle is definitely a Toy Poodle, and the Miniature Poodle a Miniature Poodle, both in balance and proportion for the Variety, diminutiveness shall be the deciding factor when all other points are equal.

*Proportion—*To insure the desirable squarely built appearance, the length of body measured from the breastbone to the point of the rump approximates the height from the highest point of the shoulders to the ground.

*Substance—*Bone and muscle of both forelegs and hindlegs are in proportion to size of dog.

Head and Expression

*(a) Eyes—*Very dark, oval in shape and set far enough apart and positioned to create an alert intelligent expression. *Major fault: eyes round, protruding, large or very light.*

*(b) Ears—*Hanging close to the head, set at or slightly below eye level. The ear leather is long, wide and thickly feathered; however, the ear fringe should not be of excessive length.

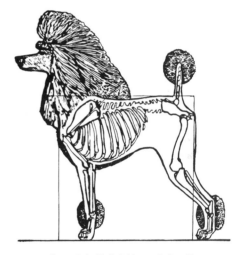

Squarely built: height equals length

Figure 9-2. Proportion.

*(c) Skull—*Moderately rounded, with a slight but definite stop. Cheekbones and muscles flat. Length from occiput to stop about the same length as of muzzle.

*(d) Muzzle—*Long, straight and fine, with slight chiseling under the eyes. Strong without lippiness. The chin definite enough to preclude snipiness. *Major fault: lack of chin.*

*Teeth—*White, strong and with a scissors bite. *Major fault: undershot, overshot, wry mouth.*

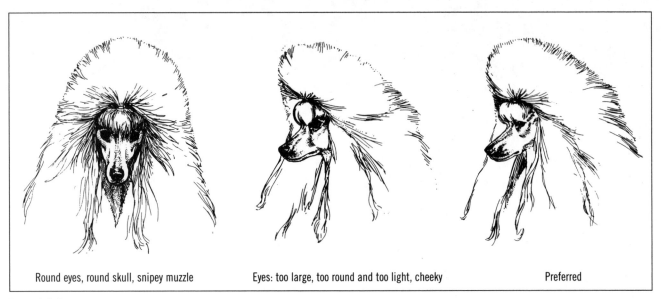

Figure 9-3. Eyes.

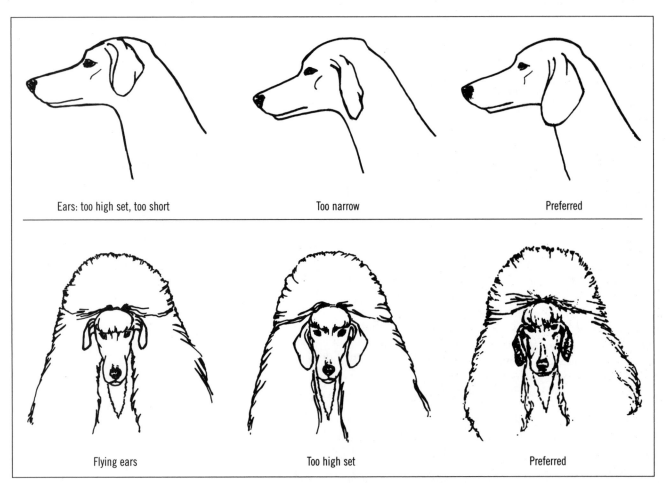

Figure 9-4. Ears.

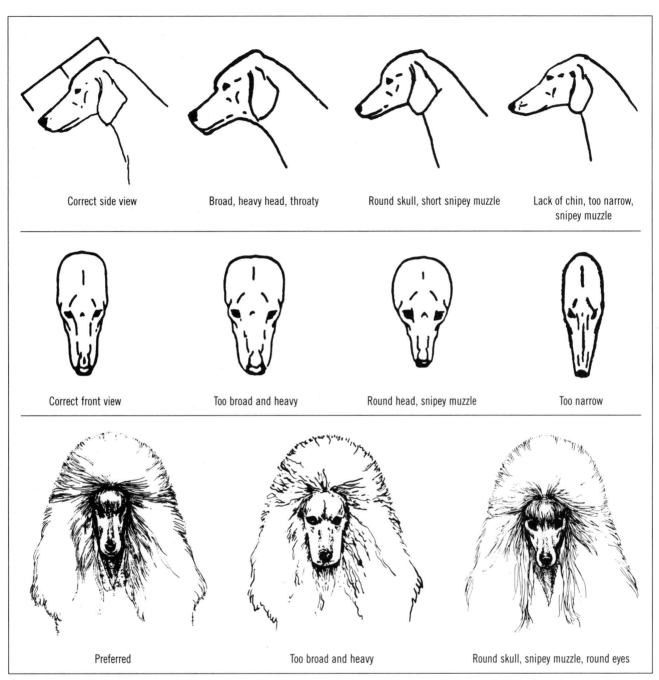

Correct side view	Broad, heavy head, throaty	Round skull, short snipey muzzle	Lack of chin, too narrow, snipey muzzle

Correct front view	Too broad and heavy	Round head, snipey muzzle	Too narrow

Preferred	Too broad and heavy	Round skull, snipey muzzle, round eyes

Figure 9-5. Skull/Muzzle.

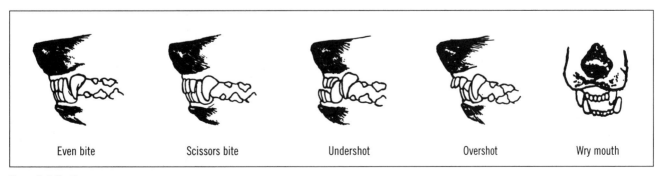

Even bite	Scissors bite	Undershot	Overshot	Wry mouth

Figure 9-6. Teeth.

Neck, Topline, Body

Neck—Well proportioned, strong and long enough to permit the head to be carried high and with dignity. Skin snug at throat. The neck rises from strong, smoothly muscled shoulders. *Major fault: ewe neck.*

The *topline* is level, neither sloping nor roached, from the highest point of the shoulder blade to the base of the tail, with the exception of a slight hollow just behind the shoulder.

Body—*(a)* Chest deep and moderately wide with well sprung ribs. *(b)* The loin is short, broad and muscular. *(c)* Tail straight, set on high and carried up, docked of sufficient length to insure a balanced outline. *Major fault: set low, curled, or carried over the back.*

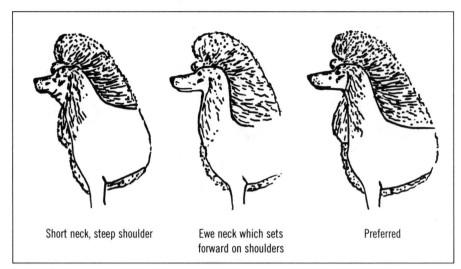

Short neck, steep shoulder

Ewe neck which sets forward on shoulders

Preferred

Figure 9-7. Neck.

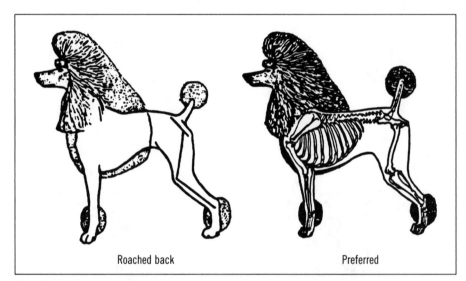

Roached back

Preferred

Figure 9-8. Topline.

Preferred: The chest is deep, its lowest point no higher than the elbows.

Lacking rib depth; too shallow in chest

Figure 9-9. Chest.

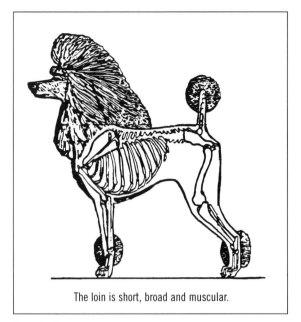

The loin is short, broad and muscular.

Figure 9-10. Loin.

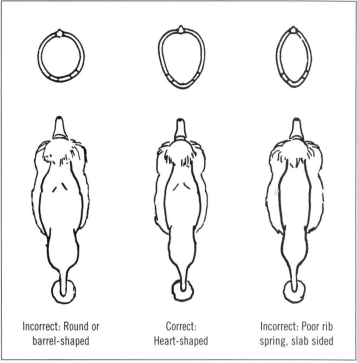

Incorrect: Round or barrel-shaped

Correct: Heart-shaped

Incorrect: Poor rib spring, slab sided

Figure 9-11. Body.

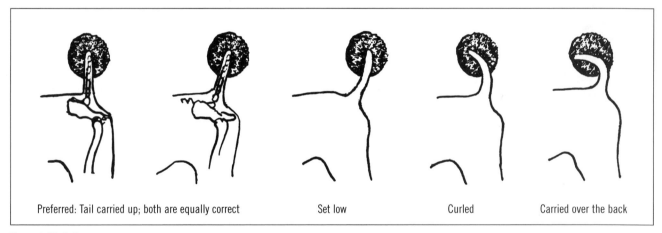

Preferred: Tail carried up; both are equally correct

Set low

Curled

Carried over the back

Figure 9-12. Tail.

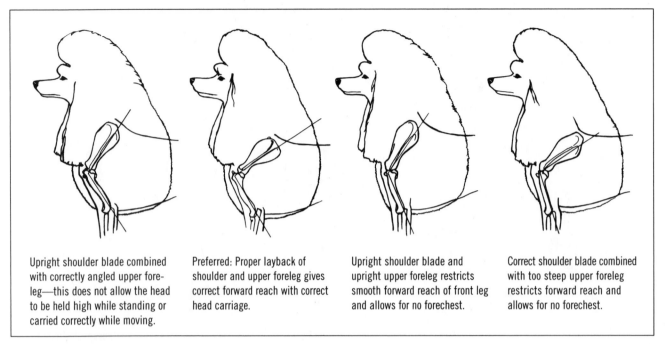

Upright shoulder blade combined with correctly angled upper foreleg—this does not allow the head to be held high while standing or carried correctly while moving.

Preferred: Proper layback of shoulder and upper foreleg gives correct forward reach with correct head carriage.

Upright shoulder blade and upright upper foreleg restricts smooth forward reach of front leg and allows for no forechest.

Correct shoulder blade combined with too steep upper foreleg restricts forward reach and allows for no forechest.

Figure 9-13. Shoulders.

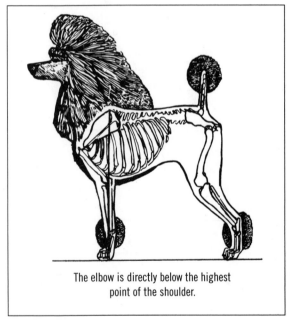

The elbow is directly below the highest point of the shoulder.

Figure 9-14. Elbow.

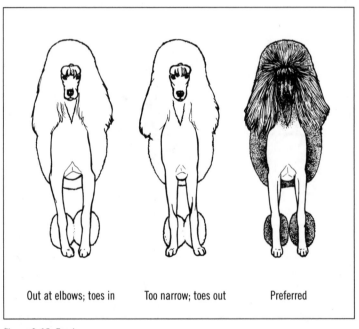

Out at elbows; toes in   Too narrow; toes out   Preferred

Figure 9-15. Forelegs.

Forequarters

Strong, smoothly muscled shoulders. The shoulder blade is well laid back and approximately the same length as the upper foreleg. *Major fault: steep shoulder.*

(a) Forelegs straight and parallel when viewed from the front. When viewed from the side, the elbow is directly below the highest point of the shoulder. The pasterns are strong. Dewclaws may be removed.

Feet

The feet are rather small, oval in shape with toes well arched and cushioned on thick firm pads. Nails short but not excessively shortened. The feet turn neither in nor out. *Major fault: paper or splay foot.*

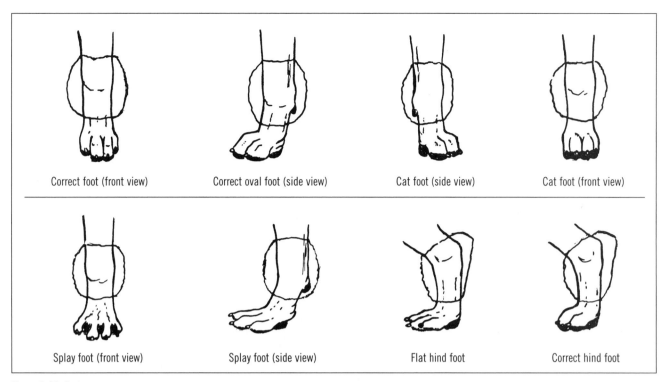

Figure 9-16. Feet.

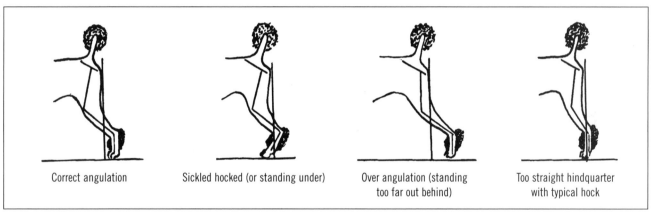

Figure 9-17. Hindquarters – side view.

Hindquarters

The angulation of the hindquarters balances that of the forequarters. Hind legs straight and parallel when viewed from the rear. Muscular with width in the region of the stifles which are well bent; femur and tibia are about equal in length; hock to heel short and perpendicular to the ground. When standing, the rear toes are only slightly behind the point of the rump. *Major fault: cow hocks.*

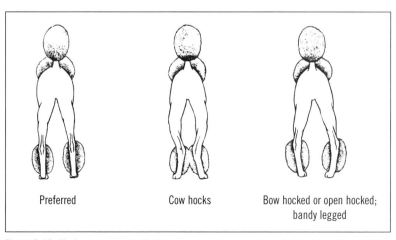

Figure 9-18. Hindquarters – rear view.

Corded Coat

Puppy clip

English Saddle clip

Continental clip

Continental clip with optional pompoms

Sporting clip

Figure 9-19. Coat.

Coat

(a) Quality—Curly: of naturally harsh texture, dense throughout. Corded: hanging in tight even cords of varying length; longer on mane or body coat, head and ears; shorter on puffs, bracelets, and pompons.

(b) Clip—A Poodle under twelve months may be shown in the "Puppy" clip. In all regular classes, Poodles twelve months or over must be shown in the "English Saddle" or "Continental" clip. In the Stud Dog and Brood Bitch classes and in a non-competitive Parade of Champions, Poodles may be shown in the "Sporting" clip. A Poodle shown in any other type of clip shall be disqualified.

(1) "Puppy"—A Poodle under 12 months may be shown in the "Puppy" clip with the coat long. The face, throat, feet and base of tail are shaved. The entire shaven foot is visible. There is a pompon on the end of the tail. In order to give a neat appearance and a smooth, unbroken line, shaping of the coat is permissible.

(2) "English Saddle"—In the English Saddle clip, the face, throat, feet, forelegs and base of tail are shaved, leaving puffs on the forelegs and a pompon on the end of the tail. The hindquarters are covered with a short blanket of hair except for a curved shaved area on each flank and two shaved bands on each hind leg. The entire

shaven foot and a portion of the shaven leg above the puff are visible. The rest of the body is left in full coat but may be shaped in order to insure overall balance.

(3) "Continental"—In the "Continental" clip, the face, throat, feet, and base of the tail are shaved. The hindquarters are shaved with pompons (optional) on the hips. The legs are shaved, leaving bracelets on the hind legs and puffs on the forelegs. There is a pompon on the end of the tail. The entire shaven foot and a portion of the shaven foreleg above the puffs are visible. The rest of the body is left in full coat but may be shaped in order to insure overall balance.

(4) "Sporting"—In the "Sporting" clip, a Poodle shall be shown with face, feet, throat and base of tail shaved, leaving a scissored cap on the top of the head and a pompon on the end of the tail. The rest of the body and legs are clipped or scissored to follow the outline of the dog leaving a short blanket of coat no longer than one inch in length. The hair on the legs may be slightly longer than that on the body.

In all clips the hair of the topknot may be left free or held in place by elastic bands. The hair is only of sufficient length to present a smooth outline. "Topknot" refers only to hair on the skull, from stop to occiput. This is the only area where elastic bands may be used.

Color

The coat is an even and solid color at the skin. In blues, grays, silvers, browns, café-au-laits, apricots and creams the coat may show varying shades of the same color. This is frequently present in the somewhat darker feathering of the ears and in the tipping of the ruff.

While clear colors are definitely preferred, such natural variation in the shading of the coat is not to be considered a fault. Brown and café-au-lait Poodles have liver-colored noses, eye-rims and lips, dark toenails and dark amber eyes. Black, blue, gray, silver, cream and white Poodles have black noses, eye-rims and lips, black or self-colored toenails, and very dark eyes. In apricots while the foregoing coloring is preferred, liver-colored noses, eye-rims and lips, and amber eyes are permitted but are not desirable. *Major fault: color of nose, lips and eye-rims incomplete, or of wrong color for color of dog.*

Parti-colored dogs shall be *disqualified*. The coat of a parti-colored dog is not an even solid color at the skin but is of two or more colors.

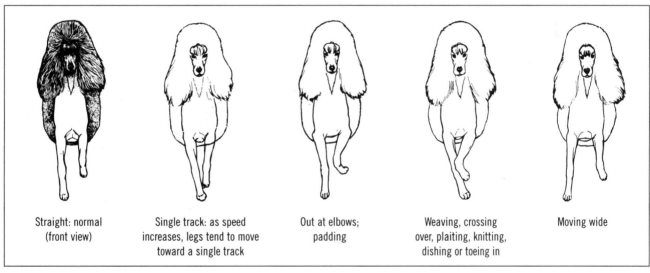

| Straight: normal (front view) | Single track: as speed increases, legs tend to move toward a single track | Out at elbows; padding | Weaving, crossing over, plaiting, knitting, dishing or toeing in | Moving wide |

Figure 9-20. Gait – front view.

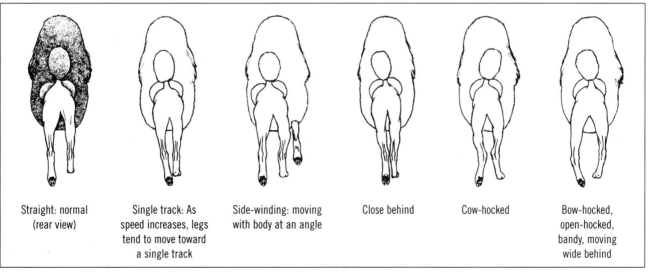

| Straight: normal (rear view) | Single track: As speed increases, legs tend to move toward a single track | Side-winding: moving with body at an angle | Close behind | Cow-hocked | Bow-hocked, open-hocked, bandy, moving wide behind |

Figure 9-21. Gait – rear view.

Correct: Trot is supported by legs on diagonal.

Incorrect: overreaching

Incorrect: hackney front; also lacks drive

Incorrect: Pace is supported by legs on the same side. The dog will rock from side to side when moving. A gait used by Poodles that do not have balanced angulation between forequarters and hindquarters.

Figure 9-22. Gait — side view.

Gait

A straightforward trot with light springy action and strong hindquarters drive. Head and tail carried up. Sound effortless movement is essential.

Temperament

Carrying himself proudly, very active, intelligent, the Poodle has about him and air of distinction and dignity peculiar to himself. *Major fault: shyness or sharpness.*

Major Faults

Any distinct deviation from the desired characteristics described in the Breed Standard.

Disqualifications

Size—A dog over or under the height limits specified shall be disqualified. *Clip*—A dog in any type of clip other than those listed under coat shall be disqualified. *Parti-colors*—The coat of a parti-colored dog is not an even solid color at the skin but of two or more colors. Parti-colored dogs shall be disqualified.

Value of Points

General appearance, temperament, carriage and condition	30
Head, expression, ears, eyes and teeth	20
Body, neck, legs, feet and tail	20
Gait	20
Coat, color and texture	10

Approved August 14, 1984
Reformatted March 27, 1990
Reproduced by permission of
The Poodle Club of America

chapter 10

INTERPRETING THE BREED STANDARD WITH EMPHASIS ON GROOMING

The standard for the Poodle is a description of the ideal of the breed. The current standard is divided into the following sections—General Appearance, Carriage and Condition; Size, Proportion and Substance; Head, Expression, Ears, Eyes and Teeth; Body, Neck, Legs, Feet and Tail; Gait; and Color and Texture—defining how the various pieces of parts of the Poodle should be. Each of these sections is assigned a point value (totaling 100) which is used by judges when they evaluate Poodles in the show ring. The Standard also lists major faults and disqualifications.

To understand the Poodle, or any breed for that matter, it is important to read the standard over and over to become familiar with the points of the breed. The descriptions of the various parts may seem rather routine, but if we zero in on the complete dog, with the pieces and parts joined together, a picture of the ideal Poodle will begin to emerge. The Poodle Club of America's illustrated standard does an excellent job of helping us to understand how Poodles should look. Once you have studied the breed standard and envisioned the ideal Poodle, when grooming, you should try to style each dog to enhance the illusion of perfection.

To be an expert groomer, you must learn to evaluate each dog individually and learn how to recognize its good points and its faults. All dogs have weak points. The perfect Poodle is yet to be born, but your objective in grooming any dog is to heighten its overall balance, good proportions and other sound points while you try

to conceal any imperfections the dog may have.

Here are some personal observations, along with additional photographs, sketches and grooming tips to help you achieve better balance and to learn how to disguise faults. Some styles or variations of styles *do* help to conceal certain faults. These are mostly tips for professional pet groomers because a prospective show exhibitor is only fooling himself or herself by showing a Poodle of poor quality. All the camouflaging in the world isn't going to fool a knowledgeable judge! However, even with a structurally sound, typey Poodle, you have to know how to stress the dog's virtues and minimize his weak points. Inferior grooming and conditioning can slow down or spoil altogether a prospective champion's chances.

All the illustrations in this chapter (except Figure 10-56) were hand-sketched by the author, who is *not* an artist! While they may look like unfinished art work, the pen and ink outlines and the silhouettes should show how you can help conceal certain structural imperfections by making some minor grooming adjustments. Many of the Poodles photographed to illustrate faults were intentionally clipped short to focus attention to their imperfections.

GENERAL APPEARANCE, CARRIAGE AND CONDITION

Active, intelligent and elegant-looking are explicit words which describe the character and appearance of the ideal Poodle. Although Poodles are generally regarded as pets or show dogs, the standards

especially still possess the physical attributes which made them remarkable water and land retrievers centuries ago. The dictionary describes elegant as "graceful, refined and polished," and this is the key to the Poodle's appearance and personality. He is elegant from top to bottom and carries himself proudly and gracefully because he knows it. His movement is fluid, never awkward or clumsy. He is squarely built. Truly, there is no more breathtaking sight than a well-groomed Poodle with his head and neck carried high.

PROPORTION

The standard calls for a squarely built dog: The length of the body measured from the breastbone to the point of the rump should approximate the height from the highest point of the shoulders to the ground. Refer again to Chapter 9, "The Official AKC Standard for the Poodle." Look at the Poodle in profile and imagine placing his body and legs (exclusive of his head and neck) into the confines of a square. If he fits into this square box, his proportions are correct. If he does not, either his body is too long and his legs too short, or vice-versa.

The Head: A Poodle's head should be attractive and balanced. To determine balance, it is necessary to examine the overall dog. A small head on a very large dog is totally out of balance, as is a big round head on a small dog. The ideal head is lean (but not too fine) and slightly peaked (Figure 10-1) and not wide or domelike. The skull should not be coarse or broad at the sides of the forehead. The "stop" refers to the slight indentation or step-up between

Figure 10-1.

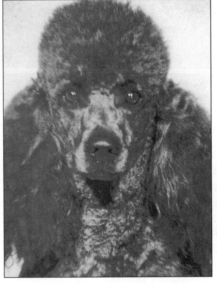

Figure 10-2.

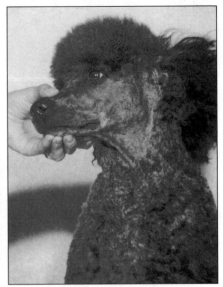

Figure 10-3.

the eyes where the muzzle and the skull meet. The stop should begin at the corners of the eyes, not below or above them.

A Poodle should have smooth, flat cheeks. Faults are thick skull, or one which is coarse at the sides of the forehead (Figures 10-2 and 10-3), high bridge between the eyes; wedge-shaped head; and cheekiness, a term that means prominent cheekbones which bulge past the eyes (Figure 10-4).

Grooming Tips: How you handle a Poodle's topknot depends on whether he is a show dog or a pet. On show dogs, the long hair on the top of the head is left full and secured with latex bands to form the topknot. Once the hair is banded, the topknot is blended into the neck hair and then shaped with shears for balance and symmetry. Instructions for putting up and banding the topknot are found in chapters 19 and 24.

On all pet clips, the Poodle's topknot is shaped round and full with scissors (Figure 10-5). It should never be wedge-shaped, broad or flat, or cut back above the eyes. Study the topknot

section before you scissor the head, as incorrect shaping will detract from the head and expression.

THE EARS

The top of the ears should be set on a line level with the corners of the eyes or slightly lower, but never higher. The hair on the ears is called the feathering, while the ear itself is called the leather. Poodle ear leathers are wide and almost fan-shaped. They should hang close to the head and, ideally, almost reach the nose when pulled forward. Faults are short or high-set ears (Figure 10-6); ears placed too far back on the head, and "flying" ears (Figure 10-7). In flying ears, the leathers are short, set horizontally, and almost stand out from the head (Figure 10-8).

Grooming Tips: When you are shaping the head on all pet styles, as you scissor across the top of each ear, if the ears are set properly (on a line level with the corner of the eyes), you want to create a definite separation between topknot and ears to outline the bottom of the topknot (Figure 10-9). After the topknot has been shaped, comb through the ear feathering,

then round the bottoms slightly with shears to remove any straggly ends. On short or high-set ears, always let the feathering grow as long as possible. Instead of scissoring a definite separation between the ears and topknot, blend the feathering into the topknot hair to create a soft look and help disguise these faults. *Never clip short or high-set ears.*

THE MUZZLE OR FOREFACE

Ideally the distance from the ear to the corner of the eye should be almost the same as the distance from the eye to the end of the muzzle (Figure 10-10). "Chiseling" is the very slight molding or indentation under the eyes. "Snipiness" means lack of sufficient chin or underjaw (Figure 10-11). When you look at a snipy dog in profile, you see a pointed muzzle lacking breadth and depth with little, if any, underjaw. "Lippiness" means a pendulous or heavy upper lip (common on the Spaniel breeds) which hangs over the lower lip.

A scissors bite, as illustrated in the official breed Standard, is one in which the outer side of the lower incisors touches the inner

Figure 10-4.

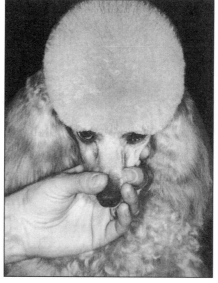

Figure 10-5.

Figure 10-6.

Figure 10-7.

Figure 10-8.

side of the upper incisors. A slightly undershot or overshot bite is no basis to reject a Poodle as a pet, but both are disqualifications for show dogs. No show Poodle will win with either an undershot bite (the front teeth, or incisors, of the lower jaw overlap or project beyond the front teeth of the upper jaw) or an overshot bite (the incisors of the upper jaw project beyond the incisors of the lower jaw, not touching the front teeth of the lower jaw, resulting in a space between the inner and outer surfaces). A wry mouth is defined as an asymmetrical alignment of upper and lower jaws, or a cross bite.

Grooming Tips: Clipping the Poodle's face adds length to the face, whereas a moustache shortens the face. Mustaches on Poodles are not as popular today as they were in the past, but they *can* be helpful in concealing mouth problems. A Poodle with large round eyes (Figure 10-12), or one with a snipy muzzle, a wry mouth or protruding teeth will look better with a moustache. Figure 10-13 shows a Poodle with a severe undershot bite. Just leaving a tuft of hair around the mouth (to be finished in a donut-style mustache)

Figure 10-9.

Figure 10-10.

Figure 10-11.

Figure 10-12.

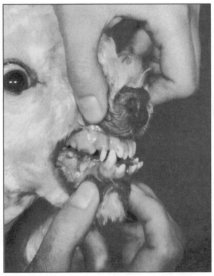

Figure 10-13.

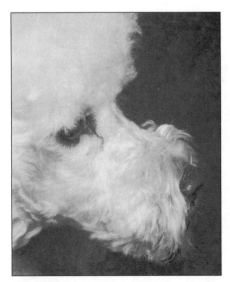

Figure 10-14.

Figure 10-15.

softens and takes the attention away from his unattractive foreface (Figure 10-14). Always keep the moustache close to the nose and away from the corners of the mouth to make it look neat (Figure 10-15), especially when the mouth is open.

THE NECK

The neck should be well-arched, strong and in balance with the head and body. There should not be any loose flaps of skin at the throat. "The elegance of a Poodle comes from many sources," says world-renowned judge Frank Sabella, "but, of all contributing factors, it would seem that a long, well-formed, well-carried neck should come first. A long neck carries an aristocratic high head and presents it for all to see. A long neck is not only part of proportion and symmetry of the dog, it seems to give this symmetry a focus and dimension." A short, thick neck makes a Poodle appear coarse. Unfortunately, a dog whose head seems to be joined to his body with no length of neck in between will never have the elegance essential to the Poodle.

Grooming tips: It's hard to disguise a short neck, but to add length to one that is not fat, choose a pet pattern where the hair is clipped off both sides of the neck (Figure 10-16). The Dutch, Town and Country, and Sweetheart are good choices for Poodles with short (but not stocky) necks. If you wish to have a more simple pattern, choose the Sporting, Lamb, Desi or any pattern with hair on the back of the neck. Clip or scissor the hair *short* on the back of the neck; clip the throat a *little* lower in front, then scissor the topknot slightly higher to add height (Figure 10-17). If the neck is short and *thick*, do the same—choose the Sporting, Lamb, Desi or any pattern with hair on the back of the neck (Figure 10-18). Clip or scissor the hair *short* on the back of the neck; clip the throat a *little* lower in front and then, if you can, shape the topknot slightly higher to add height, instead of emphasizing the fact that the dog has a short, stocky neck (Figure 10-19).

To make a very long neck look shorter and more balanced, choose a pet pattern where the hair remains on the back of the neck (Figure 10-20) instead of clipping the neck completely and calling attention to it (Figure 10-21). Clips like the Lamb, Miami, Desi (Figure 10-22) and others, are fine for Poodles with overly long necks. Leave the hair longer on the back of the neck; blend this hair with scissors, from the topline up to the topknot, to give the appearance of a properly proportioned neck. If you must use a style where the throat and back of the neck are clipped, shape the topknot into a **V** that extends into the center of the neck (Figure 10-23).

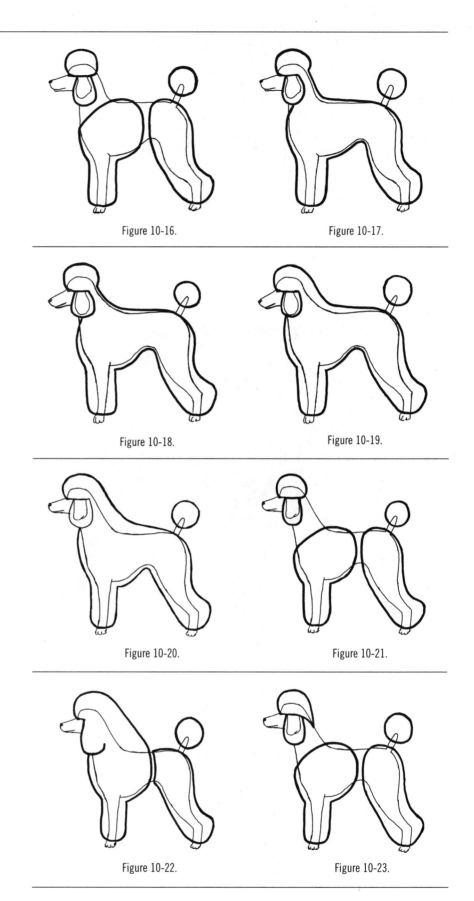

Figure 10-16.

Figure 10-17.

Figure 10-18.

Figure 10-19.

Figure 10-20.

Figure 10-21.

Figure 10-22.

Figure 10-23.

Figure 10-24.

Figure 10-25.

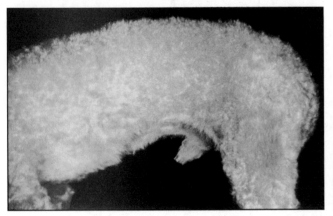

Figure 10-26.

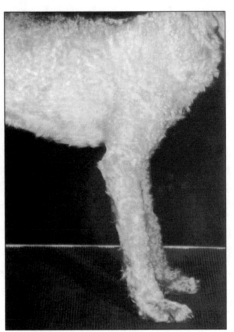

Figure 10-27.

THE BODY

The most important point to remember is that the Poodle's body should be compact. Refer back to the illustrated breed standard in chapter 9. Depth of chest is best judged from a side view of the Poodle. The brisket (sternum) line should be almost even with the elbows. Use your hands to feel the rib spring. The correct rib cage, illustrated in the official breed standard, is similar to that of an overturned rowboat, not barrel-like or slab sided. The back should be as short and as level as possible. If you run your hand from the shoulder to the base of the tail, other than a slight hollow just behind the withers, you should feel no bumps or indentations. The loins (the area between the end of the rib cage and the hips) should be short, broad and powerful. Hipbones should not protrude and should be level with the spine. The croup should be level. When the hindquarters slope too sharply, it gives the Poodle a low tail set and swings the rear framework under the body. Faults are a long back (Figure 10-24); a roach back (Figures 10-25 and 10-26), which is usually accompanied by a low tail set; a swayback, which often causes the tail to curl over the back; a shallow chest (Figure 10-27); and flat ribs.

Grooming Tips: Unfortunately, pets with long bodies, especially those with very short legs, will never have the elegant look essential to the Poodle. They will look best in styles that make the body appear shorter. The Chicago Dutch, Desi, Y, Swirl and Sweetheart clips are good choices for long-bodied dogs. In Figure 10-28, notice how the Dutch pattern, with a long, clipped straight line going from the base of the skull down the center of the back (almost to the end of the tail) adds length to the body. Then look at the Chicago Dutch (Figure 10-29) and see how this pattern make the same long body appear slightly shorter. If, however, you do want a pattern with hair on the neck, leave the hair longer on the back of the neck to make the distance between the head and tail appear shorter (Figure 10-30).

Other ways to camouflage a long body are to leave *slightly* more hair on the back of the front legs and the front of the back legs, to shorten the hair on the front of the chest and the back of the hindquarters, and to leave *slightly* more hair on the top of the back and less hair on the chest (Figure 10-31).

Pet Poodles with short bodies and very long legs look best in patterns that make the body appear longer. The Dutch and Town and Country are good styles for short-bodied dogs. When scissoring, follow the natural contour of the body, rounding the hair over the ribs and hindquarters. If the Poodle has a shallow or flat chest, gradually increase the length of hair over the ribs and under the chest.

The topline should be level from the highest point of the shoulder blade to the base of the tail (with the exception of the slight hollow just behind the shoulders). If your dog has a roach back, choose the Puppy, Sporting, Lamb, Desi or similar clip. Leave extra "fill-in" hair on top, and scissor the hair accordingly to make the topline appear level (Figure 10-32), instead of a pattern like the Dutch (Figure 10-33) or Sweetheart that would call attention to this fault.

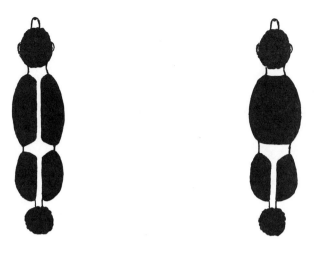

Figure 10-28.

Figure 10-29.

Figure 10-30.

Figure 10-31.

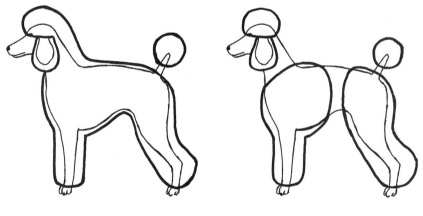

Figure 10-32.

Figure 10-33.

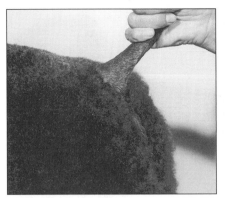

Figure 10-34.

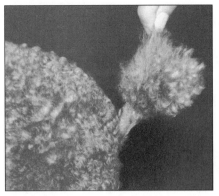

Figure 10-35.

Figure 10-36.

Figure 10-37.

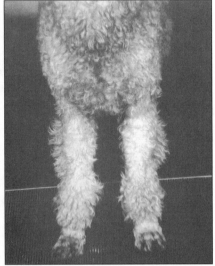

Figure 10-38.

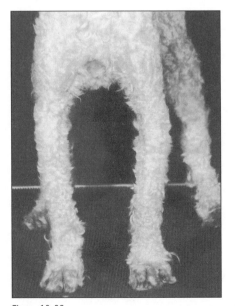

Figure 10-39.

The tail should be set high at the end of the backbone (Figure 10-34). Faults include low-set tail (Figure 10-35), a tail that curls up and is carried more or less forward over the back (squirrel tail) as on the Bichon Frise. Sketches and instructions for camouflaging improperly docked tails are in Chapter 14, "Clipping the Poodle's Tail."

THE FORELEGS

When viewed from the front of the Poodle, the forelegs should look straight; when viewed from the side (Figure 10-36), they should stand under the body. The elbows should be directly below the highest point of the shoulder blades, close to the sides of the body, and should not turn in or out. The feet should face forward and not turn in or out. Faults are short legs and legs set too far apart (Figure 10-37) or too close together (Figure 10-38). Figure 10-39 shows a Poodle with a Chippendale-like front, where the legs are out at the elbows and the pasterns are close.

Grooming Tips: To make short legs look longer, *never* expose any part of the ankles with clippers. Clip only to the end of the foot. Scissor the leg hair short. Then shorten the hair over the ribs and under the chest (Figure 10-40) instead of leaving the coat long, as shown in Figure 10-41. Try *not* to trim bracelets or puffs on short legs (Figure 10-42); doing this will make them look even shorter.

To make long, rangy legs look shorter, gradually increase the length of hair over the ribs and under the chest (Figure 10-43), instead of leaving it short (Figure 10-44). If the legs are close together, leave slightly more hair on the outside of each leg and shorten the hair on the inside (Figure 10-45), instead of scissoring as usual (Figure 10-46).

If the legs are too far apart, leave more hair on the insides (Figure 10-47) and shorten the hair on the outsides (Figure 10-48) instead of scissoring as usual.

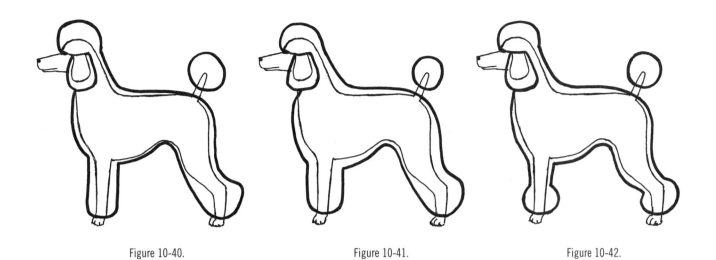

Figure 10-40.   Figure 10-41.   Figure 10-42.

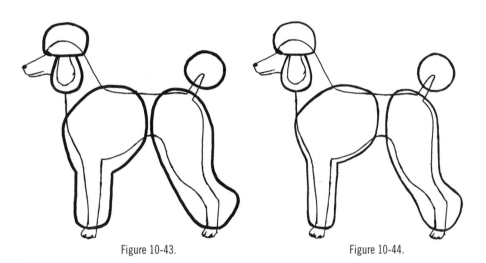

Figure 10-43.   Figure 10-44.

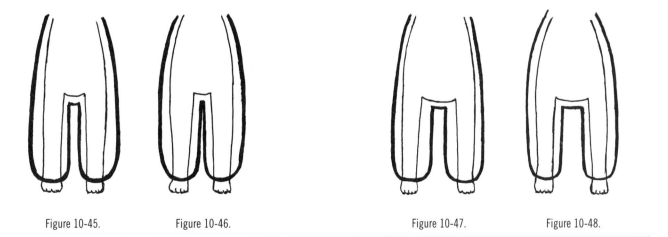

Figure 10-45.   Figure 10-46.   Figure 10-47.   Figure 10-48.

Figure 10-49.

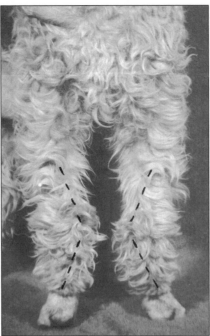

Figure 10-50.

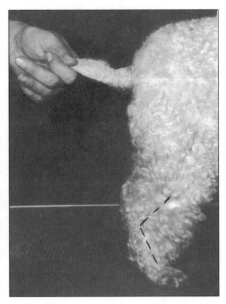

Figure 10-51.

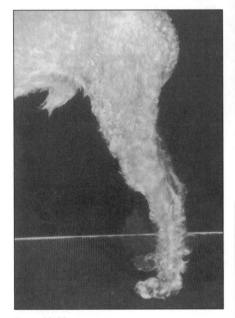

Figure 10-52.

Leonardo's Theories on Proportion and Symmetry

Around 27 B.C., Vitruvius Pollio, a Roman architect, wrote a study on the theories of proportion, one of the few technical handbooks to have survived from antiquity. Influenced by Vitruvius's reflections, Leonardo DaVinci (1452–1519) made this drawing to illustrate proportion and symmetry for his treatise on the human body. Leonardo, the most famous artist of the Italian Renaissance, wrote:

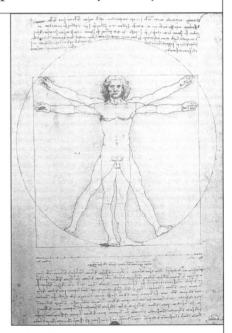

Every part of the whole must be proportionate to the whole. Thus if a man has a thick and short figure, he must be the same in all his limbs, that is to say, with short and thick arms, with wide, thick hands, and short fingers, with their joints in the aforesaid manner, and so on with the remainder. And I say the same about animals universally, reducing or *increasing them proportionately according to their diminution or increase in size. All parts of any animal will correspond to the whole.*

Figure 10-53.

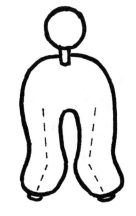

Figure 10-54.

Figure 10-55.

THE HINDQUARTERS

To assess the rear legs, the Poodle must be observed from the side. In a side view, the back legs should be well-angulated with a definite bend at the stifle joint and again at the hock joint (Figure 10-49). The thighs should be well-developed. The hocks must not be bent or curved and should not turn in or out. They should be perpendicular and close to the ground. When viewing the Poodle from the rear, the line of the leg should be straight from the hip to the foot. Faults are cow hocks (which turn in and cause the feet to turn out, giving a bow-legged appearance (Figure 10-50); sickle hocks or hocks which are bent or curved and not straight (Figure 10-51); short legs; legs set too close together or too far apart; and thin upper thighs with poor bone and muscle (Figure 10-52).

Grooming Tips: When viewing the Poodle from the rear, the line of the leg should be straight from the hip to the foot (Figure 10-53). When scissoring a cow-hocked dog, leave more hair on the outside of the leg where the hock turns in, and less hair on the inside, to make the leg look straight, as shown in Figures 10-54 and 10-55. Shorten or lengthen the hair to camouflage short or long legs.

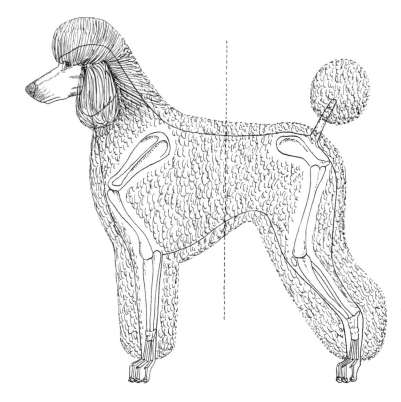

Figure 10-56.

SYMMETRY, BALANCE AND PROPORTION

Grooming Poodles is truly an art form. Each time a groomer produces a trim, on either a pet or a show dog, that person is expressing his or her artistic skills. Like a sculptor, the goal in bringing his or her work to completion is to make each creation look symmetrical, balanced, proportioned and graceful from all viewpoints.

Symmetry, balance and proportion are the most important aspects of a finished groom. These elements are not restricted to animal grooming or conformation; currently they are used in all of the arts and sciences,

Figure 10-57. Poodle A would look better if its tail and topknot were better balanced as in B.

Figure 10-58. Poodle A would look much shorter and more elegant if more hair were trimmed off the chest and the rear as on B.

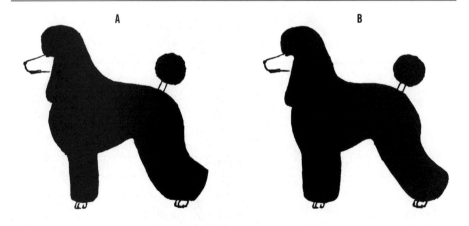

Figure 10-59. Poodle A would look more balanced with the same amount of hair on the front and back legs as on Poodle B.

including mathematics, physics, chemistry, botany, musical composition, architecture, the arts and sculpture. As you will see from the following definitions, the three terms are closely related.

Symmetry, from a grooming standpoint, means that the parts on one side of the dog correspond in size, shape and relative position to the same parts on the opposite side. Half of an animal, in other words, should be a mirror copy of the other, their parts corresponding across a dividing line.

Balance, from a grooming standpoint, means putting all the individual parts of the dog together with harmonious or pleasing results. One feature should never be so outstanding that it overshadows another. *Every part of the dog is in harmonious relationship, each one fitting together and looking aesthetically pleasing.* The head, the neck, the body, the legs and the tail individually may be exquisitely groomed, but unless these parts relate to each other harmoniously—the head with the body, legs and tail, the front to the back, one side to the other side, the top to the bottom—unless they compliment each other and make a *totally balanced* picture, their individual perfection is destroyed.

When associated with grooming, *proportion* usually refers to a harmonic relationship among the parts and between any part and the whole of the trim.

To better understand how to create the illusion, through grooming, that all the parts of the Poodle fit together in harmony with its breed standard, we must first understand the role played by our eyes. The eyes, which are said to be "the windows of the soul," are the primary means by which the brain most fully contemplates objects.

Light, shade, color, body, shape, position, distance and closeness all play an important role in what the eye sees and the brain perceives but, basically, to the human eye, all shapes converge at a central focal point. Let's apply this theory to grooming Poodles.

Since the breed Standard describes the ideal Poodle as a squarely built dog (the length of body measured from the breastbone to the point of the rump approximates the height from the highest point of the shoulders to the ground), initially you must consider the precise length and height necessary to create the illusion of a square on the dog you are grooming.

Placing an imagined vertical line in the midpoint of the square, as shown in Figure 10-56, will establish your center of attention or "focal point." There, the contours of a Poodle can be reduced to two half figures: one half from the middle backward and the other half from the middle forward. Although these two half figures are not identical, when styling a Poodle they should appear to be balanced. The center of attention should draw the eyes to the midpoint of any trim: Each and every part, line, band, strip or pattern set into the coat, on either side of the midpoint, should create the visual picture that all the dog's parts—front, rear, topknot and tail—ideally fit together.

Each Poodle has slightly different proportions which, from an artistic standpoint, must be carefully taken into account. A trim that is accurately balanced for one dog may be entirely disproportionate for another because of that dog's physical attributes. Incorrect grooming can make even the most "ideal" Poodle look out of proportion, merely by parting the hair or setting pattern lines at the wrong places, or by trimming the topknot, the tail, the bracelets and puffs too large, too small, or not in harmony with each other or the outline of the body. Leaving too much or too little coat can also affect the finished balanced look. Shortening or lengthening the coat, even by a fraction of an inch, will often better define the lines and

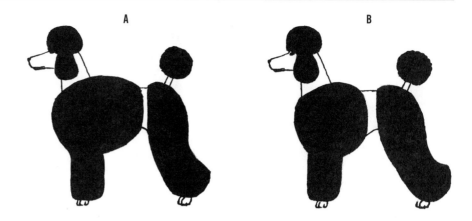

A   B

Figure 10-60. Poodle A's pattern would look more balanced by placing the "jacket" line at the last rib, as on Poodle B, instead of too far back of the last rib give the illusion of a long body.

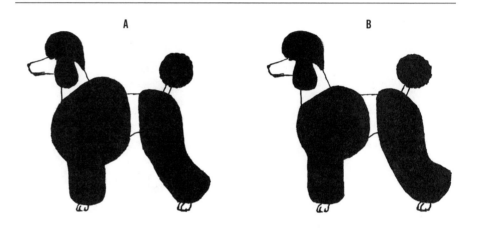

A   B

Figure 10-61. Poodle A's body pattern would look more balanced with the same amount of hair on the chest and the hindquarters as on Poodle B.

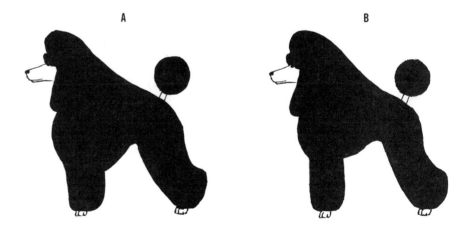

A   B

Figure 10-62. Poodle A in a Puppy clip would look shorter and more elegant if more hair were scissored off the front of the chest and under the rib cage, as on Poodle B.

Figure 10-63. Poodle A would look better with bracelets and puffs that are better proportioned and balanced, as in B.

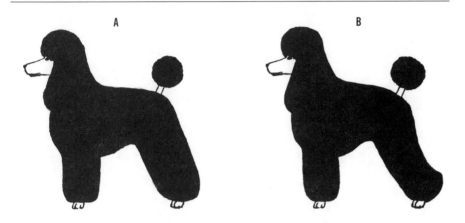

Figure 10-64. Poodle A would look less "old-fashioned" by emphasizing natural angulation in the rear as on Poodle B.

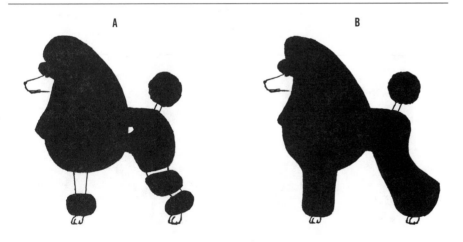

Figure 10-65. In an artistic composition, balance often depends on the arrangement of forms, that is, circles and squares. A small square form, on one side of the focal point, may be a perfectly adequate counterbalance to a larger round form on the opposite side of the focal point. This is evident in the English Saddle show trim on Poodle A and the Puppy Lion show trim on Poodle B.

shape of a finished pattern. Figures 10-57 to 10-65 show a few examples in silhouette to illustrate symmetry, balance and proportion.

CLIP

If you intend to show your Poodle in the conformation ring, only four trims are acceptable. The first is the Puppy clip that is *only* for dogs under 12 months of age. Once the Poodle becomes 1 year old, he must be shown only in the Continental or English Saddle clip. (Neither of these clips are recommended for pets as they require a great deal of time-consuming coat care and expert trimming.) In the Stud Dog and Brood Bitch classes, and in a noncompetitive Parade of Champions, a Poodle may be shown in the Sporting clip.

Among the currently popular pet styles are the Sporting, Lamb, Retriever, Town and Country, Miami, New Yorker, Dutch (and some of its variations), Sweetheart and Desi. The top and side views of these and other trims are illustrated in chapter 23. Most of these styles are easy to maintain. However, any trim that has a pattern (the Dutch, Sweetheart and Swirl, for instance) will require more frequent trimming with clippers and shears to keep the distinct pattern intact. To decide which clip is best for a Poodle, you should give some thought to the dog's comfort and your lifestyle and personal preferences. If you live in an area where fleas are a year-round problem, shorter hair—the Miami, Retriever or Sporting clip—will make it easier to prevent an infestation or treat an ongoing problem. Shorter hair will also be more comfortable to the dog in hot weather. Longer hair, naturally, will require more frequent brushing, combing and coat care to keep the dog's coat tangle free and looking good.

chapter 11

If you have studied each chapter presented so far in this book, you should have a thorough knowledge of the introductory phases of Poodle grooming: the equipment you need, how to handle your dog, how to care for the coat, how to bathe and fluff dry, how to trim the nails, how to care for the ears, eyes, teeth and anal glands and how to deal with external parasites. If you also have studied the Official AKC Standard (see chapter 9), you should have learned what the ideal Poodle should look like. After reading the important points presented in this chapter, you'll be ready to clip your Poodle.

How to Use the Clipping Instructions

Before turning to the clipping chapters, here are some suggestions to help you better understand the instructions presented there.

1) Basic instructions for clipping the feet, face, neck, tail and stomach and for shaping the topknot and styling the legs precede the instructions for the various body patterns. These instructions are presented in chapters 12 through 17. Basically, these parts are trimmed the same way, regardless of the body pattern you select.

2) If you plan to show your Poodle in the breed ring, concentrate on Part III, "Clipping the Poodle for the Show Ring," which consists of chapters 18, 19 and 20. In all regular classes, Poodles under 1 year old may be shown in the Puppy clip. Poodles 12 months of age or older must be shown in either the Continental or English Saddle clip. A Poodle in any other

trim will be disqualified. The Standard adds, however, that in the Stud Dog and Brood Bitch classes and in a noncompetitive Parade of Champions, a Poodle may be shown in the Sporting clip.

3) If you plan to show your Poodle in the Obedience ring, he may be clipped in any style.

4) Follow the instructions for setting the pattern of your choice. The chapters pertaining to clipping your Poodle for the show ring are presented first (chapters 18, 19 and 20). The chapters pertaining to clipping your pet Poodle (chapters 21, 22 and 23) appear next. In chapter 23, which provides instructions for all the pet clips, the easy-to-do pet clips, such as the Sporting, Retriever, Lamb, Miami or Summer, Town and Country, and Panda, precede the patterns that require more intricate body clipping, such as the New Yorker, Dutch, Sweetheart, Desi, Swirl, Y and T clips. Chapters 24 and 25 focus on some pet and show patterns that are popular in other countries of the world.

5) This book stresses a very important point: *setting pattern lines at specific bones*. You can use the same pattern instructions to clip any variety of Poodle—Toy, Miniature, or Standard—and not worry about correct proportions. Figure 11-1 shows the anatomy of the Poodle, which you will need to be familiar with in order to properly set a pattern.

To explain further, let's use the instructions for the Dutch clip as an example. When clipping the back of the neck, the instructions tell you to clip from the base of the skull down to where the neck

joins the body at the withers. If you were clipping a Toy Poodle, the distance from the base of the skull to where the neck joins the body may be 2 inches. On a Miniature, the distance may be 3 inches. On a Standard Poodle, the distance may be 4 to 5 inches. By clipping from bone to bone, no specific measurement is necessary, yet the pattern will be in proportion to the variety of the Poodle you are clipping. When you clip the front part of the Dutch pattern, known as the jacket, the instructions tell you to clip the line around the last rib. Thus, the jacket is formed between the shoulders and the last rib, and is in good proportion for the size of Poodle you are clipping. If you follow directions (unless the Poodle is a *very* poor specimen and considerable camouflaging is necessary), you will not set a pattern that is out of proportion.

6) When the width of the clipper blade is important to the Poodle's size, specific mention is made of this in the clipping instructions.

7) If perfect scissoring is not your strong point, clip the body hair with a snap-on comb rather than completely scissoring it. You can reduce scissoring time by using a snap-on comb to trim the body hair quickly and evenly to the exact length you want, and then neaten any uneven areas with shears.

8) On all pet clips, there is no definite rule for the length of the hair. The coat on the body, legs, topknot and tail can be as long or as short as you wish, depending on the texture of the hair and your personal preference. Keeping in mind that the trim should always appear well balanced,

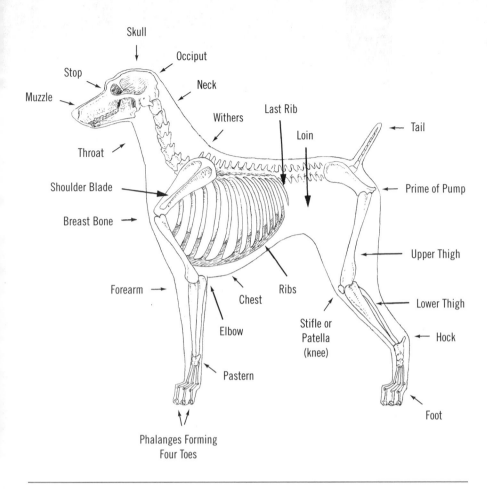

Skull

Stop

Muzzle

Occiput

Neck

Throat

Withers

Last Rib

Loin

Tail

Shoulder Blade

Breast Bone

Prime of Pump

Upper Thigh

Forearm

Chest

Ribs

Lower Thigh

Elbow

Stifle or
Patella
(knee)

Hock

Pastern

Foot

Phalanges Forming
Four Toes

Figure 11-1. Anatomy of the Poodle.

leave less hair if you prefer a shorter clip or more hair if you prefer a full coat, but never leave the coat so full that it parts and look untidy.

Preventing Clipper Burn

Clipper burn is a painful sore or rash that sometimes inflames the Poodle's sensitive areas (face, throat, underside of the tail, and genitals) after clipping. Many Poodles suffer from clipper burn every time they are clipped, while others are never bothered. Generally, white and light-colored Poodles seem to be more affected than dark-colored animals.

Clipper burn progresses like a chain reaction. First, the skin becomes red and irritated, then the dog starts scratching. If the irritated areas are ignored and not treated at this stage, the dog continues to scratch until the tender areas become raw with painful, open sores. To prevent clipper burn on a sensitive Poodle, follow these steps.

1) Don't use a fine blade on the sensitive areas, especially on a young dog. Remember, you can always take more hair off, but you can't put it back. Until you know your dog can take a closer clip, use a #10 blade when clipping a sensitive Poodle.

2) Do not clip any sensitive areas before shampooing. Instead, bathe the dog with a medicated shampoo, which can help to control clipper burn.

3) When clipping any sensitive parts after the dog is shampooed and dried, be sure the clipper blade is clean and cool. *Never clip a sensitive Poodle with a blade that is hot.* As you clip, periodically test the blade by placing it against your wrist. If it feels hot to the touch, spray the blade with Oster Kool Lube™, Laube Mr. Lube 'N Cool™ or other aerosol spray designed to cool clipper blades.

4) When clipping the sensitive areas, always hold the clipper blade *flat* against the skin. Never point the edges of the blade into the dog's skin. This is a common reason for clipper burn on the genital areas of male Poodles. Clipping underneath the back legs is an awkward job and, if the groomer holds the clippers at a slight angle instead of flat against the skin, it could cause enough irritation to start the dog scratching.

5) Do not use a dull blade or one with missing teeth to clip the sensitive areas.

6) After the dog's nails are trimmed, smooth the rough edges of each nail immediately with a file or emery board. One reason why clipper burn is a problem on the face is because a Poodle can scratch its face easily. Don't ever just hack off the ends of the nails with a trimmer and not buff the sharp edges with a file.

7) As soon as the sensitive areas are clipped, treat them with an anti-itch lotion or spray for dogs (available from most mail-order pet supply catalogs) or with Bactine™ or Vaseline Intensive Care Lotion to sooth the skin and prevent any irritation. The product you use should be greaseless so the dog will not try to rub it off.

Clipping the feet is the most difficult and demanding phase of Poodle grooming, especially for beginners. With a little patience and practice, however, you will eventually become proficient at this important part of clipping. Before you begin, here are some useful suggestions to keep in mind.

Every groomer has a preferred method of clipping feet. Some choose to sit the dog on the grooming table and to gently draw each foot forward as it is being clipped; some like to have the dog lie on his side. Other groomers prefer to have the dog stand behind them on the grooming table, looking over their shoulders, while they pull each foot forward to clip. All these methods work. The method you use to clip your Poodle's feet depends on which position is most comfortable and productive for you.

Normally, the blade you use to clip the feet will be either a #15, #30, or any of the narrow cutting blades. Narrow cutting blades like the #5/8 and #7/8 are especially useful for clipping the tiny feet of Toy Poodles. A #10, or medium blade, generally will not clip close enough to clean the hair between the toes and make the feet look really neat. However, if you are a novice, you might want to use a #10 blade the first few times until you determine how sensitive your dog's skin is. Clipping the feet too closely, especially on light-colored Poodles, may cause irritation. Most dogs will then aggravate the condition by licking and biting their feet. To help soothe sensitive areas, immediately after clipping, treat the feet with any of the topical medications

recommended in "Preventing Clipper Burn" on page 82.

Most Poodles hate to have their paws clipped, especially the front ones, and the vibration of the clippers against their feet makes them very touchy. To accustom a Poodle, especially a puppy, to the sound and pulsation, hold him in your lap, then move the clipper (while it is running but with the blade not touching the dog) gently over the feet a few times. Eventually, the dog should become accustomed to the noise.

If you do put a puppy in your lap for the first few times to get him used to the machine vibrations, as soon as the clipper-orientation is finished, move him to a sturdy grooming table. That is where anything that is involved with his grooming should always take place.

If your dog is fidgety when you first try to clip the feet, having an assistant steady the dog for a few clipping sessions will give you more confidence. The assistant should stand behind the dog to steady him. For further support, have the assistant place a hand on the hock joint while you clip each back foot, and at the elbow while you clip each front foot. However, the assistance should only be temporary. Your goal is to have your dog relax and learn to enjoy his grooming.

If your Poodle is very curious, he may put his head down to see what's going on while you're clipping the feet. If this is disturbing, you might want to protect the long ear feathering by drawing his ears back and temporarily holding them up with a small latex band as shown in Figure 12-1.

If you do make a mistake, comfort the dog immediately. Never let a dog, especially a puppy, believe you deliberately want to hurt him, especially if clipping is a new experience. Your gentle strokes and soothing words will help restore his trust in you. Remember, dogs understand not so much what you are saying as the way in which you are saying it.

You can also make clipping the feet easier for yourself and more acceptable for the dog by establishing a routine. Each time you do the feet, the order of clipping should be: front of the back feet, back of the back feet, front of the front feet and back of the front feet.

Now for the step-by-step clipping sequence.

1) Place your dog on a sturdy grooming table. My choice for the most comfortable position (for both groomer and Poodle) is for the dog to sit facing you. Gently draw one back foot forward, close to the front leg (Figure 12-2). The dog will be at ease in this position because his weight will rest on his other three legs. If your dog breaks this "sit" position at any time during the clipping session, put him back into place instantly, firmly command him to "Sit" and then continue as before.

2) Pointing the clippers upward in the direction of the leg, start near the nails and clip off all the hair from the top and sides of the foot without going between the toes (Figure 12-3). Clip only to the end of the foot, as indicated by the dotted line in Figure 12-4. Do not clip the feet any higher than the point where they join the leg. The mistake most beginners make is clipping too high up on the ankles.

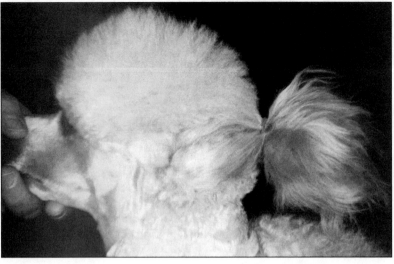

Figure 12-1.

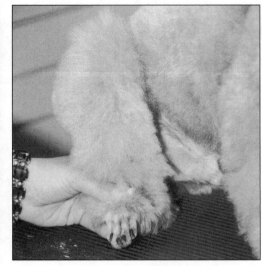

Figure 12-2.

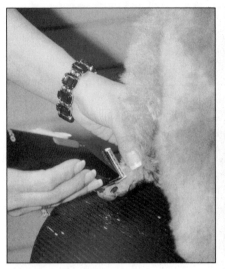

Figure 12-3.

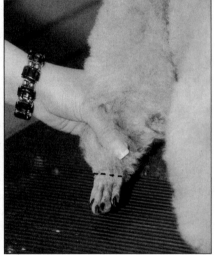

Figure 12-4.

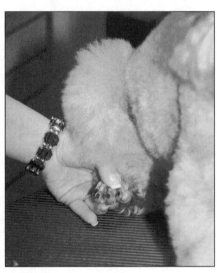

Figure 12-5.

Figure 12-4 also shows the groomer holding the long hair on leg hair upward. Doing this helps achieve a more even line around the foot and prevents clipping too high up the leg.

3) Now comes the difficult part for beginners—clipping the hair between the toes—and doing so without nicking the skin. On the underside of your Poodle's foot, there is a large pad and four smaller toe pads. Hold the foot in your hand, slip your second finger underneath, between the large

pad and the small pads, and press upward. As you do this, the toes will separate. At the same time, use your thumb on the top of the foot to further spread the toes open (Figure 12-5), one at a time.

4) Lay the edge of the blade near the nail (Figure 12-6), and remove the hair between the toes with the edge of the clipper blade, first on one side, then on the other. Even though you are using only the edge of the blade, hold it flat. Do not point the sharp edges of the teeth into the webbing. It takes a lot of

practice to master this technique and, if it is done properly, you will not nick the skin with the blade. All the toes are clipped in this manner. Clip the top of the other back foot in a similar manner.

5) The underside of each back foot is clipped with the Poodle in a standing position with the leg pulled back (Figure 12-7). Clip only to the end of the foot, making sure that the clipped line around the foot is even. It is also important to remove the hair from between the pads. Spread

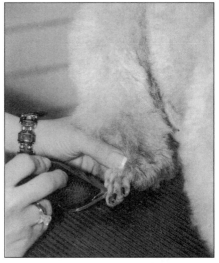
Figure 12-6.

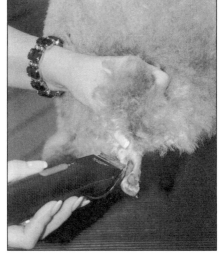
Figure 12-7.

Figure 12-8.

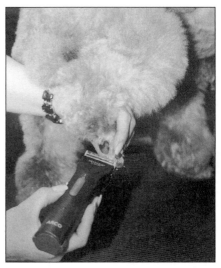
Figure 12-9.

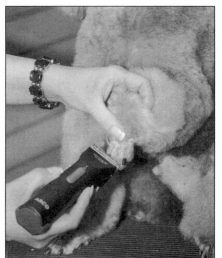
Figure 12-10.

Figure 12-11.

the outside toes apart with your thumb and second finger (Figure 12-8) while you clip the hair between the pads. The clipping here is best described as a scooping motion: The edge of the blade is held flat, and moves upward from the small pads to the large pad in an in-and-out motion (Figure 12-9).

6) The front feet are clipped with the Poodle in a sitting position, facing you, with the paw that is being clipped drawn forward

(Figure 12-10). Clip from the nails up to the end of the foot, removing all the hair from the top and sides first. Clip only to the end of the foot and not up on the ankle. Clip between the toes exactly as you did on the back feet. Spread the toes the same way, by placing your finger between the toe pads underneath and your thumb on the top of the foot (Figure 12-11). Remove all the hair between the toes with the edge of the clipper blade, taking care not to nick the skin (Figure 12-12).

7) The hair between the pads on the underside of the front foot is also clipped with the Poodle in the same sitting position. Hold the foot up and gently pull it forward. Clip to the end of the foot to make the line evenly encircle the ankle. Then spread the two end toes apart with your thumb and finger (Figure 12-13), and use the same in-and-out scooping motion to clip between the pads. The other front foot is then clipped similarly.

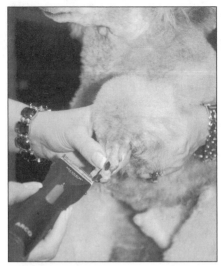

Figure 12-12.

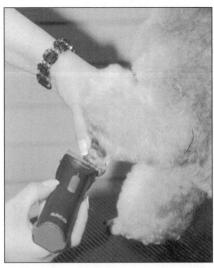

Figure 12-13.

8) After the feet are clipped, there should be no wispy hairs left around the nails. Until you become more confident, it may be easier to remove any that remain with a small cuticle scissors, but eventually you should be able to clean the feet neatly and completely with the clipper. When all four feet are finished, check to see that the clipped lines around the bottoms of the legs are even and balanced.

Generally, a Poodle's feet are clipped in most cases. However, there are various foot ailments—dermatitis; bacterial, fungal or parasitic infections; allergies; excessive licking and biting, for instance—where clipping might trigger or worsen a troublesome condition. And infrequently one may meet up with a dog to whom the foot-clipping process is so traumatic that he will not accept it without considerable commotion. In all of these situations, the solution is to leave the feet in natural condition, scissor around them to remove excess hair, then shape them round (Figure 12-14) in the Panda or Teddy Bear style. Do not remove any hair between the toes, although you may want to shorten the hair between the pads on the underside of the feet.

Figure 12-14.

chapter 13

Before attempting to clip the Poodle's face, keep in mind that some dogs have unusually sensitive skin that may become irritated as a result of being clipped. You want to take care to avoid clipper burn, the inflammation of the skin from clipping too closely. Normally, a #15, or medium-close cutting blade is preferred to clip the faces of pet Poodles, while a #30, or other close-cutting blade, is generally used for show clips. Until you know how close you can safely clip your Poodle's face, it is perhaps best to start with a #10, or medium-cutting blade. You can always switch to a closer-cutting blade if not enough hair is coming off. If the skin is easily irritated, especially on a white Poodle, you can also use two different blades: a coarser one on more sensitive areas, such as under the eyes, on the cheeks and the neck, and a finer one elsewhere.

Electric clippers do heat up during normal use, and pressing a hot blade next to the skin also can cause an irritation. To avoid this, test the blade periodically as you clip by touching it to your wrist. If it feels hot, switch to another blade, or spray the one you are using with a clipper coolant. Such products will instantly cool clipper blades, and also clean and disinfect them at the same time.

If you are an inexperienced groomer, or if this is one of your Poodle's first few trims, it is important that you proceed gently and with patience. A dog's attitude toward grooming may be contingent upon how you handle him, and how you let him know that clipping is really a pleasant experience and not something he should dread.

The sound of the clipper and the vibration against his face may frighten your Poodle at first. Start getting him comfortable with the procedure by holding the clipper (a part other than the blade) against his face. Turn on the motor and move the clipper around, but with the blade not touching the skin. Speak quietly and reassuringly as you do this. Remember that these first attempts at face clipping should be positive ones.

Clipping the Face

When you are ready to begin clipping, place the Poodle in a sitting position on a grooming table facing you. If he fusses and tries to move from this position during the session, put him back into place. Firmly command him to sit, then start clipping again. He will quickly learn what is expected of him.

Muzzling Your Poodle for Face Clipping

If your Poodle tries to bite when you clip his face, use a muzzle for protection. The best grooming muzzle is a long strip of gauze bandage. It is soft and can be tied fairly tight around the dog's mouth without cutting into the skin.

1) To make the muzzle, use a gauze bandage 2 or 3 inches wide. Cut a long strip, at least 12 inches long for a Toy Poodle, 15 inches long for a Miniature Poodle and 18 to 20 inches long for a Standard Poodle.

2) To fit the muzzle, form a large loop in the middle of the bandage, then slip the loop around the dog's muzzle just behind his nose with the knot and end ties under the chin. Then quickly tighten the loop so the dog will not be able to open his mouth.

3) Pull the ends back on each side of the face, under the ears, and tie them together in a bow knot at the base of the skull. A bow-knot closing is suggested for quick release in case the dog starts to panic. Now you can easily clip the face by sliding the muzzle forward or backward.

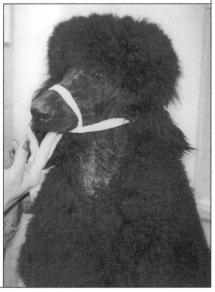

Figure 13-1.

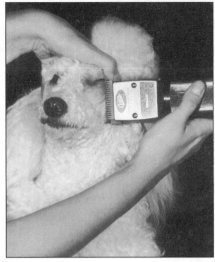

Figure 13-2.

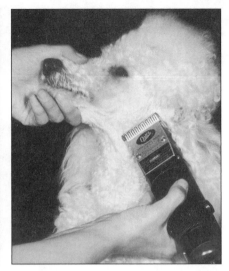

Figure 13-3.

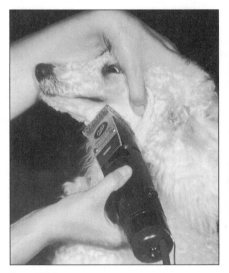

Figure 13-4.

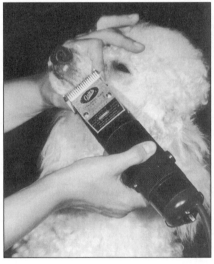

Figure 13-5.

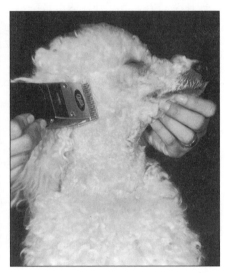

Figure 13-6.

1) The face is always clipped against the growth of hair, from the skull to the nose. Turn back the ear flap so it is out of harm's way, and hold the muzzle firmly in your free hand (Figure 13-1). The first step is to clip a straight line even with the corner of the eye. Begin in front of the ear and clip forward to the corner of the eye, not above it or below it. Hold the blade flat against the skin to avoid clipper burn. Clip off all the hair in front of the ear to make it lie as close to the head as possible. Continue clipping forward, and remove the hair on the cheek and side of the face.

2) Move the palm of your free hand to the skull, and use your thumb to gently hold the skin taut at the corner of the eye (Figure 13-2). Clip carefully under the eye. Do not remove any hair above the Poodle's eyes with the clippers; this area becomes the topknot, and is always finished with scissors. Even though you hold the blade flat against the skin, you will be using only the three or four end teeth to remove the hair. This procedure takes a little practice to master, but if you are calm and patient, you can do it!

3) Continue clipping forward on the cheek and side of the face (Figure 13-3).

4) To avoid cutting the folds of skin on the lower lip at the corner of the mouth, use your free thumb to stretch the skin back (Figure 13-4).

5) Press the jaws firmly together, and clip the remaining hair from the lips and around the nose

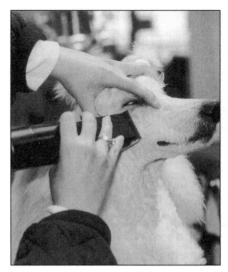

Figure 13-7.

Figure 13-8.

Figure 13-9.

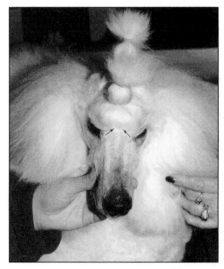

Figure 13-10.

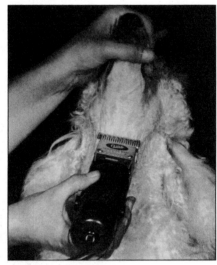

Figure 13-11.

(Figure 13-5). Hold the dog's head securely to prevent him from sticking his tongue out. It's very easy to nick the tongue, which can be very painful and traumatic to the dog.

6) Turn the dog's head and rest it against your wrist (as your arm comes around the back of the dog's head). Your thumb should be on top of the muzzle and your fingers under the jaw (Figure 13-6). Repeat the same procedure on the other side of the face. It is important to make the clipped line from the ear to the eye corner even on each side of the face, as this line sets the topknot.

7) Before clipping under the eye, move your hand from around the muzzle and place your palm on the dog's skull with your fingers pointing toward the muzzle (Figure 13-7). This leaves your thumb available to hold the skin taut at the eye corner as you did on the opposite side.

8) To avoid cutting the folds of skin on the lower lip at the corner of the mouth, use your thumb to stretch the skin back as you did on the opposite side (Figure 13-8).

9) When both sides of the face are clipped, hold the muzzle firmly in your free hand and clip a small inverted **V** (∧) shape between the eyes, using the clippers toward the muzzle (Figure 13-9).

10) The inverted **V** will enhance the dog's expression as well as add length to the muzzle. To keep it in proper proportion, the point of the **V** should be about even with the top of each eye, as shown on the Standard Poodle in show coat (Figure 13-10). Continue clipping forward until all the remaining hair on the top of the muzzle is removed.

11) Raise the head and clip upward from a spot just below the Adam's Apple to the lower lip (Figure 13-11). What you do to the neck below the Adam's Apple depends on the particular clip you choose. Instructions for clipping the neck are included at the end of this chapter (pages 90–93).

Figure 13-12. The side view of the finished French Mustache.

Figure 13-13. A three-quarters view of the finished French Mustache.

Figure 13-14. The finished view of the German mustache.

Figure 13-15. The finished front view of the Doughnut mustache.

Figure 13-16. The finished side view of the Doughnut mustache.

Clipping Mustaches and Beards

The Poodle's face may be clipped clean or styled with a small, trim mustache. Poodles shown in the breed ring must, of course, have clean-shaven faces. On all pet styles, however, a mustache is optional. Mustaches on Poodles are not as popular today as they were in the past, but they can be helpful in concealing unsightly mouth faults, most especially an undershot or overshot bite.

1) Sit the Poodle on the grooming table, facing you. Following the instructions given in the previous section, "Clipping the Face," clip each side of the face to within 1 or 2 inches of the nose (or about halfway between the corner of the mouth and the nose).

2) Clip the inverted **V** between the eyes.

3) Clip the hair on top of the nose down as far as the clipped line on the sides of the face.

4) Clip the hair on the underside of the muzzle up as far as the clipped line on each side of the face.

Note: Whatever mustache style you prefer, never set it at the corner of the mouth because it would be too large and bushy, spoiling the Poodle's expression. Always keep the mustache closer to the nose to show traces of the tapered muzzle so it will always look neat, especially when the dog's mouth is open.

Now you are ready to finish the mustache. The three most popular mustache styles are the French, German and Doughnut. Follow the instructions below for finishing the one you prefer.

THE FRENCH MUSTACHE

The French mustache has whiskers that stick out from the sides of the nose (Figures 13-12 and 13-13). The hair on the lower jaw and top of the nose is clipped off.

1) Begin by removing the hair from the top of the nose.

2) Hold the dog's head up and clip the hair from the underside of the muzzle.

3) Comb the hair on each side of the nose straight out, and scissor to a length of from ½ to 1 inch, even with the bottom of the upper lip.

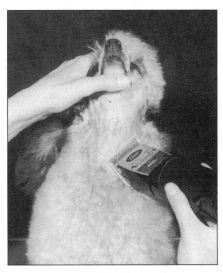
Figure 13-17. Clip the front of the neck.

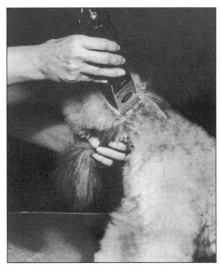
Figure 13-18. Clip the back of the neck.

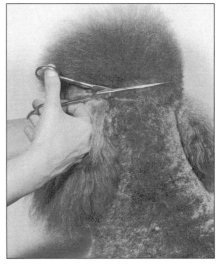
Figure 13-19. Blend the neck into the topknot.

THE GERMAN MUSTACHE

The German mustache has whiskers on each side of the nose and a beard under the jaw (Figure 13-14). Only the top of the nose is clipped clean.

1) Begin by clipping the top of the nose.

2) Comb the hair, and scissor the mustache round or tapered.

THE DOUGHNUT MUSTACHE

The Doughnut mustache has the same length of hair on the top and sides of the nose and under the jaw, to create the impression of a ring-shaped doughnut (Figures 13-15 and 13-16).

1) Begin by clipping the face to within 1 to 2 inches of the nose.

2) Comb the hair, and scissor the mustache in a round shape.

Clipping the Neck

There are two styles for clipping the throat and neck, depending on the body pattern you choose:

- The throat and front of the neck are clipped while hair remains on the sides and back of the neck.

Figure 13-20. The finished neck profile.

Figure 13-21. The finished back view of the neck.

- The front and back of the neck are clipped completely.

If you are planning to show your Poodle, you should follow the instructions for clipping the neck in Chapter 20, "The Three AKC-Recognized Show Clips." Only three clips are acceptable in all regular conformation classes: The Puppy clip, for dogs under 12 months of age, and the English Saddle or Continental clips, for dogs over 12 months of age. For these three clips, only the throat is clipped. Once you have determined the appropriate clip, consult that chapter for detailed clipping instructions.

METHOD A: CLIPPING THE THROAT AND FRONT OF THE NECK

On pet patterns, such as the Puppy, Sporting, Retriever, Lamb, Miami (or Summer), Desi, Y and Swirl clips, as well as the popular Moderne style (described in Chapter 24, "The International Scene"), only the throat and the front of the neck are clipped. The hair remains on the sides and back of the neck and is trimmed with clippers or blended with scissors to various lengths according to the pattern you select.

1) Sit the Poodle on the grooming table facing you. As this can be a

Figure 13-22. Side view of the finished neck on the Lamb clip.

Figure 13-23. Side view of the finished neck on the Desi clip.

Figure 13-24. The Modern by Mirjam van den Bosch of the Netherlands.

Figure 13-25. The Modern by Carinne Lewi of Belgium.

Figure 13-26. The Modern by Vincent Pastor of France.

Figure 13-27. The Modern by Martial Carre of France.

very sensitive area, it is very important to choose the blade that is correct for your dog's skin type. Normally, you should clip this area with a #10 blade. Don't use anything closer until you know how your Poodle will react. If your dog is extra-sensitive, however, and likely to scratch his throat after clipping, use a #9 or a #8-1/2.

2) Start an inch or so below the Adam's Apple. If the neck is short and you need to add length, start slightly lower. Pointing clippers upward, clip to the front of each ear (Figure 13-17). The clipped area either can be **V** shaped

or slightly rounded across the neck (similar to a string of pearls).

3) After the neck is clipped, comb the hair at the clipped lines upward, then scissor off any hair that extends above the line to make the pattern look neat.

4) Depending on the clip style you choose, the hair on the sides and back of the neck either is trimmed with clippers or scissored to the lengths suggested in the pattern instructions. For instance, on the Sporting, Retriever and Miami clips, because the body hair is trimmed short with clippers, the

hair on the neck is clipped with the same blade to blend in.

The Poodle should still be sitting on the grooming table to face you. Holding the muzzle in your free hand, bend the dog's head down slightly, and place the clipper blade at the base of the skull (Figure 13-18). Clip down to the point where the neck joins the body.

5) Clip the sides of the neck by lifting each ear and clipping down from under the ear to the same point.

6) Once the body is clipped to the same length, the short clipped hair

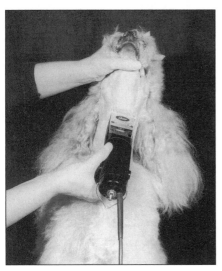

Figure 13-28. Clip the front of the neck (Step 1).

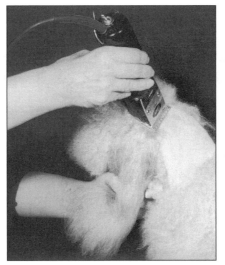

Figure 13-29. Stop clipping where the back of the neck joins the body (Step 2a).

Figure 13-30. Don't clip past the dotted line (Step 2a).

on the back of the neck is carefully blended into the topknot with scissors (Figure 13-19).

The finished results are shown in profile and from the back in Figures 13-20 through 13-23.

On the Lamb, Desi, Y and Swirl clips, the hair is much longer on the back of the neck. It can be trimmed with a snap-on comb attached over a #40 or #30 blade or with shears to blend into and balance with the body coat and the topknot.

On the most popular pet trim outside the United States, the Modern clip (see Chapter 24, "The International Scene"), the hair on the back of the neck is even longer and fuller, with the blending into the topknot starting near the withers. Examples of the Modern clip are shown in Figures 13-24 through 13-27. Notice the balance on these trims—the smooth arched line that flows from the topknot into the longer hair on the neck and down the back to create an elegant picture.

METHOD B: CLIPPING THE FRONT AND BACK OF THE NECK

On patterns like the New Yorker, Dutch, Chicago Dutch, Pittsburgh Dutch, Pajama Dutch and Sweetheart clips, the front, sides and back of the neck are clipped.

1) Begin by clipping the front of the neck as described in steps 1 through 3 of Method A, and as shown in Figure 13-28.

2) Before clipping the back and sides of the neck, you must decide how you will shape the topknot at the nape of the neck: either rounded at the base of the skull, or into a **V** shape that converges down to a point in the center of the neck. You may now wish to look through Chapter 16, "Shaping the Topknot," for more information.

a) If you choose to round the back of the topknot:

Hold the Poodle's muzzle in your free hand, bend it down slightly, and place your clippers at the base of the skull. Use a #15 blade.

Clip downward, stopping where the neck joins the body (Figure 13-29). Do not clip past that point, indicated by the dotted line shown in Figure 13-30.

b) If you choose to make the **V**-shaped topknot that converges down to a point in the center of the neck:

Scissor in the basic shape of the **V**, proportioning the tip in the center of the neck according to its length.

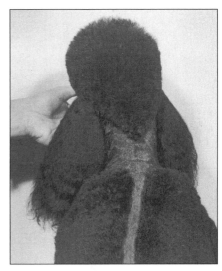

Figure 13-31. The finished view of the back of the neck with a **V** topknot.

Clip around the **V** and downward, stopping where the neck joins the body. The finished topknot is shown in Figure 13-31.

No matter how you style the back of the topknot, the line from front to back looks like a necklace would around your own neck when the neck is completely clipped. To finish any body pattern, remember to comb the neck hair upward and forward, and then to scissor off any hair that falls over the clipped line. Using curved shears here to bevel or round the edges all the way around the neck will make your pattern look neat.

chapter 14

The tail is one of the Poodle's most important features, and how it looks after grooming can enhance or spoil the overall breed profile. "Next to the head," writes Frank Sabella, celebrated former dog show handler and now a world-renowned judge, "the tail is the most expressive element of the Poodle—properly docked and groomed, with an abundant pompon, set high and carried the same, it describes all the flourish and fanfare of a gala occasion."

The Poodle Standard calls for the tail to be "straight, set on high and carried up, docked of sufficient length to insure a balanced outline." A good way to define "sufficient length to insure a balanced outline" on a pet trim is to say that after the pompon has been shaped with scissors, its proportions should just about equal the height of the dog's topknot.

On show clips, the tail is left as full and profuse as possible to balance the longer topknot that is held in place by elastic bands. You can read more about this in the instructions for the show clips: The Puppy clip (for competition), the English Saddle clip, and the Continental clip (all appear in chapter 20). For both pet and show trims, the uniformity of head and tail will help to complement the "squarely built" appearance called for in the Standard.

Clipping Properly Docked Tails

Use a #10 blade on the tail, or one that shows the natural coat color without skinning, but nothing finer unless you are positive your dog's skin can tolerate a closer clip. If it can, use a #15 blade. The area to be clipped depends on the length of the tail after docking. Generally speaking, if the tail has been docked to correct length, a good rule of thumb is to clip about one-third of the tail and leave the hair on the remaining two-thirds to be shaped with scissors into a pompon.

1) Stand your dog on the grooming table with his hindquarters facing you. Grasp the end of the tail in your free hand. Starting on the upper side, place your clippers flat against the skin and clip in to the tail's juncture with the body (Figure 14-1).

2) Clip each side of the tail in the same manner (Figure 14-2), starting from the same spot, down to where the tail joins the body. Some groomers like to clip an inverted **V** slightly forward of the base of the tail, into the body coat, as shown in Figure 14-3, to make the dog look shorter in back. If you do this, be careful not to go too far and clip off too much hair. Remember that you can always take more hair off, but it takes months to replace once removed.

3) The underside of the tail is a very sensitive area and should be clipped in the opposite direction, or from the body out to the pompon. Hold the tail in the position shown in Figure 14-4, begin above the anal opening and clip to the line in the middle. Remember: The clipped line around the middle of the tail must be even, or the pompon won't look properly shaped.

4) Although you should never clip directly over the anal opening, it is more hygienic if this area is kept free of hairs which are likely to become stained or caked with feces. This is done by carefully clipping around each side of the anal opening with the edge of the clipper blade, as shown in Figure 14-5. Notice in the photograph that even though the edge of the blade is being used, it is still being held flat. Don't clip closely below the anus unless you have chosen a clip like the Continental, Miami or other style in which the hair is shaved from the hindquarters. On pet trims such as the Lamb, Dutch and others in which hair is left on the back legs, the area below the anus is shaped with scissors.

5) Before shaping the pompon, comb the hair out toward the tail tip. Then grasp the hair in your hand, slide your fingers to the end of the tail, then scissor straight across the ends of the hair (Figure 14-6) to remove any excess or wispy ends that are out of place. When you let go, you will find that the hair around the tip of the tail is somewhat rounded.

6) The rest of the pompon is also shaped round. The best way to create the correct outline is to hold up the end of the tail with your free hand, and then fluff out the hair, almost as if you were "back-combing" it (Figure 14-7). Before beginning, take a look at the topknot to get an idea of the amount of hair necessary to skillfully balance your clip front and back.

7) Begin working with curved shears on the underside of the

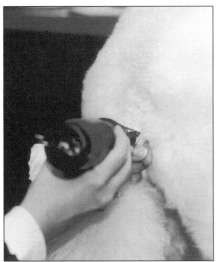

Figure 14-1.

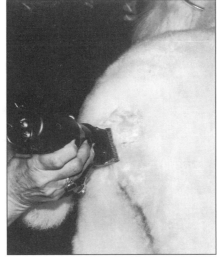

Figure 14-2.

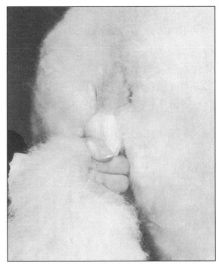

Figure 14-3.

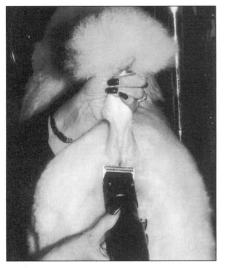

Figure 14-4.

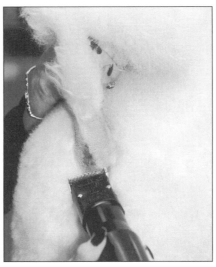

Figure 14-5.

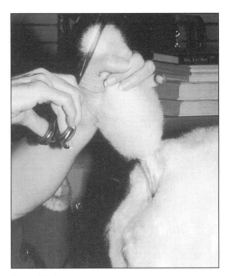

Figure 14-6.

pompon, and scissor completely around the pompon, taking off a little hair at a time, shaping it round (Figure 14-8). Stop periodically and check to see that the pompon is being shaped correctly and that you are properly balancing your clip.

Although your goal is a balanced trim, some dogs, unfortunately, have thinly coated tails which look rather "droopy" when the hair of the pompon is left too long. When confronted with such

a situation, as soon as scissoring is complete and the groomer releases the tail end, the pompon loses its shape. Compare the tail hair of the dog in Figure 14-8 with that of the dog in Figure 14-9. Taking *slightly* more hair off the latter dog would give his tail a more compact look.

Clipping Improperly Docked Tails

Some Poodles have improperly docked tails, and an expert

groomer must know how to deal with this problem to make the trim look more balanced.

The length, thickness and curvature of a Poodle's tail will determine where the pompon should be set. An improperly docked tail can be greatly enhanced by creative correction by the subtle touch of a skillful groomer. See Figures 14-10, 14-11 and 14-12.

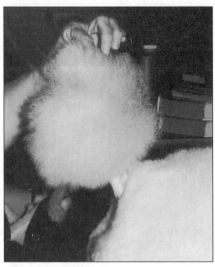

Figure 14-7.

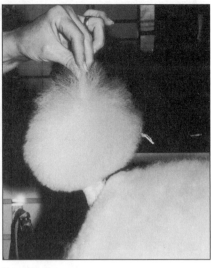

Figure 14-8.

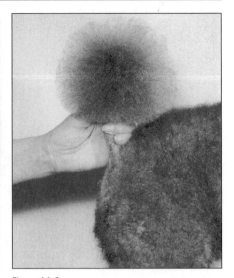

Figure 14-9.

Figure 14-10. A typical, correctly docked tail. About one-third of the tail stem is clipped to the point where the tail joins the body, while the rest is used to form the pompon.

Figure 14-11. To disguise a short tail (a common problem), move the pompon out as far towards the tail tip as possible, allowing more clipped area to create the illusion of a longer tail.

Figure 14-12. A long tail can be made to appear shorter and more balanced by reducing the amount of clipped area and positioning the pompon around the end of the tail.

chapter 15

No matter what coat pattern you choose for your Poodle, the stomach should be clipped to present a clean underline. The correct position for clipping the stomach depends on the size of your dog. It is easier to clip underneath a Toy or Miniature Poodle by lifting the dog up and holding the front feet with your free hand, as shown in Figure 15-1.

A Standard Poodle or a large or heavy Miniature should stand on the grooming table with its hindquarters facing you. Clip the right side of the stomach by lifting the right rear leg, as shown in Figure 15-2, then clip the left side of the stomach by lifting the left rear leg.

For all pet patterns, clip the stomach up to the last rib using a #15 blade. If your dog has sensitive skin, use a #10. Pointing clippers upward, start just above the genital area and clip to the middle of the dog, stopping at the last rib, as shown in Figure 15-3. Keep the clipper blade flat against the skin. The clipped area will be **U**-shaped. Gently clip around the nipples or penis without applying pressure to the clipper, taking care not to catch any folds of skin in the blade.

Before clipping the stomach for the show patterns, be sure to study the pattern instructions and determine where you will set the line for the long hair of the mane or ruff. The line should be set slightly in back of the last rib, at a spot that will make the dog look balanced. Once this line has been established, clip the stomach up to this point. The mane coat or ruff will then completely and evenly encircle the body.

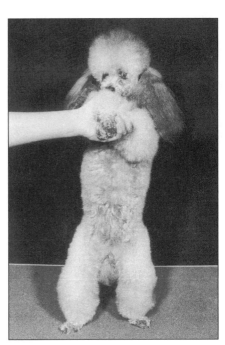

Figure 15-1.

Figure 15-2.

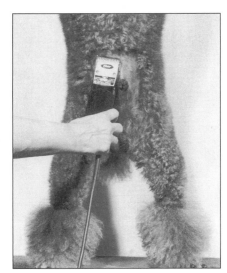

Figure 15-3.

chapter 16

Figure 16-1.

Figure 16-2.

Figure 16-3.

Figure 16-4.

Figure 16-5.

Figure 16-6.

How you fashion a Poodle's topknot depends on whether she is a show dog or a beloved companion. If you intend to show your Poodle in the breed ring, the long hair on the top of the head is left full and secured with latex bands to form the topknot. Once the hair is banded, the topknot is blended into the neck hair, and all of the mane, or long body coat, is then properly shaped for balance and symmetry. Detailed instructions for putting up and banding the topknot are given in Chapter 19, "Care of the Poodle in Show Coat."

On all the pet trims, the topknot is shaped round, with the hair in the center left slightly longer and fuller and tapering at the sides (see Figures 16-1 and 16-2). How you shape the topknot at the nape or back of the neck depends on personal preference the clip you choose. Basically, on styles that call for a clipped neck or short hair at the back of the neck (like the Dutch and its variations,

Sweetheart, Miami, Sporting and Town and Country), the topknot is either rounded (Figure 16-3) or into a **V**-shaped at the back (Figure 16-21 on page 101). On clips that call for more neck hair (like the Puppy, Lamb, Desi, Swirl, Y or Moderne), the topknot is blended into the neck hair in an unbroken line to create an overall balanced trim. Figure 16-4 shows the blending of the topknot into the neck hair on the Desi clip, and Figure 16-5 on the Lamb clip.

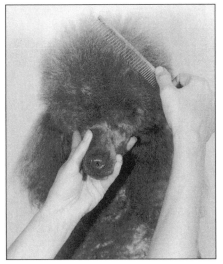

Figure 16-7.

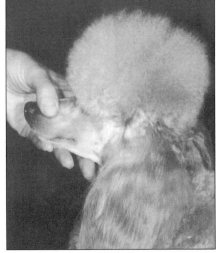

Figure 16-8.

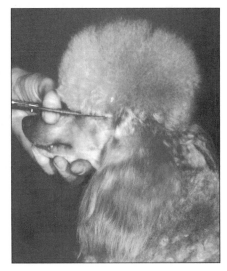

Figure 16-9.

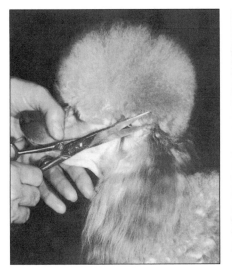

Figure 16-10.

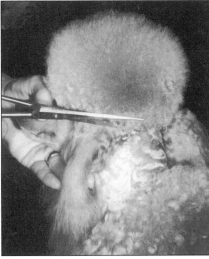

Figure 16-11.

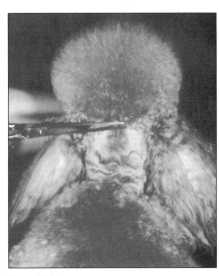

Figure 16-12.

Whatever pet clip you choose, the topknot must be properly proportioned and in balance with the coat on the body, legs and tail. If your Poodle's hair is of correct texture, leave the topknot as full as possible. A profuse, beautifully rounded headpiece is much more attractive than a flat one, but it should never be out of balance or so high that the hair parts in the middle and falls to the side. If the coat is soft, however, trim the topknot slightly shorter to prevent this from happening. Examine the Standard Poodle in Figure 16-6. Although the body and leg coat is of good texture, the topknot will need to

be shortened a little as it tends to fall to the sides. After you have groomed your Poodle a few times, you will learn the correct hair length.

For all topknot shaping, sit the Poodle on the grooming table, facing you. You must be able to see both sides of the head as you scissor. To achieve the ideal shape, it's best to view the work-in-progress not only from the front and sides, but also from the top and in profile.

You are now ready to begin, and part of your job is already done. In the initial clipping of the face,

no hair should have been clipped off above the level of the eyes. Clipping a straight line from the ear to the corner of the eye on each side of the head has automatically established the line for the topknot.

First, comb the topknot upward and forward, using light strokes to lift and fluff out the hair (Figure 16-7). This is the key to good shaping. You'll have to comb and fluff many times to coax out any straggly hairs. Don't pull these hairs out with your fingers. Comb, fluff and rescissor until you achieve the desired results.

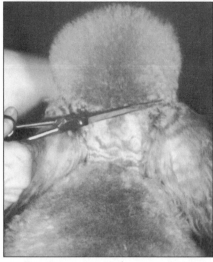

Figure 16-13.

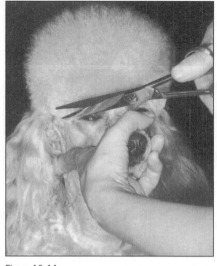

Figure 16-14.

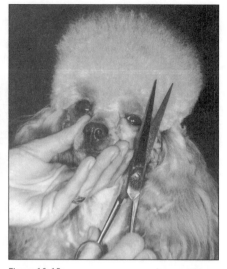

Figure 16-15.

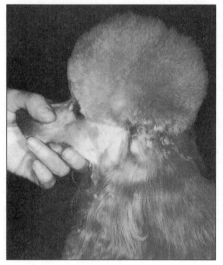

Figure 16-16.

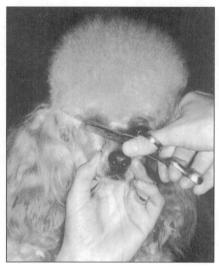

Figure 16-17.

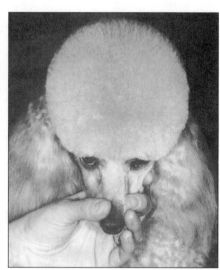

Figure 16-18.

Rounded at the Neck

1) Use straight or curved shears. Begin with the right side if you're right-handed or the left if you're left-handed. Hold the Poodle's muzzle with your free hand to steady the head (Figure 16-8).

2) Start scissoring the topknot hair at the corner of the eye, and work straight back to the ear, cutting off all the hair that falls below the clipped line from the corner of the eye to the ear (Figure 16-9).

3) Lay your shears flat against the side of the head, pointing upward, and scissor vertically up the side of the topknot to remove any hair that extends out beyond the cheekbone.

4) Fold the ear leather back, and trim off all the straggly tufts of hair in front of the opening to the ear (Figure 16-10).

5) Bring the ear leather back to its normal position, and continue scissoring in a straight line back over the ear (Figure 16-11), following the natural curve at the base of the skull (Figure 16-12), to the opposite ear (Figure 16-13), taking a little hair off at a time.

6) Back at the corner of the eye where you first started scissoring, scissor around the front of the head to the opposite ear the same way, shaping the topknot round (Figure 16-14). As you scissor across the front (between the inside corners of the eyes), notice that the bottom blade of the shears almost rests on the dog's nose. Scissor the hair above the eyes even with or *slightly* forward of the eye line (Figure 16-15).

Figure 16-16 shows the hair in front almost even with the eye line. *It should never fall behind the eye*

Figure 16-19.

Figure 16-20.

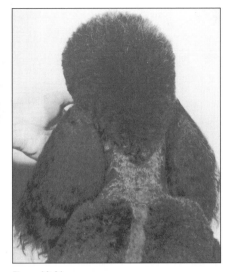

Figure 16-21.

Figure 16-22.

Figure 16-23.

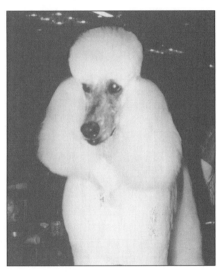

Figure 16-24.

line. Don't leave the hair too long, as it will fall forward.

7) Shape the opposite side of the topknot the same way, starting at the corner of the eye (Figure 16-17) and working straight back to the ear, cutting off all hairs that fall below the clipped line.

8) After scissoring horizontally all around the head and then vertically to remove all the hair that extends out beyond the cheekbones, shape the rest of the topknot round as shown in Figure 16-18, leaving more hair in the center of the head and tapering to the sides.

The fullness of the topknot depends on the Poodle's coat texture and your personal preference. Figure 16-19 shows a finished topknot that has been left very full and Figure 16-20 shows a shorter topknot.

V-Shaped at the Neck

Round the sides and front of the topknot as described in the previous section, but do not round the hair at the back of the neck, at the base of the skull. Instead, comb the hair outward, then shape a sharp **V** at the nape of the neck. The top of the **V** should start at the back corner of

each ear and converge down to a point in the center of the neck.

The depth of the **V** depends on each dog's length. Generally the point should be about ½ inch below the base of the skull on Toy Poodles, ¾ to 1 inch on Miniatures and 2 inches on Standards; but it should not cover more than one-third of the total neck length. As you scissor to the bottom of the **V**, taper the hair shorter until it blends in with the short hair or clipped area on the back of the neck to achieve a balanced look (Figure 16-21). Figures 16-22, 16-23 and 16-24 show finished topknots.

chapter 17

FINISHING THE EARS

Figure 17-1.

Figure 17-2.

If you are planning to show your Poodle in the breed ring, the ears are never clipped. Only the bottom edges are scissored to create a more balanced outline. On all the pet Poodle trims, however, the way the ears are finished is a matter of personal preference. They may be left with full feathering, they may be partially clipped with tassels left on the bottoms, or they may be clipped short.

Full-Feathered Ears

Fully feathered ears are required for all the show trims and are very attractive in many pet trims as well.

Once the topknot has been shaped (Figure 17-1), most professionals like to scissor a *slight* indentation at the top of the ears, just enough to show a definite separation between the topknot and the ear, as shown in Figure 17-2. To finish the ears, comb the feathering straight down. Then round the edges with your shears to neaten any straggly hairs at the bottoms or to shorten excessive length for a more balanced appearance. Make both ears even in length and shape.

Tasseled Ears

Tasseled ears are currently out of fashion; most professionals and pet owners currently prefer the elegant look of full-feathered ears. However, tasseled ears can be a sensible choice for Poodles who experience chronic heavy, waxy secretions in their ear canals which condition is then further aggravated by poor air circulation.

1) Sit the Poodle on the grooming table, facing you. Use a #15 blade. Always use the clippers in one direction, from the top of the ear downward. Never turn them the opposite way, or you will cut the flaps of skin on each side of the leather! In so doing you cause the dog considerable pain and bleeding.

2) Lay the ear flat on the palm of your hand. Start at the top of the ear and clip downward (Figure 17-3). If you prefer a full tassel, clip to the middle of the ear (Figure 17-4). If you prefer a slimmer tassel, clip to within 1 inch of the end of the leather (Figure 17-5).

3) Clip the inside of the ear as far down as you clipped the outside.

4) Press your thumb and index finger on the edge of the leather (Figure 17-6), and scissor along the edges to remove the shaggy hairs.

5) Clip the opposite ear in the same way.

6) The tassels may be left long (Figure 17-7), or shortened to a length of from 1 to 2 inches (Figure 17-8).

Fully Clipped Ears

Ears that are clipped short are good choices for country or working Poodles, especially those trimmed in the Retriever clip or the Miami clip. The hair is shortened to a length of ½ inch all over.

1) Sit the Poodle on the grooming table, facing you. Best results are obtained by using a #5F blade on clean hair.

2) Lay the ear flat on the palm of your hand. Start clipping at the top of the ear, and clip down to the end of the leather (Figure 17-9).

3) Clip the inside of the ear (Figure 17-10).

4) Press your thumb and index finger on the edge of the leather, and scissor around the ears (Figure 17-11) to neaten any untidy hairs.

5) Clip the opposite ear in the same way.

As you look through the international clips presented in Chapter 24, "The International Scene," you will notice short-clipped ears on the German clip. On the German trim, the ears are clipped in the same way as described here, except that a #10 or #9 blade is used in place of the #5F.

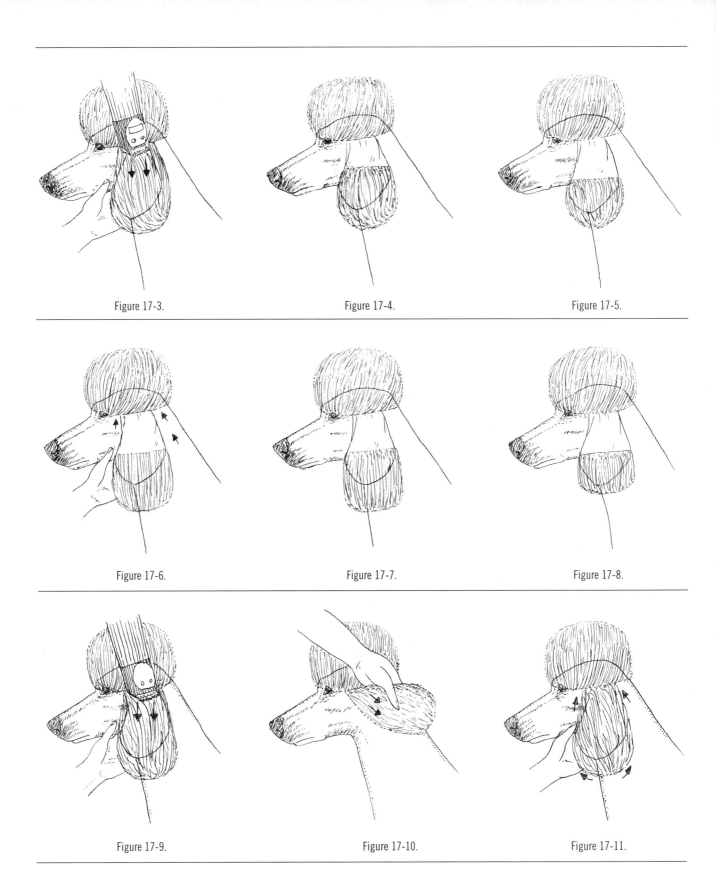

Figure 17-3.

Figure 17-4.

Figure 17-5.

Figure 17-6.

Figure 17-7.

Figure 17-8.

Figure 17-9.

Figure 17-10.

Figure 17-11.

chapter 18

THE CHANGING FASHIONS OF SHOW TRIMS

One of the most difficult parts of writing a book about trimming Poodles is to explain show grooming. It is perplexing because of several variables. Showing a Poodle in conformation competition means competing with highly skilled seasoned exhibitors, both professional and amateur. Unless you want to become quickly disillusioned, you must learn to match their talents in handling as well as grooming. Each dog is an individual, and none is faultless. Therefore, even assuming that you own a fine specimen, you must learn to evaluate your dog objectively, and then learn what is necessary to stress his virtues and minimize his weak points. Fantastic handling and grooming will not make a poor specimen into a top-winning dog. But inferior grooming and conditioning, and casual presentation, can slow down or even defeat a prospective champion's chances. Problem number one is that while it is easy to illustrate what the Puppy, Continental and English Saddle clips look like, and to generally explain how they are achieved, the way you actually clip and scissor them onto actual dogs will vary slightly depending on each Poodle's conformation.

Another problem is learning what is currently fashionable in Poodle grooming at any given time. Fashion, in the vernacular of the dog fancy, means the kind of dog being exhibited (*subtle* changes occur in every breed over time). The term *fashionable* may also be used to describe the style in which a dog is presented. You need only to glance at the following photographs to see how show grooming has changed over the decades. In the 1920s, 1930s and 1940s, Poodles were not very plush looking. In the 1950s and 1960s, they were shown with outrageously long mane coats (reaching down to the puffs on the forelegs), dripping with ear feathering and topknots which, in the show ring, were held in place with numerous elastic bands and a great deal of hair spray (which gave the dogs a lacquered appearance and their coats an artificial feel). In the mid-1970s, professional handlers and amateur exhibitors began presenting Poodles with shorter, rounder mane coats, topknots and ear feathering, enhancing the overall balance and elegance of the breed, and this practice has continued to the present. In the 1980s, a trimming trend started in the Scandinavian countries and slowly spread throughout the continent to become very popular in show rings in European countries and in other countries that are members of the FCI, or Fédération Cynologique Internationale. As shown in the final photograph of this chapter (Figure 8-12 on page 106), the Puppy Lion (or Second Puppy or Scandinavian) trim emphasizes square-looking and more angled hindquarters, with more hair left on the legs, especially the lower part of the back legs. Chapter 24, "The International Scene," contains more information about the FCI, its member countries and this trim.

Show grooming is not easy to learn. It takes great patience and considerable practice to present a dog perfectly for show. The best advice is to start by looking at photographs of winning dogs in Poodle magazines. If there is a Poodle club or all-breed club in your area, find out if they sponsor show ring training classes. These classes are good practice for both you and your dog. This is an opportunity to learn how to stack your dog (to pose or set him up to look his best), and to learn and practice the required movement patterns in a friendly atmosphere. Show ring training classes also are great for socializing puppies.

Many all-breed and specialty clubs hold puppy matches, which also are good experience for owner and dog. Before you actually enter your Poodle in a sanctioned event, plan to attend as many puppy matches and dog shows as possible in your area. Go to the grooming area and watch the handlers and exhibitors closely. Final preparation is most important, and you can learn a great deal by paying attention to how these people prepare their Poodles before they take them into the ring. Then go to the ringside and carefully watch the ring procedure: how the Poodles are hand-examined while standing quietly on the ground or on a grooming table and how the judge moves the dogs to evaluate movement. The more you observe, the more you will learn and the more proficient you can become. Soon you'll be in the ring yourself!

Figure 18-1. The 1920s.

Figure 18-2. The 1930s.

Figure 18-3. The early 1940s.

Figure 18-4. The late 1940s into the early 1950s.

Figure 18-5. The mid-1950s.

Figure 18-6. The late 1950s.

Figure 18-7. The early 1960s.

Figure 18-8. The late 1960s.

Figure 18-9. The 1970s.

Figure 18-10. The 1980s.

Figure 18-11. The 1990s.

Figure 18-12. European show trim at the turn of the twentieth century.

Figure 18-13. The corded black Standard Poodle Ch. Hastings Ten, owned by Michael Pawasarat. Corded coats are accepted in show rings in all countries of the world. The hair hangs in tight cords of varying length; longer on the mane or body coat, head and ears, and shorter on the puffs, bracelets and pompons. A great deal of maintenance is involved in growing and caring for this type of coat. Although corded Poodles were extremely fashionable in the late nineteenth century, they are hardly ever seen today. However, every now and then a few owners do exhibit them with great pride. (Photo by Ashby; courtesy of Anne Rogers Clark)

chapter 19

A Poodle must be structurally sound and in top condition if he is to be shown in the breed ring. Physical perfection for a Poodle (actually, for any breed) is achieved by nutritious food, proper exercise, fresh air and a regular brushing/bathing routine over an extended period of time. Your first concern must be feeding your Poodle a balanced diet, supplemented with all necessary vitamins and minerals. You can't expect results by simply fussing with the hair without first considering what goes inside the dog to make the coat bloom as you wish.

If you want to show your Poodle, however, he must certainly have correct coat texture. The ideal texture as described in the breed Standard is "*of naturally harsh texture, dense throughout.*" On an adult Poodle with good texture, the coat is so profuse that it seldom parts. The old adage "breeding tells" is positively true for the Poodle show prospect. Coat texture is inherited and, without the genes for producing the ideal coat, no Poodle will get it by the application of sprays, lotions or potions. Although a Poodle rarely achieves its best coat texture before 18 months of age or older, you need not guess what a puppy's coat will be like as an adult. Adult Poodles with good coats start out as puppies with good coats!

Growing and maintaining a long show coat requires many hours of work each week. You must establish a regular schedule that includes brushing, combing, bathing, nail cutting, ear cleaning, care of the teeth, executing the proper show trim and caring for the coat between shows. This routine must be followed on a daily basis.

Learning how to groom and maintain a show coat on any breed, especially on Poodles, is a demanding challenge. It takes a lot of patience and practice. The most important consideration is that you understand the breed Standard and know what an ideal Poodle should look like. If there is a Poodle club or all-breed dog club near you, become a member. Local clubs often sponsor handling and trimming classes in which you can participate. Attend as many seminars about Poodles or Poodle grooming as possible. Read all you can about Poodles. Del Dahl's *The Complete Poodle* (New York: Howell Book House, 1994) is a must read, filled with a wealth of useful information on all aspects of the breed, including grooming.

Go to as many puppy matches as possible. Attend Poodle Specialty shows or all-breed dog shows and spend time in the grooming areas. Final preparation is very important, and you can learn a great deal by observing how the Poodle handlers prepare and put the finishing touches on their dogs before they go into the ring. Then stay at ringside and watch these Poodles as they are being shown. Pay attention to the way the handlers stack their dogs, the way in which they arrange the hair, and how they constantly work with their dogs in the ring. The advice that follows will help you understand what is involved in maintaining a Poodle in show coat.

Brushing the Show Coat

Brushing is the most time-consuming part of maintaining a show coat because it must be done regularly and correctly. As previously mentioned, regular brushing achieves certain desirable results:

Figure 19-1.

It stimulates the growth of new hair and makes the coat less inclined to mat. Regular brushing keeps the skin clean and makes the dog less susceptible to skin disease and external parasites. The natural oils are distributed more evenly and the individual hairs lie more smoothly. A certain light is reflected from well-brushed hair, making it glossier than it is when brushing is neglected.

You need two different types of brushes for the show coat: a *pin brush* (with long, polished, round-tipped pins) for the mane, and a *fine-wire slicker* for the shorter hair on the rosettes or pack and the bracelets and puffs. You also need a wide-tooth comb (a Belgian half-coarse, half-medium style or any of the wide-tooth Poodle combs described in Chapter 2, "Selecting the Right Equipment") to check for tangles.

If you own a puppy, the first step is to teach the prospective show dog to lie on his side (with feet facing you) on the grooming table while his coat is being brushed, as shown in Figure 19-1. This is especially important if you are planning to have a professional handle the dog in the show ring.

Some puppies quickly learn to relax and lie still, but others can be frightened and fussy at first. If this happens, don't force your puppy down onto the table. Hold him in your lap instead, maneuvering him on his side, then brush him in that position. As soon as the puppy learns to relax, move him to the table. Ideally, you should begin the puppy's brushing, maintenance and grooming sessions as early as possible. Not only will it be good training for the young puppy, but it will also help you to learn proper care while the coat is relatively short.

The frequency of brushing a show coat depends on the age, texture and condition of the hair. Each texture varies and responds differently to grooming, as well as to the products that are used on the coat. A puppy from 4 to 10 months old usually needs to be brushed about twice a week. However, sometime between the ages of 10 and 14 months, the coat begins to change from puppy to adult texture, and the hair almost seems to mat overnight, especially on the ears, the neck and shoulders, and under the elbows. The top coat may look sparse and straggly, while what's underneath feels much thicker. During this period, you may have to brush every day to prevent mats from forming. As soon as you do find the hair beginning to mat, use your fingers to separate the clumps into smaller sections, then brush each section with a pin brush. Go through the area with a wide-tooth comb to be sure all the tangles are out. Changing of coat texture is exasperating—in fact, it separates the true exhibitor from the amateur, because it's usually the time that many owners decide they are not meant to be Poodle exhibitors and cut the dog down. Some Poodles pass through the coat change in just a few weeks; others, especially white and light-colored dogs or those with fine-textured, fragile coats, can take longer to change. Once this period has passed, however, the adult Poodle

coat is easier to maintain by keeping the dog in oil, creme rinse or conditioner, and establishing a regular brushing and bathing schedule (read more about oils and conditioners in the next section).

Hair that is being brushed should be relatively clean. Dirty hair is hard to brush and tends to tangle more easily. If the coat is dirty and matted, it is usually better to bathe the dog before you brush him. After the bath, apply a heavy creme rinse or liquid tangle remover and let either product soak into the coat for several minutes before being rinsed out. As a heavy-duty dryer blows on the hair, it will be much easier to remove the mats from the clean hair.

To brush the show coat: Remove any topknot and ear wrappers or bands. Place the dog on his side on the grooming table with his feet facing you. The long puppy coat or the mane of the Continental or English Saddle clip is always brushed using a technique called *layer-brushing* or *line-brushing*. Begin by parting the hair with your fingers lengthwise down the backbone from the head to the end of the mané at the middle of the dog (Figures 19-2 and 19-3). Always moisten the hair before you begin brushing. Never brush hair dry; that causes static electricity that can snap off the hair ends, or encourage mats to form. Spray the hair with water diluted with creme rinse or conditioner, an antistatic coat dressing, or light oil in aerosol form (such as Ring 5™ Show Coat). It's not necessary to saturate the coat, just moisten it lightly.

Once the hair is parted, use the pin brush to begin at the outer ends of the hair and work inward towards the skin, using gentle strokes (Figure 19-4). If you find a mat, separate it into smaller sections with your fingers and carefully brush them out. Hold the pin brush loosely in your hand, almost letting the handle swing like a metronome. Use your free hand to hold down the

unbrushed hair to separate it from the section being brushed (Figure 19-5). Once you reach the skin, brush outward from the part. The proper stroke is long, straight and sweeping, going beyond the hair ends to keep them from splitting or snapping off. Very little hair should come out in the brush when the correct stroke is used. But you must practice to get this right. The light "rotary" wrist action that allows you to brush for hours without tiring or pulling out coat takes time and patience to perfect.

When you have finished brushing the layer, comb through the hair with the wide-tooth comb to make sure there are no tangles. You also want to comb from the outside in towards the skin.

Make another part lengthwise about an inch below the hair you have just finished, and mist and brush that section the same way. Keep parting the hair in layers, and gradually work down to the chest until one whole side is finished. You must always keep each layer or line parted completely down to the skin. If at any time the coat becomes dry, spray it lightly. Dry hair will break!

Some owners like to start on the chest and work up to the backbone, moving the part line upward rather than downward. It makes no difference which direction you go, as long as you thoroughly brush the entire coat.

To brush the hard-to-reach spots on the chest, lift the front leg (Figure 19-6). On the shorter hair under the chest, you may wish to switch to a slicker brush. Before you turn the Poodle over to do the other side, check the hair behind the ears, on the neck and in the armpits under the front legs to be sure they are really tangle free. Then turn the Poodle over and use the same method to spray, brush and comb the other side.

The dog should sit on the table while you brush the neck

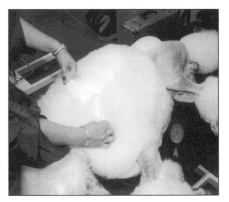

Figure 19-2.

Figure 19-3.

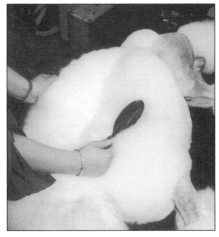

Figure 19-4.

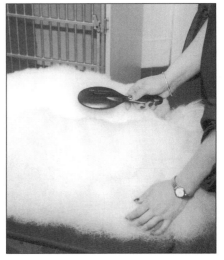

Figure 19-5.

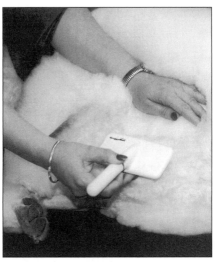

Figure 19-6.

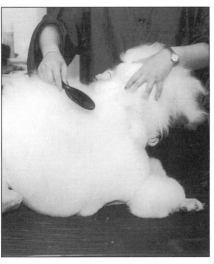

Figure 19-7.

(Figure 19-7) and the head and ears. Stand the Poodle on the grooming table to brush the front of the chest. Brush the tail with the pin brush. Switch to the fine-wire slicker to brush puppy leg hair, or the shorter hair (rosettes, pack, bracelets and puffs) of the adult show trims. After brushing, the topknot and ear fringes should be rewrapped.

Growing and Maintaining the Show Coat

To grow and maintain a Poodle's show coat, you must establish a definite routine of brushing,

bathing, drying, conditioning and, most likely, oiling, and follow this routine conscientiously to keep the hair mat free. Please keep in mind that the coat maintenance suggestions that follow are just that—suggestions. Some coats mat very quickly, others do not. Start with the information here, be guided by dog show handlers and exhibitors in your area and, eventually, you will find the routine that is correct for your Poodle's particular coat type.

UP TO 6 MONTHS

Puppies of all varieties and all colors up to 6 months of age

need to be brushed once or twice a week to keep their coats tangle free. They also need a weekly bath and blow dry to help encourage coat growth. You should not have to put a dog in oil at this age, but simply to apply a creme rinse or conditioner after the bath, working it well into the topknot, neck, shoulders and tail to prevent the hair ends from breaking. Check the hair growth in the ears and trim the nails every week. Clip the feet, face and tail regularly to accustom the puppy to the process. Start trimming the wispy ends of the coat with scissors every three to four weeks. As soon as the topknot hair starts falling forward and into the eyes, it should be banded to prevent the ends from snapping off, and to encourage growth. At this stage, using one or two bands to hold the hair in place above the eyes is all that is necessary.

BETWEEN 6 AND 10 MONTHS

Between 6 and 10 months, as the puppy grows, you will need to brush the coat more frequently between the weekly baths followed by a creme rinse or moisturizing conditioner like Ring 5 Hair Care, Bio-Groom™ Super Creme Conditioner, or #1 All Systems™ Super-Rich Protein Lotion Conditioner. During the brushing sessions, pay special attention to the hair on the neck and shoulders, the ears and under the front legs, as, at this age, these are areas that tend to mat quickly. You may wish to begin conditioning the hair with light oil in aerosol form. A protein-enriched oil adds body, eliminates flaking, and helps repair damaged hair, rather than just imparting an attractive sheen for a few days. Such a conditioner can be applied during the brushing process at least twice a week. Keep the puppy's feet, face and tail clipped and the nails trimmed short. Because the hair is growing longer and starting to become more profuse, every three to four weeks, you can do a bit more all-over shaping of the coat, as instructed in chapter 20, in the section titled "The Puppy Clip." Trimming the hair also shortens the amount of time you will spend caring for the coat. The coat on the ears will also be longer now, and you will want to band the hair or to start wrapping the topknot and ear fringes to protect them from the ravages of normal wear.

BETWEEN 10 AND 14 MONTHS— THE ADOLESCENT COAT CHANGE

During the coat change from about 10 to 14 months, the hair will most likely begin to mat excessively. Even after you thoroughly brush the hair, the mats

seem to reappear like magic. Now you must carefully inspect the coat *daily* for mats and tangles. And you will find them! White and light-colored dogs and dogs with cottony and fine coats seem to mat the most quickly, but at this stage, coats of *all varieties, colors and textures* are affected. As soon as you discover any clumps, break them apart into smaller sections with your fingers, then use the pin brush and the wide-tooth comb to work them out.

You will need to maintain your weekly bathing schedule until the coat change is complete. How you deal with the coat at this time depends on whether the dog is living as a house dog or in a kennel. If the dog is living in the house, often a heavier creme rinse or heavier Ring 5 Hair Care, Bio-Groom Super Creme Conditioner, or #1 All Systems Super-Rich Protein Lotion Conditioner treatment after the bath will help considerably to keep mats from forming. These are mixed with water according to package directions before applying, and then poured over the hair after the shampoo is rinsed out and the excess moisture toweled off. Place a small plastic basin underneath the dog while he is standing in the tub. For best results, pour the mixture over the hair and work it into the coat with your fingers to help insure even distribution. Concentrate on the mane, ears and topknot first, directing more of the mixture into the hairiest parts. Use a plastic cup to keep scooping up the mixture and pouring it over and over the coat, completely saturating the hair. Leave the mixture on the hair; do not rinse it off. Blot the excess moisture with a towel, then dry as usual. A little experimenting will determine the best dilution of creme rinse or conditioner for your dog's coat. Check the hair daily and brush it as soon as you feel mats starting to form.

USING A HEAVIER OIL

If the dog lives in a kennel and especially if you are conditioning several other Poodles at the same time, many professionals use a heavier oil at this coat-change stage to help keep the hair from breaking and mats from forming. Oil doesn't grow hair; it protects what's already there and reduces brushing time. There are several different coat oils to choose from that are very effective, including #1 All Systems Pure Lanolin Plus Skin and Hair Emollient and Wu Pi Magic™. Although each brand of oil may differ slightly, *all are mixed with water.* How much oil you add to the water depends on the length and texture of your Poodle's coat, the length of time between brushing sessions, and the climate. Start with the following proportions, then increase or decrease them when necessary: about 2 to 4 tablespoons of oil to ½ gallon of water for a Toy Poodle, about 6 to 8 tablespoons of oil to 1 gallon of water for a Miniature, and about ½ to 1 cup of oil to 1 gallon of water for a Standard. You also can add about ¼ cup of a conditioner like Ring 5 Hair Care or #1 All Systems Super-Rich Protein Lotion Conditioner to the oil-water mixture.

Just like applying conditioner, as mentioned in the preceding paragraph, the oil mixture is poured over the damp hair after the bath and the final rinse. Blot the excess moisture from the coat with a towel. Place a small plastic basin (something about the size of a dishpan or a cat litter pan) under the dog while he is standing in the tub. For best results, pour the oil mixture over the dog. Work it into the coat with your fingers (especially on the long mane) to help insure even distribution. Direct as much as possible of the surplus that drips off into the plastic basin, so you can keep scooping it up and pouring the mixture over and over the coat. Your goal is to completely saturate the coat, not just cover the top hair. Do not rinse off the oil. Let it soak into the coat for a few minutes, then blot the excess moisture again with a towel. Dry the hair as usual with a conventional stand dryer. Try not to use a high-velocity dryer after oiling; it will only blow the mixture down and off the hair shafts.

A little experimenting will determine the most effective dilution of conditioner or oil for your dog. If the dog is being shown every weekend, you're going to want a lighter and more diluted mix than on one that is growing hair and not going to be shown for a while. (As you will read in the next section, "Beyond the Coat Change— Caring for the Adult Coat," you also may wish to continue using a heavier oil depending on your Poodle's coat type.)

If the dog lives in the house, you will have to use an even lighter dilution of conditioner or oil to keep the furniture and carpets from becoming stained. If you prefer not to pour any conditioner or oil mixture into the coat of a house dog, you can use a lighter oil from an aerosol can (Show Ring or Bio-Groom Mink Oil Conditioner, for instance). This can be applied while you are layer-brushing the hair. If you opt for the lighter oil in aerosol form, however, you will have to brush more frequently.

Putting an oil mixture into the coat over an extended time period causes certain problems. Oil attracts dirt and is extremely messy, so the dog *must* be bathed on a regular basis. The prolonged use of oil tends to soften all coat textures. In some cases, prolonged used causes the skin to flake excessively. If this happens, you must then take your dog out of oil until the skin condition returns to normal. A medicated or antiseborrheic shampoo, followed by a nonoily conditioner can be used for relief. *When you take a Poodle out of oil, pay very close attention to the coat.* Traces of oil will ooze from the pores for

a week or so after the shampoo and cause huge clumps of mats to form. You must examine the coat faithfully at least once a day and brush it when necessary. If the dog is white or light-colored, sprinkling some grooming powder designed for soft textured coats (not harsh-textured or double coats) or cornstarch into the hair may help to absorb the oil faster.

BEYOND THE COAT CHANGE— CARING FOR THE ADULT COAT

When the coat change is complete, the adult coat will be much easier to maintain. By now your Poodle should be either in the Continental or English Saddle trim; getting rid of the long puppy hair on the hindquarters will lessen the time you have to spend maintaining the coat. As the coat reaches maturity, you can stretch the bathing schedule from one to two weeks (if the dog is not being shown). The coat can be maintained in Ring 5 Hair Care, #1 All Systems Super-Rich Protein Lotion Conditioner, Bio-Groom Super Creme Conditioner or similar product. Depending on the coat type, you may opt for a heavier oil. Generally, adult coats only need brushing once a week to keep the hair from matting. However, depending on your Poodle's coat type and color, his hair may need to be brushed and bathed more often. Just be sure to keep checking for mats and tangles, and brush out any clumps as you as you find them.

Wrappers and bands are generally taken out weekly. The hair is checked for tangles, brushed, and then rewrapped or rebanded. Dogs that rub or chew their wrappers or bands will need to be checked more often. Nails are always kept short.

Do remember that oil is used only between shows, and must be completely shampooed from the hair before a dog is exhibited in the breed ring.

Depending on your Poodle's color and coat type, the hair should be bathed from one to three days before a show. Bathing softens the hair and shampooing beforehand (even a day or so) helps to restore the coat's natural harshness. If your Poodle is white or light-colored, however, you may have to rebathe the rosettes or pack, bracelets, puffs and tail the day before the show to restore that fresh, crisp appearance. Follow the shampoo with a *light* conditioner or creme rinse. If the dog is put down in an oil mixture, a special degreasing shampoo or detergent may be necessary to completely remove the oil from the coat. Most dog show concessionaires sell shampoos designed to wash out excessive oils, such as #1 All Systems Super-Cleaning and Conditioning Shampoo; or the following mixture has been used for years by professionals to remove oil: In an empty gallon jug, pour 1 quart of Liquid Lux™ dish detergent. Add 4 ounces of USP glycerine and 4 ounces of white vinegar. Fill the jug to the top with water and shake well. *Use this mixture only if your usual dog shampoo is not strong enough to effectively remove the oil or you can't find a special degreasing shampoo formulated for dogs.*

If the Poodle is dark-colored, all the required clipper work (face, feet, tail, hindquarters, etc.) should ideally be done two or three days before the show with a #40 blade. Be careful not to clipper burn the skin. Using a #40 blade several days ahead of the show lets just enough hair grow back to give a neat, velvety look to the skin by show time. If the Poodle is white or light-colored or cannot take a close clip with a #40 blade, use a #30 or #15, and do all necessary clipper work the day before the show. To avoid irritation after clipping, especially if you use a #40 blade, always swab the skin with an anti-itch lotion made for dogs or with Bactine or Vaseline Intensive Care Lotion.

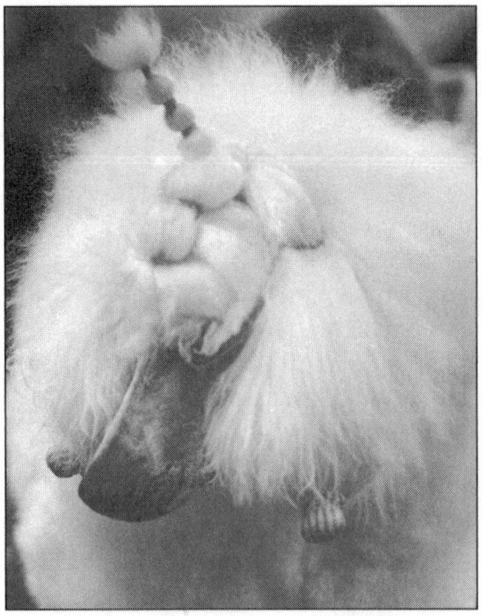

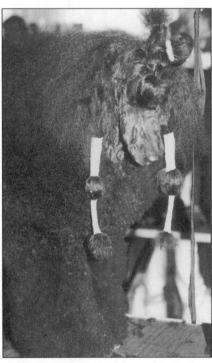

Figure 19-8.

Figure 19-9.

Figure 19-10.

Figure 19-11.

Care of the Topknot and Ears

On both young Poodles (as the coat is growing) and on mature dogs between shows, it is necessary to wrap or band the topknot and the ear fringes. This will protect the long hair from falling into the eyes or the mouth, from being broken or chewed off, from hanging into the dog's food or water and from being dragged on the ground or rubbed against furniture. There are many different ways to wrap or band, as you can see in Figures 19-8, 19-9, 19-10 and 19-11. The method you use depends primarily on your dog: some Poodles are better with wrappers, others should be done with bands and still others do better with a combination of both. You'll have to experiment a bit to find out which is best for your Poodle. If you use wrappers, it is necessary to choose the correct material. Usually, some type of soft plastic is the most popular. Most dog show concessionaires sell precut plastic wrappers (usually 12 in a package), or you could make your own using Baggies™ or any light plastic trash/garbage bags. Occasionally one sees other materials used for wrappers, such as nylon tulle, Saran Wrap™, Handi-Wrap™, Handiwipes™, Vet Wrap®, waxed paper and florist's paper being used. Again, because you will get different results depending on your Poodle's coat texture, the climate and humidity, you'll need to experiment to learn which material works best, or to ask fellow breeders and exhibitors in your area for some guidance.

Figure 19-12.

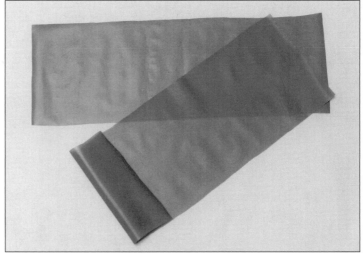

Figure 19-13.

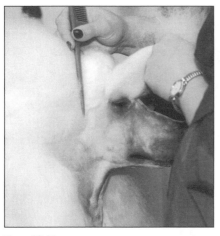

Figure 19-14.

Figure 19-15.

HOW TO KEEP THE TOPKNOT HAIR FROM BREAKING

The long hair of the topknot may be wrapped or banded to keep it from breaking. The hair should be clean, dry and thoroughly brushed with no tangles before wrapping or banding. The dog can be in creme rinse, Hair Care, Super Creme Conditioner, Super-Rich Protein Lotion Conditioner, or oil. When wrapping or banding the topknot, it is best to start in front, above the eyes, and work backward (Figure 19-12).

WRAPPING THE TOPKNOT

Let's begin with *wrapping* the topknot. Use precut soft plastic wraps or make your own by cutting several oblong shapes, generally about 6 to 8 inches long and 4 to 5 inches wide, depending on the Poodle's variety and hair length (Figure 19-13). Each wrap should be wide enough to fold lengthwise into thirds around the topknot hair, and long enough to reach beyond the ends of the hair. Once you become familiar with the topknot wrapping procedure on your dog, you will learn the correct size for the wrappers.

The first section of hair to be wrapped starts above the eyes and extends about halfway back to the ear. Use a knitting needle or the tip of a rat-tail comb to make a straight part across the top of the head, as shown in Figure 19-14. Comb through this section of hair to make it straight before you wrap it.

Although not mandatory at this point, some professionals take an additional step to protect the hair at the end of the wrapper to keep it from matting too quickly. They fold a thin strip of self-adhering cotton around the hair after it has been combed straight. Most professionals use Miss Webril™, Salon Curl™ or Beauty Coil cotton banding. These can be obtained at any beauty supply house. If you choose to do this, tear off about a 2- to 3-inch strip and wrap it around the hair, as shown in Figure 19-15.

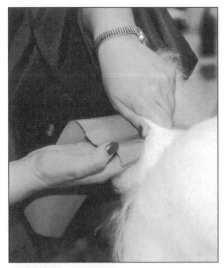

Figure 19-16.

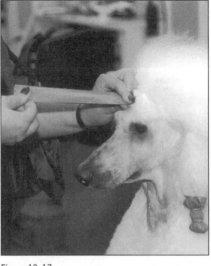

Figure 19-17.

Figure 19-18.

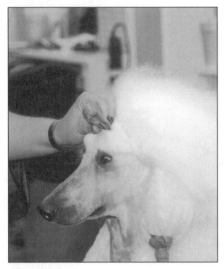

Figure 19-19.

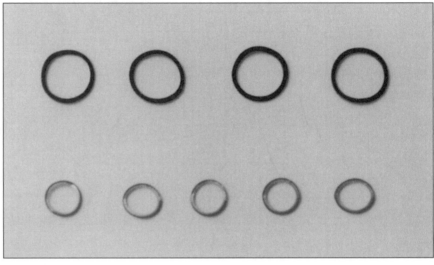

Figure 19-20.

Place your soft plastic wrapper behind the hair and close to the skin (if you have used a strip of cotton, the wrapper goes *over* the cotton), as shown in Figure 19-16. Twisting the hair *slightly* will help it stay in the wrapper. Fold the wrapper into thirds lengthwise around the hair, as shown in Figure 19-17. Be sure the hair inside is straight. Next, fold the wrapper downward in half (Figure 19-18), and then fold it downward in half again (Figure 19-19). At this point, you will have made a little packet about 1 inch to 1½ inches long. Fasten the folded packet with two rubber bands (small enough to turn only

three or four times), one at the top and one at the bottom. Most dog show handlers and exhibitors use No. 8 rubber bands, or the kind that are used to band horses' manes, for fastening. These are shown on the top row of Figure 19-20 and can be purchased from most dog show concessionaires, at horse shows, or at stationery stores. Wrap the hair neatly and firmly so the packets don't fall apart, but not so tight that they pull up and distort the eyes.

For the next wrap, make another straight part from in front of one ear across the skull to the front of the other ear (Figure 19-21). Make sure the part is straight and

that you are *not* including any hair from the top of either ear in the wrap (Figure 19-22). The second wrap is wrapped around the hair (Figure 19-23) and fastened in the same manner as the first wrap by folding it in half (Figure 19-24) and half again (Figure 19-25). Depending on the length of hair and personal preference, you can add more wraps extending down the neck. Figure 19-26 shows a third and fourth wrap, and Figure 19-27 shows the long hair wrapped almost to the end of the mane. If the hair is very long and thick on an adult dog, you may wish to divide each section into two packets.

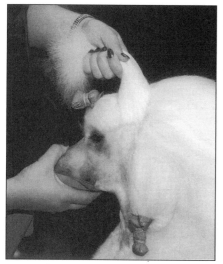

Figure 19-21.

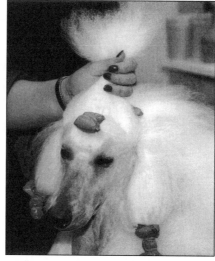

Figure 19-22.

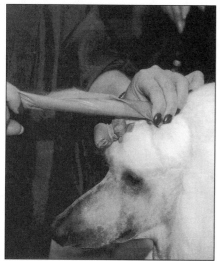

Figure 19-23.

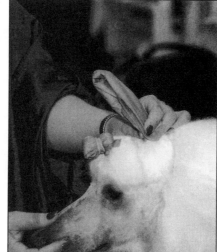

Figure 19-24.

Figure 19-25.

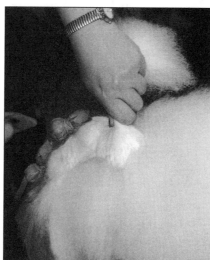

Figure 19-26.

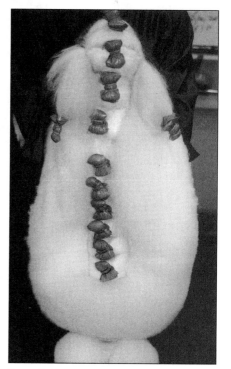

Figure 19-27.

BANDING THE TOPKNOT

Some Poodles fuss when their topknots are wrapped. They rub their heads on the floor or in their crates, and do other destructive things to pull out the wrappers, which can cause a great deal of damage. If this happens, you should consider banding the topknot to protect the hair. Basically the topknot hair is parted in the same manner, only small bands are used instead of plastic wraps. There are so many different ways to band the topknot that an entire chapter could be devoted to the subject. The following method seems the easiest to accomplish.

As previously instructed, the first section of hair to be banded starts above the eyes and extends about halfway back to the ears. Use a knitting needle or the tip of a rat-tail comb to make a part straight across the top of the head. Comb through this section of hair to be sure it is straight before putting in the band. Hold the hair up in one hand, as shown in Figure 19-28, while you use the other to fasten the band around it close to the skull (it will be tight, but eased later).

Use bands that are small enough to turn only three to four times. Small latex dental bands, about ¼ inch to ½ inch in diameter, are good choices for Toy and Miniature Poodles; larger latex bands, about ⅜ inch in diameter, or No. 8 rubber bands are good for Standard Poodles (shown in Figure 19-20 on page 114). Do keep in mind that what you use on any dog will be influenced by the texture and density of the hair. Latex dental bands are softer and cause less hair breakage than rubber bands. Learn to turn your bands from side to side, rather than from front to back. If your Poodle has a very heavy coat, to keep the hair from breaking, you might want to divide the first section in half and put in two bands. On a soft puppy coat, especially, hair tends to slip

out of a single-banded section more easily than if that section is divided into two.

For the second section to be banded, make another straight part from in front of one ear across the skull to the front of the opposite ear. Make sure that the part is straight and that you are not including any hair from the top of either ear into the band. As you did before, comb through the hair to be sure it is straight, then put in the band (Figure 19-29).

The third section to be banded goes from the top of the ear across the skull (near the occipital bone) to the top of the other ear. *Be sure the hair is parted at the top of each ear and that no ear hair is caught up in the band.* Figure 19-30 shows the third and fourth banded sections.

To keep the topknot in place, you should connect the bands of hair to prevent them from falling forward. Grasp the first and second sections together, pull them back from the face and band them together, as shown in Figure 19-31. Check the front of the topknot and if it is too tightly banded above the eyes, loosen it slightly with your fingers so the dog is comfortable (Figure 19-32).

If the hair is long, you may want to band the first two sections to the third and fourth sections, as shown in Figure 19-33. Depending on the hair length and personal preference, you can add more bands extending down the neck (Figure 19-34).

When the hair is very long, it is necessary to use additional bands around the hair, in ½-inch-long to 1-inch-long spaces above the first one, forming a pigtail, as shown in the photographs in this section. When you have finished banding, spray a protein or mink oil conditioner or dab a little Wella™ Kolestral on the ends of the hair to moisturize them to reduce breakage.

PROTECTING THE HAIR ON THE EARS

The long hair on the ears should be clean, dry and thoroughly brushed with no trace of tangles before wrapping or banding. The dog can be in creme rinse, Hair Care, Super-Rich Protein Lotion Conditioner, Super Creme Conditioner or oil.

WRAPPING THE EAR FRINGES

Let's begin with wrapping the ear fringes. *You only want to wrap the long hair that falls below the ear leather, never on any part of the ear itself.* Use two precut soft plastic wraps or make your own by cutting two oblong shapes, generally about 6 to 8 inches long and 4 to 5 inches wide, depending on the dog's variety and hair length. Each wrap should be wide enough to fold tubular fashion around the ear, and long enough to reach from the tip of the ear leather down past the ends of the long hair. If you prefer, you may also use VetWrap®, a self-adhering elastic wrap (Figure 19-35, bottom), to wrap the ears.

Before applying the wrappers, brush and comb the hair on the ears, making sure it hangs straight down. Be sure you are wrapping only the long ear fringes and *no hair originating from the neck.*

Just as you did on the topknot, before putting on the plastic wrap some handlers and exhibitors often take an extra step to protect the hair at the top of the wrapper to keep it from becoming dirty or matted too quickly. To do this, wrap a thin strip of self-adhering cotton webbing (Miss Webril, Beauty Coil or Salon Curl, also shown in Figure 19-35, top) around the ear hair after it has been combed straight, a little below the ear leather. If you do this, tear off a strip of the cotton banding and wrap it around the ear hair just *below the tip of the leather,* as shown in Figure 19-36.

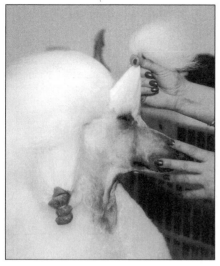

Figure 19-28.

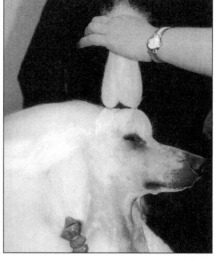

Figure 19-29.

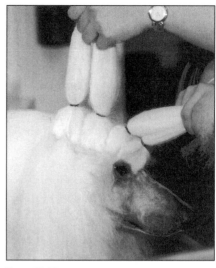

Figure 19-30.

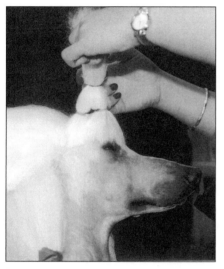

Figure 19-31.

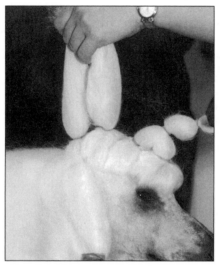

Figure 19-32.

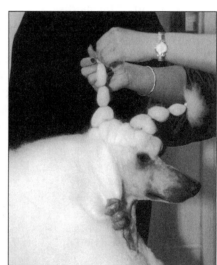

Figure 19-33.

Figure 19-34.

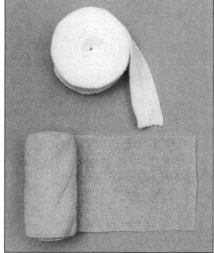

Figure 19-35.

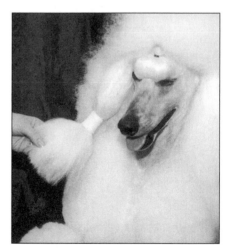

Figure 19-36.

Place a wrapper behind the long hair below the ear leather (if you use cotton, place the wrapper over it). Fold the wrapper lengthwise into thirds (Figure 19-37), forming a tube. Next, fold the wrapper upward in half (Figure 19-38), then fold it in half again (Figure 19-39). Fasten the folded plastic with two small rubber bands, one at the top of the packet and one at the bottom of the packet (Figure 19-40). Again, most professionals use No. 8 rubber bands, or bands for fastening horse manes. Wrap the hair neatly and firmly so the packets don't fall apart, but not so tight that they pull the hair and cause the Poodle any discomfort. If the hair is very long and thick on an adult dog, divide it into two sections. Wrap the opposite ear in the same manner.

After each ear is wrapped, check to see that the packet is not pressing on the ear leather. Pass the teeth of a comb or the tip of a rat-tail comb through the hair *between the wrapper and tip of the ear leather*, as shown in Figure 19-41. If the comb cannot go through the hair at the bottom of the ear leather easily, the wrapper is too high and must be lowered immediately! *When a wrapper is placed too high, the blood circulation is being interrupted and the ear will be severely damaged if the wrapper is not adjusted.* You can also protect the ear feathering with VetWrap, wrapping the long ear fringes as shown in Figures 19-42 and 19-43. Once applied, VetWrap eliminates the need for fasteners.

Your Poodle may try to chew off the wrappers. To discourage him, wrap another strip of cotton banding, soaked in Grannick's Bitter Apple™, Sour Grapes™ or Tabasco Sauce™, over the plastic packet.

BANDING THE EAR FRINGES
Another way to protect the long hair on the ears is to band it instead of using wrappers. Before banding the hair, brush and comb the hair straight down, making sure it is tangle free. Just as with banding the topknot, choose bands that are small enough for you to wind around the hair only three or four times (bands that must be twisted around the hair too many times will cause breakage). Again, what you choose depends on the density of the hair, but generally small latex dental bands are preferred for Toys and Miniatures and larger latex dental or No. 8 rubber bands are the choice for Standard Poodles.

The long hair is sectioned off as shown in Figure 19-44. Grasp the ear with your free hand and use your other hand to twist the band around the hair. The first band should be placed just below the end of the ear leather and *not on the tip of the leather itself.*

When the hair is very long, it will be necessary to use additional bands around the hair, several inches below the first one, as shown in Figures 19-45 and 19-46. Set small spaces between the bands so that as many hair ends as possible are kept under control. Pass the teeth of your comb through the hair between the band and the tip of the ear leather. As with the packet, if the comb cannot pass through easily, the band is too high and must be lowered immediately.

TIPS FOR WRAPPING AND BANDING
- Do not wrap or band topknot hair or ear fringes that are wet or dirty.
- Examine the wrappers and/or bands every day. How often they need to be changed depends on the length and texture of your Poodle's coat, how you house the dog, and the climate in which you live. In most cases, wraps and/or bands need to be changed once or twice a week. Poodle coats that are changing from puppy to adult texture and thin,

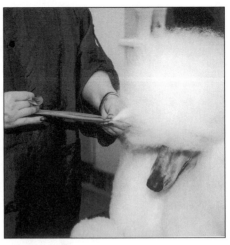

Figure 19-37.

cottony coat textures tend to mat more easily and frequently and may need changing every day or two.

- When you take out the wrappers or bands, brush the hair as carefully as possible. If you find any tangles, carefully separate them with your fingers, mist the hair lightly with water mixed with a little creme rinse, then brush it with a pin brush. If there are no tangles, simply brush and comb the hair straight and rewrap or reband.
- The correct way to remove bands is to slip the end tooth of a comb under the band, to lift it and pull it out and away from the hair. The band will usually snap apart when you do this. If it does not, cut it with blunt tipped scissors. Pulling the band away from the hair will prevent you from mistakenly cutting any of the long hair.
- If your dog is in oil, check the bands frequently. They tend to absorb oil and break easily.
- Observing handlers and exhibitors at dog shows is an excellent learning experience. You'll see many different techniques for wrapping and banding topknots and ears.

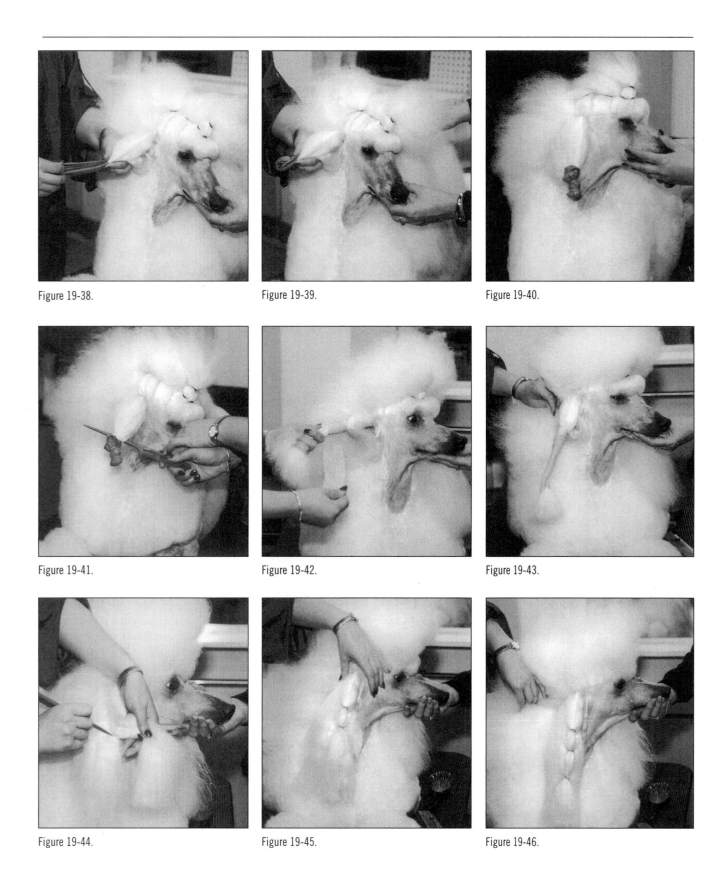

Figure 19-38.

Figure 19-39.

Figure 19-40.

Figure 19-41.

Figure 19-42.

Figure 19-43.

Figure 19-44.

Figure 19-45.

Figure 19-46.

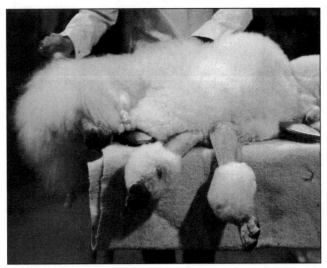

Figure 19-47.

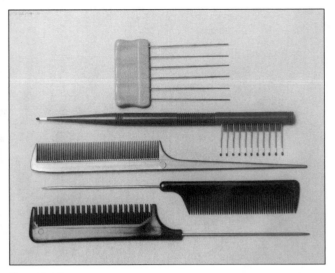

Figure 19-48.

Grooming and Final Touches at Dog Shows

Prepare your tack box the evening before the show including, of course, the tools and supplies you will need to prepare the dog for the ring. These normally include show leads, pin brushes and slicker brushes, Belgian combs and wide-tooth combs, straight and curved shears, a knitting needle or rat-tail comb, latex and rubber bands, old scissors for cutting out bands, new plastic wrappers (to rewrap topknot and ears after the show), styling mousse, hair spray, and a trigger spray bottle filled with water or an antistatic nonoily coat dressing. Once the dog is bathed before the show, you do not want to brush the hair with any product that contains oil. An antistatic spray (like Ring 5 Coat Gloss or #1 All Systems Hair Re-Vitalizer Anti-Static Coat Spray) will eliminate any static electricity in the coat and reduce flyaway hair, keeping it where it should for the final scissoring touches.

Plan to arrive at the show well ahead of the scheduled judging time. This lets you set up your grooming table and tack box, exercise your dog and then pre-

pare him for the ring in a leisurely manner. If you arrive too late and put your dog together at breakneck speed, you may both be unnerved by the time your class is called, and when he goes into the ring he will perform accordingly.

Begin preparing the dog by brushing the mane as long and straight as possible. Place your dog on his side on the grooming table (Figure 19-47) so he can relax while you use the pin brush to brush the hair in layers. Moisten each layer lightly with water or nonoily coat dressing. It's not necessary to heavily spray the coat; you just want to add a little moisture to prevent static electricity and to help the brush pass through the hair easily. To avoid over-wetting, try spraying a mist above the coat, letting it float down and settle onto the hair. When one side is completely brushed, turn the Poodle over and brush the other side. A good routine to follow is to brush the right side of the dog first and the left side of the dog (the side the judge sees) last. If the judge's side is brushed last, it generally looks fresher and straighter. Stand the dog up to brush the tail with the pin brush, then brush the rosettes or pack and the puffs and bracelets with

the fine-wire slicker. If the tail, bracelets and rosettes are not very profuse, work a *little* styling mousse into them to add volume.

Before beginning the final shaping with the shears and arranging the topknot, put the show lead *into* the coat. To do this, tilt the Poodle's head downward and part the hair *to the skin* from the base of one ear across the back of the neck to the base of the other ear. Use a knitting needle, the tip of a rat-tail comb, or position an index finger behind each ear and slide each across the neck until they join. Place the show lead around the Poodle's neck and slide it down to the part at the skin. Push the neck hair back up to render the back of the lead invisible. At the front of the neck, fold the lead up under the chin and band it to keep it out of the way while you complete the finishing touches.

Comb the rosettes or the pack and the bracelets, pulling the hair up and out, and rescissor any areas that need touching up. Fluff out the tail with your comb and shake it to loosen any wispy ends. Hold up the tip of the tail (the way it will be in the ring), then rescissor if necessary to the desired full, round shape.

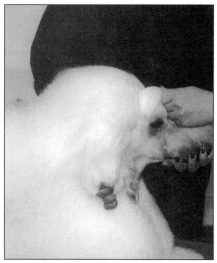

Figure 19-49.

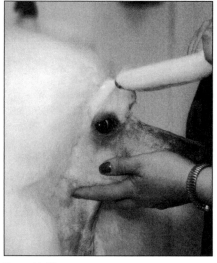

Figure 19-50.

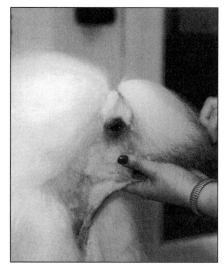

Figure 19-51.

THE TOPKNOT

Take out the wrappers or old banding on the topknot and brush the hair, using a spray of water or nonoily coat dressing. Before finishing the topknot, comb through the hair to be sure it is straight and that there are no waves from the wrappers or bands. Your Poodle must hold his head still while you put up the topknot; if he does not, have an assistant available to steady him.

How many sections of the topknot you band will depend on the length and texture of your Poodle's coat. The previous breed Standard (approved in 1978) specified that the topknot may "be held in place by no more than three elastic bands." Today, while there is generally greater tolerance regarding the number of bands allowed, don't go overboard either. Keep in mind that the Poodle Standard states that the topknot, from the stop to the occiput, is the only area where elastic bands may be used.

Putting up the topknot is probably the most difficult part of preparing a Poodle for the show ring to explain. Nothing makes a Poodle look more glamorous or more elegant than a beautifully prepared topknot. It is the focal point that pulls the entire trim together, and your goal is to create a topknot that enhances the individual dog's expression. You can't change the conformation of the head or how the features are shaped, but you can create some subtle illusions. Study the instructions and photographs that follow. You can also learn a great deal by studying the various techniques used by top handlers and exhibitors at the shows.

PUTTING UP THE TOPKNOT

There are several different types of combs and picks that might be used to put up the topknot (Figure 19-48).

1) To put in the first band (Figure 19-49), part the front section of hair. Make the part with a knitting needle or the tip of a rat-tail comb. The part starts above the outside corner of one eye (about ½ inch on a Toy, ¾ inch on a Miniature, and 1 inch or so on a Standard) and goes straight across the skull to the same spot behind the outside corner of the other eye.

2) Comb this section of hair straight and then put a small rubber band at the center and twist it from side to side no more than three times (Figure 19-50). Use small latex dental bands for Toys and Miniatures and larger dental bands or No. 8 rubber bands for Standards. Don't worry if the hair seems tightly banded above the eyes; you will loosen this with your fingers when you fashion the "bubble."

3) Pull the first banded section forward toward the nose (Figure 19-51).

4) To put in the second band, part another section of hair behind the first topknot (Figure 19-52). This part starts in front of one ear and goes straight across the skull to the front of the other ear. Comb the hair straight and band it as previously described.

5) Pull the second section forward (Figure 19-53).

6) To put in the third band, make another part straight across the occiput (Figure 19-54). *Be sure no ear hair is included in this section.* Comb and band this section.

7) When you have finished, three sections of hair have been banded (Figure 19-55).

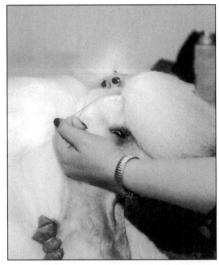
Figure 19-52.

Figure 19-53.

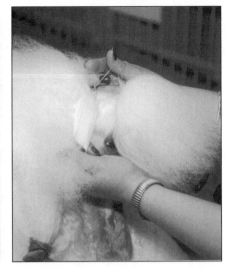
Figure 19-54.

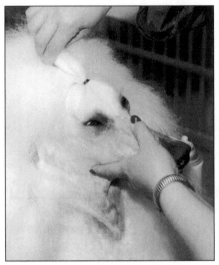
Figure 19-55.

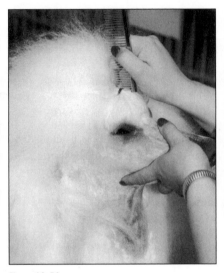
Figure 19-56.

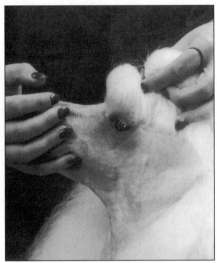
Figure 19-57.

8) Next comes the hard part; making the bubble over the eyes to enhance the expression. Begin by putting the end tooth of your comb under the first band, and pull it backward (Figure 19-56).

9) To fashion a bubble that gives the illusion of a long, lean head takes considerable practice and patience. The best way to make the bubble is to hold the dog's muzzle in your free hand (Figure 19-57). Grasp the hair at the *back* of the band with the fingers of

your other hand and pull backward. When you release your fingers, the bubble will emerge.

10) The bubble will probably need further shaping. To do this, use your thumb and index finger to hold the bubble on each side while you further adjust it (Figure 19-58). If you are not getting the expression you desire, cut the latex and begin again.

11) Figure 19-59 shows the front view of the finished bubble. If any wispy ends stick out of the band,

put a little hair spray or styling gel on your fingers and carefully rub them on the bubble to keep the hair in place.

12) To add more height above the bubble, take the entire first band of hair and all of the second one and band them together (Figure 19-60). If the hair is very long, you can take a few hairs from each band and attach them to the next band to further secure the topknot.

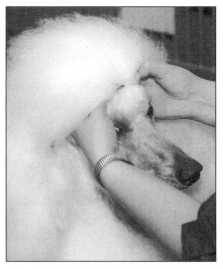

Figure 19-58.

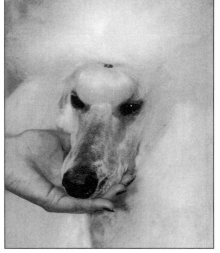

Figure 19-59.

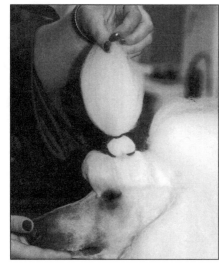

Figure 19-60.

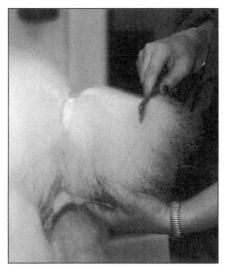

Figure 19-61.

Figure 19-62.

13) Once the topknot is banded and the bubble is in place, depending on the illusion you wish to create, there are two ways of finishing the topknot: working from front to back or working from back to front. In this series of photographs, the topknot is being finished from front to back. Have the dog sit facing you. Begin by parting a very thin layer of hair above the eyes, combing it forward (Figure 19-61).

14) Use a little hair spray to hold the topknot in place (Figure 19-62). Instead of spraying the tips of the hair, you want to spray lightly into the base of the coat, near the skin. Although most hair sprays do a good holding job, Grande Finale™ seems to be the brand preferred by professionals because it leaves the hair full-bodied but natural looking. Be sensible and do not over-spray! A light misting deep into the hair will add volume and control; the ends will feel natural, not sticky or like shellac, when

the judge examines the dog. After spraying, use the tip of a rat-tail comb or a hair pick to lift the hair upward, forward and outward. Keep working backward, a thin layer at a time, combing the hair upward, forward and outward. After combing each layer, lightly spray the hair deep into the base of the coat, then use the rat-tail comb or hair pick to lift the hair. After spraying, use the tip of a rat-tail comb or a hair pick to lift the hair upward, forward, and outward.

Figure 19-63.

Figure 19-64.

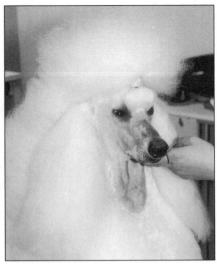

Figure 19-65.

Figure 19-66.

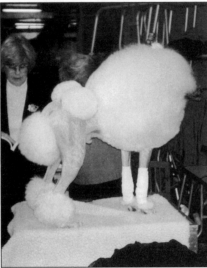

Figure 19-67.

Figure 19-68.

15) When you reach the back of the neck, use your comb to fan the hair upward and forward, and blend the hair of the topknot in with the neck coat to give height to the dog's neck (Figure 19-63). If you need to add body, put a *little* hair spray into the mane coat. How much hair spray you use depends on several factors, most importantly on your dog's coat texture and the humidity level on the day of the show. As previously mentioned, instead of spraying the tips of the hair, you want to comb the hair forward layer by layer and spray lightly into the base of the coat. Keep combing and pulling the hair up and out as you work down over the shoulders to the end of the mane.

16) If the topknot hair is too long, it should be scissored to balance with the length of hair on the mane.

Figure 19-64 shows the front view of the finished topknot with the hair fanned out to frame the face. Notice the importance of the bubble and how it becomes the base of the frame.

When properly shaped, the hair of the topknot and neck can make a Poodle appear shorter in back, add length to the neck and create the illusion of height. Figure 19-65 shows a three-quarter view of the topknot. On this style topknot, the hair has been back combed on either side.

Figure 19-66 shows another style of finishing in which the topknot is fanned out to frame the face.

THE FINISHING TOUCHES

With the topknot in place and the mane coat combed upward and forward, now is the time to use your shears to remove any stray ends and make the outline as elegant as possible.

Remove the bands or wrappers from the ears and brush out the ear fringes, again using a fine mist spray of water or coat dressing. You may scissor off any wispy ends at the bottom of the fringes

to even them. Finish by fanning out the long hair on each ear; apply a little hair spray to your hands and stroke down the ears to keep the hair hanging straight. Check to see that every part of the trim is in balance. After a light all-over misting of Grand Finale (please cover your Poodle's eyes with your free hand when spraying the front of the topknot), you're just about ready for the ring!

Always take your comb with you into the ring; keep it in a pocket or slipped through your belt. While your Poodle is in the ring, you want to always preserve his glamorous and elegant look. After each time the dog is moved, you should flick the comb through the hair, bringing it upward and forward from the end of the mane to the neck. Keep the topknot up and fanned out, and comb the long ear hair straight down, so it lies flat against the sides of the head.

The Day After the Show

If you are showing your dog every week, on the day after the show, you must remove any hair spray, mousse, styling product or powder that you put into the hair. You also want to remove any dirt, debris or pollution picked up at the show. The easiest way to cleanse the coat of these contaminants that tend to bond themselves to the hair is to bathe the dog with a product called Pre-Wash. Rinse off the Pre-Wash thoroughly, then shampoo the hair as usual, and rinse thoroughly once again. Follow with a creme rinse or conditioner to keep the hair from tangling, then blow dry as usual. Wrap or band the topknot and ears. Then shampoo the dog again at the end of the week for the next show.

One final suggestion: A common problem among male Poodles in show coat, especially those that are white or light-colored, is staining. During the act of lifting their back legs to urinate, the front bracelets can become sticky and stained. To prevent this from

happening between shows, you can protect the front bracelets by wrapping VetWrap around them (Figure 19-67) or by slipping on a protective covering (Figure 19-68). These are sold by most dog show concessionaires.

Glossary of Show Coat Terms

Clipped or Shaved Bands: The areas between the bracelets on the back legs.

Bloom: The sheen of the coat in prime condition.

Bracelets: The rounded tufts of hair left on each back leg of the Continental and English Saddle clips.

Conformation: The form and structure, make and shape; arrangement of the parts in conformity with a breed Standard.

Crescents or "Kidney Patches": Terms used to describe the curved clipped area on each side of the flank of the English Saddle pattern.

Feathering or Fringes: The longer hair on the ears.

Mane: The long, profuse hair on the neck, shoulders, ribs and chest that is shaped round. Also called the ruff.

Occiput: The posterior or back point of the skull.

Pack or Saddle: The closely trimmed hindquarters of the English Saddle pattern.

Pompon: The rounded tuft of hair left on the end of the tail.

Puffs: The rounded tuft of hair left on the bottom of each foreleg on the Continental and English Saddle clips.

Rosettes: The rounded tufts of hair left over the hips on the Continental clip.

Topknot: The long hair on the top of the head from the stop to the occiput.

If you intend to show your Poodle in the conformation ring, there are four recognized show clips. The first is the Puppy clip, which is acceptable only for dogs under 12 months of age. Once a Poodle is one year old, it must be shown only in the English Saddle or Continental clip. Both clips are not practical for pets, as they require a great deal of expert and time-consuming coat care. All three of these clips are presented in this chapter.

In the Stud Dog and Brood Bitch classes and in a noncompetitive Parade of Champions only, a Poodle may be shown in the Sporting clip. See pages 151–52 for instructions for that clip, one of the most popular pet styles.

The Puppy Clip (for Competition)

Figure 20-1.

The Puppy clip (Figure 20-1) is one of the three styles recognized by the American Kennel Club and the Poodle Club of America for all regular show conformation classes. A Poodle may be shown in Puppy trim up to the age of 12 months. As described in the breed Standard, *"the face, throat, feet and base of the tail are shaved. The entire shaven foot is visible. There is a pompon on the tail. In order to give a neat appearance and a smooth unbroken line, shaping of* the coat is permissible.*"* After 12 months of age, a Poodle that is being shown in the conformation ring must be trimmed in either the English Saddle or Continental clip.

The Puppy clip is a charming trim but one of the most difficult to

Figure 20-2.

Figure 20-3.

Figure 20-4.

explain in detail since it evolves constantly as a puppy grows to maturity. "Puppies change a lot during the time they are in puppy trim," writes Del Dahl, in *The Complete Poodle*. "They grow throughout that period and they grow a lot of hair. That means you really have to rethink your trim every two or three weeks. In fact, it is like trimming a different dog each time you do it." To determine a balanced image that appeals to you, Mr. Dahl suggests that it will be beneficial to study photographs of Poodles in Puppy trim and to observe puppies at shows (especially as the handlers and exhibitors are preparing them for the ring). "You will discover, if you haven't already," he adds, "that there is considerable variation in the trims that puppies wear in the ring."

Most breeders start basic clipping at an early age to get a puppy used to being handled and to start accepting the sound of the running clipper. Figure 20-2 shows a baby Miniature puppy ready for his first experience with the clipper. At this age, no other trimming is necessary. Other than to brush the hair with a soft brush and the tiniest bit of body shaping to accustom the puppy to the process, shown in Figure 20-3, no other grooming is required. As the same

puppy grows a little older and the coat starts growing longer, the wispy ends of the hair need to be evened off as shown in Figure 20-4. As the dog matures and the coat grows even longer, as shown on the 11-month-old white Standard puppy in Figure 20-5, much more shaping with shears becomes necessary.

Establishing a regular brushing, bathing and coat maintenance routine is a most important part of show grooming for puppies, especially as their hair grows longer in preparation for their graduation into the Continental or English Saddle clip. Be sure to carefully study the advice in Chapter 19, "Care of the Poodle in Show Coat."

For a dark-colored Poodle, most professionals like to trim the clipped areas with a #40 blade about three to four days before a show. This gives a little time for the shaved areas to grow back looking velvety smooth by show time. For light-colored Poodles, or those that cannot take a close clip with a #40, use a #15 or a #30 blade, and clip the day before the show. To avoid irritation after clipping, especially if you use a #40 blade, swab the skin with an anti-itch lotion made for dogs, or with a little Bactine™ or Vaseline™ Intensive Care Lotion.

Read more about this under "Preventing Clipper Burn" (page 82). Here are the basic instructions for the Puppy clip for the show ring.

1) Bathe the Poodle and blow dry the hair straight.

2) Follow instructions for clipping the feet. Clip to the end of each foot; *not* up on the ankles. While the Standard states that the entire shaven foot should be visible, until you have mastered the silhouette you desire, it's better to leave the clipped line lower rather than to take too much off.

3) Follow instructions for clipping the face. On the sides of the head, be sure the clipped line is straight between the outer corner of the eye to the ear. This sets the topknot line on each side. Clip an inverted **V** between the eyes as shown in Figure 20-6.

4) Clip the tail and shape the pompon. On all the show clips, you want to leave as much hair as possible to shape into a pompon. A good rule is to clip about one-quarter of the tail and leave the hair on the remaining three-quarters to be shaped into the pompon. Stand your dog on the grooming table with hindquarters facing you. Grasp the end of the tail in your free hand (Figure 20-7).

Figure 20-5.

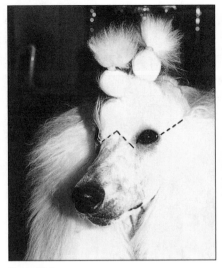

Figure 20-6.

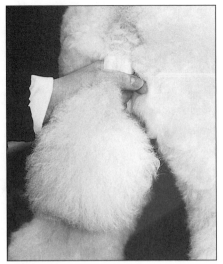

Figure 20-7.

Figure 20-8.

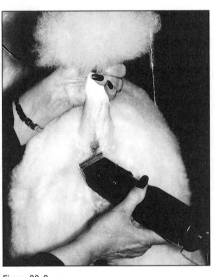

Figure 20-9.

Figure 20-10.

Starting on the upper side, place your clippers flat against the skin and clip in to the tail's juncture with the body. Most professionals like to clip an inverted **V** slightly forward of the base of the tail, into the body coat (Figure 20-8) to make the dog look shorter in back. If you do this, be careful not to go too far and clip off too much hair. Remember that you can always take more hair off, but it takes months to replace. The underside of the tail is a very sensitive area and should be clipped in the opposite direction, from the body out to the pompon line (Figure 20-9). Remember that the clipped line around the tail must be even or the pompon won't look properly shaped.

5) Hold the tip of the tail in your free hand as it will be held in the ring and fluff the hair out with a comb (Figure 20-10). Grasp the hair in your hand, slide your fingers to the end of the tail and scissor straight across to remove any excess length or wispy ends (Figure 20-11). Use curved shears to shape the pompon very full and round (Figure 20-12). The degree of fullness and roundness of the pompon depends, of course, on the puppy's age and the amount of hair there is to work with.

6) Place the Poodle in a sitting position facing you to clip the throat. It should be trimmed into a **V** shape (Figure 20-13). Start at a point at the middle of the throat, a little below the Adam's Apple, and clip each side of the neck up to the front of the ear. Because this is a sensitive area, if your Poodle clipper burns easily, set the **V** in the opposite direction, by starting at the base of the ear and clipping downward to the middle of the throat. Adjust the **V** upward or downward, depending on the length of your Poodle's neck. Brushing a little soft white grooming powder or cornstarch

Figure 20-11.

Figure 20-12.

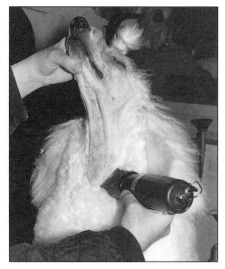

Figure 20-13.

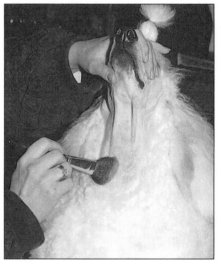

Figure 20-14.

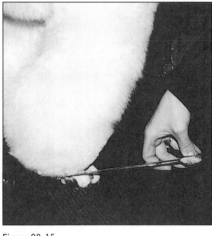

Figure 20-15.

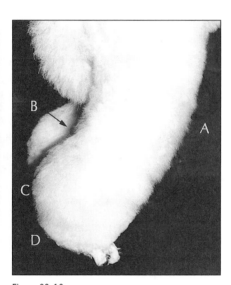

Figure 20-16.

on the neck, as shown in Figure 20-14, will help to soften a closely clipped look.

7) Clip the stomach. Pointing clipper upward, start just above the testicles or vulva, and clip up to the last rib.

8) The scissoring work on the Puppy trim is rather difficult to explain. Study Figure 20-1 carefully. Actually, very little hair is scissored off the body with the exception of the hindquarters and around the base of the tail. The rest of the coat remains long, with only the untidy top hair scissored off to get the shape shown in

Figure 20-1. As a puppy's coat grows longer to be transformed into the Continental or English Saddle clip (with a long mane) at one year, the ends become straggly. Because hair does not grow evenly, about once a month the straggly ends must be evened off and shaped with shears to help strengthen the hair and to give the Poodle a smooth, balanced and finished appearance. This type of scissoring work is called *tipping* and does not greatly alter the length of the coat. Consider it a sort of pruning. If you let a bush grow wild, its strength dissipates, but when you prune it, the branches grow

stronger and healthier. That, in effect, is what you are doing to the puppy's hair, and it will respond the same was as that bush does.

Begin scissoring the puppy's rear first. Stand the puppy on the grooming table with hindquarters facing you. Start by shaping the back legs. If you are right-handed, do the leg at your right first. If you are left-handed, start at the left side. Comb the hair downward and outward, as the puppy coat naturally falls. Scissor off any hairs that fall below the clipped line around the foot (Figure 20-15). Then shape the leg. This seems easiest to do by

Figure 20-17.

Figure 20-18.

Figure 20-19.

starting at the ankle and working up to the point where the back leg joins the body. Hold your shears flat against the hair you are working on—do not point the tips of the blade into the coat—and start shaping, taking a little hair off at a time. Always move your shears smoothly in a vertical direction, either upward or downward, never horizontally, as this almost causes notches in the coat.

9) When you finish shaping one part of the leg, begin again at the ankle and trim another section up to this point. Work completely around the leg in this manner, following the Poodle's natural conformation, emphasizing angulation above the hock joint and at the curve of the stifle. Study Figure 20-16. The shaping should accent the natural curve of the stifle joint at point A. Point B is trimmed in and comes outward again at the hock at point C, and then it *slightly* angles downward to point D. Lift the opposite leg to scissor any hard-to-reach areas on the inside. If you are not satisfied with the shape, recomb the hair and begin again. Scissor the other back leg, making it even in size and shape.

10) Next, shape the hair on the hindquarters and around the base of the tail. Every Poodle exhibitor has his or her favorite way of

trimming this part. If you are a beginner, the easiest way is to comb the body hair up and out to fluff the coat. Begin scissoring upward from where the back leg joins the body. Shape the hair below the base of the tail short but round, to keep the puppy from looking long-bodied. Using Figure 20-1 as a guide, curve and increase the length of the hair as you scissor from the tail toward the hipbones. No matter what technique you use to shape this area, the hindquarters should blend gradually into the longer hair on the back and over the ribs.

There should be no signs of a break in the mane coat.

The remaining hair on the body is tipped slightly with scissors to remove untidy ends and give the coat a smooth, balanced and finished appearance. Although you are only tipping the hair, keep in mind that your goal is a *neat, elegant and balanced outline*. Leaving too much hair in certain places can make a puppy look too bulky, too short and thick, or too long in body.

11) Comb the hair on the front legs downward and outward, as it naturally falls. Scissor off the straggly ends that fall below the clipped line around the feet. Then scissor each front leg into the

cylindrical shape shown in Figure 20-1. Comb the hair on the front of the chest upward. The coat here should be shorter and slightly curved, as shown in the photos in this chapter. Leaving too much hair adds undesirable length to the Poodle's body.

12) Put up the topknot. Photographs and instructions for doing this are in Chapter 19, "Care of the Poodle in Show Coat." Then comb the topknot upward and outward to blend with the neck hair. On young puppies, a few short hairs above the eyes often will slip out of the band. To remedy this, put a little hair spray or styling gel on your fingers and carefully rub them over the wispy ends to hold them in place. For older puppies with longer hair, it may be necessary to divide the topknot into two sections as instructed in chapter 19.

THE FINISHED PRODUCT

Because the Puppy clip is so much a study in subtlety, I close this section with three showing a well-executed Puppy clip on a silver Miniature (Figure 20-17), a white Standard (Figure 20-18) and a black Toy (Figure 20-19). Observation sharpens the eye, which in turn strengthens the expertise of the groomer.

The English Saddle Clip

The English Saddle clip (Figure 20-20) is one of the three styles recognized by the American Kennel Club and the Poodle Club of America for all regular show conformation classes.

The Poodle Standard states "in the English Saddle clip, the face, throat, feet, forelegs and base of the tail are shaved, leaving puffs on the forelegs and a pompon on the end of the tail. The hindquarters are covered with a short blanket of hair except for a curved shaved area on each flank and two shaved bands on each hind leg. The entire shaven foot and a portion of the shaven leg above the puff are visible. The rest of the body is left in full coat but may be shaped in order to ensure overall balance."

Establishing a regular brushing, bathing and coat maintenance routine is a most important part of show grooming. Be sure to carefully study the advice in Chapter 19, "Care of the Poodle in Show Coat." If you are a beginner and have never attempted the English Saddle clip, here is some advice. The English Saddle is the *most* difficult of the show clips to execute. It requires superior scissoring and clipping skills and takes more time than any other trim to accomplish. Although the basic pattern for this clip is the same for all Poodles, the placement of the lines and the finishing touches depend on the proportions of each individual Poodle. It's very easy to make mistakes if you are not accustomed to dealing with a long show coat—errors that can take months and months of waiting for the hair to grow back. To set the pattern initially, you might consider having a professional handler trim your Poodle into the English Saddle clip, establishing the lines that are correct for your particular dog, and *then* start trimming. No matter

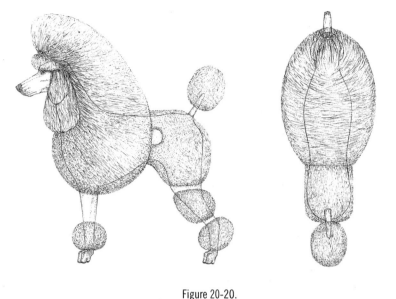

Figure 20-20.

how much accurate step-by-step grooming information you read, it is never the same as *seeing* it done.

If a Poodle is dark-colored, most professionals like to trim the clipped areas with a #40 blade about three to four days before a show. This allows the shaved areas to grow back looking velvety smooth by the day of the show. If a Poodle is white or light-colored, or can't take a close clip with a #40 blade, use a #15 or #30 blade, and do all of the clipping the day before the show. To avoid irritation after clipping, especially if you use a #40 blade, swab the skin with a canine anti-itch lotion, or with a little Bactine or Vaseline Intensive Care Lotion. Read more about this subject in "Preventing Clipper Burn" on page 82.

1) Bathe and blow dry the hair straight.

2) Follow instructions for clipping the feet. Clip to the end of the foot; *not* up on the ankles. While the standard states that the entire shaven foot should be visible, until

you master the look you desire, it's better to leave the clipped line lower rather than to take too much off.

3) Follow instructions for clipping the face. On the sides of the head, be sure the clipped line is *straight* between the outer corner of the eye to the ear, as shown in Figure 20-21. This automatically sets the topknot line on each side.

4) Clip the tail and shape the pompon. On all the show clips, you want to leave as much hair as possible to shape into a pompon. A good rule is to clip about one-quarter of the tail and leave hair on the remaining three-quarters to be shaped into the pompon. Stand your dog on the grooming table with the hindquarters facing you. Hold the end of the tail in your free hand. Starting on the upper side, place your clippers flat against the skin and clip in to the tail's juncture with the body. Some handlers and exhibitors like to clip an inverted **V** slightly forward of the base of the tail, into the body coat to make the dog look shorter in back. If you do this, be careful

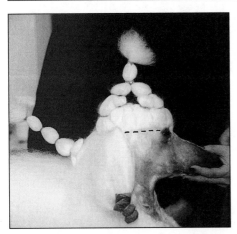

Figure 20-21.

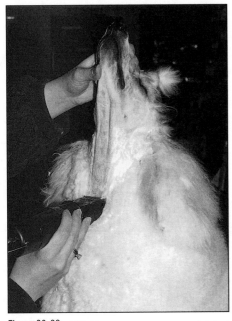

Figure 20-22.

not to go too far and clip off too much hair. Clip the sides of the tail in to the tail's juncture to the body. The underside of the tail is a very sensitive area and should be clipped in the opposite direction, from the body out to the pompon. The clipped line around the tail must be even or the pompon won't look properly shaped. Hold the tip of the tail in your free hand (the way it will be in the ring) and fluff the hair out with a comb. Use curved shears to shape the pompon very full and round. (See Figures 20-7 through 20-12 in the section titled "The Puppy Clip for Competition" on pages 128–29.)

5) Place the Poodle in a sitting position facing you to clip the throat. It should be trimmed into a V shape, as shown in Figure 20-22. Start at a point in the middle of the throat, a little below the Adam's Apple, and clip each side of the neck up to the front of each ear. Because this is a sensitive area, if your Poodle clipper burns easily, make the V in the opposite direction, by starting at the base of the ear and clipping downward to the middle of the throat. Adjust the V upward or downward, depending on the length of your Poodle's neck.

6) Stand the Poodle on the grooming table. The first step in the English Saddle clip is to make a part completely around the dog in back of the last rib with a knitting needle or tip of a rat-tail comb. The hair in front of the part, called the *mane,* will remain long (to be shaped round, later on). The hair in back of the part, called the *pack* or *saddle,* will be scissored into a short plush finish. It's complex to explain exactly *where* on your dog's body to part the hair. It should be separated where it keeps the dog in balance, and this spot varies with the individual dog. Try making the part ½ inch in back of the last rib on a Toy Poodle, about 1 inch in back of the last rib on a Miniature, and

about 1½ to 2 inches in back of the last rib on a Standard. Then step back and look at the dog. If he looks out of balance, adjust the part line forward or backward. It's usually necessary to experiment a little until the dog looks balanced. Once the part is made, brush the hair in front of the part upward. To protect it and keep it out of the way while you trim the hindquarters, especially if you are a beginner, push the long hair forward and spray it with a little hair spray, or wrap a strip of VetWrap around the back and under the chest.

7) Comb the hair on the back and scissor it a little shorter, to make it easier to visualize where you're going to set the pack and form the back bracelets.

8) Clip the stomach. Pointing clippers upward, start just above the testicles or vulva, and clip up to the part line near the middle of the dog.

9) Study Figure 20-23 of the Poodle in English Saddle clip. Notice that the hindquarters are covered with short, plush hair, except for a crescent-shape clipped area on each flank and two clipped bands on each back leg. There is a bracelet below the hock joint and one above the hock joint, ending at the stifle joint.

The bands between the bracelets are always set first with shears and then clipped in. Begin by setting the lower band to form the bottom bracelet. Starting just above the hock joint, scissor a narrow band completely around the leg from Point 1 to Point 2 in Figure 20-23. Notice in this side-view sketch that the band slopes downward from the back to the front of the leg. It is not necessary to clip a Toy, but if you are working on a Miniature or Standard Poodle, use one of the narrow cutting blades to clip carefully over the scissored area. Pointing clippers upward, shave around the leg in short strokes, making

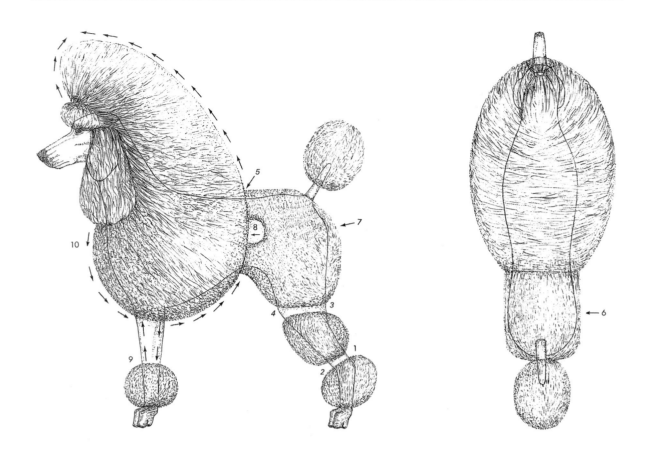

Figure 20-23. Execute the pattern for the English Saddle clip in the direction shown by the arrows.

the band about ¼ inch wide. The leg is hollowed above the hock bone, so you must place your finger on the opposite side of the leg when you clip and press the hollowed part forward.

10) Clip the upper band. Use your fingers to feel for the center of the stifle joint. Scissor another band at this spot, completely around the leg at the same level, from Point 3 to Point 4 in Figure 20-23. You may have to place the band *slightly* higher or lower if your Poodle is short- or long-legged. Once again, if you are trimming a Miniature or Standard Poodle, point clippers upward and clip around the leg, at exactly the same level, in short strokes, making the upper band about ¼ inch wide.

11) Clip the bands on the other hind leg. Make sure both legs are even. When viewing the dog from behind, both clipped bands should be symmetrical lines from across one leg to the other.

12) Comb the hair below the hock joint on each back leg to begin shaping the bottom bracelet. Comb the hair down, then scissor around the clipped line to remove any untidy ends. If the dog does not have great feet, leave a *little* more hair at the bottom of the bracelet for camouflage. Then comb the hair up and scissor off any untidy hairs above the shaved band. Comb the hair outward, then use curved shears to shape each bracelet. When viewed from the side, the bottom bracelets are more oval than round in shape,

sloping downwards from the back of the leg towards the front, emphasizing angulation. When viewed from behind, the bracelets should make the legs appear straight and parallel.

13) Shape the upper bracelet. This bracelet is slightly larger than the lower one. Comb the hair down and scissor off any untidy hairs that fall below the clipped line at the bottom of the bracelet. Comb the hair up, and scissor off any hair that extends over the clipped band around the stifle joint. Fluff out the hair with your comb, then, using curved or straight shears, trim the bracelet into a modified oval shape shown in Figure 20-23. Hold your shears flat against the hair you are working on, taking a little hair off at a time. Do not dig into the coat with the points of the shear. Don't pull out the hair with your fingers or you will spoil the plush look. If you are not satisfied with the shape of the bracelet, recomb the hair and begin scissoring again. Scissor the upper bracelet on the opposite leg even in size and shape.

There are several ways to camouflage subtle faults here (you should not show a dog with major faults). If the dog is a little wide in the rear, leave more hair on the insides of the bracelets and less hair on the outsides. If the dog is a little narrow behind, do the opposite, leaving more hair on the outsides of the bracelets and less on the insides. If the hocks tend to turn in (causing the feet to turn out, build up the hair on the outside of the bottom bracelet and shorten the hair on the inside. If the hocks turn out slightly (causing the feet to turn in), do the reverse. If the dog hocks are slightly curved and not straight up and down, lengthen the hair at the bottom of each rosette to make the hocks appear straight. Of course, all these steps should be done in a subtle, not obvious, manner.

14) Comb the hair on the top of the pack upward. The pack should join the mane with only the part line as a separation, as indicated by Point 5 in Figure 20-23. The top and sides of the pack are shaped square and flat (Point 6 in Figure 20-23). It seems easier to begin by scissoring the top of the pack (from the base of the tail up to the mane) flat. Comb the hair upward and outward to lift it as much as possible, then scissor it flat and plush to a length of about ½ to 1 inch, depending on the variety of your Poodle. Comb the hair outward and downward on the hindquarters under the tail. This part of the pack is scissored to appear slightly rounded (Point 7 in Figure 20-23) and blends gradually with the flat, squared

top part in front of the tail. Comb the hair down at the clipped band around the stifle joint, then scissor off untidy hairs that fall below the shaved band.

15) To complete the pack, clip a crescent-shaped indentation (sometimes called the *kidney patch*) over the flank on each side of the dog, between the top and underside of the body (although closer to the topline). Clipping the crescents can be confusing for beginners. The front of each crescent connects to the part line at the mane (Point 8 in Figure 20-23). The circular part of the crescent should not extend back beyond the point where the rear leg joins the body. If you are unsure of yourself, mark the shape of the indentation with chalk, or scissor the line into the hair. Then clip the crescent using one of the narrow cutting blades to avoid making a mistake. Comb the hair near the clipped areas forward, and scissor off untidy ends that obscure the crescent shape.

16) Turn the Poodle around to stand facing you to clip the puffs on the forelegs, which should be in balance with the bracelets on the rear leg. Begin at a point level with the lower rear bracelet, and clip the front and sides of each foreleg up to the point of the elbow (Point 9 in Figure 20-23). To take off the hair evenly, clip the back side of each foreleg in the opposite direction, from the point of the elbow down to the bracelet line. If you are a beginner and are unsure of where to begin clipping, stand the dog the way you will pose him in the ring. Then scissor a little mark in the hair, even with the rear bracelets. You might even want to set the front puffs a little higher than usual until you determine the correct line. You can always move the line downward, but it can take months of growing hair to move it upward!

17) Comb the hair on each front puff. Comb the hair down and scissor around the foot to remove any straggly hairs that fall below the clipped line. As you did on the rear, if the dog does not have ideal feet, leave a *little* more hair at the bottom for camouflage. Then comb the hair up, and scissor off any untidy hairs above the clipped line around the leg. Fluff out the hair with a comb and then shape the puffs with curved shears. The front bracelets should be longer from top to bottom than they are wide. They are beveled at the top and at the bottom with curved shears and trimmed into the shape you see in Figure 20-23. When you have finished, the puffs on the front legs and the bracelets on the rear legs should be in proportion to each other and create the illusion that the legs and feet are straight and parallel when viewed from the front of the back of the dog.

18) Stand the Poodle on the grooming table the way you will pose him in the ring. Comb the mane outward for its final shaping. Study Figure 20-23 and notice that the mane is shaped into a round ball. The length of the mane varies with the individual dog. You can make shaping easier by the way you prepare the long hair. Begin by combing it upward and outward around the neck. As your hand moves backwards, comb the hair upward and slightly forward toward the head. Comb the sides of the body outward and slightly forward. Comb the hair on the chest outward and downward, and on the underbody downward and forward. As you scissor and shape the mane, think of circles and balls. Essentially you will be drawing a circle, only you're doing it with shears (Point 10 in Figure 20-23). Use curved or straight shears. Hold them flat against the hair; don't point the tips into the coat. Most professionals begin to shape the mane

Figure 20-24. On the English Saddle clip the pack may be straight or curly. Here you see a curly pack on a Standard Poodle. Although curly packs are not seen very often in the show ring, they are easy to accomplish. After shampooing and rinsing your Poodle, instead of blow-drying the hair on the pack straight, let it dry naturally. The hair will tend to curl. When you have finished putting your trim together, fill a spray bottle with water. Mist the pack hair with water while you lightly tap it down with a pin brush. The more you mist the pack with water and tap it down with your brush, the tighter the curls will be.

Figure 20-25. Ch. Midnight Gambler of Shikarah, black Miniature Poodle owned by Javier Blanco and David Allen, Madrid, Spain.

Figure 20-26. Ch. Alekai Mikimoto on Fifth, white Standard Poodle owned by Karen Lefrak and handled by Wendell Sammett.

round by starting underneath and scissoring upward. Trim the hair around and under the elbow fairly short and tight. You don't want excess hair in this area to dangle or flip out while the dog is moving around the ring. When you reach the front of the chest, shape it round and tight. An excessive amount of hair here will make the dog look dumpy and long in body. If the Poodle has a straight front, however, be careful! Taking off too much hair will call attention to this fault. You also want to lift each ear and trim the mane a little shorter underneath to make the ears lay flat against the body coat.

19) Put up the topknot. Instructions and photographs for doing this are in Chapter 19, "Care of the Poodle in Show Coat." If the topknot is too long, it may be trimmed shorter to create a better balance to the mane and to frame the head.

20) Brush and comb the ear feathering downward. Trim off any uneven ends with your shears, if necessary.

THE FINISHED PRODUCT

On all the show clips, your goal is a Poodle that is elegant and regal-looking, like the Poodles in Figures 20-24, 20-25 and 20-26. Everything should be balanced and fit perfectly together in harmony with the breed Standard: the tail with the topknot, the front puffs with the back bracelets, the pack with the mane, the mane blending into the topknot, and the topknot framing the face and making the head look as long and refined as possible. Don't get carried away with excessive coat. An extravagant amount of hair may seem glamorous, but too much can make a Poodle appear coarse and thickset, the exact opposite of the elegant-looking dog described in the breed Standard.

For another view of the English Saddle Clip, see Figure 24-19 on page 204.

The Continental Clip

The Continental clip (Figure 20-27) is one of the three styles recognized by the American Kennel Club and the Poodle Club of America for all regular show conformation classes. It is interesting to note that the Continental clip is the oldest recorded Poodle clip, first described by Gervase Markham in 1621.

The Poodle Standard states "in the Continental Clip, the face, throat, feet and base of the tail are shaved. The hindquarters are shaved with pompons (optional) on the hips. The legs are shaved, leaving bracelets on the hindlegs and puffs on the forelegs. There is a pompon at the end of the tail. The entire shaven foot and a portion of the shaven foreleg above the puff are visible. The rest of the body is left in full coat but may be shaped to insure overall balance."

Establishing a regular brushing, bathing and coat maintenance routine is a most important part of show grooming. Be sure to carefully study the advice in the Chapter 19, "Care of the Poodle in Show Coat." If you are new to Poodle grooming and have never attempted the Continental clip, here is a little advice. Although the basic pattern for this clip (and the English Saddle) is the same for all Poodle varieties, the placement of the lines and the finishing touches depend on the proportions of each individual Poodle. It's *so* easy to make mistakes if you are not accustomed to dealing with a long show coat—errors that can take months and months of waiting for the hair to grow back. To set the pattern initially, you might consider having a professional handler or an experienced owner-handler trim your Poodle into the Continental clip, establishing the lines that are correct for your particular dog, and *then* start trimming the dog yourself. No

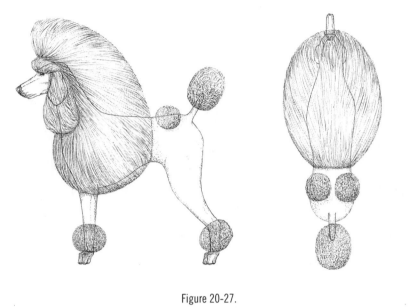

Figure 20-27.

matter how much accurate step-by-step grooming information you read, it is never the same as *seeing* the grooming actually being done.

For a dark-colored Poodle, most professionals like to trim the clipped areas with a #40 blade about three to four days before a show. This allows the shaved areas to grow back looking velvety smooth by the day of the show. If the Poodle is white or light-colored, or can't take a close clip with a #40, use a #15 or #30 blade, and do all of the clipping the day before the show. To avoid irritation after clipping, especially if you use a #40 blade, swab the skin with an anti-itch lotion made for dogs, or with a little Bactine or Vaseline Intensive Care Lotion. Read more about this subject in "Preventing Clipper Burn" on page 82.

1) Bathe the Poodle and blow dry the hair straight.

2) Follow instructions for clipping the feet. Clip to the end of the foot; *not* up on the ankles. While the Standard states that the entire shaven foot should be visible, until

you master the trim you desire, it's better to leave the clipped line lower rather than to take too much off.

3) Follow instructions for clipping the face. On the sides of the head, be sure the clipped line is straight between the outer corner of the eye to the ear. This automatically sets the topknot line on each side. See Figure 20-6 on page 128 in "The Puppy Clip (for Competition)."

4) Clip the tail and shape the pompon. On all the show clips, you want to leave as much hair as possible to shape into a pompon. See Figures 20-6 through 20-12 on pages 128–129, in the section titled "The Puppy Clip (for Competition)." A good rule is to clip about one-quarter of the tail and leave the hair on the remaining three-quarters to be shaped into the pompon. Stand your dog on the grooming table with its hindquarters facing you. Grasp the end of the tail in your free hand. Starting on the upper side, place your clippers flat against the skin and clip in to the tail's juncture with the body. Clip the sides of the tail in the same manner. The underside of the tail is a very sensitive area, and should be clipped in the opposite direction, or from the body out to the pompon.

The clipped line around the tail must be even or the pompon won't look properly shaped. Hold the tip of the tail in your free hand (the way it will be in the ring) and fluff the hair out with a comb. Use curved shears to shape the pompon very full and round. Figure 20-28 shows a pompon that has been beautifully shaped.

5) Place the Poodle in a sitting position facing you to clip the throat. It is trimmed into a **V** shape. Start at a point in the middle of the throat, a little below the Adam's Apple, and clip each side of the neck up to the front of each ear. Because this is a sensitive area, if your Poodle clipper burns easily, set the **V** in the opposite direction, by starting at the base of the ear and clipping downward to the middle of the throat. Adjust the **V** upward or downward, depending on the length of your Poodle's neck. See Figures 20-13 and 20-14 on page 129 in the section titled "The Puppy Clip (for Competition)."

6) Stand the Poodle on the grooming table. The first step in the Continental clip is to make a part completely around the dog behind the last rib with a knitting needle or the tip of a rat-tail comb. The hair in front of the part, the mane or ruff, will remain long (to be shaped round, later). The hair behind the part, on the hindquarters, will be shaved off except for two rosettes over the hipbones. It's tricky to explain exactly *where* on the dog's body to part the hair. It should be separated where it keeps the dog in balance, and this spot varies with the individual dog. Try making the part ½ inch in back of the last rib on a Toy Poodle, about 1 inch in back of the last rib on a Miniature, and about 1½ to 2

inches in back of the last rib on a Standard. Then step back and look at the dog. If he appears out of balance, move the part forward or backward. It's often necessary to experiment a little until the dog looks balanced and pleasing to the eye. Once the part is made, brush the hair in front of the part upward. To protect it and keep it out of the way while you shave the hindquarters, especially if you are a beginner, push the long hair forward and spray it with some hair spray, or wrap a wide strip of VetWrap around the back and under the chest.

7) Study Figure 20-27, and notice that the hindquarters are clipped close, with a bracelet on each back leg and a rosette (optional) above each hip. Begin pattern work by shaving the back legs. Pointing clippers upward, begin about ½ inch above the hock joint on a Toy or Miniature Poodle and about 1 inch on a Standard, and clip up to the hindquarters as indicated by the arrows in Figure 20-29. To emphasize angulation, slant the clipped line slightly downward at the front of the leg. Remove all the hair on the outside and inside of the back leg. Clip the opposite leg.

8) Clip the stomach. Pointing clippers upward, start just above the testicles or vulva, and clip to the part line near the middle of the dog.

9) The next step is to clip a rosette on each side of the hindquarters. Depending on the variety of the Poodle you are clipping, rosettes should be spaced about ¼ to 1 inch apart and placed immediately over the middle of the hipbone. Study Figure 20-29 and notice the placement of the rosettes on the top and side of the dog. If the Poodle you are clipping has a less-than-ideal tail-set, however, you will want to move the rosettes slightly backward. If the topline is slightly roached or arched, move

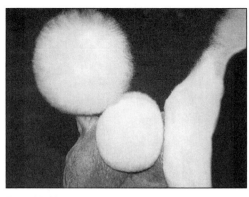

Figure 20-28.

the rosettes slightly forward, keeping less distance between them and the mane. If the dog is a little long in body, place the rosettes higher on the hips, make them slightly larger in size and keep each front edge close to the mane.

10) Begin by clipping a narrow strip (about the same width as the base of the tail) from the base of the tail straight up the backbone, stopping at the line of the mane, as indicated by the arrows in Figure 20-29. To correctly proportion the width of the strip, use a #5/8 blade on a Toy Poodle, a #7/8 blade on a Miniature Poodle, and a #40 on a Standard. Be sure the dog stands straight. If he is fidgety, have someone steady his front so the strip is not off-center. The size of the rosettes should fit the dog. Generally on a Toy Poodle the rosettes are about 1½ inches in diameter; on a Miniature Poodle, they are about 2½ to 3 inches in diameter; and on a Standard, from 3½ to 4 inches in diameter. They can be increased or decreased in size in accordance with the dog's conformation. Clipping round rosettes freehand and making them even in size, shape and placement is rather difficult. Most professionals use an object as a template or guide: a plastic cup or jar, an aerosol can lid, or anything nonbreakable with an opening the diameter of the desired width. Hold the template against the hair

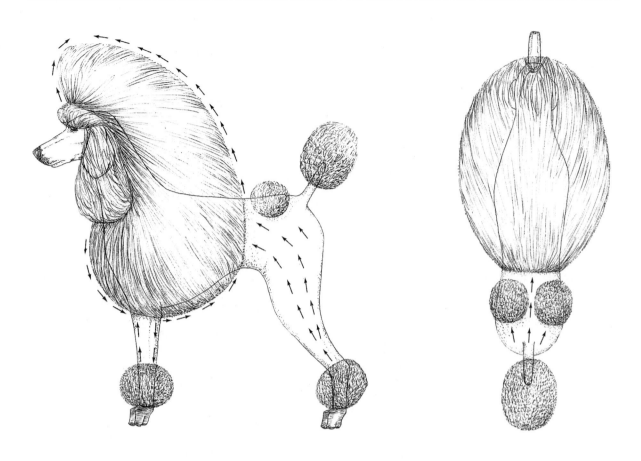

Figure 20-29. Execute the pattern for the Continental clip in the direction shown by the arrows, making allowance for the individual dog's faults and virtues.

and trim around the edges with scissors. Once you have made two basically round shapes, then trim around them with clippers.

11) With the #40 blade, clip the remaining hair around each rosette up to the part line near the middle of the dog.

12) Comb each rosette upward and outward to lift the hair as much as possible. Scissor around each one to emphasize its round shape, as shown in Figure 20-30, then shape the top to look slightly domed. Trim the basic round outline first, working in a circular motion and taking off a little hair at a time. Once you have the correct shape, the rosettes can be refined. Although they should be

slightly domed on top, you want to keep them fairly low in height. Rosettes that are too high will create the illusion that the dog is high in the rear and that his neck is short. Both rosettes must be even in size and shape.

13) If rosettes are not desired, shave the hindquarters up to the part line.

14) Comb the hair below the hock joint on each back leg. Begin shaping the bracelet by combing the hair down, then scissoring around the clipped line around the foot, to remove any untidy ends. If the dog's feet are less than ideal, leave a little more hair at the bottom of the bracelet for camouflage. Then comb the hair up, and scissor

off any untidy hairs above the clipped line around the leg. Comb the hair outward, then shape each bracelet with curved shears. When viewed from the side, as shown in Figure 20-31, each bracelet is more oval than round in shape, sloping downward from the back of the leg towards the front, emphasizing angulation. Figure 20-31 also illustrates good balance between the bracelets and the rosettes. When viewed from the back, the bracelets should make the legs appear straight and parallel.

There are several different ways to camouflage subtle faults here (remember, you shouldn't show a dog with major faults). If the dog is a little wide in the rear, leave more hair on the insides of the

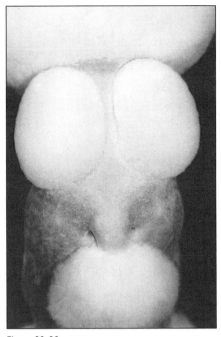

Figure 20-30.

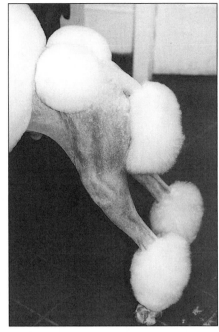

Figure 20-31.

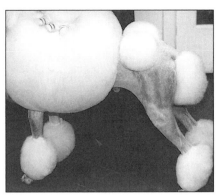

Figure 20-32.

bracelets and less hair on the out-sides. If the dog is slightly narrow behind, do the opposite, leaving more hair on the outsides of the bracelets and less hair on the insides. If the hocks tend to turn in (causing the feet to turn out), build up the hair on the outside and shorten the hair on the inside as you shape each bracelet. If the hocks turn out (causing the feet to turn in), do the reverse. If the hocks are slightly bent or curved and not straight up and down, lengthen the hair at the bottom of each rosette to make the hocks appear straight. Under these circumstances, you might want to forget about the Continental clip entirely and choose the English Saddle clip instead.

15) Turn the Poodle around to stand facing you to clip the puffs on the forelegs, which should be in balance with those on the hocks. Begin at a point level with the rear bracelets, and clip the front and sides of each foreleg up to the point of the elbow. To take off the hair evenly, clip the back side of each foreleg in the opposite direction, from the point of the

elbow down to the top of the puff, as indicated by the arrows in Figure 20-29. If you are a beginner and unsure of where to begin clip-ping, stand the dog the way you will pose him in the ring. Then scissor a little mark in the hair (even with the rear bracelets).

16) Comb the hair on each front puff. Comb the hair down, and scissor around the foot to remove any straggly hairs that fall below the clipped line. As you did on the rear, if the dog doesn't have great feet, leave a little more hair at the bottom for camouflage. Then comb the hair up, and scissor off any untidy hairs above the clipped line around the leg. Fluff out the hair with a comb, then shape the puffs with curved shears. They are more rounded in shape than the bracelets on the back legs, tapering slightly at the bottom. The puffs on the front legs and the bracelets on the rear legs should be in proportion to each other, as shown in Figure 20-32, and create the illusion that the legs and feet are straight and parallel when viewed from the front or the back of the dog.

17) Stand the Poodle on the grooming table in the manner you will pose him in the ring. Comb the mane outward for its final scissoring. Study Figure 20-29 again, and notice that the mane is shaped into a round ball. The length of the mane varies with the individual dog. You can make shaping easier by the way you prepare the long hair. Begin by combing it upward and outward around the neck. As your hand moves backward, comb the hair upward and slightly forward toward the head. Comb the sides of the body outward and slightly forward. Comb the hair on the chest outward and downward, and on the underbody downward and forward. As you scissor and shape the mane, think of circles and balls. Essentially you want to draw a circle, but you're doing it with shears. Use curved or straight shears. Hold the blades flat against the hair, and don't point the tips into the coat. Most professionals find it easier to shape the mane round by starting underneath and scissoring upward. Trim the hair around and under the elbow fairly

Figure 20-33. Ch. Baliwick Awesome Blossom, brown Toy, owned by Ianthe Bloomquist.

Figure 20-34. American and Canadian Ch. Dacher Braylane Bluechip, white Miniature, owned by Mary and Charles Woodward; Shaunna Bernardin, handler.

Figure 20-35. Ch. Legacy's Made in the Shade, black Standard; Christina Pawlosky, handler.

Figure 20-36. Ch. Dreamcatcher's My Bella Jewel, white Standard, owned by Christopher Zecco; Kaz Hosaka, handler.

short and tight. You don't want excess hair in this area to dangle or flip out while the dog is moving around the ring. When you reach the front of the chest, shape it round and tight. An excessive amount of hair here will make the dog look dumpy and long-bodied. If your Poodle has a straight front, however, be careful here. Taking off too much hair will call attention to this fault! You also want to lift each ear and trim the mane a little shorter underneath to make the ears lie flat against the body coat.

18) Put up the topknot. Instructions and photographs for doing this are in Chapter 19, "Care of the Poodle in Show Coat." If the topknot is too long, it may be scissored shorter to create a better balance to the mane and to frame the head.

For another view of the Continental clip, see the illustration of the Lion clip (Figure 24-17) on page 202.

19) Brush and comb the ear feathering downward. Trim off any uneven ends with your shears, if necessary.

THE FINISHED PRODUCT

Your goal is a Poodle that is elegant and proud looking like the ones in Figures 20-33, 20-34, 20-35 and 20-36. Everything should be balanced and fit perfectly together in harmony with the breed Standard: the tail with the topknot, the front puffs with the back bracelets, the rosettes balanced in size and shape and not too high, the topknot framing the face and blending into a mane of correct length. Don't get carried away with excessive coat. An extravagant amount of hair may seem glamorous, but too much can make a Poodle appear coarse and thickset, the exact opposite of the elegant looking dog described in the breed Standard.

chapter 21

INTRODUCTION TO THE "PET" POODLE TRIMS

The styles and patterns that appear in the following chapters are called pet trims because they are for designed for Poodles that are pets, not for Poodles that will be shown in the breed ring. None of the clips in this group are permitted in the conformation ring with one exception: the Sporting clip. The official AKC Standard for the Poodle states that "in the Stud Dog and Brood Bitch classes and in a non-competitive Parade of Champions, Poodles may be shown in the 'Sporting' clip."

The easy-to-do pet clips, such as the Puppy, Sporting, Retriever, Lamb, Miami (or Summer)and Panda, are presented before the clips that require more intricate body clipping, such as the Town and Country, New Yorker, Dutch (and all its variations), Sweetheart, Desi, Swirl, Y and T.

As you study the diagrams accompanying the instructions for the easy-to-do clips, keep in mind that most of these are styles on which the face, feet, throat and base of the tail are clipped. Longer hair is left on the head, which is shaped with scissors into a topknot, and also on the end of the tail, which is shaped into a pompon. The rest of the body and legs are clipped or scissored to follow the contour of the dog, leaving an overall covering of hair that can vary in length considerably with the style of clip chosen. On the majority of the pet clips, as you will see on the diagrams, the leg hair is usually slightly longer than the body coat. The front legs are shaped like cylinders, parallel and straight, and the back legs are shaped to emphasize angulation.

If you are new to grooming, the easy-to-do clips are the trims to begin with to gain confidence in using your clippers and scissors. Once you have mastered the basics of balance and are creating flowing lines that blend into each other in good proportion, you can graduate to the more complex body patterns.

The grooming of pet Poodles has changed dramatically since the first edition of this book was written. Years ago, the hair on the body was scissored very full and round, topknots were often shaped to look like balloons, ears were frequently clipped bare with little tassels of hair left hanging at the bottoms, and thick moustaches were popular. In addition, the hair on the legs was either left full and shaped into pantaloons (which made the Poodle look like it was wearing baggy trousers) or left with an abundance of hair over the hips which tapered down to the ankles in a triangular shape like a "leg-of-mutton" sleeve.

Today, emphasis is placed on balance and symmetry. Coats are no longer abundantly bouffant. Lines are neat and crisp, ideally creating the illusion that *every* part of the Poodle blends together in harmony with its breed Standard: the front to the back, one side to the other side, the front legs to the back legs, and the topknot to the tail. One part should never be so exaggerated that it overshadows another. The ideal Poodle is a squarely built dog. The length of the body measured from the breastbone to the point of the rump approximates the height from the highest point of the shoulders to the ground.

Once you have studied the breed Standard (chapter 9) and visualized the ideal Poodle, you should try to style each dog to enhance the illusion of perfection. *All* dogs have weak points, so your objective in trimming is to heighten overall balance while you try to conceal any imperfections the dog may have.

Arranging hair, whether human or animal, is an art. The role of today's successful pet stylist can be compared to that of today's human hair stylist. Not every woman looks good wearing the same hairdo. A great-looking style is proportioned to each woman's particular head and body. Her face shape, head size, neck length, body proportions, height, weight, age and hair texture are all important considerations when choosing a flattering style. Each situation is entirely individual. Moreover, the chosen hairdo should be easy to care for and suit the individual's lifestyle. If you have studied Chapter 10, "Interpreting the Breed Standard with Emphasis on Grooming," you already know that these also are important considerations when styling Poodles.

Good Poodle grooming must always emphasize correct proportion and the illusion of a square. If a dog is not proportioned correctly, his trim can be adjusted to enhance the balance and proportion that the eye sees, thereby minimizing his faults and emphasizing this attributes. As Del Dahl comments in *The Complete Poodle*, "It doesn't change the dog; it only changes how you see it."

chapter 22

Figure 22-1.

The Poodle's legs are shaped the same way for most pet clips, with the exception of the Miami (or Summer) clip. If you study the illustrations of all the different pet trims (except the Miami), you will see that on the back legs, the shape follows the natural conformation of the leg, emphasizing the angulation above the hock joint and the curve of the stifle joint. The front legs are shaped like cylinders, straight from the top to the bottom on all sides, not tapering to the feet or wedge-shaped. To distinguish this leg shape from the variations shown at the end of this chapter, I will refer to this style as *full-coated.* How much hair you leave on full-coated legs depends on several factors: personal preference, the dog's lifestyle, the pattern you select, the length of hair you leave on the body (the trim must always be in balance) and the texture of the coat. Texture plays a very important role in finishing. Harsh, dense hair is fairly thick in diameter and holds together better than coats of less substantial texture. Fine, thin hair

is slightly smaller in diameter and, when allowed to grow too long, doesn't hold its shape and quickly becomes limp. When it is trimmed shorter, however, fine hair looks neater, appears to be thicker and holds its shape much better. Under any circumstances, as you will see by examining the illustrations of all the pet styles (except the Miami), the hair on the legs is always slightly longer than that on the body. On pet trims, the body hair is never longer than the leg hair.

There are two methods of finishing the legs:

- Shaping them by hand-scissoring

- Skimming through the hair with a snap-on comb fitted over a #40 blade and then trimming any uneven ends with shears (see page 19 for information on snap-on combs)

Personally, I think it is easier to start by finishing the back legs—shaping one, then the other—and then moving on to finish the front legs.

Method 1: Hand Scissoring

If you intend to shape your Poodle's legs with scissors, your goal is to achieve a smooth, plush finish. Study the finished legs in Figure 22-1, especially take note of the area above each foot, indicated by the arrows. Notice that the bottom line of the leg is even and slightly rounded. Most groomers call this area the cuff. If you are a beginner, it is easier to set the cuff first, and then to shape the rest of the leg.

SETTING THE CUFFS

1) To make a round cuff, begin by combing the hair around the ankle straight down.

2) Holding your shears in the position shown in Figures 22-2 and 22-3, scissor completely around the ankle to trim off any hairs that fall below the clipped line above the foot.

3) Comb the hair outward, and you have created a natural round cuff, as shown in Figure 22-4. Using curved shears here will create a lovely rounded effect.

SHAPING THE LEGS

1) Fluff the hair upward and outward before beginning to shape the leg itself. Some groomers (including the author) like to start at the ankle and work up to the hip; others prefer doing the reverse. With experience, you will choose whichever approach is most comfortable for you. Whichever method you choose, hold your shears flat against the hair you are working on—*do not* point the blade tips into the coat— and start shaping, taking a little hair off at a time. Always move your shears *smoothly* in a vertical direction, either upward or downward, never in a horizontal or angled direction—which almost always causes notches in the coat. The fastest and most efficient way to achieve the correct outline is to concentrate on one part of the leg at a time; that is, start at the ankle and scissor a line up to the hip.

2) Adjacent to the part you just finished, begin again at the ankle and scissor another line up to the hip. Continue this process around the leg until it takes shape. Do not move about erratically when scissoring, but maintain an organized, methodical approach to your work.

3) Scissor the hard-to-reach areas on the inside of the back leg using either of two positions: gently lifting the leg you are working on and pulling it backward, or lifting the opposite leg with your free hand. When scissoring near the vulva or testicles, place your free hand over them for protection. There is no excuse for nicking the genitals. The dog will never forget it and will likely be skittish and uncooperative during any future grooming operations.

4) To achieve the desirable velvety smooth finish, don't pull out straggly hairs with your fingertips. Instead, fluff the hair upward and outward every so often with your comb to ease out any untidy ends, then rescissor the area. Some groomers also like to gently shake the leg during the shaping process to encourage the hair to stand out straight. (See the section titled "Developing the Correct Scissoring Technique" in chapter 2 for more information.) Remember, your goal is to end up with an even, plush finish with the shape shown in the accompanying illustration.

5) The back legs should show correct angulation. Study Figure 22-5. The shaping should accentuate the natural curve of the stifle at point A. Point B is trimmed in and comes outward again at the hock at point C, and then it *slightly* angles downward to point D. (If the dog you are trimming lacks rear angulation, leave additional hair at the top of the hock, at point C, and at the front of the stifle, at point A. Then scissor the hair a little shorter below the tail and down the leg to the hock.) When viewed from the rear, the legs should look parallel, as shown in Figure 22-6. This shape is typically the way groomers in the United States and Canada style pet Poodle legs.

Tips from the Pros: Making Perfect Cuffs

Most professional pet stylists use this fast and foolproof way to shape the cuffs round at the bottom of the legs.

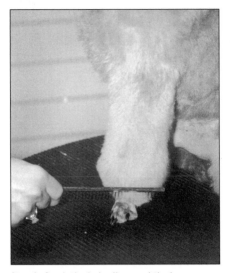

Step 1. Comb the hair all around the leg straight down.

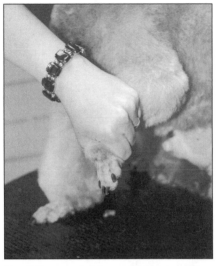

Step 2. Clasp your hand around the leg hair with your thumb and index finger, then slide your hand downward towards the foot.

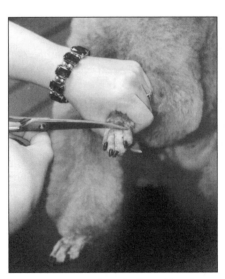

Step 3. Holding your shears in the position shown, scissor an even line completely around the ankle. Your goal is to trim off all the hair that falls below the clipped line above the foot. Using curved shears here will create a lovely rounded effect.

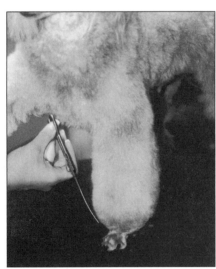

Step 4. After scissoring, release your hand, and comb the leg hair outward and upward. You have created a natural round cuff and are ready to shape the rest of the leg.

6) When the leg is completely shaped to the hip, start blending the longer leg hair into the shorter body hair. Use curved shears here, if you have them. Keep combing upward and scissoring the hair until the line from the leg hair blends smoothly into the body coat, creating an overall balanced look. There should a gradual flow of hair in proportion with the overall profile, with no excess

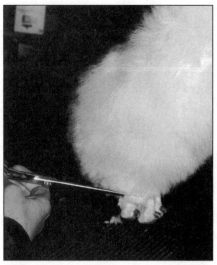

Figure 22-2.

Figure 22-3.

Figure 22-4.

coat that puffs out to make the dog look "hippy." Scissor the other back leg, making it even in size and shape. The hair on the rear beneath the tail should be trimmed tight to make the dog appear as short in back as possible.

7) Turn the dog around to stand facing you. Shape the front legs by first making a neat cuff at the bottom of each leg, exactly as you did on both rear legs. Comb the hair around the ankle straight down, then scissor off any hairs that fall below the clipped line above the foot. Comb the hair outward, and the cuff will be round.

8) Hold your Poodle's front leg in your hand, extend it towards you (Figure 22-7), and fluff the leg hair up and out with your comb. The front legs are scissored to appear cylindrical in shape, straight from top to bottom on all sides, as shown in Figures 22-8 and 22-9, *not* tapering to the foot. This shape is typically the way American and Canadian groomers style the legs. As you did on the rear legs, hold your shears flat against the hair you are trimming— *do not* point the tips of the blade into the coat—and start shaping by taking a little hair off at a time. Always move your shears in a

vertical upward or downward direction, never across the coat. Again, you can achieve the correct cylindrical shape by scissoring methodically. Begin at the ankle and trim one section of hair up to the elbow; then, adjacent to where you just finished, repeat the process. Continue in the same manner all around the leg. Remember to fluff the leg hair up and out with your comb to ease out any uneven hairs, then rescissor. You can also take hold of the paw, pull it forward, and gently shake the leg during the shaping process to encourage uneven hairs to stand out straight.

9) To scissor the hair on the hard-to-reach areas under the front leg, lift the leg on which you are working, and pull it gently forward. When you put the leg down, check the elbow: There should be no hollows or tufts of hair sticking out. Scissor the other front leg, making sure it is even in size and shape, and that both legs are in balance with the back legs.

10) Comb the hair between the front legs and chest upward. Shape these areas, gradually blending the hair up to the front of the neck. The hair here should be short and slightly curved, not overly rounded

or so long as to add length to the Poodle's body, or so flat as to resemble a Fox Terrier front. Figure 22-5 also provides a clearer illustration of the shoulder layback and the outline for which you are striving.

Balance and symmetry are essential when finishing the legs. It bears repeating that each back leg should be even in size and shape, as should each front leg. More importantly, the back legs and front legs should also be in balance with each other. Figures 22-10 and 22-11, taken at a grooming competition, show excellent examples of proper shaping and balance.

Method 2:
Snap-on Comb

If you have difficulty scissoring or if speed is a consideration, you can use a snap-on comb attached to a #40 blade to take off the excess hair, and then shape any untidy ends with shears. Choose a snap-on attachment that leaves the leg hair longer than the body coat (see page 19).

1) Stand the dog on the grooming table. Beginning on the back legs, use the snap-on comb to blend the hair over the hips into a smooth

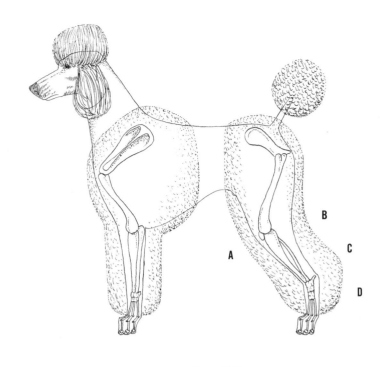

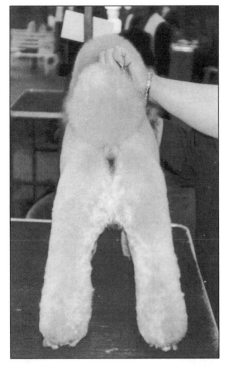

Figure 22-5.

Figure 22-6.

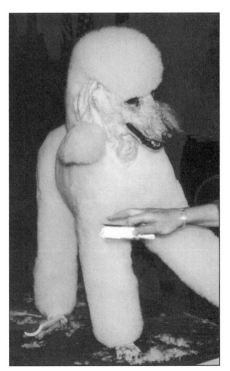

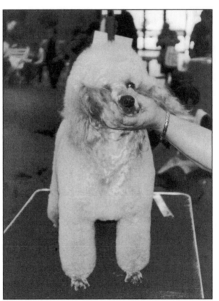

Figure 22-9.

Figure 22-8.

Figure 22-7.

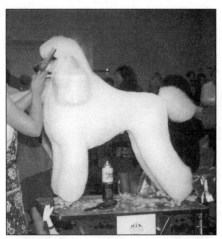

Figure 22-10.

Figure 22-11.

Figure 22-12.

Figure 22-13.

line that flows down the outsides and insides of the legs. When you have finished, comb the hair at the bottom of the leg straight down on all sides, and scissor off any straggly hairs that fall below the clipped line around the ankles. Comb the hair outward, and you will have created a round cuff at the bottom of the leg. Fluff out the leg hair and scissor off any uneven lines, shaping the legs instructed in Method 1.

2) On the front legs, use the snap-on attachment to blend the hair in a smooth line that flows over the shoulders and down each leg. Create the cuff at the bottom, then fluff the hair on the leg and scissor off any uneven lines, shaping the legs in Method 1.

Remember: The areas where the body and leg hair meet must always be carefully blended to prevent a noticeable difference in length.

International Differences

Since this book is international in scope, it must be mentioned here that there are slight differences in the way groomers from the United States, Canada and other countries style the legs. As mentioned earlier in this chapter, on North American pets, from a side view, the shaping of the back leg closely follows the natural conformation, emphasizing the angulation above the hock joint and the curve of the stifle joint (Figure 22-12). On pet Poodles from other nations, especially European countries, from a side view, the hair on the hindquarters extends slightly out from the tail and then curves inward (where it is scissored shorter). The hair then curves outward again and angles downward in back, with more fullness beginning near the stifle joint, as shown in Figure 22-13.

When viewed from the rear, the back legs should look parallel. The typical American and Canadian styling was shown in Figure 22-6 (page 145). Groomers in other countries tend to leave more hair on the bottoms of the

legs, below the hock joint (in correct proportion, of course), as shown in Figure 22-14. The same is true of the front legs. While they are shaped like cylinders, straight from top to bottom in the United States and Canada (Figures 22-8 and 22-11), Europeans also scissor cylindrical shapes but leave slightly more hair on the bottoms (Figures 22-15 and 22-16). See Chapter 24, "The International Scene," for more information.

The Leg Variations

The following four leg variations may be used with any pet clip in place of the full-coated leg styles described at the beginning of this chapter. Even though some may be considered old-fashioned, they are included here, as they are seen on pet Poodles from time to time.

THE BELL BOTTOM

1) Clip the Poodle's feet, face, tail, stomach, neck and the selected body pattern. Clip or scissor the body hair following the pattern instructions.

2) Stand the dog on the grooming table with its hindquarters facing you. The bell-bottom leg is achieved with scissors, but preliminary combing of the leg hair is most

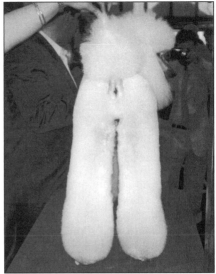

Figure 22-14.

Figure 22-15.

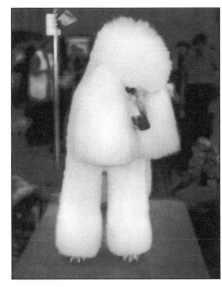

Figure 22-16.

important to the finished shape, as shown in Figure 22-17. Unlike the full-coated leg shape described earlier in this chapter, the fullest part of the leg is the hair at the ankle. Fluff the hair outward from the leg. Do not comb upward, for you will not be able to scissor the modified "bell" shape. Begin scissoring at the hip, following the natural curve of the leg at the stifle joint. As you work down to the hock joint, gradually increase the length of hair until you reach the widest part of the bell at the ankle. Comb the hair downward as you scissor near the ankle. Keep combing and scissoring until you create the desired shape. Finally, scissor all four legs and make them even.

THE BOLERO

1) Clip the Poodle's feet, face, tail, stomach, neck and the selected body pattern. Scissor the body hair following the pattern instructions.

2) Stand the dog on the grooming table with the hindquarters facing you. At the hock joint, point your clippers upward, using a #15 or any of the narrow cutting blades,

and clip a narrow strip around the leg. Make the band about ¼ inch wide on Toy Poodles, about ½ inch wide on Miniatures and about 1 inch wide on Standards. Scissor the hair below each clipped band into a puff. Fluff out the hair above each clipped band with your comb. Scissor off any hairs that fall below the clipped strip, then shape the rest of each leg, as shown in Figure 22-18, following the dog's natural conformation and emphasizing the curve of the stifle joint.

3) Turn the dog around to stand facing you. Notice on the illustration that the clipped bands and puffs on the front legs are lined up evenly with those on the back legs. To avoid making a mistake, use chalk or make a tiny notch in the hair with your shears to mark the spot on each leg where you want to begin clipping. Point your clippers upward, and clip a band of corresponding size completely around each front leg. Scissor the front puffs, making them even in size and shape with those on the back legs. Comb the hair above the clipped bands and trim each into the desired shape.

THE FIFTH AVENUE

1) Clip the Poodle's feet, face, tail, stomach, neck and the selected body pattern. Scissor the body hair following pattern instructions.

2) Stand the dog on the grooming table with the hindquarters facing you. Comb the hair on the back legs upward and outward to fluff the coat. Scissor each back leg as instructed earlier in this chapter, following the dog's natural conformation, emphasizing angulation above the hock joint and the curve of the stifle joint.

3) Turn the dog around to stand facing you. In this variation, as shown in Figure 22-19, a puff is trimmed on each front leg. Start about 1½ inches above the clipped line around the ankle on a Toy Poodle, about 2 to 3 inches on a Miniature and about 3 to 4 inches on a Standard. Clip the front and sides of each front leg up to the elbow with a #15 blade. To take off the hair evenly, clip the back of each front leg in the opposite direction, from the elbow down to the puff with the same blade. Fluff out the hair below the clipped area with a comb, then

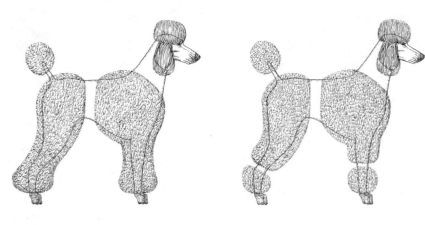

Figure 22-17. The Bell Bottom.

Figure 22-18. The Bolero.

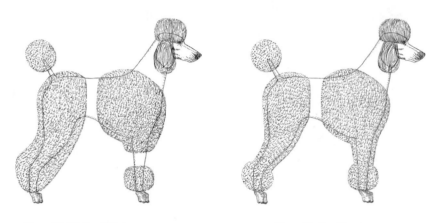

Figure 22-19. The Fifth Avenue.

Figure 20. The Miami.

shape the puff with your shears. Comb the hair on the front of the chest and at the elbows, then scissor any untidy ends that fall below the clipped lines to make the pattern look neat.

THE MIAMI

1) Clip the Poodle's feet, face, tail, stomach, neck and the selected body pattern. Regardless of which pattern you choose, the body hair must always be trimmed short with the Miami leg variation, to blend in with the shorter leg hair, as shown in Figure 22-20.

2) Stand the Poodle on the grooming table with the hindquarters facing you. With a #4 or #5 blade (for a longer length, use a snap-on comb over a #40 blade), clip the outside and inside of each back leg down to the hock joint. Shape the hair below each hock joint into a puff with your shears. Begin by combing the hair downward toward the foot, then scissor off any untidy ends that fall below the clipped line around the ankle. Comb the puff up and scissor any uneven hairs that extend above the clipped line around the hock joint. Fluff out the hair with your comb. Shape each puff with scissors to a length of about 1½ to 2 inches in diameter on a Toy Poodle, 2 to 3 inches in diameter on a Miniature and 3 to 4 inches in diameter on a Standard. Make the back puffs even in size and shape.

3) Turn the Poodle around to stand facing you. Comb out the front legs. To line up the front puffs evenly with those on the back legs, scissor a spot in the hair where each puff will begin. Then, with the same blade you used on the back legs, clip each front leg down to the puff line. Scissor each front puff even in size and shape with those on the back legs.

Pet Poodles can be trimmed into hundreds of styles and variations. Among the currently popular pet styles are the Sporting, Lamb, Retriever, Miami (or Summer), Dutch (and some of its variations), Desi, Sweetheart (or Heart), Swirl and Panda. Instructions and illustrations for all of these styles and variations are included in this chapter, as well as a few others: the Puppy clip (for pets) and the Town and Country, New Yorker and Y.

The Puppy Clip (for Pets)

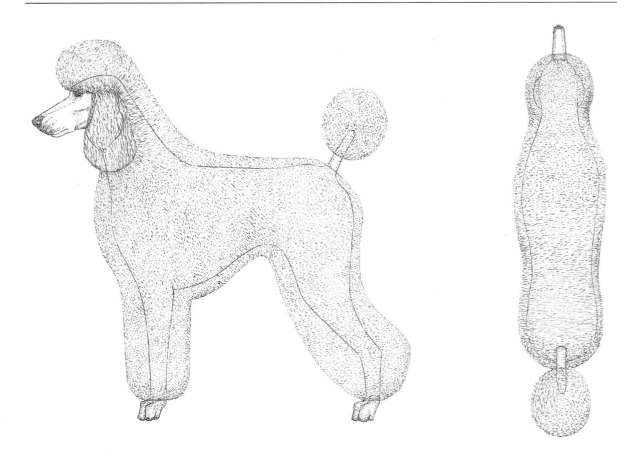

Figure 23-1. The Puppy clip for pets.

The Puppy clip (Figure 23-1) is a charming style that is used on pet Poodles until they are old enough to be trimmed into one of the more mature clips. Because fine, soft puppy hair falls flat and loses its style quickly, it does not adapt well to the more sophisticated pet patterns mentioned in this book until there is enough length, body and volume to the coat. Describing how to execute the Puppy clip in step-by-step detail is difficult because the trim develops gradually as the puppy progresses from babyhood to its first birthday.

By the time Poodle puppies leave their mothers and litter mates for new homes, most have had their feet, face and tail clipped clean. If a Poodle is very young, say six to eight weeks old, this will have been done by the breeder. The reason is that, until they are fully immunized, baby puppies should

Figure 23-2. Before basic clipping.

Figure 23-3. After clipping face, feet and tail.

Figure 23-4. Finishing the clipped area under the throat.

Figure 23-5. An older puppy requiring major shaping with shears.

not go to grooming salons where they can easily come into contact with other dogs. Most breeders start basic clipping at an early age to get a puppy used to being handled and to start accepting the sound of the running clipper. At this early age, no other trimming is necessary. Other than to brush the hair with a soft brush to make it look glossy and keep it from tangling, the coat is left at its existing length.

As a puppy grows older, however, and the hair starts growing longer, wispy ends appear, which must be evened off with shears approximately every four weeks. This type of scissoring is called *tipping* and does not greatly alter the length of the coat. Consider it a sort of pruning. If you let a bush grow wild, its strength dissipates; but when you prune it, the branches grow stronger and healthier. In effect, that is what you are doing

to the puppy's hair, encouraging it to grow into a young adult coat that is as healthy and dense as possible. Figure 23-2 shows a 12-week-old puppy before basic clipping. Figure 23-3 shows the same puppy after the face, feet and tail have been clipped. Other than brushing the hair, no other trimming was done.

As a puppy continues to mature, the stomach can be clipped up to the last rib with a #10 or #9 blade (See Chapter 17, "Clipping the Stomach") and the throat/front of the neck can be clipped with a #10 or #9 blade. Keeping in mind that the throat is a potentially sensitive area, be sure to use the correct blade for your dog's skin type. You may wish to use a #8-1/2 or #7F blade at first. Hold the puppy's muzzle in your free hand and gently lift the head upward. Start an inch or so below the Adam's Apple. Pointing clippers upward, as shown in Figure 23-4, clip to the front of each ear. The clipped area can be **V** shaped or slightly rounded across the neck like a necklace.

When the coat grows longer and starts becoming more profuse,

you can do a bit more all-over shaping with shears. How much scissoring is required depends on the puppy's age. Figure 23-5 shows an older puppy after face, feet and tail have been clipped and before scissoring. As you can see, at this age, major shaping with shears is necessary. The hair at the bottom of each leg (just above the clipped line around the foot) is evened and slightly rounded. The hair on the legs and body is fluffed up and out with a comb, and then shaped with shears to present a well-groomed, finished appearance, following the natural lines of the body. On the back legs, a slight indentation is scissored above the hock joint to show angulation. The hair below the base of the tail is scissored a little shorter to keep the puppy from appearing long-bodied. As you can see in Figure 23-1, the shape gradually curves upward to blend in with the body coat. The front legs are scissored into cylindrical shapes. A pompon is shaped at the end of the tail and the topknot is scissored round in front to keep the hair from falling into the eyes.

The Sporting Clip

The Sporting clip (Figure 23-6) is one of the four show trims recognized by the American Kennel Club. It is acceptable for Poodles that are shown in the Stud Dog and Brood Bitch classes, and in a noncompetitive Parade of Champions at Specialty shows. The Sporting clip also is one of the most popular trims for pets because it is smart looking and easy for new groomers to execute and to maintain.

1) Bathe and fluff dry your Poodle.

2) Follow the instructions in chapter 12 for clipping the feet.

3) Follow the instructions in chapter 13 for clipping the face.

4) Follow the instructions in chapter 14 for clipping the tail and shaping the pompon.

5) Follow the instructions in chapter 15 for clipping the stomach. Clip up to the last rib.

6) Sit the dog on the grooming table, facing you. When clipping the throat and front of the neck, you must choose the blade that is correct for the dog's skin type, as this can be a very sensitive area. Normally, you should clip this area with a #10 or #9 blade. If the Poodle is sensitive, however, and likely to scratch his throat after clipping, use a #8-1/2 or #7F blade. Start an inch or so below the Adam's Apple. If you need to add length to the neck, start slightly lower. Pointing clippers upward, clip to the front of each ear. The clipped area can be **V** shaped or slightly rounded across the neck like a string of pearls. After the neck is clipped, comb the hair at the clipped line upwards, then scissor off any hair that extends above the line to make the pattern look neat. See the section titled "Clipping the Neck" in chapter 13 for photographs.

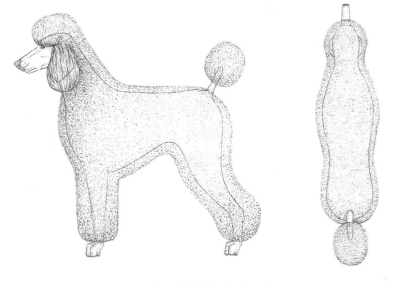

Figure 23-6. The Sporting clip.

7) Stand the Poodle on the grooming table. The hair on the back of the neck and body is clipped off to an even length of from ½ inch to 1 inch depending on the blade being used. Use a snap-on comb attached over a #40 or #30 blade (see page 19 for comb numbers and resulting hair lengths). In the absence of snap-on combs, use a #4F or #5F blade. Start at the base of the skull and clip the hair from the back and sides of the neck. (For a more stylish look on pets, leave a little extra fill-in hair on the back of the neck to slightly enhance the arch of the neck when you shape the topknot later.) Then clip down the center of the back to the base of the tail as shown in Figure 23-9 of a silver Poodle. Using clippers in the same direction, trim off all the hair on top of the body, clipping in long sweeping strokes (Figure 23-8). Do not use clippers below the shoulders and hips, indicated by the dotted lines in Figure 23-7. Clip around these areas then clip the hair between the shoulders and hips on each side of the dog.

Note: F blades are designed to be used on clean hair. If you are

rough-cutting dirty hair, use a #2, #3 or #4 blade; after the dog has been bathed and fluff dried, go over the body again with the appropriate F blade for a more velvety finish.

8) Now lift the front leg on each side and clip the hair under the chest from under the leg to the last rib with the same blade. To tighten the loose armpit skin, stretch the leg forward (Figure 23-10). When you have finished clipping, the hair should be an even length all over the body, with the exception of longer hair on the shoulders and hips, which will be used for blending when the legs are finished.

9) Stand the dog on the grooming table with the hindquarters facing you. Follow the instructions in chapter 22 for finishing the back legs. Fluff up the hair on the hindquarters with a comb, and continue scissoring upward, smoothly blending any longer hair at the top of the legs into the shorter body hair. Skimming over the top of the leg with clippers (Figure 23-11) also will help to smooth the blending.

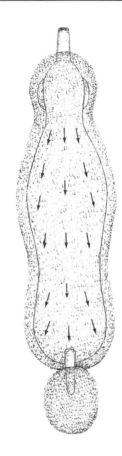

Figure 23-7.

Figure 23-8.

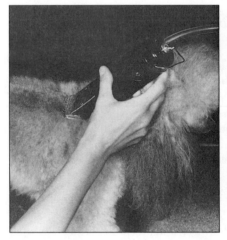

Figure 23-9.

Figure 23-10.

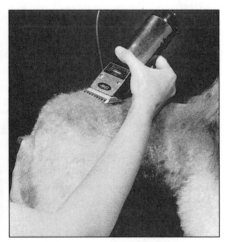

Figure 23-11.

10) Turn the dog around to stand facing you. Follow the instructions in chapter 22 for finishing the front legs. Comb the hair at the shoulders upward. Blend this hair with the short body hair exactly as you did over the hips, by combing the hair up and blending with

clippers and scissors until the line is smooth and sleek.

11) Sit the Poodle on the grooming table, facing you. Comb the hair on the head upward and forward, and follow the instructions in chapter 16 for shaping the topknot. When working at the base

of the skull, remember to blend the topknot hair with the short hair on the neck.

12) Comb the ear feathering downward, and round the ends with scissors to remove any straggly hairs or excessive length for an overall balanced appearance.

The Retriever Clip

Figure 23-12. The Retriever clip.

In the Retriever clip (Figure 23-12) the hair is trimmed very short all over the body and legs, with a scissored topknot and tail. It is, of course, the easiest clip in which to maintain a Poodle. As the hair is trimmed to a uniform overall shortness, this style is a good choice for brood bitches and for Poodles that work in the field or in water. Popular worldwide, the Retriever clip is also called the Curly clip, the Astrakhan, the Karakul, and the Pecorella Persiana (the Italian Persian Lamb variation which is traditionally worn with a donut moustache).

1) Follow the instructions for clipping the feet in chapter 12.

2) Follow the instructions for clipping the face in chapter 13.

3) Follow the instructions for clipping and scissoring the tail in chapter 14. A pompon is optional.

4) Follow the instructions for clipping the stomach in chapter 15. Clip up to the middle of the dog, stopping at the last rib.

5) Sit the Poodle on the grooming table, facing you. Clip the front of the neck with a #10 or #9 blade. If your Poodle is sensitive and likely to scratch at his throat after clipping, use a #8-1/2 or #7. Start an inch or so below the Adam's Apple. Pointing clippers upward, clip to the front of each ear. The clipped area can be **V** shaped or slightly rounded across

the neck like a string of pearls. (See more information and illustrations in chapter 13.)

6) Stand the dog on the grooming table. Depending on how short you want the hair to be, use a #2F, #3F or #4F or a #1 snap-on comb over a #30 or #40 blade. Starting at the base of the skull and going towards the tail, clip off all the hair on the neck, shoulders, back, ribs, hips and under the chest. (For a more stylish look, leave a little extra fill-in hair on the back of the neck to slightly enhance the arch of neck when you shape the topknot.) Use your clippers in long, sweeping strokes in one direction. When clipping under the each front leg, stretch the leg forward to tighten the loose skin, preventing it being nipped by the blade.

Note: F blades are designed to be used on clean hair. If you are rough-cutting dirty hair, use a #2, #3 or #4 blade; after the dog has been bathed and fluff dried, go over the body and legs again with the appropriate F blade for a more velvety finish.

7) Lift up the ear feathering and clip downward, removing the hair on the sides of the neck and the chest. Continue clipping down the outside and inside of each front leg to the ankle.

8) Stand the dog with hindquarters facing you. Use the same blade to start at the hips and clip the outside and underside of each back leg, down to the ankle.

9) Brush up the hair on the body and legs that you just clipped. Scissor around the clipped line above each foot to remove any untidy ends. Then use your shears to neaten any uneven clipped areas and to make them look velvety.

10) Sit the Poodle on the grooming table, facing you. Comb the hair on the head upward and forward. Follow instructions in chapter 16 for shaping the topknot.

11) Comb the ear feathering downward, and round the ends with scissors to remove any untidy ends or excessive length for an overall balanced appearance. On this trim, the hair on the ears also may be clipped short. See chapter 17 for shorter ear styles.

The Lamb Clip

The Lamb clip (Figure 23-13), currently one of the most popular pet styles, is a classic and elegant trim that has the added advantage of being easy to maintain. It is similar in appearance to the Sporting clip, except that the coat is longer and fuller.

1) Bathe and fluff dry your Poodle.

2) Follow the instructions for clipping the feet in chapter 12.

3) Follow the instructions for clipping the face in chapter 13.

4) Follow the instructions for clipping and scissoring the tail in chapter 14.

5) Follow the instructions for clipping the stomach in chapter 15. Clip up to the middle of the dog, stopping at the last rib.

6) Clip the front of the neck. Sit the Poodle on the grooming table, facing you. When clipping the throat and front of the neck, be sure to choose the correct blade for your dog's skin type, as this can be a sensitive area. Normally, you should clip with a #10 or #9 blade. If your Poodle is sensitive, however, and prone to scratching his throat after clipping, use a #8-1/2 or #7F. Start an inch or so below the Adam's Apple. Pointing clippers upward, clip to the front of each ear. The clipped area can be **V** shaped, or slightly rounded across the neck like a necklace would be around your own neck. See the photographs in chapter 13.

7) Study Figure 23-14 and then look again at the finished Sporting clip in Figure 23-6. The body coat on the *true* Lamb clip is trimmed with scissors to an even length all over. To speed up the process, however, professionals often use a snap-on comb attachment over a #30 or #40 blade. The length of the hair is a matter of personal preference although,

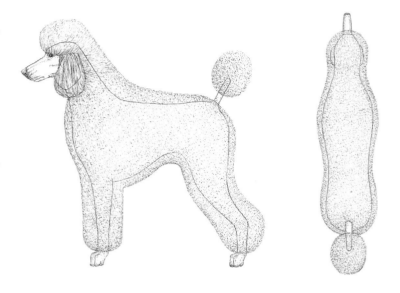

Figure 23-13. The Lamb clip.

as you can see by comparing both clips, it should be longer on the Lamb clip. Generally, the body hair should be about ½ inch long on a Toy Poodle, about 1 inch long on a Miniature Poodle, and about 2 inches long on a Standard Poodle. Keeping overall balance in mind, these measurements can be increased or decreased according to the size of the individual dog.

8) Stand the Poodle on the grooming table. As previously mentioned, the body coat is trimmed to an overall even length. You can accomplish this in either of two methods:

• By scissoring the body coat to the preferred length

• To speed up the scissoring process, by trimming off the excess hair with a medium to long snap-on comb attachment (see page 19 for comb numbers and resulting hair lengths) over a #30 or #40 blade, fluffing the coat up and out with a comb, and then finishing by shaping any uneven areas with your shears.

Most professionals find it faster and easier to use the latter method. If

you choose that method, starting at the base of the skull and clipping towards the tail, use the snap-on comb attachment (over a #30 or #40 blade) to shorten the hair on the back and sides of the neck and down the back to the tail, as directed by the arrows in Figure 23-14. When using clippers over the shoulders and hips, skim over these areas, leaving the hair a little longer. This hair will be used for blending later when the legs are scissored. Clip the hair between the shoulders and hips on each side of the dog, as also shown in Figure 23-14. Always use your clippers in one direction, and in long, sweeping strokes.

9) Now lift the front leg on each side and shorten the chest hair from under the leg to the last rib. To tighten the loose armpit skin, stretch the leg forward. When you have finished clipping, any excessively long hair should be shortened all over the body, with the exception of the slightly longer hair over the shoulders and hips.

10) Stand the dog on the grooming table with hindquarters facing you. Follow the instructions for finishing the back legs in chapter 22.

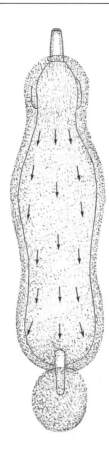

Figure 23-14. Execute the pattern for the Lamb clip in the direction shown by the arrows.

Figure 23-15. Ann Martin, of Sacramento, California, one of America's top competition groomers, is shown here with a beautiful rendering of the Lamb clip on a white Standard Poodle. (Shutter Pup)

11) Fluff up the hair on the hips and hindquarters with your comb. Continue scissoring upward, smoothly blending the longer hair at the top of the legs into the slightly shorter body hair. At this point, you only will need to fluff the body hair up and out and then to scissor finish any areas where the snap-on comb may have left a rough outline. Keep fluffing the body hair up and out and scissoring off a little hair at a time, following the natural contours of the dog, as you scissor forward on the back, over the ribs, the chest and shoulders. The most important point about the Lamb clip is to *scissor the hair to an overall even length.*

12) Stand the Poodle facing you. Follow the instructions for shaping and finishing the front legs in chapter 22.

13) As you scissor upward on the front of the chest, from shoulder to shoulder, blend the leg hair evenly into the body coat. Just as you did on the hindquarters, the lines from the tops of the front legs should flow smoothly upward into the shorter body coat, with no breaks in the hair. Scissor any remaining long hair between the front legs to the same length as the rest of the body.

14) Sit the Poodle facing you. Comb the hair on the head upward and forward, and follow the instructions for shaping the topknot in chapter 16.

15) Comb the ear feathering downward, then round the edges with scissors to remove any wispy hairs or excessive length for an overall balanced appearance.

Figure 23-15 shows a wonderful example of the finished Lamb clip.

The Miami Clip

The Miami clip (Figure 23-16) is very stylish yet easy to maintain. The body and most of the area on all four legs are clipped short. The top-knot and tail are shaped with scissors, as are the puffs on the bottoms of the legs. The Miami clip is an excellent choice for Poodles that live in warm climates. Because this clip is so popular around the world, it is also known by many other names: Summer, Clown, Bikini, Ponjola, Palm Springs and San Tropez.

1) Bathe and fluff dry your Poodle.

2) Follow the instructions for clipping the feet in chapter 12.

3) Follow the instructions for clipping the face in chapter 13.

4) Following instructions for clipping and scissoring the tail in chapter 14.

5) Follow the instructions for clipping the stomach in chapter 15. Clip up to the middle of the dog, stopping at the last rib.

6) Clip the front of the neck. Sit the Poodle on the grooming table, facing you. When clipping the throat and front of the neck, be sure to choose the correct blade for the dog's skin type, as this can be a sensitive area. Normally, you should clip with a #10 or #9 blade. If your Poodle is sensitive, however, and likely to scratch at his throat after clipping, use a #8-1/2 or #7F. Start an inch or so below the Adam's Apple. Pointing clippers upward, clip to the front of each ear. The clipped area can be **V** shaped or slightly rounded across the neck like a string of pearls. See the section titled "Clipping the Neck" in chapter 13 for photographs.

7) Stand the dog on the grooming table. Depending on how short you want the hair to be, use a

Figure 23-16. The Miami clip.

#3-3/4F, #4F, #5F or #7F blade. Starting at the base of the skull and going towards the tail, clip off all the hair on the neck, shoulders, back, ribs, hips and under the chest, as directed by the arrows in Figure 23-17 and shown in Figure 23-18. Use clippers in one direction and in long smooth strokes. When clipping under the front legs, stretch the leg forward to prevent any loose folds of skin from catching in the blade and being cut.

Note: F blades are designed to be used on clean hair. If you are rough-cutting on dirty hair, use a 3-3/4, #4, #5 or #7 blade; after the dog has been bathed and fluff-dried, go over the body and legs again with the appropriate F blade for a more velvety finish.

8) Start under each ear and clip downward, removing the hair on the sides of the neck and down the front of the chest as directed by the arrows in Figure 23-17.

9) Stand the Poodle on the grooming table with his hindquarters facing you. With the same blade, start at the hips and clip the top

and underside of each back leg down to the hock joint. The best way to clip this area without making a mistake and taking off too much hair is to wrap your free hand securely around the leg at the hock joint, as shown in Figure 23-19, then clip downward. This not only protects the hair below the hock joint (which forms the puff on the back leg), but also keeps the leg in place and prevents the dog from moving suddenly.

10) Turn the Poodle to stand facing you. The trickiest part of the Miami clip is setting the puffs on the front legs. They must be evenly lined up with the puffs on the back legs. If they are higher or lower, the trim will look out of balance. Before clipping, use chalk or make a tiny scissor notch in the coat (Figure 23-20) to mark the spot on each leg where you want the puff to begin. Then, with the same blade, clip the front legs from the shoulders down to your mark. Again, the easiest way to avoid taking off too much hair is to wrap your free hand securely around the leg (protecting the hair below your mark) and clipping

Figure 23-17. Executing the Miami clip requires directing
the electric clipper in the direction shown by the arrows.

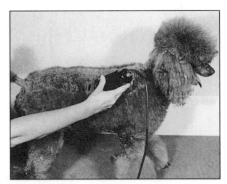

Figure 23-18.

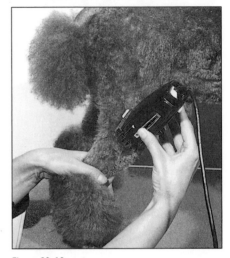

Figure 23-19.

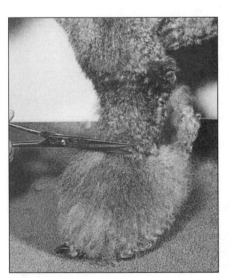

Figure 23-20.

Figure 23-21.

down to the point where you are
holding the leg, as shown in
Figure 23-21.

11) The hair below the hock joint
on each back leg is scissored into

a puff. Use curved shears, if you
have them, for this. Begin by
combing the hair straight down
toward the foot, then scissor
around the ankle (Figure 23-22)
to remove any untidy ends. Then

comb the hair straight up and
scissor off any uneven hairs that
extend above the clipped line
around the hock (Figure 23-23).
If you have used curved shears,
the line at the top and bottom of
the puff will be partially beveled
already. Fluff out the hair with a
comb before beginning to shape
the rest of the puff, then scissor
(Figure 23-24). Figure 23-25
shows a side view of the correct
shape. Because of the conformation of the leg at the hock joint,
the puffs are shaped upward at
the back, making them slightly
oval instead of completely round.
This also enhances the look of
more angulation. From behind,
the puff looks rounded with a
slightly oval appearance. If you
are a beginner, it may take a little
time to get the puffs looking right,
but eventually, with practice, you
will learn how to shape them
correctly. The more often you do

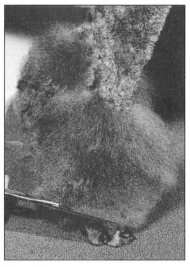

Figure 22-22.

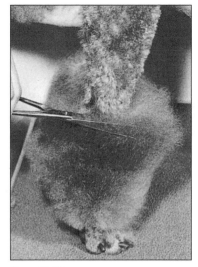

Figure 23-23.

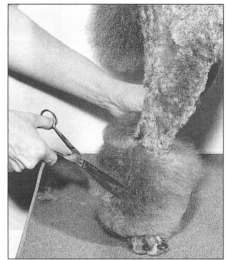

Figure 23-24.

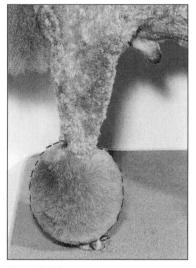

Figure 23-25.

Figure 23-26. The Summer Miami clip.

it, the easier it will become. Keep fluffing the hair out with the comb and taking a little hair off at a time. The bracelets on each leg should be even in size and shape and, when viewed from the side or behind, make the legs look parallel and the feet straight.

12) Shape the front puffs, preferably with curved shears. As you did on the back legs, comb the coat straight down toward the foot, then scissor around the ankle to remove any hair that falls below the clipped line. Then comb the hair straight up, and scissor

off any uneven hairs that extend above the clipped line. Fluff out the hair with your comb, then scissor into shape completely around the leg. The puffs should be slightly oval in shape, and in balance with those on the back legs.

13) Sit the Poodle on the grooming table, facing you. Comb and fluff the topknot hair upward, and follow the instructions in chapter 16 for shaping the topknot.

14) Comb the ear feathering downward, and round the ends with your shears to remove any straggly hairs or excessive length

for an overall balanced appearance. For ear styles with shorter hair, see chapter 17.

The Summer Miami

The Summer Miami clip (Figure 23-26) is an excellent hot-weather clip and it can also be used on badly matted Poodles that must be clipped very short for coat restoration. This variation differs only in the length of body and leg hair. Instead of using the #3-3/4F, #4F, #5F or #7F, trim the hair shorter, with a #8-1/2, #9, or #10 blade.

The Town and Country Clip

The Town and Country clip (Figure 23-27) closely resembles the Dutch clip (page 170). Actually, in certain areas, the Town and Country clip is sometimes called the Royal Dutch clip. The difference between the two styles is in the setting of one pattern line: The jacket line of the Dutch clip is set at the last rib, and on the Town and Country, the jacket is set slightly forward, closer to the shoulders and front legs. Compare Figure 23-27 to Figure 23-43 (page 169) and see how similar they are.

1) Bathe and fluff dry your Poodle.

2) Follow the instructions for clipping the feet in chapter 12.

3) Follow the instructions for clipping the face in chapter 13.

4) Follow the instructions for clipping and scissoring the tail in chapter 14.

5) Follow the instructions for clipping the stomach in chapter 15. For the moment, clip up to the middle of the dog, stopping at the last rib.

6) Sit the Poodle on the grooming table, facing you, to clip the back of the neck. Before beginning, decide how you want to shape the topknot at the nape of the neck: either rounded at the base of the skull or into a **V** shape that converges down to a point in the center of the neck. At this time, you may wish to review Chapter 16, "Shaping the Topknot." If you choose to round the back of the topknot, hold the Poodle's muzzle in your free hand, bend it down slightly and place clippers at the base of the skull. Using a #15 blade, clip down to the point where the neck joins the body. Do *not* clip below that point. If you choose to

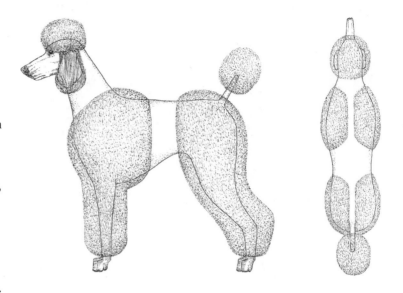

Figure 23-27. The Town and Country clip.

make the **V**, scissor in the basic shape, proportioning the tip in the center of the neck according to its length, then clip around the **V** and down to the point where the neck joins the body. Clip the sides of the neck by lifting each ear and clipping down from under the ear to the same point.

7) Next, clip the front of the neck with a #10 blade. If your Poodle is sensitive, however, and likely to scratch his throat after clipping, use a #9 or #8-1/2. Pointing clippers upward, start an inch or so below the Adam's Apple and clip to the front of each ear. When the neck is completely clipped, the line around it, from front to back, looks like a necklace would around your own neck. See the section titled "Clipping the Neck" in chapter 13 for photographs.

8) Stand the Poodle with his hindquarters facing you to begin setting the pattern. The first step in setting the Town and Country pattern is to clip a narrow strip (about the same width as the base of the tail) from the tail up the

center of the back to the neck. To correctly proportion the width of the strip to the variety of Poodle you are clipping, use a #5/8 blade on a Toy, a #7/8 on a Miniature and a #10 (or #15 blade if you like a closer clip) on a Standard. Start your clippers at the base of the tail and clip straight up the center of the back to the neck, as directed by the arrows in Figure 23-28. If the dog is fussy, have someone steady his front so the strip is not off-center. If you are worried about making the line straight, clip halfway, from the base of the tail to the middle of the dog, then stop. Check to see that the clipped strip is straight. If it is, continue clipping the strip up to the neck. If it is not, make any minor adjustments, then continue.

9) The next step is to make a circular cut over each side of the hindquarters. Start at the center strip, about 1 to 2 inches forward of the hipbones and, with the same blade, clip a circular cut on the side of the dog as indicated by the arrows in Figure 23-28. To assure balance and proportion,

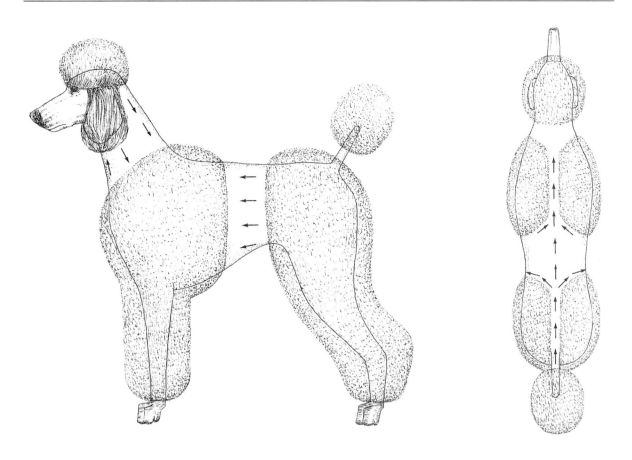

Figure 23-28. Execute the pattern for the Town and Country clip in the direction shown by the arrows.

these measurements can be increased or decreased depending on the size of the dog. Then clip a circular cut over the other side of the dog that exactly matches the first side. *Always* start your circular cuts in front of the hipbones to keep the clipped line over the loins *forward* of the point where the back legs meet the body. Round the corners of the pattern line with your clippers.

10) Start again at the center strip several inches *behind* the front legs, and clip a circular cut on each side of the ribs to form the jacket, as shown in Figure 23-28. Clip off all the hair between the pattern lines on the hindquarters and over the ribs. Clip the hair under the chest to complete the pattern. Again, these measurements can be increased or decreased

depending on the size of the individual dog. Ideally, you are striving to keep the body pattern in balance.

11) Once the body pattern is set, be sure that all clipped areas are the same length, especially if you have used one of the narrow cutting blades to clip the center strip. When used against the growth of hair, these tend to cut close. For a professional finish, all clipped areas should look even and smooth.

12) Stand the dog with his hindquarters facing you. Comb the hair on the back legs up and out to lift and fluff the coat. Follow the instructions in chapter 22 for finishing the back legs. Make both back legs even in size and shape.

13) Comb the hair on the hips and hindquarters. Continue scissoring upward, blending the hair to flow smoothly into the hindquarters, following the natural contours of the dog's body. When shaping the hair at the clipped strip and pattern lines over the hindquarters, fluff it up and out with your comb, then scissor off the untidy hair that falls over the clipped lines. Then use curved shears to bevel, or slightly round, the edges all around the pattern, to remove any sharp lines and create a soft look.

14) Now shape the front. Fluff out the hair on the back, ribs, shoulders and chest with your comb. Begin shaping the jacket by scissoring off any long hair that falls over the clipped strip and pattern lines over the ribs. Next, bevel the edges all the way around the pattern to remove any sharp lines and create a soft look. Scissor the jacket to the same length as the hair on the hindquarters, following the natural contours of the body. Scissor the hair under the chest to the same length. Turn the dog to stand facing you, and shape the front of the chest slightly round, from shoulder to shoulder. Don't leave the hair too long here; it will make the body look long and heavy. Comb the hair up at the clipped line around the neck. Scissor off any hair that falls over the clipped line to make the pattern look neat, then use curved shears to bevel the edges all the way around to remove any sharp lines.

15) Have the Poodle stand facing you. Follow the instructions in chapter 22 for shaping and finishing the front legs.

16) Sit the Poodle to face you. Comb the hair on the head upward and forward, and follow the instructions in chapter 16 for shaping the topknot.

17) Comb the ear feathering downward, then round the edges with scissors to remove any untidy hairs or excessive length for an overall balanced appearance.

Note: You may find it easier to use a medium to long snap-on comb attachment (see page 19 for comb numbers and resulting hair lengths) *over a #30 or #40 blade to remove excess coat and outline the body hair to an overall even length. If the coat is tangle-free, you can use a snap-on comb either before or after shampooing and fluff drying. Once the hair has been reduced to more workable proportions and the basic profile has been blocked in, then set your pattern. Afterwards, fluff the hair up and out with your comb, and finish by hand scissoring.*

The Panda (or Teddy Bear) Clip

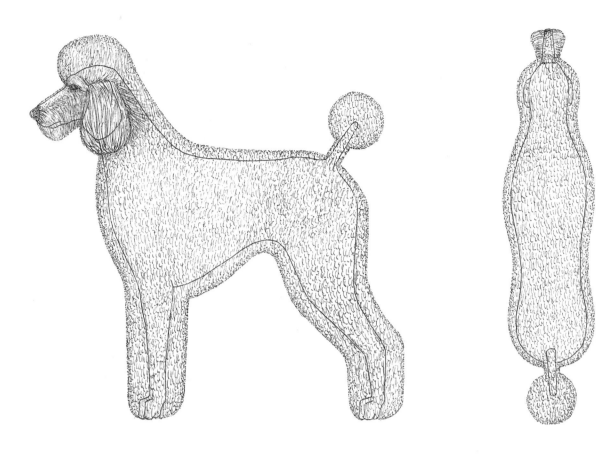

Figure 23-29. The Panda or Teddy Bear clip.

The Panda, or Teddy Bear, clip (Figure 23-29) is ideal for owners who dislike Poodle trims on which the feet, face and tail are closely clipped. It also is a good choice for Poodles that constantly struggle during feet or face clipping, for dogs with foot allergies that are worsened by shaving, for older Poodles and for various Poodle crossbreeds (Cocker/Poodle or Terrier/Poodle, for instance) that neither resemble either distinct breed, nor have true Poodle coat texture. The attractiveness of this trim is that it gives the dog a casual, yet charming, look.

1) Bathe and fluff dry your dog.

2) Clip the hair from between the pads on the underside of each foot. Do not clip the tops of the feet or between the toes.

3) A clipped tail with a pompon at the end is optional. If this is the look you want, follow the instructions for clipping and scissoring the tail in chapter 14. If no clipping is desired, scissor the tail to a length of about 1 inch all over, with or without a pompon at the end.

4) Follow the instructions for clipping the stomach in chapter 15. Clip up to the middle of the dog, stopping at the last rib.

5) Stand the Poodle on the grooming table to face you. Ideally, the look you are trying to achieve is that of a neat and natural-looking dog, almost resembling the Bichon Frise, with no closely clipped areas. The hair on the front and back of the neck and the top and underside of the body is clipped or scissored to a length of about 1 inch.

Clipping the hair to this length is best accomplished with a medium to long snap-on comb (see page 19 for comb numbers and resulting hair lengths) attached to a #30 or #40 blade. This will remove the excess coat and outline the hair to an overall even length. *All* the clipping is done with the growth of hair, from the head to the tail and down the legs. Begin at the base of the skull, and clip the hair on the back and sides of the neck.

Figure 23-30. The Panda or Teddy Bear clip is a good choice for this Cocker-Poodle crossbreed. While not distinctly resembling either breed, his coat is more Poodle-like, but soft-textured, especially around the head.

Figure 23-31. After being bathed and fluff dried, the tail is scissored to a length of about 1 inch all over with no pompon. The back feet are shaped round; the back legs and hindquarters are shaped with scissors. At the top of the leg, the hair blends smoothly into the hindquarters, following the natural contours of the dog's body.

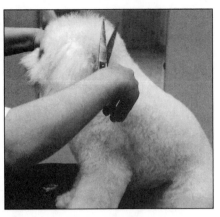

Figure 23-32. Here the groomer is scissoring forward at the back of the neck to create a smooth line that flows into the topknot.

Figure 23-33. Ideally, even though the face is not clipped, you still want to fashion a "Poodley" topknot, following the natural round shape of the skull with more hair remaining in the center of the head and tapering to the sides. However, the finished look of the topknot depends on the coat texture. On this dog, the coat tends to part in the center because of its extreme softness.

Then clip down the middle of the back to the base of the tail. Shorten the hair all over the body and under the chest. Clip over the hindquarters and partially down the back legs. Gently lift up the head and clip downward from the throat to the chest. Clip over the shoulders down to the elbows. When you have finished trimming with the snap-on comb, the hair should be about 1 to 2 inches long, depending on the variety of your Poodle, with longer hair remaining only on the legs, face and head.

6) If you choose to hand scissor the body instead of clipping, begin by fluffing the hair up and out with your comb. Scissor to an even, overall length: the back, over the hips, over the ribs and underneath the chest, over the shoulders, under the ears and down the throat, to give a plush appearance, resembling the look of the Bichon Frise.

7) Stand the dog on the table with the hindquarters facing you. Fluff the hair on the back legs up and out with your comb. Lift the foot and scissor the coat underneath level with the foot pads.

Then scissor neatly around each foot to remove any untidy ends and shape the paw round. Do not remove any hair between the toes. Shape each leg evenly all over, as instructed in Chapter 22, "Styling and Finishing the Legs," following the dog's natural conformation by showing angulation above the hock joint and the curve of the stifle joint.

8) As you scissor upward toward the body, blend the leg hair evenly into the body coat. The lines should flow smoothly from one area into the other, with no breaks in the hair. Scissor the hair under the tail fairly short. This will make the dog look shorter in body and help to keep the anal area clean.

9) Turn the dog around to stand facing you. Fluff the hair on the front legs up and out with your comb. Scissor neatly around each foot to remove any untidy ends, then shape the paw round. As on the rear, do not remove any hair between the toes. Scissor each front leg evenly into cylindrical shapes as instructed in Chapter 22, "Styling and Finishing the

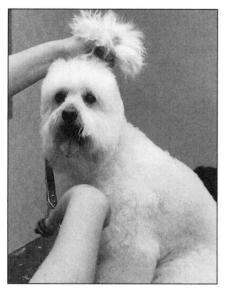

Figure 23-34. Here the dog's ears are lifted in preparation for scissoring the head. The hair has been trimmed short at the stop and the inside corner of each eye. It increases gradually in length toward the sides of the face.

Figure 23-35. The finished Panda clip.

Figure 23-36. Here the Panda or Teddy Bear clip is shown on a silver Standard Poodle with a very dense coat.

Legs," keeping them in balance with the back legs. As you scissor upward toward the chest and shoulders, blend the leg hair evenly into the body coat. Again, the lines should flow smoothly from one area into the other, with no breaks in the hair. Scissor any remaining long hair between the front legs to the same length as the rest of the body.

10) Sit the dog on the grooming table to face you. All the head work is done with shears. Begin by combing out the facial hair. Then use blunt-tipped shears to trim an indentation (like an inverted **V**) between the eyes. The hair here should be short. After the **V** is formed, shorten the hair at the inside corners of each eye with shears, going across the bridge of the nose and under the eyes, gradually increasing the length of hair as you scissor toward the sides of the face and the ears. Lift each ear as you scissor neatly underneath, to make them lie close to the head when they hang in a

natural position. Comb the moustache and beard hair and shape it into the German style, as illustrated on page 90.

11) Comb the topknot hair upward and slightly forward. Shorten the topknot in front to prevent hair from falling into the eyes. Then shape the rest of the head. On this trim, the topknot follows the natural round shape of the skull, with more hair remaining in the center of the head, then tapering to the sides. The hair at the back of the skull blends into the hair on the neck. At the sides of the head, the topknot blends into the ear feathering. Unlike most other Poodle styles, on the Panda trim there is *little* or no scissored separation between the topknot and the ears.

12) Comb the ear feathering downward, and round the ends with your shears to remove any untidy hairs or excessive length for an overall balanced appearance.

Figure 23-37. The charm of the Panda clip is that the finished look will always vary depending on the dog's coat texture and conformation. Here the clip is shown on a crossbreed Poodle with an undocked tail. Because of her long tail, the model in her Panda clip looks very much like a Bichon Frise.

The New Yorker Clip

The New Yorker clip (Figure 23-38), also known as the Banded clip, is easy to trim and to manage. Beginners who are anxious to try pattern setting will find the New Yorker a good choice to start with.

1) Bathe and fluff dry your Poodle.

2) Follow the instructions for clipping the feet in chapter 12.

3) Follow the instructions for clipping the face in chapter 13.

4) Follow the instructions for clipping and scissoring the tail in chapter 14.

5) Follow the instructions for clipping the stomach in chapter 15. Clip up to the middle of the dog, stopping at the last rib.

6) Sit the dog on the grooming table, facing you, to clip the back of the neck. Before beginning, however, you must decide how you intend to shape the topknot at the nape of the neck: either rounded at the base of the skull, or into a **V** shape that converges down to a point in the center of the neck. At this time, you may wish to review Chapter 16, "Shaping the Topknot." If you choose to round the back of the topknot, hold the Poodle's muzzle with your free hand, bend it down slightly, and place clippers at the base of the skull. Using a #15 blade, clip down to the point where the neck joins the body. Do *not* clip below that point. If you choose to make the **V**, scissor in the basic shape, proportioning the tip properly in the center of the neck according to its length, then clip with the #15 blade around the **V** and down to the point where the neck joins the body. Clip the back of the neck, working from ear to ear, using your clippers from the base of the skull to where the neck joins the

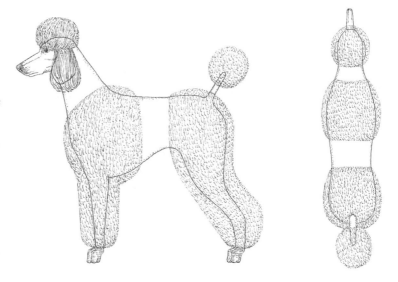

Figure 23-38. The New Yorker clip.

body. Clip the sides of the neck by lifting each ear and clipping down from under the ear to the same point on each side. See photographs illustrating these steps in the section titled "Clipping the Neck" in chapter 13.

7) Next, clip the front of the neck with a #10 blade. If your Poodle is sensitive, however, and likely to scratch at his throat after clipping, use a #9 or #8-1/2. Pointing clippers upward, start an inch or so below the Adam's Apple, and clip to the front of each ear. When the neck is completely clipped, the line from front to back looks like a necklace. Again, refer to chapter 13 for photographs illustrating this step.

8) Stand the Poodle with his hindquarters facing you to begin setting the pattern. Approximately ¾ inch in front of the hipbones on a Toy Poodle, 1 inch on a Miniature Poodle and 2 inches on a Standard Poodle, make a part across the Poodle's back. Be sure the part is *forward* of the hipbones, otherwise the pattern will be totally out of

balance. With a #10 blade (or #15 if you like a closer clip), start at the part and clip forward to the front of the dog, stopping about an inch or two behind the back legs, as shown in Figure 23-39. Keep clipping from the part line toward the front of the dog until you have clipped an even, wide band around the Poodle's middle (Figure 23-39). Clip the hair under the chest to complete the band. Be sure the clipped lines are straight. Make sure there are no untidy hairs within the band you just clipped.

9) Stand the dog with his hindquarters facing you. Comb the hair on the back legs up and out to lift and fluff the coat. Follow the instructions in chapter 22 for shaping and finishing the back legs. Make both back legs even in size and shape.

10) Comb the hair on the hips and hindquarters. Start at the top of the leg and scissor upward, blending the hair to flow smoothly into the hindquarters, following the natural contours of the dog's body. When shaping the hair at

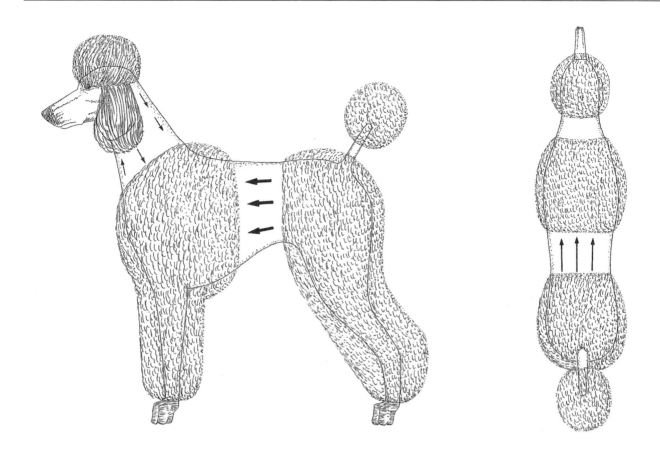

Figure 23-39. Execute the pattern for the New Yorker clip in the direction shown by the arrows.

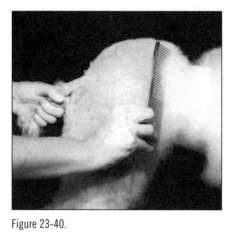

Figure 23-40.

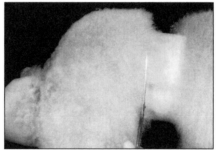

Figure 23-41.

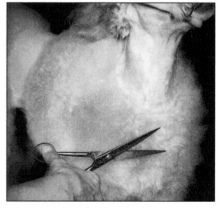

Figure 23-42.

the clipped line forward of the hip bones, fluff it up and forward with your comb, as shown in Figure 23-40, then scissor off the untidy hair that falls in front of the clipped area to form precise pattern lines. Then bevel (or slightly round) the edges all the way around the pattern, as shown in Figure 23-41, to remove any sharp lines and create a soft look. Using curved scissors will speed up the beveling process.

11) Now shape the front. Fluff out the hair on the jacket (the back, ribs, shoulders and chest) with your comb. Begin shaping by scissoring off any superfluous hair that falls over the clipped pattern line at the ribs. Then bevel the edges all the way around the pattern to remove any sharp lines and create a soft look. Next, scissor the jacket to the same length as the hair on the hindquarters,

following the natural contours of the body. Scissor the hair under the chest to the same length. Turn the dog to stand facing you, and shape the front of the chest slightly round, from shoulder to shoulder (Figure 23-42). Don't leave the hair too long here; it will make the body look long and heavy. Comb the hair up at the clipped line around the neck. Scissor off any hair that falls over the clipped line to make the pattern look neat, then bevel the edges all the way around to remove any sharp lines.

12) Have the Poodle stand facing you. Follow the instructions for shaping and finishing the front legs in chapter 22.

13) Sit the Poodle facing you. Comb the hair on the head upward and forward and follow the instructions for shaping the topknot in chapter 16.

14) Comb the ear feathering downward, then round the edges with scissors to remove any untidy hairs or excessive length for an overall balanced appearance.

Note: You may wish to use a medium to long snap-on comb attachment (see page 19 for comb numbers and resulting hair lengths) over a #30 or #40 blade to remove excess coat and outline the body hair to an overall even length. If the coat is tangle-free, you can use a snap-on comb either before or after shampooing and fluff drying. Once the hair has been reduced to more workable proportions, and the basic profile has been blocked in, then set the pattern. Afterward, fluff the hair up and out with your comb, and finish by hand scissoring.

The Dutch Clip

The Dutch clip (Figure 23-43) has been one of the most popular styles for pet Poodles for many decades. In the 1940s and 1950s, when it was truly in vogue, the legs were shaped into puffy pantaloons to create the effect of a Dutchman's baggy trousers, thus the source of the name. Today, although the Dutch clip is not as fashionable as it used to be, a more balanced version, displaying the elegant lines of the body, is favored by professional pet stylists. Around the world, this trim is called many different names, among them the Zazou clip in France, the Francesina clip in Italy and the Jas en Broek in The Netherlands (see page 213). Four variations of the Dutch clip are presented after these instructions.

1) Bathe and fluff dry your Poodle.

2) Follow the instructions for clipping the feet in chapter 12.

3) Follow the instructions for clipping the face in chapter 13.

4) Follow the instructions for clipping and scissoring the tail in chapter 14.

5) Follow the instructions for clipping the stomach in chapter 15. Clip up to the middle of the dog, stopping at the last rib.

6) Sit the dog on the grooming table, facing you, to clip the back of the neck. Before beginning, you must decide how to shape the topknot at the nape of the neck: either rounded at the base of the skull, or into a **V** shape that converges down to a point in the center of the neck. At this time, you may wish to review Chapter 16, "Shaping the Topknot." If you choose to round the back of the topknot, hold the Poodle's muzzle in your free hand, bend it down slightly, and place clippers at the

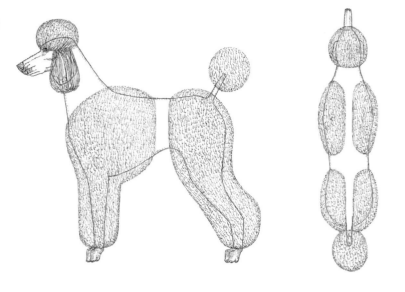

Figure 23-43. The Dutch clip.

base of the skull. Using a #15 blade, clip down to the point where the neck joins the body. Do *not* clip below that point. If you choose to make the **V**, scissor in the basic shape, proportioning the tip in the center of the neck according to its length, then clip around the **V** and down to the point where the neck joins the body. Clip the sides of the neck by lifting each ear and clipping down from under the ear to the same point on the other side. See the photographs in the section titled "Clipping the Neck" in chapter 13.

7) Clip the front of the neck with a #10 blade. If your Poodle is sensitive, however, and likely to scratch at his throat after clipping, use a #9 or #8-1/2. Pointing clippers upward, start an inch or so below the Adam's Apple, and clip to the front of each ear. When the neck is completely clipped, the line from front to back looks like a necklace. See the photographs in chapter 13.

8) Stand the Poodle with his hindquarters facing you to begin

setting the pattern. The first step in setting the Dutch pattern is to clip a narrow strip from the tail straight up the center of the back to the neck. The mistake most beginners make is clipping the strip too wide; it should be about the same width as the base of the tail. To correctly proportion the width of the strip to the variety of Poodle, use a #5/8 blade on a Toy, a #7/8 on a Miniature, and a #10 (or #15 if you like a closer clip) on a Standard. Start your clippers at the base of the tail and clip straight up the center of the back to the neck, as indicated by the arrows in Figure 23-44. Be sure your Poodle stands still while you clip the strip from tail to head. If the dog is fidgety, have someone steady his front so the strip is not off-center. If you are worried about making a straight line, clip halfway, from the base of the tail to the middle of the dog, then stop. Check to see that the clipped strip is straight. If it is, continue clipping the strip up to the neck. If it is not straight, make any minor adjustments, then continue. Figure 23-45 shows the strip after clipping. (The hair that falls over the

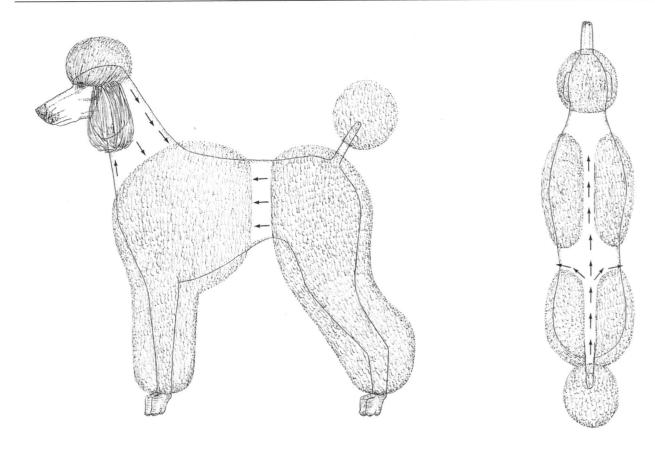

Figure 23-44. Execute the pattern for the Dutch clip in the direction shown by the arrows.

clipped lines will be shaped with shears later.)

9) The next step is to make a circular cut over the hindquarters on each side. Start at the center strip, about 1 to 2 inches forward of the hipbones and, with the same blade, clip a circular cut over the side of the dog (as indicated in Figure 23-44). To assure balance and proportion, these measurements can be increased or decreased depending on the size of the dog. Then clip a strip on the other side of the dog that exactly matches the first side. *Always* start your circular cuts in front of the hipbones to keep the clipped line on the loins *forward* of the point where the back legs meet the body. The corners of the pattern lines should be slightly rounded with clippers.

10) To complete the pattern, use the same blade to clip from the circular cuts on each side of the hindquarters forward, over the loin to the last rib as indicated by the arrows in Figure 23-44. If you have clipped the stomach up to the last rib, as instructed in step 5, the clipped line at the ribs now completely encircles the Poodle's middle and the jacket is formed. Round off the corners of the pattern lines with your clippers.

11) Once the body pattern has been set, be sure that all trimmed areas have been clipped to the same length, especially if you have used one of the narrow cutting blades to clip the center strip. When used against the growth of hair, these tend to cut close. For that professional finish, all clipped areas must look even and smooth.

12) Stand the dog with his hindquarters facing you. Comb the hair on the back legs up and out to lift and fluff the coat. Follow the instructions for shaping and finishing the back legs in chapter 22. Make both back legs even in size and shape.

13) Comb the hair on the hips and hindquarters. Start at the top of the leg and scissor upward, blending the hair to flow smoothly into the hindquarters, following the natural contours of the dog's body. When shaping the hair at the clipped strip and pattern lines over the hindquarters, fluff it up and out with your comb, then scissor off the untidy hair that falls over into the clipped areas (Figure 23-45) to form precise and clean pattern lines. Then use curved shears to bevel, or slightly round, the edges all the way

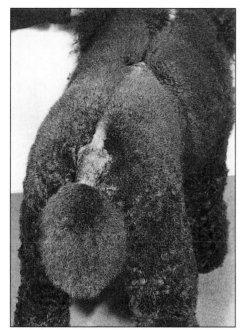

Figure 23-45.

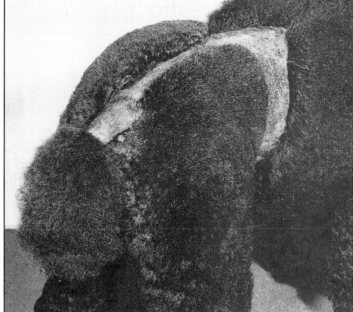

Figure 23-46.

around the pattern, as shown in Figure 23-46, to remove any sharp lines and create a soft look.

14) Now shape the front. Fluff out the hair on the jacket (the back, ribs, shoulders and chest) with your comb. Begin shaping by scissoring off any long hair that falls over the clipped strip and the pattern lines around the last rib. Next, bevel the edges all the way around the pattern to remove any sharp lines and create a soft look. Scissor the jacket to the same length as the hair on the hindquarters, following the natural contours of the body. Scissor the hair under the chest to the same length. Turn the dog to stand facing you, and shape the front of the chest slightly round, from shoulder to shoulder. Don't leave too much hair here; it will only make the body look long and heavy. Comb the hair

up at the clipped line around the neck. Scissor off any hair that falls over the clipped line to make the pattern look neat, then use curved shears to bevel the edges all the way around to remove any sharp lines.

15) Have the Poodle stand facing you. Follow the instructions for shaping and finishing the front legs in chapter 22.

16) Sit the Poodle facing you. Comb the hair on the head upward and forward, and follow the instructions for shaping the topknot in chapter 16.

17) Comb the ear feathering downward, then round the edges with scissors to remove any untidy hairs or excessive length for an overall balanced appearance.

Note: On the Dutch clip and its four variations that follow, you may find it easier to use a medium to long snap-on comb attachment (see page 19 for comb numbers and resulting hair lengths) over a #30 or #40 blade to remove excess coat and to outline the body hair to an overall even length. If the coat is tangle-free, you can use a snap-on comb either before or after shampooing and fluff drying. Once the hair has been reduced to more workable proportions and the basic profile is blocked in, then set the pattern. Afterwards, fluff the hair up and out with your comb, and finish by hand-scissoring.

The Chicago Dutch (A Variation of the Dutch Clip)

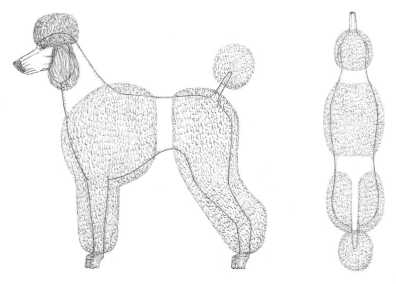

On this popular variation, the Poodle's feet, face, tail, stomach and neck are clipped exactly the same as instructed for the Dutch clip. The only difference is in the setting of the body pattern: Instead of a clipped strip that runs from the base of the tail straight up the backbone to the neck, on the Chicago Dutch (Figure 23-47), the strip is clipped from the base of the tail up the backbone *only to the last rib*, as you can see the top view in the figure. Here is how to clip the body pattern.

1) Stand the Poodle with his hindquarters facing you. Use your comb to make a part completely around the dog's middle at the last rib. Be sure the part is even. Starting at the base of the tail, clip a strip straight up the center of the back, between the hipbones, to the part line at the last rib, as directed by the arrows in Figure 23-48. To correctly proportion the width of the strip to the variety of the Poodle, use a #5/8 blade on Toys, a #7/8 blade on Miniatures and a #10 blade (or #15 if you like a closer clip) on Standards.

2) The next step in the Chicago Dutch is to make a circular cut on each side of the hindquarters to complete the pattern. Start at the center strip, about 1 to 2 inches forward of the hipbones and, with the same blade, clip a circular cut on the side of the dog as indicated in Figure 23-48. Then clip a strip on the other side of the dog that exactly matches the first side. To assure total balance and proportion, these guidelines can be increased or decreased in accordance with the dog's size.

3) Using the same blade, clip the hair on the dog's middle between the circular cuts on each side of

Figure 23-47. The Chicago Dutch.

the hindquarters and the part line around the last rib, as directed by the arrows in Figure 23-48. Be sure the clipped lines are straight and that there are no untidy hairs between the circular cuts.

4) Once the body pattern has been set, be sure that all trimmed areas are clipped to the same length, especially if you have used one of the narrow cutting blades to clip the center strip. When used against the growth of the hair, these tend to cut close. For a professional finish, all clipped areas should look even and smooth.

5) Shape and finish the back legs and hindquarters with your shears as instructed in steps 12 and 13 for the Dutch clip. Remember that there should be a smooth flowing of lines from the body coat down the leg and that the coat should be beveled at the pattern lines to look smooth. Practice will help you learn to bevel the hair where it meets the clipped areas into the sculptured look perfected by professional pet stylists.

6) Comb the hair on the back, over the ribs and on the shoulders and chest up and out to fluff the coat. Scissor the jacket to the same length as the hindquarters, following the natural contours of the dog's body.

7) Shape and finish the front legs with your shears as previously instructed in steps 14 and 15 for the Dutch clip. There should be a smooth flowing of the lines from the body coat down the leg, and the hair should be beveled at the pattern lines with curved shears to look smooth.

8) Sit the Poodle on the grooming table, facing you. Comb the hair on the head upward and forward, and follow the instructions for shaping the topknot in chapter 16.

9) Comb the ear feathering downward, then round the ends with your shears to remove any straggly hairs or excessive length for an overall balanced appearance.

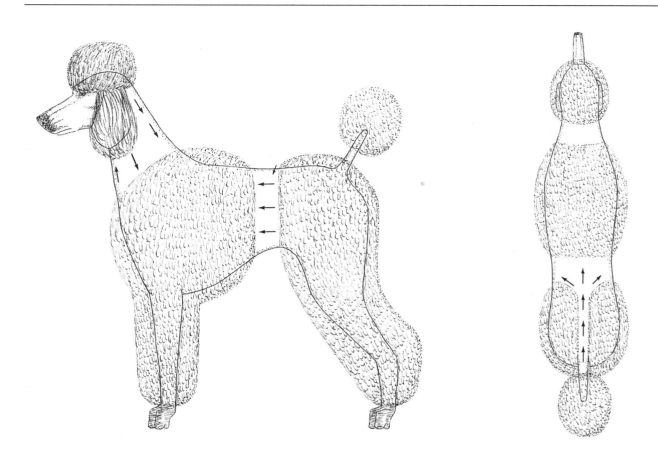

Figure 23-48. Execute the pattern for the Chicago Dutch in the direction shown by the arrows.

The Pittsburgh Dutch (A Variation of the Dutch Clip)

On this variation, the Poodle's feet, face, stomach and neck are clipped exactly the same as instructed under the Dutch clip. The only difference is in the setting of the body pattern: Instead of a clipped strip that begins at the base of the tail and runs straight up the backbone to the neck, on the Pittsburgh Dutch (Figure 23-49), the strip begins at the last rib. Follow these instructions to set the body pattern.

1) Stand the Poodle with his hindquarters facing you. Use your comb to make a part completely around the hindquarters. Start about 1 inch in front of the hipbones on a Toy poodle, and from 1 to 2 inches on a Miniature or Standard Poodle. Be sure the part is even. To assure total balance and proportion, these guidelines can be increased or decreased in accordance with the dog's size.

2) Using a #10 blade (or #15 blade if you like a closer clip), start at the part line in front of the hipbones, and clip forward until you reach the last rib. Clip off all the hair on each side of the loin from the part line up to the last rib, making a clipped band around the middle of the Poodle. Be sure the clipped lines are straight and that there are no untidy hairs within the band you just clipped.

3) Now you are ready to finish clipping the pattern. Use a #5/8 blade on a Toy Poodle, a #7/8 blade on a Miniature and a #10 (or #15 if you like a closer clip) on a Standard. Start at the last rib and clip a narrow strip up the center of the back to the neck, as indicated by the arrows in Figure 23-50. Be sure the dog stands still while you clip the strip. If he is fidgety, have someone steady his front so the strip is not off-center.

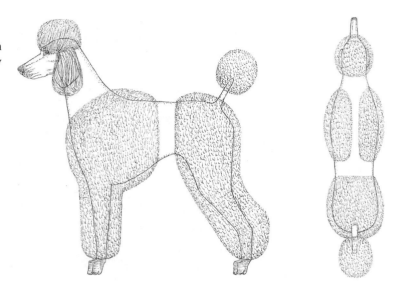

Figure 23-49. The Pittsburgh Dutch.

Use the corner of the clipper blade to round the edges of the strip at the last rib.

4) Once the body pattern has been set, be sure that all trimmed areas are clipped to the same length, especially if you have used one of the narrow cutting blades to clip the center strip. When used against the growth of hair, these tend to cut close.

5) Shape and finish the back legs and hindquarters with your shears as previously instructed for the Dutch clip. Remember that there should be a smooth flowing of lines from the shorter body coat into the longer leg hair. When scissoring near the pattern line, fluff the coat up and out with your comb, then trim off any untidy hairs. Use curved shears to bevel the coat at the pattern line to soften any sharp edges.

6) Comb the hair over the ribs and on the shoulders and chest up and out to fluff the coat. Scissor the jacket to the same length as the hindquarters, following the natural contours of the body. Use your comb to fluff up the hair on each side of the center strip and around the pattern line encircling the ribs. Then used curved shears to scissor around these clipped lines to bevel the hair and soften any sharp edges. Comb the hair up at the clipped line around the neck. Use curved shears to scissor around the neck to bevel the hair and soften any sharp edges.

7) Shape and finish the front legs with your shears, as previously instructed in the Dutch clip. As on the hindquarters, there should be a smooth blending from the short body hair into the longer leg hair.

8) Sit the Poodle on the grooming table, facing you. Comb the hair on the head upward and forward, then follow the instructions for shaping the topknot in chapter 16.

9) Comb the ear feathering downward, then round the ends with your shears to remove any straggly hairs or excessive length for an overall balanced appearance.

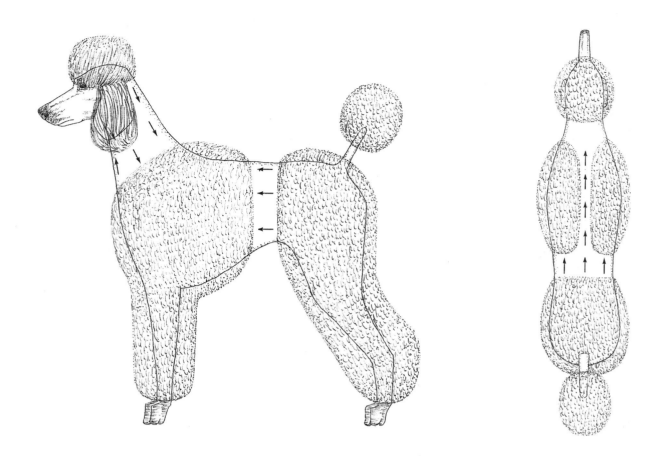

Figure 23-50. Execute the pattern for the Pittsburgh Dutch in the direction shown by the arrows.

The Criss-Cross Dutch (A Variation of the Dutch Clip)

On this variation, the Poodle's feet, face, tail, stomach and neck are clipped in exactly the same manner as instructed under the Dutch clip. There is a slight difference in the setting of the body pattern: When viewed from the top, on the Criss-Cross Dutch (Figure 23-51), the Poodle has a cross in the middle of his back. Here is how to clip the body pattern.

1) Stand the Poodle with his hindquarters facing you. The first step is to clip a narrow strip from the base of the tail straight up the center of the back to the neck, as directed by the arrows in Figure 23-52. To correctly proportion the width of the strip to the variety of Poodle you are clipping, use a #5/8 blade on Toy Poodles, a #7/8 blade on Miniature Poodles and a #10 blade (or #15 if you like a closer clip) on Standards. Be sure the dog stands still when you clip the strip from tail to head. If he is fidgety, have someone steady his front so the strip is not off-center. If you are worried about clipping a straight line, clip halfway, from the base of the tail to the middle of the dog, then stop. Check to see that the line is straight. If it is, continue clipping the strip up to the neck.

2) The next step is to clip a narrow strip around the middle of the dog to complete the pattern. It's easier if you part the hair first with a comb. Make an even part completely around the dog's middle, just in back of the last rib. Then, using the same blade, clip the strip around each side of the dog, as indicated in Figure 23-52. Use the corner of the blade to round the edges of the strips at the center of the back and the neck.

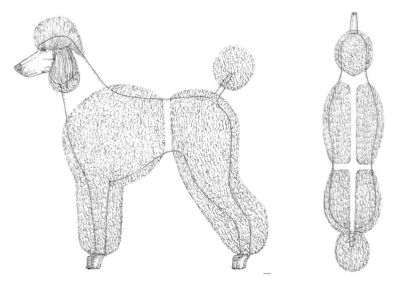

Figure 23-51. The Criss-Cross Dutch.

3) Shape and finish the back legs with your shears as instructed in steps 12 and 13 for the Dutch clip.

4) Fluff out the hair on the hips and hindquarters with your comb. Shape the hindquarters, following the natural contours of the body, keeping in mind that the hair on the body should flow smoothly down to blend with the longer hair on the legs. When shaping the hair near the edges of the clipped strip, comb it up and out, then scissor off all the hair that falls over the clipped lines to make the pattern look neat. Use curved shears to bevel the hair at pattern lines to soften any sharp edges.

5) Comb the hair on the back, over the ribs and on the shoulders and chest up and out to fluff the coat. Scissor the jacket to the same length as the hindquarters, following the natural contours of the body.

6) Shape and finish the front legs with your shears as instructed in steps 14 and 15 for the Dutch clip. As on the hindquarters, there

should be a smooth flowing of the lines from the shorter body coat to blend with the longer leg hair. When shaping near the edges of the clipped strip up the center of the back and around the neck, comb the coat up and out, then scissor off all the hair that falls over the clipped lines to make the pattern look neat. Use curved shears to bevel the hair at the pattern lines to soften any sharp edges.

7) Sit the Poodle on the grooming table, facing you. Comb the hair on the head upward and forward, and follow the instructions for shaping the topknot in chapter 16.

8) Comb the ear feathering downward, then round the ends with your shears to remove any straggly hairs or excessive length for an overall balanced appearance.

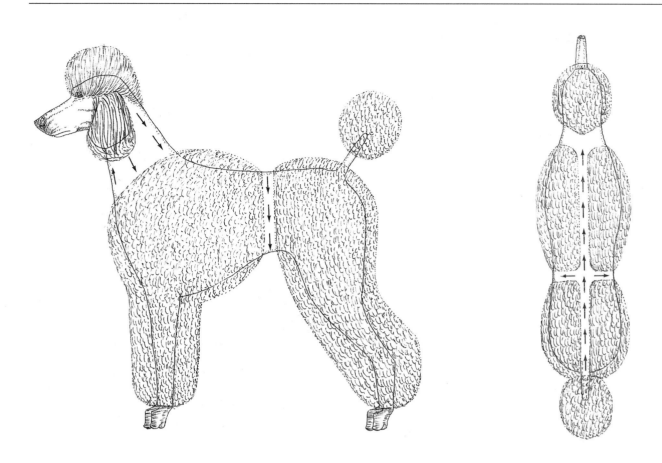

Figure 23-52. Execute the pattern for the Criss-Cross Dutch in the direction shown by the arrows.

The Pajama Dutch (A Variation of the Dutch Clip)

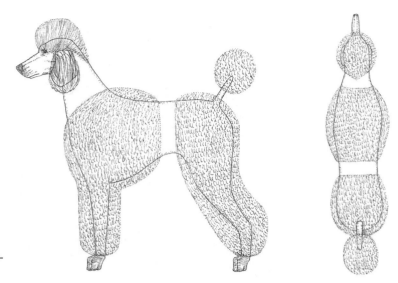

Figure 23-53. The Pajama Dutch.

On this variation, the Poodle's feet, face, tail, stomach and neck are clipped the same as instructed under the Dutch clip. The only difference is in the setting of the body pattern: There is no narrow clipped strip that runs from the base of the tail up the backbone to the neck, only a clipped band around the middle of the dog. The Pajama Dutch (Figure 23-53) also bears a resemblance to the New Yorker clip (Figure 23-38); on that style, however, the clipped band is much broader. Follow these instructions to set the body pattern.

1) Stand the Poodle with his hindquarters facing you. Use your comb to make a part completely around the hindquarters. Start about 1 inch in front of the hip-bones on Toy Poodles, and from 1 to 2 inches on Miniatures or Standard Poodles. To assure total balance and proportion, these guidelines can be increased or decreased in accordance with the dog's size. Be sure the part is even. Using a #10 blade (or #15 if you like a closer clip), clip forward from the part line and stop just before you reach the last rib. Keep clipping from the part line, over the loins, up to the last rib until you have made a wide clipped band around the middle of the Poodle, as indicated by the arrows in Figure 23-54. Be sure the clipped lines are straight and that there are no untidy hairs within the band you just clipped.

2) Shape and finish the back legs and hindquarters with your shears as instructed in steps 12 and 13 for the Dutch clip. Remember that there should be a smooth flowing of lines from the shorter body coat into the longer leg hair. When shaping the coat near the clipped band, comb it up and out, then scissor off any untidy hairs that fall over the pattern line. Use curved shears to bevel the hair at the pattern lines to soften any sharp edges.

3) Comb the hair on the back, over the ribs, on the shoulders and chest up and out to fluff the coat. Scissor the jacket to the same length as the hindquarters, following the natural contours of the body.

4) Shape and finish the front legs with your shears as instructed in steps 14 and 15 for the Dutch clip. As on the hindquarters, there should be a smooth flowing of the lines from the shorter body coat blending into the longer leg hair. Use curved shears to bevel the hair at the pattern lines to soften any sharp edges.

5) Sit the Poodle on the grooming table, facing you. Comb the hair on the head upward and forward, and follow the instructions for shaping the topknot in chapter 16.

6) Comb the ear feathering down-ward, then round the ends with your shears to remove any straggly hairs or excessive length for an overall balanced appearance.

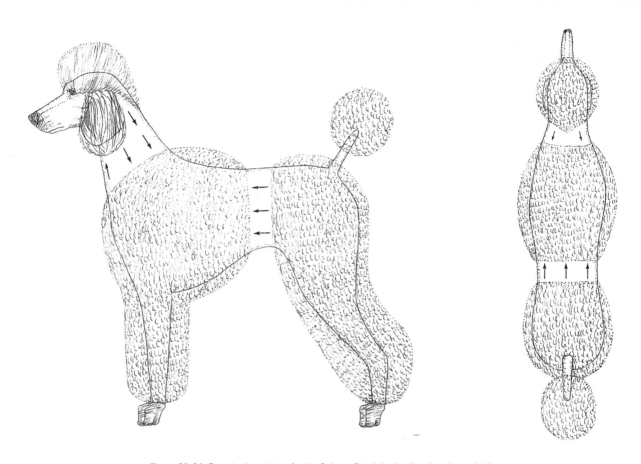

Figure 23-54. Execute the pattern for the Pajama Dutch in the direction shown by the arrows.

The Sweetheart or Heart Clip

The Sweetheart or Heart clip (Figure 23-55) is a stylish trim. With its soft heart-shaped lines, it looks lovely regardless of whether the Poodle wearing it is a Toy, Miniature or Standard.

1) Bathe and fluff dry your Poodle.

2) Follow the instructions for clipping the feet in chapter 12.

3) Follow the instructions for clipping the face in chapter 13.

4) Follow the instructions for clipping and scissoring the tail in chapter 14.

5) Follow the instructions for clipping the stomach in chapter 15. Clip up to the middle of the dog, stopping at the last rib.

6) Sit the dog on the grooming table, facing you, to clip the back of the neck. Before beginning, decide how you want to shape the topknot at the nape of the neck: either rounded at the base of the skull, or into a **V** shape that converges down to a point in the center of the neck. At this time, you may wish to review Chapter 16, "Shaping the Topknot." If you choose to round the back of the topknot, hold the Poodle's muzzle in your free hand, bend it down slightly, and place clippers at the base of the skull. Using a #15 blade, clip down to the point where the neck joins the body. Do *not* go below that point. If you choose to make the **V**, scissor in the basic shape, proportioning the tip in the center of the neck according to its length, then clip around the **V** and down to the point where the neck joins the body. Clip the sides of the neck by lifting each ear and clipping down from under the ear to the same point on both sides. Photographs showing how to complete these steps are in the section titled "Clipping the Neck" in chapter 13.

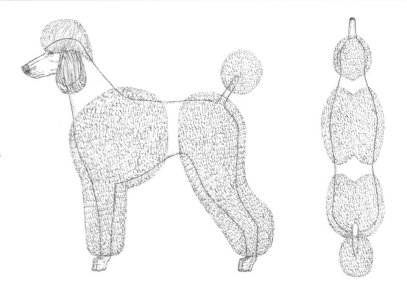

Figure 23-55. The Sweetheart or Heart clip.

7) Next, clip the front of the neck with a #10 blade. If your Poodle is sensitive, however, and likely to scratch at his throat after clipping, use a #9 or #8-1/2 blade. Pointing clippers upward, start an inch or so below the Adam's Apple, and clip to the front of each ear. When the neck is finished, the line around it looks like a string of pearls you would wear around your own neck. (See the photographs in chapter 13.)

8) Stand the Poodle with his hindquarters facing you to begin setting the pattern. Study Figure 23-56 and notice that two heart shapes are clipped on the back.

Approximately 1 inch in front of the hipbones on a Toy Poodle, 2 inches on a Miniature Poodle and 3 inches on a Standard Poodle, make a part across the back. Be sure the part is *forward* of the hipbones, otherwise the pattern will be totally out of balance. Use a #10 blade and, starting at the part line as shown in Figure 23-56, clip forward, stopping just about at the last rib. Make a band completely around the dog's middle by clipping from the part line up to the last rib. Be sure the clipped lines are straight and that there are no untidy hairs within the band you just clipped.

9) Now you are ready to shape the hearts. Study the top view shown in Figure 23-55. The point of each heart must be in the center of the back; if they are off-center the pattern will look unbalanced. If you are a beginner, to avoid making mistakes with the clippers, try sculpting in the points of the hearts with your shears beforehand. Then use the edge of the clipper blade to clip the heart points.

10) Stand the dog with his hindquarters facing you. Comb the hair on the back legs up and out to lift and fluff the coat. Follow the instructions for shaping and finishing the back legs in chapter 22. Make both back legs even in size and shape.

11) Fluff out the hair on the hips and hindquarters with your comb. Continue scissoring upward, blending the hair to flow smoothly into the hindquarters. When scissoring around the clipped heart,

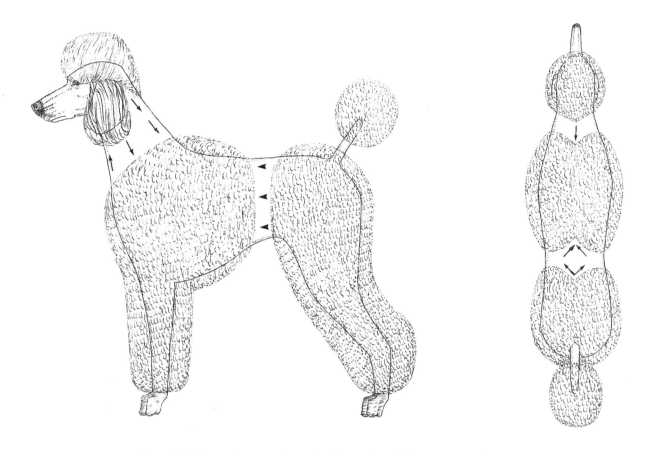

Figure 23-56. Execute the pattern for the Sweetheart or Heart clip in the direction shown by the arrows.

comb the hair up and forward, then cut off any untidy hairs that fall over the clipped lines to make your pattern clean and precise. Use curved shears to bevel, or slightly round, the edges all the way around the heart to remove any sharp lines and create a soft look.

12) Next, shape the front. Fluff out the hair on the back, ribs, shoulders and chest with your comb. Begin shaping by scissoring off any untidy hairs that fall over the clipped heart and the pattern lines around the last rib. Bevel the edges all the way around the pattern to remove any sharp lines and create a soft look. Scissor the jacket to the same length as the hair on the hindquarters, following the natural contours of the body. Scissor the hair under the chest to a balanced, even length. Turn the dog to stand facing you, and shape the front

of the chest slightly round from shoulder to shoulder. Leaving the hair too long here will make the body look long and heavy. Comb the hair up at the clipped line around the neck. Scissor off any hair that falls over the clipped line to make the pattern look neat, then use curved shears to bevel the edges all the way round to remove any sharp lines.

13) Have the Poodle stand facing you. Follow the instructions for shaping and finishing the front legs in chapter 22. Be sure to make both front legs even in size and shape, and see that they are in balance with the back legs.

14) Sit the Poodle to face you. Comb the hair on the head upward and forward, and follow the instructions for shaping the topknot in chapter 16.

15) Comb the ear feathering downward, then round the edges with scissors to remove any untidy hairs or excessive length for an overall balanced appearance. See chapter 17 for more information about finishing the ears.

Note: You may find it easier to use a medium to long snap-on comb attachment (see page 19 for comb numbers and resulting hair lengths) over a #30 or #40 blade to remove excess coat and outline the hair to an overall even length. If the coat is tangle-free, you can use a snap-on comb either before or after shampooing and fluff drying. Once the hair has been reduced to more workable proportions and the basic profile has been blocked in, then clip in the pattern. Afterwards, fluff the hair up and out with your comb, and finish by hand-scissoring.

The Desi Clip

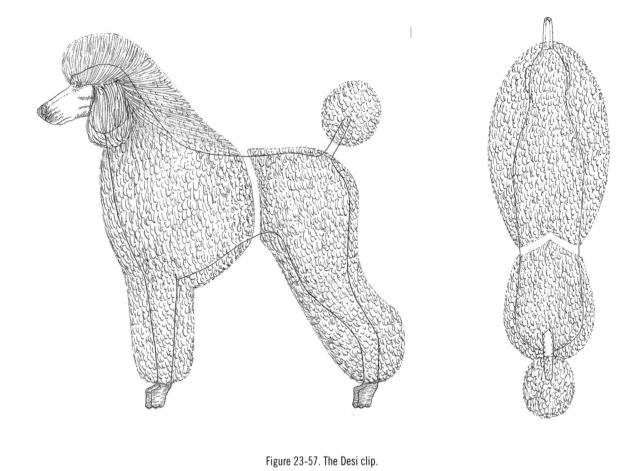

Figure 23-57. The Desi clip.

The Desi clip (Figure 23-57) was designed by Elizabeth Paul of Satellite Beach, Florida, one of the world's top-winning competition pet stylists. Liz created the Desi clip as an elegant pet version of the English Puppy Lion clip (see Figure 24-1 in Chapter 24, "The International Scene"), currently one of the most popular trims seen in the British show ring. Like the Puppy Lion clip, there is a long mane in front with short hair on the hindquarters, but everything is scissored to a shorter, more manageable length. The Desi trim requires expert scissor work and a practiced eye to achieve balance and symmetry.

1) Bathe and fluff dry your Poodle.

2) Follow the instructions for clipping the feet in chapter 12.

3) Follow the instructions for clipping the face in chapter 13.

4) Follow the instructions for clipping and scissoring the tail in chapter 14. As you can see in the top view of the Desi clip (Figure 23-57), the base of the tail should be clipped to an inverted **V**.

Sit the dog on the grooming table, facing you, to clip the front of the neck. Choose the blade that is correct for your dog's skin type, as this can be a very sensitive area. Normally you should use a #10 or a #9 blade. If your Poodle is sensitive, however, and prone to scratching at his throat after clipping, use a #9 or #8-1/2.

Pointing clippers upward, start an inch or so above the Adam's Apple, and clip to the front of each ear. The clipped area can be **V** shaped or slightly rounded across the neck like a string of pearls. (See the photographs in the section titled "Clipping the Neck" in chapter 13.)

5) Stand the Poodle to face you to begin setting the body pattern. Study Figure 23-57. Notice that the pattern line encircles the last rib, *curving around the rib*, and ends in an inverted **V** in the center of the back. Setting this pattern line around a dog's waist is not easy. Therefore, if you are attempting the Desi for the first time, especially on a Poodle with an abundance of coat, the easiest way to fix the pattern is to cut the line in with curved shears, and then set it with clippers. Once the basic line is scissored in, use a #5/8 or #7/8 blade to clip it.

6) Shape the top of the hindquarters. Comb the hair up and out. Shape this area short and level with your shears. Scissor the hair tight under the tail to make the dog appear as short in back as possible.

7) Comb the hair on the back legs up and out to lift and fluff the coat. Follow the instructions for shaping and finishing the back legs in chapter 22. Make both legs even in size and shape. At the top of each leg, scissor upward, blending the hair to flow smoothly into the hindquarters, following the natural contours of the dog's body. When shaping the hair at the clipped pattern line, fluff it up and forward with your comb, then scissor off any untidy hairs that fall over the clipped line. Then use curved shears to bevel the edges around the pattern to remove any sharp lines, creating a soft look.

8) The next step is to shape the mane in front. Begin by combing the hair at the pattern line encircling the last rib. Use curved shears to scissor off untidy hairs that fall in back of the clipped line. Next, bevel the edges all the way around the pattern with curved shears to remove any sharp lines and create a soft look in the front.

9) The mane is shaped round with curved shears. The hair increases in length as you work forward to the neck. The length of the mane hair is a matter of personal preference. A fuller mane is more pleasing to the eye, but it is more difficult to maintain between trimmings. Once you become familiar with the Desi clip, you will learn from experience which length is best for your dog.

Round the hair under the chest, then turn the dog to stand facing you and shape the front of the chest round, from shoulder to shoulder. As you did under the tail, keep the hair on the chest short and tight to avoid making the dog look long in body. Lift each ear leather, and scissor underneath to complete the round mane.

10) Follow the instructions for shaping and finishing the front legs in chapter 22.

11) Sit the Poodle to face you. Fluff the hair on the head upward and forward with your comb, and follow basic instructions for finishing the topknot. Before you begin, study Figure 23-57 again. To balance the topknot with the mane and create a smooth arched line that flows into the longer hair on the neck, the topknot is shaped a little wider and fuller than usual. In front of the eyes, it is as clean as usual, but leans *slightly* forward. When the topknot is shaped in this manner, it adds reach of neck and height to the dog, creating a very elegant finished picture.

12) Comb the ear feathering downward, then round the edges with scissors to remove any untidy hairs or excessive length for an overall balanced appearance.

Note: Although the final look may not be as plush looking as a complete scissor finish, you can use a medium to long snap-on comb attachment (see page 19 for comb numbers and resulting hair lengths) over a #30 or #40 blade to remove excess coat and reduce the hair to more workable proportions. When doing this, however, you must leave extra length on the back of the neck, to blend the topknot and neck into the mane. Fluff the hair up and out with your comb and then used curved shears to achieve a balanced shape.

Figure 23-58. Elizabeth Paul, of Pampered Paws, Satellite Beach, Florida, designed the Desi clip. One of the world's premier competition groomers, Liz has won over 45 "Best Groomed Dog" and "Best All-Around Groomer" wins and is the only person to win the coveted title of "Intergroom International Groomer of the Year" three times. As of the publication date of this book, Liz has been a member of every GroomTeam USA squad since 1989, bringing home many medals for the United States. Pictured with Liz is Jerry Schinberg, organizer of the All-American Grooming Show, which is held annually in August in the Greater Chicago area. Mr. Schinberg's contest and seminar, first organized in 1973, is the oldest annual pet grooming event.

The Y Clip

This eye-catching style was designed by Kathy Rose, of Boynton Beach, Florida, a multiple grooming competition winner and member of four different GroomTeam USA squads that represented American pet stylists in world team competition. If you like the look of the Lamb clip, the Y clip (Figure 23-59) is a charming alternative that adds a little extra pizzazz. Actually, all you need do is style your Poodle in the Lamb clip, and then trim in the **Y** pattern with a #5/8, #7/8 or #10 blade. The Y clip is easy to maintain and is attractive on Poodles of all sizes and conformation.

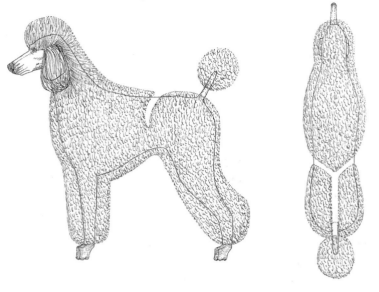

Figure 23-59. The Y clip.

1) Bathe and fluff dry your Poodle.

2) Follow the instructions for clipping the feet in chapter 12.

3) Follow the instructions for clipping the face in chapter 13.

4) Follow the instructions for clipping and scissoring the tail in chapter 14.

5) Follow the instructions for clipping the stomach in chapter 15. Clip up to the middle of the dog, stopping at the last rib.

6) Clip the front of the neck with a #10 or #9 blade. Sit the Poodle on the grooming table, facing you. Keeping in mind that this can be a very sensitive area, be sure to use the correct blade for your dog's skin type. If your Poodle is sensitive and prone to scratching at his throat after clipping, use a #7F or #8-1/2 blade. Start an inch or so below the Adam's Apple. Pointing clippers upward, clip to the front of each ear. The clipped area can be **V** shaped or slightly rounded (like a necklace) across the neck. (See the photographs in the section titled "Clipping the Neck" in chapter 13.)

7) The easiest way to execute the **Y** pattern is to trim the body to an overall even length, as you would do for the Lamb trim, and *afterwards clip in the* **Y** *with a narrow cutting blade*. Follow steps 8 and 9 of the Lamb clip on page 155 for trimming the body hair. You can accomplish this by either of two methods:

   a) Scissoring the body coat to an overall length: about ½ inch long on a Toy Poodle, 1 inch long on a Miniature Poodle and 2 inches long on a Standard Poodle. Keeping overall balance in mind, these estimated hair lengths can be increased or decreased according to the size of the dog.

   b) Shortening the overall body coat to the lengths previously suggested by clipping with a medium to long snap-on comb attachment (see page 19 for comb numbers and resulting hair lengths) over a #30 or #40 blade.

8) Once the body coat is outlined to an overall even length, you are ready to clip the **Y**. The first step in setting the pattern is to clip a narrow strip, starting at the base of the tail, up the center of the backbone, stopping just before you reach the last rib at the middle of the dog, as shown in Figure 23-60. To correctly proportion the width of the strip to the variety of the dog, use a #5/8 blade on a Toy Poodle, a #7/8 blade on a Miniature Poodle and a #10 blade (or #15 if you prefer a closer clip) on a Standard Poodle.

9) The next step is to clip the branches of the **Y** on each side of the dog. Starting at the center strip, about ½ to 2 inches forward of the hipbones (depending on the variety of the Poodle), use the same blade to clip a forward-and-downward curved strip, as shown from the top and in profile in Figure 23-60, on each side of the dog. *The end of each branch of the* **Y** *should arc slightly backward, almost tapering to a point,* and

Figure 23-60. Execute the pattern for the Y clip in the direction shown by the arrows.

should fall just below the broadest point of the Poodle's rib cage.

10) Stand the dog on the grooming table with hindquarters facing you. Follow the instructions for finishing the back legs in chapter 22.

11) Fluff up the hair on the hips and hindquarters with your comb. Continue scissoring upward, smoothly blending the longer hair at the top of the legs into the slightly shorter body hair. At this point, if you have shortened the body coat to an overall even length by scissoring or by clipping with a snap-on comb attachment, you will only need to fluff the coat up and out and lightly scissor finish any uneven areas. When shaping the hair at the clipped strip up the backbone and the

branches of the **Y**, fluff it up and out with your comb, and scissor off any untidy hairs that fall over the clipped areas to form crisp, precise pattern lines. Then use curved shears to bevel, or slightly round, the edges all the way around the pattern to remove any sharp lines and create a soft look. Keep fluffing the body hair up and out and scissoring off a little hair at a time, following the natural contours of the dog, as you scissor forward on the back and over the ribs, the chest and shoulders.

12) Have the Poodle stand facing you. Follow the instructions for shaping and finishing the front legs in chapter 22.

13) As you scissor upward on the front of the chest, from shoulder

to shoulder, blend the leg hair evenly into the body coat. Just as you did on the hindquarters, the lines from the tops of the front legs should flow smoothly upward into the shorter body coat, with no breaks in the hair. Scissor any remaining long hair between the front legs to the same length as the rest of the body.

14) Sit the Poodle to face you. Comb the hair on the head upward and forward, and follow the instructions for shaping the topknot in chapter 16.

15) Comb the ear feathering downward, then round the edges with scissors to remove any wispy hairs or excessive length for an overall balanced appearance.

The Swirl Clip

The elegant Swirl clip (Figure 23-61) was designed by Kathleen Putman, of Plano, Texas, a member of five different GroomTeam USA squads that represented American pet stylists in world team competition. This artistic pattern, with the swirl curving around the middle of the Poodle, can be trimmed in two ways: the first with the curve pointing towards the hindquarters and the second with the curve pointing towards the front of the dog. The Swirl clip requires proficient clipper and scissor work along with a practiced eye to achieve balance and symmetry. Beginning groomers should not attempt either pattern of the Swirl clip until they master the art of clipping narrow pattern lines and making them even in position, size and shape on both sides of the Poodle's body.

The Swirl clip is best accomplished by first styling the Poodle in the Lamb clip and then trimming in the narrow curving lines with a #5/8 or #7/8 blade.

1) Bathe and fluff dry your Poodle.

2) Follow the instructions for clipping the feet in chapter 12.

3) Follow the instructions for clipping the face in chapter 13.

4) Follow the instructions for clipping and scissoring the tail in chapter 14.

5) Follow the instructions for clipping the stomach in chapter 15. Clip up to the middle of the dog, stopping at the last rib.

6) Clip the front of the neck with a #10 or #9 blade. Sit the Poodle on the grooming table, facing you. Keeping in mind that this can be a very sensitive area, be sure to use

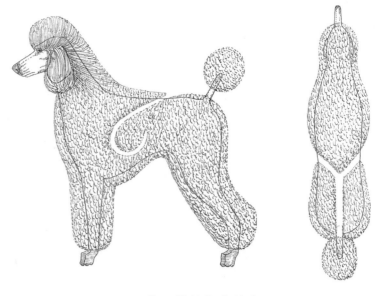

Figure 23-61. The Swirl clip.

the correct blade for your dog's skin type. If your Poodle is sensitive and prone to scratch at his throat after clipping, use an #8-1/2 or a #7F. Start an inch or so below the Adam's Apple. Pointing clippers upward, clip to the front of each ear. The clipped area can be **V** shaped or slightly rounded (like a necklace) across the neck. (See the section titled "Clipping the Neck" in chapter 13.)

7) The most efficient way to execute the Swirl is to trim the body first to an overall even length, as you would do for the Lamb clip, and *afterwards clip in the pattern lines with a narrow cutting blade.* Follow steps 8 and 9 of the Lamb clip on page 155 for trimming the body coat. You can accomplish this by either of two methods:

a) Scissoring the body coat to an overall length: about ½ inch long on a Toy Poodle, 1 inch long on a Miniature Poodle and 2 inches long on a Standard Poodle. Keeping overall balance in mind, these estimated hair lengths can

be increased or decreased according to the size of the dog.

b) Shortening the overall body coat to the lengths previously suggested by clipping with a medium to long snap-on comb attachment (see page 19 for comb numbers and resulting hair lengths) over a #30 or #40 blade.

8) Once the body coat is outlined to an overall even length, you are ready to clip the Swirl pattern. The first step is to clip a narrow strip, starting at the base of the tail, up the center of the backbone, stopping an inch or so behind the last rib, as shown in Figure 23-62. Use a #5/8 blade on a Toy Poodle and a #7/8 blade on a Miniature or Standard Poodle.

9) Now comes the tough part—clipping the curved line on each side of the Poodle. Even the most experienced groomers find it difficult to clip the narrow swirling lines freehand and make them even in placement, size

Figure 23-62. Execute the pattern for the Swirl clip in the direction shown by the arrows.

and shape. Consequently, most professionals use some object as a template or guide: a large plastic soda cup for a Standard Poodle, for instance, or an aerosol can lid for a Miniature or Toy Poodle make excellent templates. Place your template in the center of the Poodle's side. Hold it in place and, with the same narrow blade, clip about two-thirds of the way around the template, as indicated by the arrows in Figure 23-62.

10) Connect the swirl to the narrow strip you have already clipped up the backbone, as shown from the top in Figure 23-62.

11) Repeat these steps on the other side of the Poodle. When you have finished, the two sides should join together in a **V** where they meet the narrow strip up the

center of the back, as also shown in the top view of Figure 23-62.

12) Stand the dog on the grooming table with hindquarters facing you. Follow the instructions for finishing the back legs in chapter 22.

13) Fluff up the hair on the hips and hindquarters with your comb. Continue scissoring upward, smoothly blending the longer hair at the top of the legs into the slightly shorter body hair. At this point, if you have shortened the body coat to an overall even length with shears or a snap-on comb attachment, you will only need to fluff the coat up and out and lightly scissor any uneven areas. When shaping the hair at the clipped strip up the backbone and around the curving lines on the sides, fluff it up and out with

your comb, and scissor off the untidy hairs that fall over the clipped areas to form crisp, precise pattern lines. Then use curved shears to bevel, or slightly round, the edges all the way around the pattern to remove any sharp lines, creating a soft look. Keep fluffing the body hair up and out and scissoring off a little hair at a time, following the natural contours of the dog, as you scissor forward on the back, over the ribs, the chest and shoulders.

14) Have the Poodle stand facing you. Follow the instructions for shaping and finishing the front legs in chapter 22.

15) As you scissor upward on the front of the chest, from shoulder to shoulder, blend the leg hair evenly into the body coat. Just as

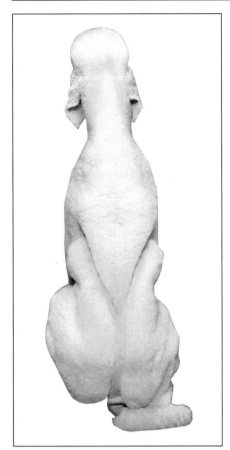

Figure 23-63. Photo courtesy of *Pet Stylist* magazine.

Figure 23-64. Photo courtesy of *Pet Stylist* magazine.

you did on the hindquarters, the lines from the tops of the front legs should flow smoothly upward into the shorter body coat, with no breaks in the hair. Scissor any remaining long hair between the front legs to the same length as the rest of the body.

16) Sit the Poodle facing you. Comb the hair on the head upward and forward, and follow the instructions for shaping the top-knot in chapter 16.

17) Comb the ear feathering downward, then round the edges with scissors to remove any wispy hairs or excessive length for an overall balanced appearance.

Figures 23-63 and 23-64 show the top and side views of the finished Swirl clip.

The Swirl Variation

1) Complete steps 1 through 7 as instructed for the Swirl clip.

2) Study Figure 23-65. Notice that this swirl starts with an inverted **V** in the center of the back. The pattern line almost encircles the last rib. The easiest way to start the pattern is to cut in the inverted **V** with shears as indicated by the small arrows in Figure 23-66, and then set it with clippers.

3) Now comes the difficult part: clipping the swirl on each side of the Poodle. Even the most experienced groomers find it difficult to clip the narrow swirling lines freehand and make them even in placement, size and shape. Therefore, you should use an object as a template or guide, as

described in step 9 of the Swirl clip. Place your template in the center of the Poodle's side with the back edge lined up with the last rib. Hold it in place. Using a #5/8 blade on a Toy Poodle and a #7/8 blade on a Miniature or Standard Poodle, clip about two-thirds of the way around the template, as indicated by the arrows in Figure 23-66.

4) Repeat these steps on the opposite side of the Poodle. When you have finished, the two sides should join together at the inverted **V** in the center of the back.

5) Complete steps 12 through 17 as instructed for the Swirl clip.

Figure 23-65. The Swirl variation.

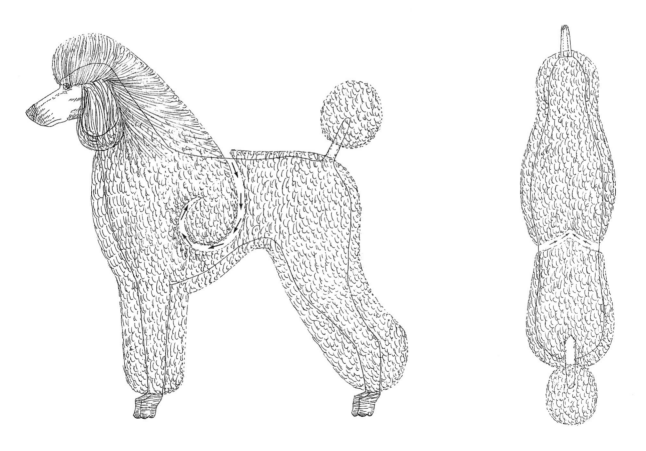

Figure 23-66. Execute the pattern for the Swirl variation in the direction shown by the arrows.

Elegant Finishing Touches

Figure 23-67.

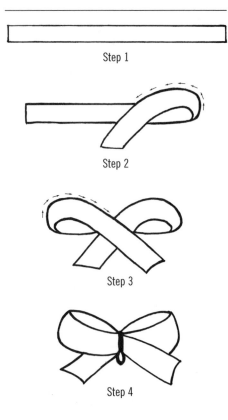

Step 1

Step 2

Step 3

Step 4

Figure 23-68. Four steps to fashioning Poodle bows.

The use of finishing touches for pets—bows and bandannas—is strictly a matter of personal preference. Many pet owners like to add a smart finishing touch to match their dog's collar and leash or a favorite outfit. You can buy bows and bandannas in different fabrics and designs, although making your own is very easy and a great way to express your creativity.

BOWS

Ear bows are most popular for pet Poodles. A bow can be tied or fastened by a latex band to the ear feathering, at the top of the ear just below the topknot and/or to a little tuft of hair on the hip, as shown in Figure 23-67. The best type of ribbon to use is nonfraying satin acetate florist's ribbon, which is available by the roll from most mail-order pet supply catalogs. The selection is dazzling: solid-colored ribbon in brilliant shades or fancy ribbons patterned with checkerboards, stripes, polka dots, paw prints, doggie bones, confetti, glitter or holiday themes.

Everyone has his or her favorite way of making hair bows, but you can make one in a few seconds (that will stay firmly attached to the hair when applied correctly), by following these steps.

1) To make the most basic bow, start with a piece of ribbon from 8 to 14 inches long, depending on the dog's size (step 1 in Figure 23-68). Generally, a 6- to 8-inch-long ribbon makes a balanced bow for Toys, a 10- to 12-inch ribbon is good for Miniatures and a 14-inch ribbon or slightly longer is best for Standards.

2) Fold the right end to the center to make a loop on the right side

(step 2 in Figure 23-68), holding the loop in place with your fingers.

3) Fold the left end to the center, and make a loop on the left side, as shown in step 3 in Figure 23-68, holding both loops in place with your fingers.

4) Secure the bow in place either by tying in the center with a thin strip of ribbon or by twisting a small latex band around the center (step 4 in Figure 23-68). One end of the latex band loops through the other and holds the bow in place. It might take a little practice to pass one end of the band through the other, but with a little dedication you can learn to do it.

For a really elegant effect, use two or three ribbons in harmonizing colors or use one solid and one plaid, checked or patterned ribbon for each bow. You can also use brightly colored yarn in place of ribbon. For a pretty and soft touch, after the yarn bow is attached, use a fine comb to carefully comb out the end pieces of the yarn.

Some finished bows are shown in Figure 23-69. This kind of bow can be applied easily to the dog's hair by the loop of the band that holds the ribbon together.

To fasten the bow to the ear, pull out a few strands of the long hair at the top center of the ear (Figure 23-70). Attach the bow to the strands of hair (bow on the outside, ribbon or latex band underneath). Slide the bow up to the top of the ear (Figure 23-71), then tie the ribbon around the feathering or twist the loop of the latex band around the hair, taking care that there is no skin caught up in the band (Figure 23-72). Bows attached to the feathering in this manner will not injure the ear

Figure 23-69.

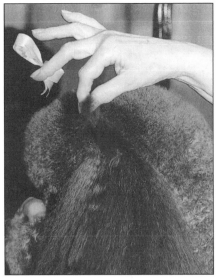

Figure 23-70.

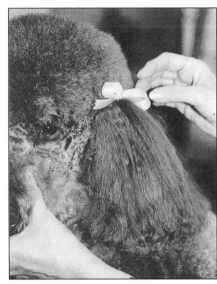

Figure 23-71.

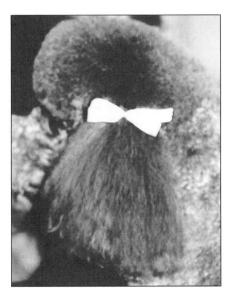

Figure 23-72.

Figure 23-73.

Figure 23-74.

leather and will stay firmly attached until the band is snipped away with scissors.

You can also buy assortments of lovely handcrafted bows already tied to latex bands in different designs, fabrics and trim (ribbon, tulle, netting, satin roses, tiny seed pearls and beads) at pet stores and from mail-order pet supply catalogs.

BANDANNAS

You can also buy bandannas in bright attractive prints or seasonal motifs at pet stores or from most mail-order pet supply catalogs. Each bandanna is about 22 inches square and made of machine-washable cotton. This size is suitable for Standard Poodles. You can fold each bandanna and wear it as is, or cut it in half with pinking shears to make two triangle-shaped bandannas, or into quarters to make four smaller bandannas.

It's easy to make your own bandannas by using brightly colored cotton or cotton-blend material and cutting them into triangles of various sizes with pinking shears (Figure 23-73). Figure 23-74 shows a Standard Poodle wearing a bandanna.

chapter 24

This chapter is devoted to the show clips and pet patterns that are popular in countries other than the United States and Canada. A few of the styles closely or exactly resemble some of the American clips described in the previous chapters, although in the accompanying illustrations and photographs, you will see that there are distinct nuances in fashion from country to country.

If you are interested in trying one of these elegant trims, the instructions for clipping the Poodle's face, feet and tail are basically the same the world over. The face is closely clipped from the ear to the outer corner of the eye on both sides of the head, as instructed in Chapter 13, "Clipping the Poodle's Face and Neck." The muzzle may be clipped clean (officially, the breed Standard of the FCI (Fédération Cynologique Internationale) states that one centimeter of coat may be left on the lower jaw, but this really is out of date) or, on pet dogs, styled with a moustache. The hair on the throat and front of the neck is clipped from just below the Adam's Apple to the corner of each ear in a **V** or **U** shape. The feet are clipped the same as described in Chapter 12, "Clipping the Poodle's Feet." The tail is clipped and styled the same as described in Chapter 14, "Clipping the Poodle's Tail," and the hair on the tail is shaped with scissors into a round pompon. Groomers in most foreign countries prefer clipping a **V** shape at the base of the tail, slightly into the dog's topline, to enhance the appearance of a short back. The stomach is clipped up to the last rib, the same as instructed in Chapter 15, "Clipping the Poodle's Stomach."

While American trimming methods and styles have affected show and pet grooming in other countries of the world, it is the Scandinavian styling (especially on the European continent) that has been most influential. Correct execution of the elegant, flashy international styles, especially of the Puppy Lion clip—the most popular show trim overseas—requires an eye for balance, proportion, symmetry, and correct angulation, and the talent for artistic scissoring to create a beautifully shaped coat.

The United Kingdom and The Kennel Club Poodle Standard

Dog shows in the United Kingdom are governed by The Kennel Club in London, England, the world's oldest authoritative body dealing with dog breeds and breed Standards. The Kennel Club recognizes over 180 dog breeds, which are classified into six variety Groups. All three Poodle varieties are classified in the Utility Group, which is most like the Non-Sporting Group in the United States.

The Kennel Club Standard

The Poodle Standard approved by The Kennel Club describes the coat and color as follows:

COAT

Very profuse and dense; of good harsh texture. All short hair close, thick and curly. It is strongly recommended that the traditional lion clip be adhered to.

COLOUR

All solid colours. White and creams to have black nose, lips and eye rims, black toenails desirable. Browns to have dark amber eyes, dark liver nose, lips, eye rims and toenails. Apricots to have dark eyes with black points or deep amber eyes with liver points. Blacks, silvers and blues to have black nose, lips, eye rims and toenails. Creams, apricots, browns, silvers and blues may show varying shades of the same colour up to 18 months. Clear colours preferred.

The Show Trims in the United Kingdom

Poodles, like all breeds, can begin to compete at the age of six months. The following trims are accepted in the show ring in the United Kingdom:

- The Full Puppy trim
- The Puppy Lion trim
- The Continental Lion trim
- The Traditional Lion or English Saddle trim

THE FULL PUPPY TRIM

This trim is occasionally seen on younger puppies. Currently, few exhibitors choose the Full Puppy trim; they prefer the Puppy Lion style instead. Like the American Puppy clip for the show ring described in chapter 20, the Poodle's feet, face and tail are clipped. The tail hair is shaped with scissors into a round pompon. The stomach is clipped to the last rib with a #15 blade. The hair on the legs, the body and the head is fluffed up and out with a comb, then trimmed slightly into a crisp, natural outline. Also, like the American Puppy trim, very little hair is scissored off the body with the exception of the hindquarters and around the base of the tail. The rest of the coat remains long, with only the untidy ends scissored off to achieve the correct outline. As the coat grows longer, it is shaped slightly shorter from the base of the tail, and gradually increases in length toward the neck and head. The ear feathering is left long; any untidy edges are rounded with scissors. When the topknot is long enough, it is put up in latex bands to keep the hair from breaking or falling into the eyes (see Figure 24-2 on page 197).

THE PUPPY LION TRIM

The Puppy Lion trim (Figure 24-1) is currently the most popular trim seen in the international show ring. It is equally popular among all three Poodle varieties. This elegant

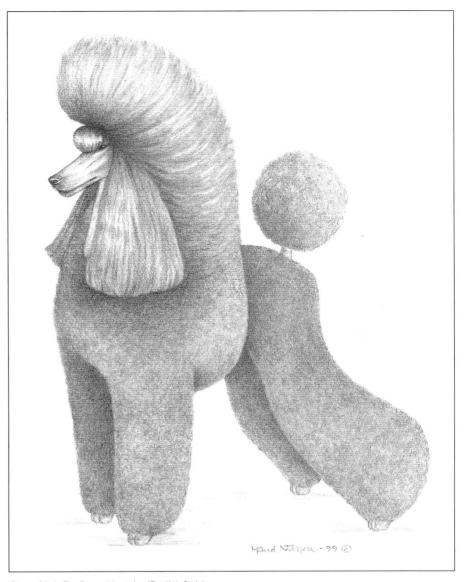

Figure 24-1. The Puppy Lion trim (English Style).

trim, in particular, requires an eye for balance, proportion and symmetry. And, because the Puppy Lion trim requires the Poodle to be scissored all over, it also requires the scissoring talent to create a stylishly shaped coat. There are two slightly different outlines for the Puppy Lion clip: the English style and the Scandinavian style. On the English style, shown in Figure 24-1, the hindquarters are somewhat rounded, while on the Scandinavian style, the hindquarters are more angular and more hair is left on the bottoms of the legs (see Figure 24-3 on page 198). Here are

the grooming instructions for the English version of the Puppy Lion clip.

1) Begin by bathing the dog, then blow drying the coat straight (see Chapter 6, "Bathing and Drying a Poodle in Show Coat"). Clip the feet and face as instructed in chapters 12 and 13, respectively, of this book.

2) Clip the tail and shape the pompon. On all the show clips, you want to leave as much hair as possible to shape into the pompon. A good rule is to clip about one-quarter of the tail and leave the hair on the remaining three-quarters to be shaped into the pompon. The base of the tail should be clipped into an inverted **V**.

3) Clip the front of the neck with a #15 blade. Pointing clippers upward, start an inch or so below the Adam's Apple, and clip to the front of each ear. The clipped area can be **V**-shaped or slightly rounded. (See photographs in the sections "The Puppy Clip for Show" or "The Continental Clip" in chapter 20.)

4) Stand the Poodle to begin setting the body pattern line. Study Figure 24-1. The dividing line between the long coat of the mane and the shorter hair of the hindquarters is set just behind the last rib, near the middle of the dog or central focal point. It's difficult to explain *exactly* where to part the hair. It should be separated where it maintains the dog's balance, and this varies with the individual dog. Try making the part ½ inch in back of the last rib on a Toy Poodle, about 1 inch in back of the last rib on a Miniature, and about 1½ to 2 inches in back of the last rib on a Standard.

5) Take the end tooth of your comb or a knitting needle and make a part slightly behind the last rib, up one side, over the back and down the other side. Making a straight part line around a Poodle's middle is not easy. If you are trying this for the first time, especially on a Poodle with a great deal of coat, use some hair spray to hold the long mane forward, or try wrapping a long strip of VetWrap or gauze bandage around the body at this point to hold it down. This will help to separate the long hair in

front from the hair on the hindquarters that will be scissored short.

If you are *not* sure that the part is in the right place, set the line a little farther back to avoid making a mistake. You can always move it forward, but it can take months of growing more hair to move it back. Once you are sure the part line is even and in the right place, cut around the line with scissors to define the part. Then remove the gauze wrapping.

6) Shape the top of the hindquarters. The top and sides of the hindquarters join the mane with *only* the part line (made with the end tooth of a comb or a knitting needle) as the separation. If made correctly, the part line should barely be visible. Fluff the hair up and out with your comb. Shape this area short and level with your scissors. Scissor the hair tight under the tail to make the dog look short in body.

7) Comb the hair on the back legs up and out to lift and fluff the coat. The back legs are shaped very much like a well-angulated Lamb clip. Just how much angulation you scissor in, however, depends on the individual requirements of each dog. To achieve the desirable velvety smooth finish, don't pull out straggly hairs with your fingertips. Instead, fluff the hair upward and outward every so often with your comb to ease out any untidy ends, then scissor the area again. Some groomers also like to gently shake the leg during the shaping process to encourage the hair to stand out straight. Make both rear legs even in size and shape. You can

learn a lot about shaping the hindquarters and the mane by taking a good look at the Poodles in the show ring in your country.

8) The next step is to shape the mane in front. Fluff the hair up and out with your comb. The mane is best scissored with curved shears to the round shape shown in Figure 24-1. Round the hair under the chest, then turn the dog to stand facing you to shape the area across the front of the chest round. As you did under the tail, keep the hair fairly short and tight to avoid making the dog look long in body.

9) The front legs are shaped like cylinders, straight from the top to the bottom on all sides. Be sure both front legs are even in size and shape and that they are in balance with the rear legs.

10) The topknot is left full and held in place with elastic bands. See the section titled "Putting Up the Topknot on the Show Trims" on pages 205–206 for photographs showing how to put up and spray the topknot; also see Chapter 19, "Care of the Poodle in Show Coat." When you have finished scissoring the Puppy Lion clip, everything should look properly balanced and proportioned, with long topknot flowing into the neck and mane, square body, deep brisket, well-angulated rear, and the tail balanced with the head.

As you will see later in this chapter, the Scandinavian version of this trim is *much* more exaggerated. The hindquarters are more angled and the bottoms of the legs are much fuller.

THE CONTINENTAL LION TRIM

The Continental Lion trim, out of style for some years, has recently become more popular in the United Kingdom. This is the same style as the American Continental clip with traditional mane shaped to form a ball appearance, hindquarters shaved, a round rosette over each hip, a puff on each front leg and a bracelet on each rear leg. In the United Kingdom, the Continental trim is seen mostly on Standard Poodles, who carry more coat. It is not often seen on Toy Poodles. For more information, see the section titled "The Continental Clip" in chapter 20 and Figure 24-17 on page 202.

THE TRADITIONAL LION OR ENGLISH SADDLE TRIM

The Traditional Lion or English Saddle trim is the same as the American English Saddle clip with a closely scissored pack or saddle over the loins and hips, bracelets on the stifle and hock joints and one puff on each front leg. Currently in the show ring, it is seen most often on Miniature Poodles, occasionally on Toy Poodles and only rarely on Standard Poodles. This is because the traditional Lion clip, writes Eileen Geeson in *The Complete Standard Poodle*, (New York: Howell Book House, 1998) "takes far longer than any other in order to achieve excellence. It takes longer to dry, longer to groom, and a lot longer to scissor than the Continental Lion. When the result is achieved through clipping, the clipping is more difficult and the scissoring is artistically demanding." She adds, however, that this is a beautiful trim for the show dog and, on a white Standard Poodle, looks especially spectacular. For more information, see the section

titled "The English Saddle Clip" in chapter 20 and Figure 24-19 on page 204.

THE MOST POPULAR PET TRIMS IN THE UNITED KINGDOM

Styles for pet Poodles in the United Kingdom are very similar to some American trims previously described. Current British trends in pet trimming favor practical yet stylish clips that are easy to maintain, rather than fancy patterns. The most popular are the Lamb trim, the Clown (the same as the American Miami clip), the Teddy Bear and the Dutch (although currently the Dutch is somewhat out of favor). Basically, all these clips are executed in the same manner as described in chapter 23.

The Fédération Cynologique Internationale

Dog shows in most countries of the world (except the United States, the United Kingdom and Canada) fall under the authority of the Fédération Cynologique Internationale (FCI), headquartered in Thuin, Belgium. Many countries come under FCI rules, some of them being: Belgium, France, the Netherlands, Germany, Austria, Spain, Portugal, Denmark, Sweden, Norway, Finland, Hungary, Ireland, Italy, Israel, Monaco, Morocco, Poland, Slovenia, Switzerland, Greece, Bulgaria, the Czech Republic, Latvia, Lithuania, Russia, Ukraine, South Africa, Zimbabwe, South Korea, India, Sri Lanka, Malaysia, Japan, Philippines, Taiwan, Thailand, Hong Kong, Australia, New Zealand, Argentina, Brazil, Chile, Columbia, Ecuador, Peru, Uruguay, Venezuela, Mexico, the

Republic of Panama, Costa Rica, Guatemala, Honduras, Puerto Rico and the Dominican Republic.

The Fédération Cynologique Internationale includes both members and contract partners (one member per country) that each issue their own pedigrees and train their own judges. Because each country has its own kennel club, there are minor national differences that extend even to grooming styles. In the show rings of the countries governed by FCI regulations, one often sees slightly different variations of the authorized trims.

The FCI recognizes over 330 dog breeds, which are classified into 10 Groups. Each breed is the "property" of a specific country (France, for instance, "owns" the Poodle Standard). The "owner" countries write the breed Standards in cooperation with the Standards and Scientific Commissions of the FCI. These Standards are the reference on which the judges base themselves when judging at shows held in FCI member countries. All three Poodle varieties are placed in Group 9: *Chiens d'agrément et de compagnie*, or Companions and Toys. The portion of the FCI Poodle Standard for coat and accepted clips is included on page 196.

The FCI Show Trims

In countries under the jurisdiction of the FCI, dogs can begin to compete in shows at the age of nine months. The Puppy clip, the Lion (or Continental) clip and the English Saddle clip are all well-known in FCI show rings around the world although, at the moment, the Puppy Lion (done in the Scandinavian fashion) is the most popular.

COAT

Color Poodles with 'Curly' or 'Corded' coats: black, white, brown, gray and apricot.

- The brown color must be pure, quite dark, uniform and warm. The graduations in the brown shades must not go either to the beige or to its lighter derivatives. Neither must the shade of the brown color be close to black, as seen in the 'tête de nègre' or the 'aubergine'.

- The gray color must be uniform. The graduations in he gray color must not show traces of black or white.

- The apricot color must be uniform, neither tending towards the beige or the cream, neither to the red or the auburn, nor to the brown colors or their derivatives.

CLIP

'Lion Clip' *The curly and the corded Poodles are clipped on the hindquarters up to the ribs. Also clipped: the top and bottom part of the muzzle starting from the lower eyelids; the cheeks; the fore and hind legs, leaving bracelets on the hindlegs and puffs on the forelegs and the optional pompons on the hindquarters; the tail is shaved except for a round or oblong pompon at the tip. Leaving the moustache is recommended, Keeping hair on the front legs, called "trousers" is admitted.*

'Modern Clip' *In this clip, the hair may be left on all four legs, provided the following standards are respected:*

1) The following shall be clipped:

- The lower part of the front legs from the nails to the tip of the dewclaw; the lower part of the

hindlegs to the same height as the front legs. Machine clipping, limited to the toes only, is permitted.

- The head and tail will be clipped the same as in the Lion Clip. In this style of clip the following exceptions are allowed: (1) The presence of short hair beneath the lower jaw, however, not exceeding the length of 1 centimeter with the lower line (profile) cut parallel to the lower jaw. The beard called 'goat's beard' is not acceptable. (2) Absence of the pompon on the tail (but this will slightly diminish the rating for coat texture).

2) Shortened coat: On the body, to show on the back line a moiré (silk) effect more or less of at least 1 centimeter long. The length of the coat shall be progressively increased around the ribs and upper parts of the legs.

3) Regularized hair:

a) On the head, which stays with a casque (topknot) of reasonable height, as well as on the neck, descending behind the neck to the withers, and in front, without discontinuity down to the shaven part of the foot following a slightly slanting line from the point of the sternum downward. On the upper part of the ears and up to a third of their maximum length, the hair may be cut with scissors or shaved in the direction of the hair. The lower part is left covered with hair of a length increasing progressively from top to bottom, to end up in fringes which can be adjusted.

b) On the legs, "trousers: marking a distinct transition with the shaven part of the feet. The length of the hair increases

progressively upwards to show on the shoulder as on the thigh a length of 4 to 7 centimeters on straightened hair, in proportion with the size of the dog but avoiding any "bouffant." The trousers on the back legs must allow the typical angulation of the Poodle to be seen. All other fancy clips which do not comply with these normal standards are eliminatory. Whatever the standard outline obtained through the grooming, it must never influence the classification at the dog shows, all dogs of the same class shall be judged and placed together.

'English Clip' *Add to the Lion clip motifs on the hindquarters, i.e. bracelets and cuffs. On the head: a topknot. For this clip, the moustache is optional. Absence of demarcation on the hair on the hindquarters is tolerated. The topknot is optional.*

TEXTURE OF THE COAT

Curly Coated Poodle *Abundant hairs of fine texture, woolly and curly, elastic and resistant to pressure of the hand. It must be thick, dense, of uniform length, forming even curls that are generally combed. The coat hard to the touch giving an impression of horsehair is undesirable and shall be demoted in favor of the regular texture.*

Corded Poodle *Abundant hair of fine texture, woolly and dense, forming the characteristic cords of even length. These should be at least 20 centimeters in length. The longer they are, the more they are appreciated. The cords on each side of the head may be tied up by a ribbon above the ears, and those on the body parted on each side to avoid an untidy coat.*

THE FULL PUPPY CLIP

As in the United Kingdom the Full Puppy clip (Figure 24-2), is occasionally seen on younger puppies. Currently, few exhibitors are choosing the Full Puppy trim; they prefer the Puppy Lion style instead. Like the American Puppy clip described in chapter 20 and the English Full Puppy clip, the Poodle's feet, face and tail are clipped. The stomach is clipped to the last rib with a #15 blade. The tail hair is shaped with curved scissors into a round or oblong pompon. The hair on the legs, the body and the head is fluffed up and out with a comb, and then trimmed into a crisp natural outline. As the coat grows longer, it is shaped slightly shorter from the base of the tail and gradually increases in length toward the neck and head. The ear feathering is left long; any untidy edges are rounded with scissors. Just like the American and English versions of the Puppy clip, the topknot is put up in latex bands.

THE PUPPY LION OR SECOND PUPPY CLIP (SCANDINAVIAN)

The Puppy Lion or Second Puppy clip (also known by several other names including the Scandinavian trim, the Swedish trim, the Nordic trim, and the Lowen-Schur) is not easy to produce because it requires expert scissoring all over. Basically, in the FCI countries, the Puppy Lion pattern (Figure 24-3) is set in the same manner as previously instructed in the "Show Trims in the United Kingdom" section of this chapter, with the dividing line between the long mane and the shorter hindquarters set slightly behind at the last rib. The top and sides of the hindquarters are separated from the mane by the part line (made with the end tooth of a comb or a knitting needle) around the middle of the dog. The principal difference is in the shaping of the hindquarters and the legs. The hindquarters are squared, angulation is greatly

Figure 24-2. The Full Puppy clip.

emphasized, and the bottoms of the legs are left much fuller—in some cases, so full that the feet cannot be seen.

Study Figure 24-4, paying attention to how the hair overlays the Poodle's outline. Notice that the hair on the top of the hindquarters is scissored short, level and square-shaped. It extends slightly out from the tail (still very short), then curves and angles sharply downward in back, with the fullness beginning near the stifle joint. Again, just how much angulation is sculpted in depends on the individual dog. The hair under

the tail is scissored tight to make the dog appear short in body. Notice, too, in all the photographs of the Puppy Lion clip in this chapter, that the hindquarters have a velvety, smooth appearance.

The mane in front is best scissored with curved shears to the round shape shown in Figure 24-3. As with the area under the tail, the hair on the chest is kept fairly short to avoid making the dog look long in body. The front legs are shaped like cylinders, as usual; however, while they sometimes are not as full, they still must be in balance with the rear legs.

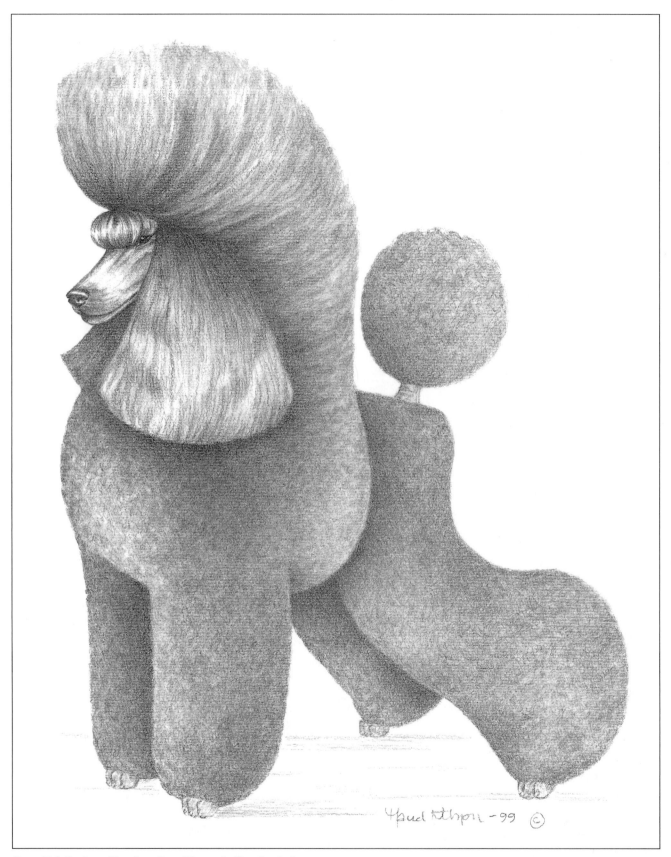

Figure 24-3. The Puppy Lion clip or Second Puppy clip (Scandinavian).

Figure 24-4. Styling diagram for the Scandinavian Puppy Lion illustrated by Kitty Dekeersgieter (Belgium).

Figure 24-5. Notice the profile differences between the Scandinavian Puppy Lion, English Puppy Lion, Full Puppy and European-T clips.
(Illustrations by Kitty Dekeersgieter)

Figure 24-7. The long hair in front is trimmed with curved shears into a round shape. On this dog, the topknot has been put up and the ears brushed out, ready for the show ring.

Figure 24-6.

Figure 24-8. Here is another view of the Scandinavian Puppy Lion on a multi-champion brown Miniature Poodle from Germany at a recent World Dog Show.

Figure 24-9. The Standard Poodle Ch. Avatar Biscaya with Anders Rosell (Sweden).

Figure 24-10. The Standard Poodle Ch. Avatar Arabica with Anders Rosell (Sweden).

Figure 24-11. Jean-Francois Vanaken (Belgium) breeder, owner and handler of the famous "des Super Supers" Poodles.

Figure 24-12. A Russian version of the Puppy Lion clip.

Figure 24-13. Italian, Luxembourg and International Ch. Racketeer Dance With A Stranger, Italy's top Poodle for 1995, owned, groomed and handled by Lorena Merati.

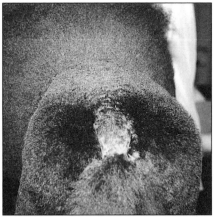

Figure 24-14. A close-up view of the same dog showing the square shape of the hindquarters (grooming by Ms. Merati).

Figure 24-15. A rear view of the same dog.

The topknot is left full and held in place with elastic bands in the manner described in Chapter 19, "Care of the Poodle in Show Coat," or in the section titled "Putting up the Topknot on the Show Trims" later in this chapter.

The Puppy Lion (Scandinavian version) requires expert scissoring all over, as is evident on the dog shown in Figure 24-6.

There are slight nuances from country to country as shown in Figures 24-6 through 24-13. There is a very thin dividing part between the long mane and the shorter hindquarters that is set behind the last rib. Occasionally, one sees no dividing line between the end of the long mane hair and the beginning of the short hair on the hindquarters. In all instances, however, the hair on the hindquarters is scissored short, level and square-shaped on top. It then extends slightly out from the tail, hugs the natural curves of the leg below the tail and then angles sharply downward. The white Miniature Poodle in Figure 24-6 is being readied for competition at a recent World Dog Show models the trim.

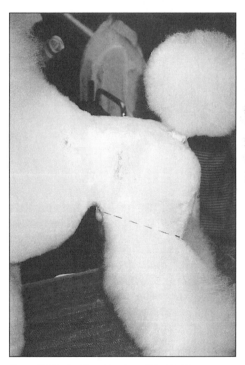

Figure 24-16. Another side view of the hind legs. On the Scandinavian version of the Puppy Lion clip, angulation is greatly emphasized as is apparent in the previous photographs. To achieve the correct line, the hair extends slightly out from the tail, then curves inward (where it is scissored shorter) and angles downward, as shown here, with the fullness beginning near the stifle joint.

Figure 24-17. The Lion clip.

THE LION CLIP

The Lion clip (Figure 24-17, also known in various countries as the Continental, the Leoncina, the Lion Continental à l'Américaine and the Leão) is done exactly the same as the American Continental trim. A variation of the Lion clip, without the rosettes on the hips, shown in Figure 24-18, is occasionally seen. For more information, see the section titled "The Continental Clip" in chapter 20.

THE ENGLISH SADDLE CLIP

The English Saddle clip (Figure 24-19, also known as the Lion à l'Anglaise and the Tosa à Inglesa) is done exactly the same as the American English Saddle trim. It is acceptable in the show ring, but not very popular at the moment. For more information, see the section titled "The English Saddle Clip" in chapter 20.

PUTTING UP THE TOPKNOT ON THE SHOW TRIMS

Topknots on the show clips can be put up in either of two manners: (1) by working from front to back or (2) by working from back to front. Chapter 19, "Care of the Poodle in Show Coat," contains a sequence of photographs and instructions explaining how to put up the topknot by working from front to back. In the first technique, the groomer starts at the front, above the bubble, and separates the hair from side to side into slender layers, arranging each layer forward and upward, while lightly spraying deep into the hair to hold it in place.

In the second technique, the groomer does the exact opposite. He or she starts down the neck and back, and separates the hair from side to side into slender layers, arranging each layer *backward* and *upward*, while lightly spraying deep into the hair to keep them in place.

Figures 24-20 through 24-37 illustrate the sequence of steps for the back-to-front technique.

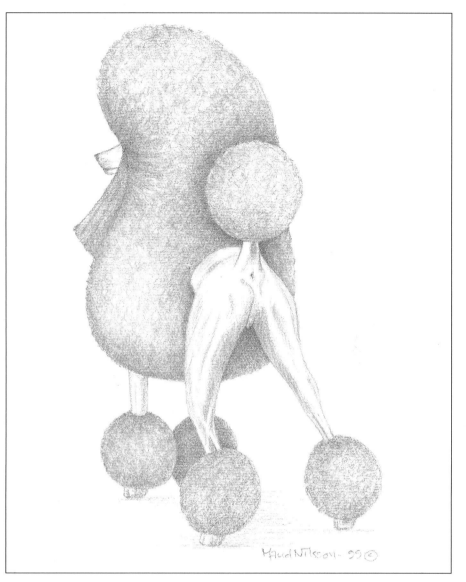

Figure 24-18. The Lion clip variation.

Figure 24-19. The English Saddle clip.

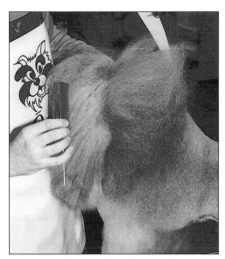

Figure 24-20. On this silver Miniature, the hair above the eyes has already been parted into two sections and banded in a manner similar to that described in chapter 19. A bubble that puffs out slightly has also been formed above the eyes. Then all the hair was brought forward toward the nose, as shown here, in preparation for finishing the topknot.

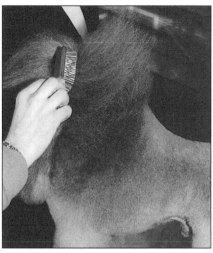

Figure 24-21. The hair on the neck, behind the separation that you see, has already been parted from side to side, thin layer by thin layer, and lightly sprayed to add body. Then each layer was brushed backward, upward and outward.

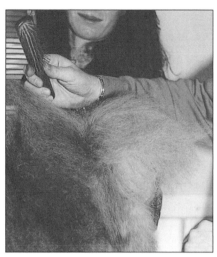

Figure 24-22. Working forward, each thin layer is separated, then brushed or combed backward, towards the center and upward. At this point, starting to direct the hair towards the center helps to create the illusion of a long neck.

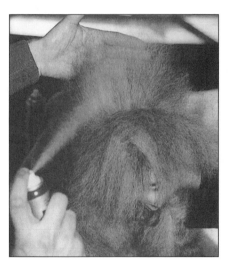

Figure 24-23. A little hair spray will hold each layer in place. Instead of spraying the top of the hair, you want to direct the spray into the base of the coat. A light misting deep in the hair will add volume and control, and the hair ends will not feel sticky.

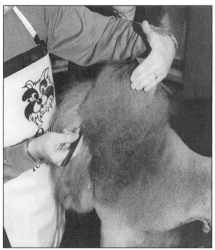

Figure 24-24. After spraying, use the tip of a rat-tail comb or hair pick to lift each layer of hair in the same direction: backward, to the center and upward.

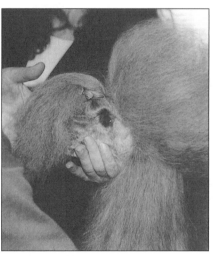

Figure 24-25. Keep working forward in this manner.

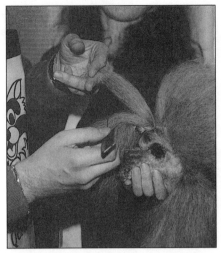

Figure 24-26. When you reach the latex bands above the eyes, part the hair as usual into tiny layers.

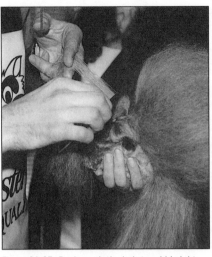

Figure 24-27. Back-comb the hair to add height, then spray.

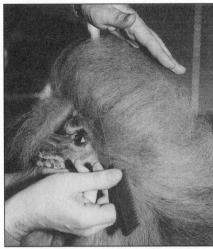

Figure 24-28. Use the tip of a rat-tail comb or hair pick to again lift and fan out each layer backward, to the center and upward.

Figure 24-29. Do the same for the layer immediately above the bubble.

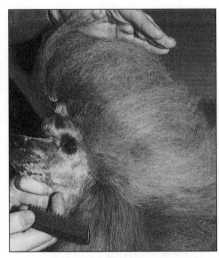

Figure 24-30. Spray the hair, then use the comb or hair pick to lift the hair.

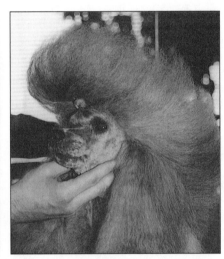

Figure 24-31. The finished topknot. If the topknot is too long, it should be scissored to balance with the length of hair on the main coat. The topknot always should be in balance with and blend with the rest of the body coat.

Figure 24-32. Another view of a finished topknot on a white Miniature Poodle.

Figure 24-33. The Modern clip.

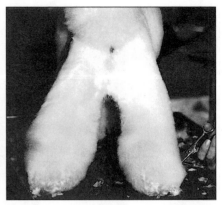

Figure 24-34. The Modern clip is one of the most popular international styles because it is a very elegant-looking and flattering trim for Poodles of all sizes and shapes. Here, the feet, face and tail have been clipped. The hair had been fluffed out with a comb and is ready for shaping.

Figure 24-35. Shaping the hindquarters. When viewed from the side, the shape of the back legs follows the natural conformation of the leg, emphasizing the angulation above the hock joint and the curve of the stifle joint.

Figure 24-36. Here, the back legs are being scissored. From a rear view, notice that even though the hair on the legs will be left very full, the fullness is at the bottoms of the legs, not at the hip area. When viewed from behind, the back legs should look parallel. The hair under the tail is scissored tight to make the dog look short in body.

THE MODERN CLIP

The Modern clip is also accepted for show by the FCI. As you can see in Figures 24-33 through 24-44, on this style there is no separation between the hindquarters and the mane, but a smooth unbroken line from topknot to the base of the tail. Even though it does not happen often, a Poodle in Modern clip can compete in the regular classes and win its championship. This trim is especially popular in Germany. Poodle clubs in that country often hold special "Modeschur" or "Modern Schur" shows at which only dogs clipped in the Modern style can compete.

Throughout Europe, South America and Asia, the Modern clip (also known in different countries as the Moderne, Moderna, Modeschur and Modern Schur) is one of the most popular styles for pet Poodles. This is because in Europe, in particular, dogs take a larger part in daily life than they normally do in the United States. Dogs are routinely permitted in restaurants and shops and on public transportation; consequently their owners like them to be smartly groomed. The Modern clip is so popular because it is a practical trim, very easy to care for, and yet elegant for a companion Poodle. It is also an excellent choice for Poodles of all sizes and shapes because, in the scissoring process, the groomer can conceal faults when necessary. The Modern clip most closely resembles the American Lamb clip, but it is executed with European flair.

In Figures 24-34 through 24-41, a French groomer trims the Modern clip in the contest ring at the MilanGroom international competition. His white Miniature Poodle has been shampooed and fluff dried and is ready for trimming.

Like most international trims, there are slight differences in the finished look from country to country. Figures 24-42, 24-43 and 24-44 offer some other examples.

SCISSORING THE LEGS

When scissoring the legs on all pet styles described in the international section, the goal is to achieve an even, plush finish. From the side, the back legs should show angulation, as seen on the Standard Poodle shown in Figure 24-45.

When viewed from the rear, the legs should look parallel (Figures 24-44 and 24-46). While the hair length is a matter of personal preference, on most pet styles the legs generally are trimmed slightly shorter than on the show clips to make it easier for the pet owner to care for the dog between professional groomings. However, the bottoms of the legs, below the hock joint, are left full, but in correct proportion. The leg hair blends smoothly into the body

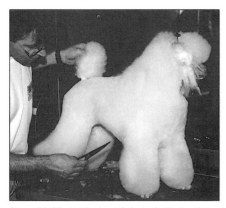

Figure 24-37. A side view of the body. Notice that the hair blends smoothly from the back legs into the body coat. The front legs are scissored to appear cylindrical in shape, straight from top to bottom on all sides. The hair on the chest should be short and slightly curved. Leaving too much hair on the chest adds length to the body.

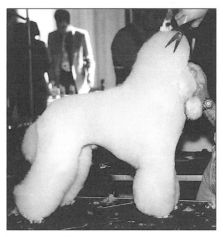

Figure 24-38. The topknot is shaped round and full, blending smoothly into the longer hair on the back of the neck.

Figure 24-39. A three-quarter view of the topknot.

Figure 24-40. A front view of the finished topknot.

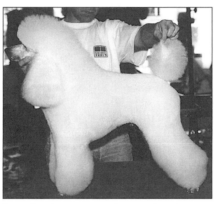

Figure 24-41. A side view of the finished Modern clip. As you can see, there is a smooth unbroken line from topknot to the base of the tail.

Figure 24-42. The Modern clip by Mirjam van den Bosch (The Netherlands).

Figure 24-43. The Modern clip by Sylvie Guinchard (France).

Figure 24-44. A rear view of Sylvie's Poodle.

Figure 24-45. This dog has been scissored by Kitty Dekeersgieter of Kortrijk, Belgium.

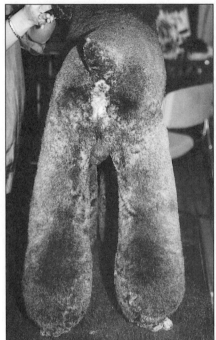

Figure 24-46.

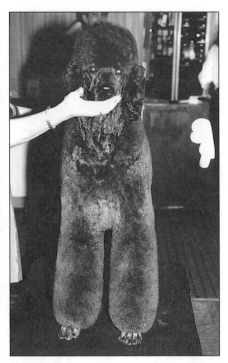

Figure 24-47.

coat, creating an overall balanced look. There should be a gradual flow of hair in proportion with the overall profile, with no excess coat that puffs out to make the dog look "hippy." The hair below the tail is always trimmed close to give the dog a short-backed look.

On all pet styles, the front legs are shaped like cylinders, straight from the top to the bottom, with slightly more hair left on the bottoms (Figure 24-47). Both front legs should be even in size and shape and in balance with the back legs. The hair blends smoothly into the body coat. Just as you do on the hindquarters, there should be a gradual flow of hair in proportion with the overall profile, with no excess coat that puffs out to make the shoulders look "loaded." The hair on the front of the chest should be short and slightly rounded, not overly

rounded or so long as to add length to the Poodle's body.

Some Popular International Pet Clips

Some other popular pet trims are illustrated in Figures 24-48 through 24-54. Figure 24-48 shows the German clip, a charming trim in which the ears and tail are clipped short (most often with a #10 blade), and the topknot and legs are shaped with scissors to appear very full-coated. The face usually sports a profuse, German-style mustache. This trim is seen occasionally in grooming contest rings in the United States. Figure 24-49 shows a variation of the German clip with "terrier"-style feet that are not clipped. Figure 24-50, the Model, and Figure 24-51, the Fox, illustrate clips that are well-known in the Benelux countries (Belgium, The

Netherlands and Luxembourg). Figure 24-52 shows the San Tropez, one of the most favored pet trims around the world, especially in countries with warm climates. In the United States, we know it as the Miami (or Summer) clip, described in chapter 23. Figure 24-53 shows the European T-Clip. This trim is popular in many countries because, when the hair on the head, back of the neck and over the shoulders and ribs is allowed to grow longer, it can easily be converted into any style of show clip. In the Scandanavian countries, the European T-Clip is also known as the Toilette 60. Figure 24-55, the Zazou or Jas en Broek, is the same popular trim that is known as the Dutch clip in the United States. Keep in mind that these popular trims may be known by other names in various countries of the world.

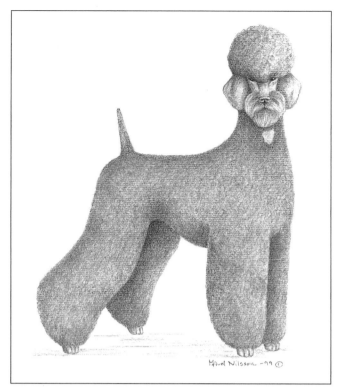

Figure 24-48. The German clip (also called the Karakul or Tonte Allemande).

Figure 24-49. A variation of the German clip on which the feet are not clipped.

Figure 24-50. The Model (also known as the Jeugdmodel or Mouton).

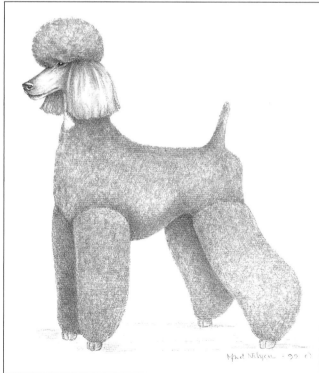

Figure 24-51. The Fox (also called the Mod Fox).

Figure 24-52. The San Tropez (also known as the Kaal met Sokken).

Figure 24-53. The European T-Clip.

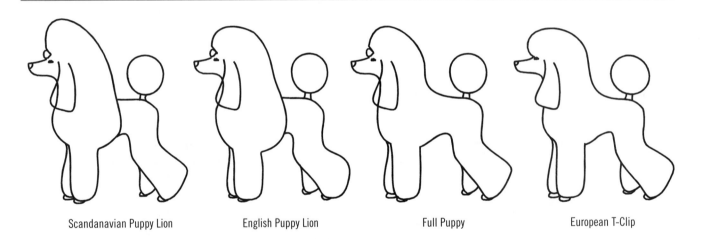

Scandanavian Puppy Lion   English Puppy Lion   Full Puppy   European T-Clip

Figure 24-54. In profile view, you can see that these four clips are very similar. Chart by Kitty Dekeersgieter.

Figure 24-55. The Zazou or the Jas en Broek (the equivalent of the Dutch clip).

Figure 25-1. Manufacturers and distributors display and sell their products and equipment at grooming shows throughout the world. Groomers can observe the state of the art today in products, services and techniques, and can preview what's on the drawing board for tomorrow. Here, Gregory Crisp, president of Double-K Industries, explains all about professional hair dryers to a group of interested professionals.

Figure 25-2. Grooming shows are an excellent place for professional groomers to see and handle a variety of scissors, shears, finger and thumb guards and other tools that can make their work day more efficient.

Even after becoming a professional pet stylist, your quest for knowledge does not stop. You should continually keep aware of the constant progress in the grooming world. Because new techniques and trends in dog care are constantly emerging, many professionals consider it a must to attend grooming conventions on a regular basis, to sharpen both their technical skills and business acumen. Grooming conventions are events where educational programs, hands-on demonstrations, competitions and trade shows take place concurrently at the same venue. These are great places to meet and exchange ideas with other professionals who share your interest in grooming as a career.

The Top Grooming Conventions

At most of these events, groomers come not only to see grooming demonstrations given by breed experts, but also to observe or participate in competition grooming. Manufacturers and distributors of grooming products and equipment regularly attend these conventions, so pet stylists also have the opportunity to see and handle the newest products and equipment—shears, brushes, combs, hair dryers, tables, shampoos and other hair preparations—that make them more knowledgeable professionals and enhance their operating efficiency. You shouldn't have to travel far to get involved yourself. Grooming conventions are held throughout the United States and Canada during practically every month of the year. Some are produced by

independent organizers; others are organized by regional grooming associations. The largest shows in the United States are Intergroom (New Jersey), Groom Expo (Pennsylvania and California), the All American Grooming Contest (Illinois), the New England Pet Grooming Professionals (Massachusetts), the National Dog Groomers Association of America (Florida, Kentucky and Missouri), the Southern California Groomers Association (California), the Atlanta Pet Fair (Georgia), the U.S. Pet-Pro Classic (Texas) and Backer Associates/Groom and Board (New Jersey and Illinois).

There also are grooming associations in many states that hold smaller, regional events and/or competitions, as well as promoters who organize single-day grooming seminars on a variety of business-related and technique-oriented subjects. If you have never attended a grooming show or seminar, a local or state event may be the place for you to start.

How to Learn About Grooming Conventions

The best way to learn about upcoming national and international grooming shows and single-day regional seminars is to check the "Calendar of Events" in various trade magazines and newsletters for groomers (some addresses are listed in the Appendix). These usually list the dates and locations of shows three months or so before the events take place. Also listed will be the name, address, telephone and fax number of the person to contact for more information.

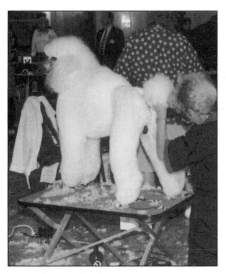

Figure 25-3. Elizabeth Paul, Satellite Beach, Florida.

Figure 25-4. Shaunna Bernardin, Calgary, Alberta, Canada.

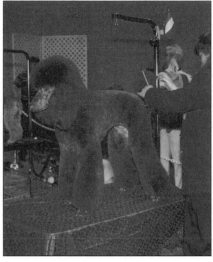

Figure 25-5. Paola Acco, Venice, Italy.

Grooming Contests

If you've ever marveled at the way handlers and exhibitors prepare their dogs for the show ring, you're in for a treat when you sit ringside at a grooming competition and watch the contestants magically transform their raggle-taggle entries into dogs of incredible beauty. It's really quite fascinating!

After attending a few conventions and carefully watching what happens in the contest ring, you may even decide to compete yourself. Professional groomers, like dog show exhibitors, have their own "show circuit." Unlike dog shows, these are contests in which only the dog's *grooming* is judged, not its conformation (although indirectly conformation *is* important, because you would not want to compete with a poor specimen that requires time-consuming corrective grooming).

PREPARING TO COMPETE

Competing at a grooming contest requires months of homework. It's not just a matter of the few hours a groomer spends in the ring, but the advance preparation required if you want to become a winner. This includes choosing the right

dog, growing the dog's coat to the correct length, learning how to do the best work under pressure, practicing to finish the trim within the required amount of time, prepping the dog correctly and achieving the right frame of mind to compete.

New competitors can win if they are skillful groomers. A lot depends on individual circumstances, but the greatest difficulties at first seem to be nervousness and finishing an entry properly in the time allotted. Even the most seasoned competitors admit to having been very tense the first time they groomed in front of spectators and that the time limit for completing their trim passed too quickly.

Before a contest, you can take various steps to help improve your efficiency. In the ring, you will be given a certain time limit (specified in the contest rules) to complete your grooming. Therefore, start by timing yourself to learn how long it takes you to finish your chosen trim. Then constructively evaluate your finished work. Expertise is more important than speed, but if the trim is hard to complete in the time allotted, try to reduce

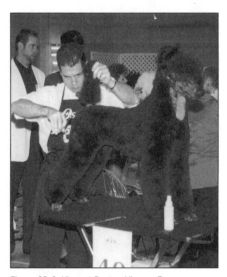

Figure 25-6. Vincent Pastor, Vienne, France.

Figure 25-7. The International Poodle Class at Intergroom.

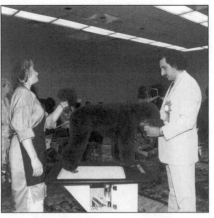

Figure 25-8. Umberto Lehmann of Milan, Italy, judging a Poodle at Intergroom.

Figure 25-9. Beth Paynter, of Planet Poodle, Wall, New Jersey, the first Champion of the "Rags to Riches" competition, sponsored by Double-K Industries. Contestants in this special competition must start with very hairy dogs—16 weeks hair growth beyond a normal grooming. However, they are permitted to clip the hair on the face and genitals (for sanitary reasons) up to 6 weeks prior to the start of the competition. With Beth, from left to right: Gregory Crisp, Double-K Industries, Sarah Hawks (USA), Umberto Lehmann (Italy), Monique Janssens (Belgium) and Elizabeth Paul (USA), judges.

Figure 25-10. Sue Zecco, of Paxton, Massachusetts, "Intergroom International Groomer of the Year, 1998," pictured with all the trophies and rosettes she won at the show. On her way to the top title, Sue won the Laube International World Class Poodle Challenge (and the title "World Champion Poodle Groomer") and "Best Groomer-American Classes." In addition to the beautiful trophies and rosettes, Sue took home several thousand dollars in cash.

the time spent on basics, which will give you more time for finishing, or else choose a less complicated style.

ENTERING A CONTEST

For your first experience, select a show that will be convenient for you to get to, one where the pressure of competing won't be too formidable. Write and request a catalog or brochure describing the contest rules and the classes that you can enter. This will also contain all the additional information you need to know about the show, such as the location, hours and list of judges; and it will also include entry forms for the contest. Most grooming shows take place at motels or hotels. Make your reservation early, for it's always more relaxing and convenient for you and your dogs to stay at the contest site.

CONTEST RULES AND CLASSES

Like dog shows, grooming contests are governed by rules. It is very important to read the official rules carefully for they will differ slightly from contest to contest. Regarding Poodles, for instance, at some contests, all three varieties are groomed in the same class.

At other shows, Standard Poodles are judged in one class while Miniatures and Toys are judged in another class. And occasionally, you will find a Non-Sporting class, in which all three varieties of Poodles are judged with Bichons Frises and other breeds of the Non-Sporting Group.

Most shows offer at least two levels of competition: Division A, which is open to all contestants (and where all the top winners compete), and Division B, restricted to groomers who have not previously competed or who have not previously won three first placements. If you are a new competitor, Division B is definitely the place to start!

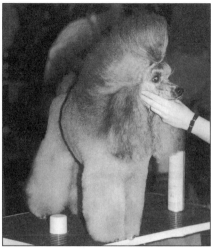

Figure 25-11. Oster European Invitational Tournament of Champions 2000, Berlin, Germany. Left to right; Anders Rosell (Sweden), judge; Natalia Fomicheva (Russia), judge; Christina Gregor, Ferruccio Soave (Italy), Champion; Shirlee Kalstone; Denys Lorrain (France), judge.

Figure 25-12. Romana Divisova of the Czech Republic, with her silver Miniature Poodle at Pragobest.

Rules will vary in the amount of time allotted for the various classes. You may have 1½ hours to complete a Miniature Poodle at one contest, for instance, while at another you may get 2 hours. All competitions require a minimum hair growth on dogs that are to be trimmed; some require six weeks' growth of hair, others eight weeks' growth. Read the contest rules carefully before you fill out the entry form. If the information is unclear, call the show organizer to learn exactly what is required.

JUDGES AND JUDGING PROCEDURES

The judging procedure also varies. At some contests, you will find one judge for each class, while at others, you will see a panel of two or three judges per class. Each contest organizer decides how many judges he or she will use per class. Whether it's one person or a panel per class, judges are selected on their knowledge of correct breed profiles and grooming procedures, good judgement, honesty and integrity.

The term *breed profile* is not the same as *breed Standard*. An official breed Standard is a written description of the ideal dog of

each recognized breed, point by point, which serves as a word pattern by which dogs are judged at AKC-licensed shows. A breed Standard is composed of sections defining the correct structure of, among other parts, the head, neck, body, forequarters, hindquarters, feet and tail, as well as the correct coat texture and color. A breed profile is the established visual appearance or outline of the ideal dog of each recognized breed when it is groomed correctly. It is based on the *correct* grooming patterns approved by the various national breed clubs and seen on champion dogs in the show ring. The first prerequisite of any competitor is to learn correct breed profiles. Attending dog shows and taking profile photographs and head-study shots of the various breeds will help you visualize what is correct.

Here is a brief overview of what takes place in the contest ring. Your competition dog should be shampooed and fluff dried before you enter the ring (this can be done the day before the competition or early in the morning on the day of the competition). The dog's coat should be free of tangles; the judge should be able to easily

comb through the coat. The rules at most contests usually allow you to also clip the dog's toenails and to clean its ears in advance.

Plan to arrive at the contest ring at least 20 minutes before prejudging begins. You will need time to set up your equipment, plug in your clippers and especially to get the dog comfortably settled on the grooming table—and to calm yourself down, too.

Prejudging always occurs prior to the official start of each class. The judge(s) will examine the dogs to determine the overall cleanliness and general condition of each dog's skin and coat. Dogs with insufficient coat growth, skin disease, fleas or other problems may be dismissed at this point. After the contest starts, the judge(s) will observe the contestants not only to evaluate their grooming techniques but also to determine that the dogs are handled humanely. Rough handling is usually penalized, as are clipper burns, nicks, cuts and other evidence of unprofessional conduct.

At the end of each class, the judge(s) will examine each dog individually, combing through the coat, before making their final

Figure 25-13. A view of the trophy table at Ciseaux d'or, organized by Mijo and Guy Klein, an international competition and seminar that takes place in the south of France.

Figure 25-14. MilanGroom, an international competition and seminar organized by Umberto Lehmann, takes places annually in Milan, Italy. In 1998, the winner of Best Groomed Dog in Show was Lorena Merati with Italian, Luxembourg and International Champion Racketeer Dance with a Stranger.

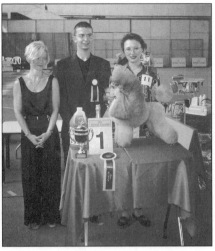

Figure 25-15. Grooming contests are becoming popular in Russia and some of them are held in conjunction with all-breed dog shows. Here judges Natalia Fomitcheva and Roman Fomine award "Best Groomed Dog in Show" at a 1999 competition in Moscow.

Figure 25-16. The 1996 Oster International Invitational Tournament of Champions winner Mirjam van den Bosch from Dieren, The Netherlands. Left to right: John Davenport, Oster Professional Products, Marita Rodgers (England), Marie-France Sequino (France) and Christina Pawlosky (USA), judges.

decisions. In the Poodle class, the judges take into consideration the following:

- The suitability of the trim to the dog's conformation and breed profile
- The quality of clipping and scissoring; the correct placement of pattern lines
- The smoothness of the finish
- Proportion, balance and symmetry

Mistakes that can keep a contestant from winning a placement in a hotly contested class include:

- Uneven pattern lines
- Tangles left in the hair
- Sloppy clipping between the toes and foot pads
- An unbalanced trim (the topknot and tail out of balance with the rest of the trim or the hair left longer on one side of the dog than the other)
- Dirty ears
- Choppy clipping or scissoring

When you do compete, make each contest a learning experience. If you don't win a class placement, ask the judge to evaluate your work so you can do better the next time.

INTERNATIONAL EVENTS

Contest winners often take home thousands of dollars in cash. In the United States, many sponsors offer substantial cash prizes, handsome trophies and beautiful rosettes. Grooming contests are not only popular in the United States, but also around the world. Competitions are organized in many countries, including Canada, England, France, Italy, Germany, Belgium, Holland, Denmark, Spain, Portugal, the Czech Republic, Russia, Argentina, Australia, New Zealand, Japan, Thailand and the Republic of China.

Over the past few years, the great interest in grooming competitions around the world has prompted Oster™ Professional Products to sponsor two very special events: the International Invitational Tournament of Champions and the European Invitational Tournament of Champions. These two competitions have given grooming a big boost, since it is considered the highest honor to be invited to compete, and the number of invitations issued are very limited. In the international tournament, 30 of the world's top-winning groomers are invited to compete once a year for the title of "Oster World Champion." Invitations are based on the groomer's contest wins during the previous year. The champion takes home a substantial amount of cash and an elegant trophy. The European tournament is similar, except that the 30 invited competitors are top winners from various European countries who compete for the title of "Oster Europa Champion." To win either title is the dream of all groomers.

In addition to regular competitions and invitational tournaments previously described, a special World Team Grooming Competition, held every second year (until 1997, it was held annually), moves between countries. In this exciting event, teams of highly skilled groomers from various nations compete against each other for the World Championship.

GROOMTEAM USA

As a result of the World Team Championships, a wonderful program, GroomTeam USA, was implemented in this country during the late 1980s. A group of movers and shakers in the professional grooming industry joined together to help formalize the selection process for the American team. This selection process was implemented with the creation of a point system: groomers could compete at sanctioned contests throughout the United States and be awarded a certain number of points for their wins, based on the number of dogs in competition. This has proven a fair and enormously successful project over the years. The Committee tabulates the points throughout the calendar

year (now every second year), and the six groomers with the most points become members of the squad that represents the United States at world competitions. Through the generous sponsorship of a number of concerned manufacturers, enough money is contributed to pay all entry fees and travel expenses for the entire team. It is a matter of great pride for the GroomTeam that American squads have won the World Championships many different times in many different countries. As a result of the GroomTeam USA program, regional and national competition has intensified in the USA with many groomers trying to become members of the American Team.

You may find competing to be one of the most enjoyably *tense* experiences you've ever had. You may even aspire to become a member of GroomTeam USA. On the other hand, however, even if you don't plan to compete, do go to contests as an observer. Spectators say that just watching the precision work that takes place in the ring makes them more proficient!

Figure 25-17. The 1998 Oster International Invitational Tournament of Champions winner Ann Martin, Sacramento, California. Left to right: Denys Lorrain (France), judge; Christina Pawlosky, Oster Professional Products; Masahiro Tsujihara (Japan), judge; Geri Kelly (USA), judge; and David Vallin, Oster Professional Products.

Figure 25-18. Grooming contests are excellent places to view the latest styles, especially artistic designs created by some of the world's most talented groomers. Diane Betelak of Heads and Tails Professional Grooming, Liverpool, New York, competing at the New *England Professional Pet Groomers Association, showing the beautiful "Sky Clip" that she designed.*

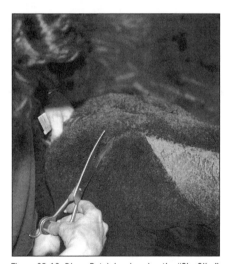

Figure 25-19. Diane Betelak scissoring the "Sky Clip."

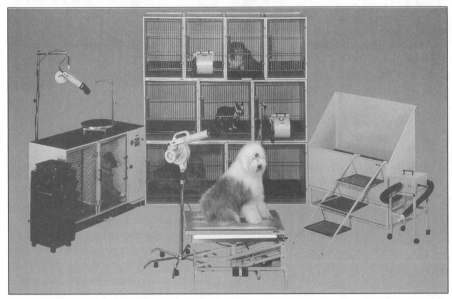

Figure 26-1. It's easy to equip a professional salon today. Some manufacturers offer total grooming packages that include every piece of state-of-the art equipment (in your choice of several standard and custom designer colors) needed to run a modern, profitable shop. Pictured here is the "Total Groom" system from Edemco Dryers, Inc., showing (left to right) The Force High-Velocity Dryer; stainless steel tub with back splash wall and animal restrainer; pet steps; nine-unit modular cage system (two shown with clamp-on cage dryers) with waste trays and floor grills; stand dryer; double-cage drying cabinet (dries up to eight dogs per hour) with grooming table top and table-mount dryer; grooming cart (for equipment storage) and, in the center, an electric table with soft diffused light that illuminates all of the dog. (Edemco Dryers, Inc.)

Figure 26-2. The complete salon system from PetLift, Ltd. is also available in your choice of several standard or custom designer colors. Left to right: roll-about caddy with tool panel; electric grooming table available in three different models (standard black top; 360-degree rotating top, or opaque Lucite lighted top); nine-unit modular cage system; wall-hung work station; walk-in shower bath with a ramp that provides easy access; tub rack; and hydraulic grooming table with clamp-on post. (PetLift Ltd.)

Groomers—working in grooming salons, boarding and breeding kennels and veterinary hospitals, as well as out of private homes and mobile units—are busier than ever before and grooming a greater variety of breeds. Dog owners have become more knowledgeable about general care, and clean, well-groomed animals are an important part of today's family life. Next to the owner, a groomer usually is the person most familiar with and to a dog. The groomer sees most groomable breeds more often than a veterinarian, often on a monthly schedule. All this has generated a demand for more groomers and promoted the growth of the profession.

Grooming is an art that requires talent and training. A groomer's skill must include knowledge of anatomy; of handling and managing dogs and cats; of grooming techniques (combing, brushing, bathing, drying, clipping, scissoring, thinning, stripping and plucking); and of other aspects of hygiene such as trimming nails, cleaning ears and eyes, skin health care, coat care and maintenance and dealing with external parasites. Today, the pet animal grooming field is as sophisticated as the human beauty business. To be successful, a groomer must be familiar with the many breeds of dogs and cats, and know how each is groomed in accordance with style and breed Standards. To ensure that clients will return again and again, a groomer *must* consistently turn out *quality* grooming. Nothing pleases customers more than to see their pets well-groomed and well-treated, especially when the pets wag their tails at the sight of the groomer or the sound of the groomer's voice!

If you have enjoyed grooming your own dog and are thinking about becoming a professional groomer, it takes time. Start by consulting books about various breeds and especially focus on the grooming chapters to get an idea of what is required, then contact a grooming school or a professional groomer to inquire about formal training. Many schools throughout the United States and Canada—indeed the world—offer courses in groomer training. Most are licensed by their individual states as private vocational schools. *Groom & Board* magazine (see the Appendix) maintains up-to-date listings of the many grooming schools currently in operation. Do keep in mind that it will take time to learn how to properly groom the various breeds of dogs. And don't forget about grooming cats. Many groomers limit their business only to dogs and miss a lot of potential customers.

The major factors to consider before setting up an area for grooming professionally are the design and decoration of both the work room and reception area. Regardless of whether you are planning to open a new grooming salon or to add grooming services to an established boarding or hobby kennel, you don't need a lot of space to start. A small, well-planned "step-saving" area that contains the proper equipment will make grooming easier, faster and less tiring for you and any employees you might hire in the future.

A bright, airy grooming area and reception room will impress your clients. Light colors either in paint, wallpaper or wall paneling create a cheerful atmosphere and make it easier from a contrast standpoint to groom dogs. Dark colors make the atmosphere dull and also make rooms look smaller than they really are. It's also important to choose floor coverings that are easy to mop and disinfect. Neutral colors, which do not readily show the soil between cleanings, are the best choice.

Good lighting and adequate electrical power (with ample outlets in strategic locations) are other musts. Electric usage in a grooming shop is high, considering the clippers, dryers, lighting fixtures, air conditioning and other equipment that constantly will be in use. An electrician can advise you on what is necessary to support the many electrical accessories used in the normal course of grooming. Consulting with an electrician before you go into business will save you considerable time, frustration and short circuits!

Arrange your reception area so that your telephone, appointment book, computer, client card filing system, and business cards are all within easy reach. When you arrange to have telephone service installed, be sure to add a cordless extension phone in your grooming room near your grooming table. When you are working alone, you should *never* have to stop in the middle of grooming, put the pet back in its cage and go to the reception area to answer the phone each time it rings. If you are bathing or drying a dog alone, leave a short message on your answering machine saying that you can't come to the phone at the moment because you are caring for an animal and that you will return the call as soon as you are able.

It's also a good idea to plan a reception area that is separated from your work room by a wall or panel. Clients should *not* be permitted to enter the grooming room because they will disrupt your work schedule. Many groomers install a "Dutch door" between the two areas. Such a door consists of two units horizontally divided so that the upper part can be opened while the lower part remains closed, allowing you to observe activities in the reception area, or to talk to customers without leaving the work area.

Furnish the reception area with several chairs, a coffee table or an end table so that clients can be comfortable while they wait for their dogs. Place copies of the latest dog magazines and books about dog-related subjects on the coffee table. Framed photographs or prints of dogs and cats, of dog show or grooming contest wins, or of your grooming work; trophies and ribbons from dog shows or grooming contests; and championship certificates and other memorabilia, all prominently displayed, will establish you as an active member of the dog world in the eyes of your clients.

When you greet your customers, you want to convey the aura of professionalism. The first impression your clients will have of your shop is your appearance. We are called "professional" groomers, therefore we should look the part. You (and your employees) should look neat and clean and wear a clean grooming uniform, lab coat or jacket. Today, many companies specialize in fashionable groomer uniforms: color-coordinated jumpsuits, jumpers, unisex jackets, shirts, tops and pants in brilliant colors, made of durable fabrics that shed hair and water easily. These can be ordered through most mail-order groomer supply catalogs.

When you plan your work area, set aside (preferably against a wall) an area for caging, for you must confine the dogs that come to you for grooming. They must be kept under control at all times; if they are allowed to get together, a fight could develop. Regardless of whether you select portable wire cages that stack on top of each other or a unit of multiple fiberglass or stainless steel models (which are easy to clean and disinfect), you should have sufficient caging available at all times. And be sure to have caging in various sizes to accommodate the breeds you will groom. Large dogs should not be squeezed into small cages where they will be uncomfortable. Fasten a metal ID-card holder or clip on the front of each cage. These will hold 4 × 6-inch or 5 × 8-inch cards which should identify the animals being caged and the work to be done on each (more about this later).

Tools of the Trade

If you are new to the grooming world and about to open your first shop, you need to assemble the proper equipment to groom efficiently. Everything you purchase should be of top quality; it will last longer and perform better. The tools and supplies you will need include the following: bathing tub, cages to house the dogs that will be in your shop, grooming tables (with posts and loops), hair dryers, clippers, clipper blades, snap-on combs, clipper oil and blade cleaner, regular shears and thinning shears, brushes and combs, mat-removing tools, shampoos, conditioners and rinses, dips, muzzles for dogs and cats, and supplies for finishing touches, such as ribbon by the roll (to make your own bows), latex bands for attaching them, or pre-made bows, neckerchiefs or bandannas.

You also must have certain backup supplies—clippers, clipper blades, scissors—so that as your business increases, and your blades and shears become dull and need to be sharpened, you will still have enough equipment to do your job properly and efficiently while other tools are out being serviced. Keep in mind that certain tools will occasionally need to be replaced: nail trimmers become dull, long brush pins or bristles begin to sink into their rubber base, bent-wire slicker brushes become loose and out of shape. All of these cause you to expend more effort to achieve results that may lead to hand and arm fatigue.

Grooming Tables and Their Placement

Your grooming tables should be sturdy enough to accommodate large, heavy breeds and should raise and lower smoothly (most from a low of 19 inches to a high of 40 inches from the floor) by foot pump or electric pedal so you can comfortably groom dogs of various heights. Thanks to some progressive manufacturers, it's no longer necessary to bend over to groom small breeds or to break your back lifting heavy dogs onto a table.

Place your grooming tables in the brightest part of the workroom. Each table should be equipped with a grooming post and loop and some other device to steady fussy dogs while they are being trimmed. For instance, special grooming saddles, haunch holders and body supports are available that prevent dogs from sitting or lying down. Plan to have your tools and supplies close at hand. Some adjustable tables come with storage drawers to hold combs, clipper blades and other small tools when not in use. Otherwise your shears, clippers, other small implements, and ribbons should be mounted on pegboard on the wall near your grooming table. You can also buy magnetic holders that attach to the wall or table to hold your clipper blades safely and securely. Tools should never be left lying on a grooming table as they can be accidentally knocked off by a dog, resulting in some rather expensive, avoidable repairs. Supplies also can be kept on racks or wall shelves near the table, or in a polystyrene grooming cart or beauty shop tray on rollers so that everything you need is within easy reach. A comfortable, adjustable stool will permit you to sit during certain portions of the grooming procedure. It's also a good idea to use anti-fatigue floor mats where you stand most often.

Many groomers like to put a mirror on the wall behind their grooming tables. Since it's necessary to look at the overall profile of the dog as you are trimming, a carefully placed mirror gives you a better perspective than can be obtained by just leaning back and looking at your work.

Every grooming table should be equipped with a post and loop. Occasionally a groomer may be called away in the middle of a grooming session. When this kind of interruption occurs, the animal should never be left to stand free on the table because he will almost certainly decide to jump off and injure himself or, worse yet, escape through the door.

Bathing Facilities

Shampooing dogs is probably the most basic and frequent service a groomer provides, therefore your bathing facilities should be both efficient and comfortable. You can have a conventional porcelain bathtub set waist high so you don't have to bend over or, better yet, you can install a stainless-steel bathtub specifically designed for animal groomers. The most popular models come equipped with a powerful spray, a wide drain with a special hair strainer basket that catches loose hairs and prevents clogging, a backsplash behind the tub to protect the wall, ample storage cabinets above and below for towel and bottle storage, and a shampoo dispensing system with adjustable trigger sprays. One professional tub made by PetLift has a built-in ramp at one end, with a trolley that slides forward and backward. Pull it out, lift the guillotine door, and the dog walks right up the ramp and into the tub without the groomer having to lift or strain. This tub is wide enough for the groomer to turn large dogs around in and lead them out and back down to the ramp.

If you opt for a conventional porcelain tub, be sure to enclose three sides in tile. With this configuration, the area remains clean and dry and eliminates the development of dry rot and places for bacteria to multiply. It's also easier to control fussy dogs. Be sure your tub is equipped with an efficient spray hose (thorough rinsing is even more important than sudsing), as well as some form of footing on the bottom, such as wooden slats, nonskid strips, or a rubber mat, to keep dogs from slipping. An anchored slip lead, a choke chain and lead, or some other control device in the tub will help steady unruly animals and keep them from jumping out while you are working on them. Don't forget a wire drain cover to keep hair from clogging up your drains. Shampoos and rinses may flow from overhead dispensing systems, or they may be stored along with your towels on nearby shelves so you can keep one hand firmly on a dog while you reach for supplies with the other. Busy grooming shops use several tubs to prevent pile-ups during peak periods. Naturally, you will need plenty of towels.

Your choices of shampoos, rinses and conditioners are a matter of personal preference, of course, and you will undoubtedly use a variety of them as well as flea and tick dips. Just remember to wear the proper protective equipment, such as aprons and rubber gloves, when applying flea and tick dips to pets. Recent case studies, reported by Rebecca Stanevich and Christine Romani-Ruby, found that many groomers who apply pesticides had dermal exposures of the hands and forearms as well as respiratory exposures, yet they often failed to use any protection.

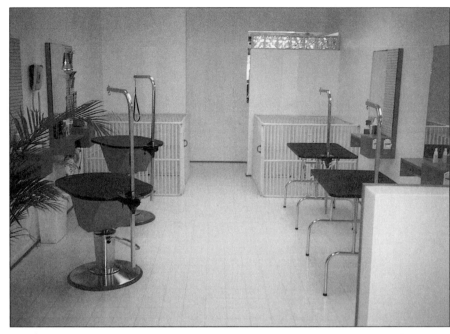

Figure 26-3. A well-planned grooming room containing the proper equipment will make your work easier and less tiring. You don't need a lot of space. Here is an excellent example of a small "step-saving" grooming salon. The front of the room contains holding pens to confine large dogs. Both hydraulic and portable tables are used for grooming in the center of the room. Behind each table is a wall styling station with a mirror that allows the groomer to view his or her work from many angles. (PetLift Ltd.)

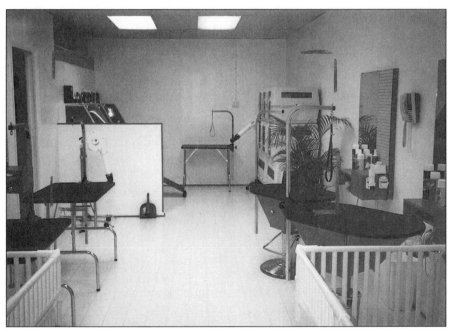

Figure 26-4. The bathing (two tubs) and drying area is located in the rear, flanked by portable Vari-Kennels to confine small- and medium-size dogs. (PetLift Ltd.)

Figure 26-5. Wall styling stations are designed to keep grooming supplies within easy reach. In addition to the mirror, there is a wide strip of pegboard for immediate use items, a Formica work top with a large drawer, a clipper holder and utility rack for ribbons and paper towels. (PetLift Ltd.)

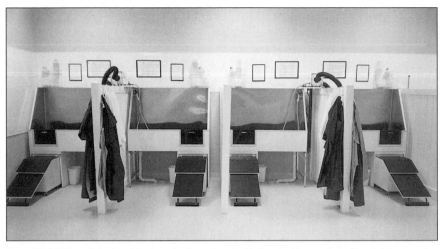

Figure 26-6. This well-designed larger salon is equipped with four bathing stations. The stainless-steel tubs have high back splashes and side walls and roll-in/walk-up ramps with sure footing. The ramps provide easy access to the tubs and fold up and out of the way when not in use. Also notice the placement of two high-velocity dryers (with flexible hoses) above the tubs, allowing the groomer to blast the excess water down and off the hair shaft after the bath while the dog stands in the tub. (PetLift Ltd.)

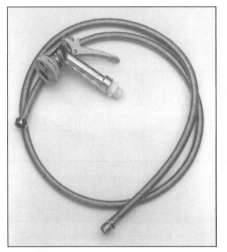

Figure 26-7. A professional spray hose with an efficient nozzle is a must in a grooming salon. Choose one with a grip that prevents hand fatigue and with different spray types that allow you to alter the water pattern and force. (PetLift Ltd.)

Figure 26-8. The large stainless-steel tubs features a high back splash and side walls and a roll-in/walk-up ramp. Inside each tub is a professional spray hose and a control device to help steady unruly dogs and keep them from jumping out. Products used during the bath and towels are within easy reach. Professionals don't have to lift large or heavy breeds into bathtubs or onto tables. The Petlift Showerbath features an access door and built-in ramp for easy entrance into or exit from the tub. (PetLift Ltd.)

The Drying Area

Once dogs are removed from the tub after a bath, they should be dried in a separate drying area. Electric hair dryers not only speed up drying time but also help to add a more finished look to the final grooming of long-coated breeds. Professional pet stylists and dog show handlers use stand dryers, high-velocity dryers and cage dryers to dry various breeds.

Long-haired breeds are usually fluff dried with powerful variable-flow stand or high-velocity dryers, while those with shorter or smooth coats are often cage dried. Most professionals agree that the final appearance of a fluff-dried dog is preferable to that of a cage-dried dog. To completely fluff dry certain "hairy" breeds, however, would take a great deal of time, which would call for additional charges. To compensate, most groomers use a combination of drying techniques involving cage dryers, high-velocity and heat dryers to achieve a lovely professional finish. Health conditions and anatomy also are important in judging which drying method should be used in each case. Dogs with cardiac or respiratory problems, dogs that are prone to seizures, and Pekinese and other breeds with brachycephalic heads (large round skulls with broad, very short and flat noses) should *never* be cage dried. Their nasal bones are small, and there is a tendency toward breathing difficulties in poorly ventilated areas.

Stand and high-velocity dryers are described at length in Chapter 2, "Selecting the Right Equipment." Cage dryers are specially designed to be attached to a cage by brackets and are used to dry smooth-coated and certain medium-coated breeds to save time. Some are shown in Figure 26-12. Like stand dryers, most cage models have a strong air output and can dry a dog quickly. Most feature the same

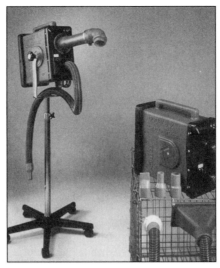

Figure 26-9. Fast and efficient drying is important, especially on heavy-coated breeds or those that are fluff dried. Electric dryers not only speed up drying time but also help to add a more finished look to the final grooming of long-coated dogs. In addition to stand dryers, groomers who will be drying dogs with long or heavy coats should invest in a high-velocity dryer, such as Double-K Industries' ChallengAir 850, that sweeps the excess water from wet hair. In most cases, this can be done after the final rinse, while the dog is still standing in the tub. (Double-K Industries)

Figure 26-11. Another professional model is this triple-headed cage dryer designed by Rapid Electric, with three separate thermostats, three separate heating elements and three individual control hoses, permitting groomers to cage dry several dogs simultaneously. (Rapid Electric)

Figure 26-10. The use of cage dryers depends on the breeds you will groom in your salon because only certain breeds, primarily those with short hair, can be dried adequately with a cage dryer. Dryers that fit all standard grooming cages, such as Double-K Industries' ChallengeAir 560, offer variable heat and air control. The temperature inside the cage is regulated to prevent hyperthermia (excessive heat) and hypothermia (low body temperature). (Double-K Industries)

Figure 26-12. Great advances have been made recently in the design of professional cage dryers. For instance, the PetLift Aqua-Dri 2000, available in various sizes, can run all day without producing excessive heat. The drying process works because of the large volume of air passing through the dryer, not by a dependence on high heat. It's impossible for the pet or groomer to get burned.

Multiple-cage dryers have separate thermostats, separate heating elements and separate hoses with individual controls. If you are drying several dogs at once, you can switch them all on. Individual controls let you use only as much electricity as you need. (Petlift Ltd.)

Figure 26-13. Edemco's Pet Step attaches to the grooming table or tub to get any large or heavy dog into place without injuring your back. Once the dog is on the table or in the tub, the Pet Step folds up. (Edemco Dryers, Inc.)

variable air volume and temperature control as the stand models. Cage dryers are safe and effective, but some precautions should be observed when they are used:

- Be sure the air circulates freely through the sides or front of the cage. If the cage is made of metal, do not cover the top and sides with towels in an effort to make the dog dry faster, as the animal could suffocate.

- Check the dog often—wet animals sometimes try to get as close as possible to the heat source. Be careful that the dog does not lean on any metal parts of the cage where the dryer is attached.

Cage drying is not recommended for breeds that are normally fluff dried, such as Poodles and Bichons Frises, or breeds with long, flowing coats like Afghan Hounds, American Cocker Spaniels, Lhasa Apsos, Maltese, Shih Tzu and Yorkshire Terriers; these dogs should be layer brushed as they dry to make their coats hang straight.

Sanitation

It is most important to maintain a clean, fresh-smelling and sanitary environment in your shop. There is no excuse for offensive odors or piles of dirty hair on the floor. Your work room and all the equipment in it should be cleaned and disinfected regularly. Cages, table tops and floors should be scrubbed and disinfected at the end of each day. Combs, brushes, clippers, blades, shears and other grooming tools should be cleaned and made ready for the next day's use. The floors should be kept as clean as possible. Pick up accumulations of hair frequently with an industrial shop vacuum so that it doesn't build up. Dirty hair begins to smell quickly. An electric deodorizer will help eliminate any disagreeable odors—doggy or otherwise.

Actually, you don't have to spend valuable time sweeping up dirty hair. Today, many groomers use special vacuum systems designed for professionals. Systems like Clipper Vac™ (manufactured by MDC Romani, Inc.) or Shear Magic™ (manufactured by Metro (Metropolitan Vacuum Clearner Company) are designed with heads that can be mounted on any clipper. Fastened to the head mount is a lightweight flexible hose, the other end of which is attached to a collection box (Clipper Vac) or any standard shop or home vacuum (Shear Magic). The hair being clipped is drawn into the hose and, in turn, into the collection box instead of falling to the floor. The vacuum lift helps you clip through tangles and under mats to better remove animal dander and saliva, dead hair and parasites and their eggs the instant the hair is cut. The constant air circulation also helps to keep clipper blades cool, no matter how long the clipper operates. Fine hairs are also kept from jamming the blades. Hair control systems such as these help to

reduce other indoor airborne contaminants—bacteria, viruses, molds and mildew, pesticides, fungicides, certain organic compounds (found in aerosol products) and tobacco smoke—that can circulate through your shop.

Appointments and Prices

One of the first details to consider before opening a dog grooming salon is to establish an efficient appointment schedule. You must plan your days efficiently so that you won't be over- or under-booked. Most groomers prefer the Week-at-a-Glance™-type appointment book which breaks down the days, hour by hour, on a weekly basis. One that is especially designed for groomers, John Stazko's Unit Grooming Appointment Book, is available from many mail-order groomer supply catalogs.

Prices for show grooming will depend, of course, on whether you are just trimming a dog for a show or whether you are boarding and conditioning that same dog in addition to its grooming. The prices you charge for grooming pets should be based on complete groomings (usually computed from four to five weeks between appointments) and are also based on overhead, the amount of time involved and, to some degree, on prevailing prices in your area. A complete grooming should include a brush and comb out, nail trim, ear cleaning, shampoo and drying, and clipping, scissoring, thinning or hand-stripping. Most groomers charge extra if a pet goes beyond the four to five week period, and also for insecticidal dips, medicated baths, skin conditioners or hot oil treatments, and for badly matted dogs (if they are not shaved down). Remember to establish separate prices for shampoos, flea dips, nail trims, and other basic grooming operations, as various short-coated will be brought into your salon from time to time for these individual services.

Make a list of charges for all the breeds you will groom and post it where everyone can see. Charge the same prices for grooming so that no one can accuse you of asking for more or less from someone else. It is reasonable to discuss charges with potential customers over the phone, but *never* commit yourself to a definite price for working on a dog that you or your employees have not hand examined. Tell the prospective client what your price ranges are, but reserve the right to charge extra when necessary.

A Fixed Schedule

A successful grooming business is run in an orderly manner. The majority of dogs to be groomed should arrive early in the morning. It's more relaxing to know that you can begin rough-cutting or mat removing early in the day. Most groomers like to have all rough-cutting, bathing and drying finished by early afternoon. Any dirty hair is cleaned away and wet towels are popped into a washing machine or hamper. You then have the rest of the day to finish your work in a clean environment. Of course, a customer often will call and want you to trim his or her dog that very day. While every groomer occasionally squeezes a dog or two into the shop schedule at off hours of the day, animals that constantly come and go interrupt your work pattern.

Finished dogs should be picked up at specified times during the day. You'll need to be firm about this with clients, otherwise some will arrive too early and expect to watch you finish grooming (which usually causes their dogs to become over-anxious about going home!) or too late and you'll be waiting after business hours for clients to collect their dogs. Late pickups are fairly common when you work out of your home or a kennel adjoining your home.

When a dog arrives for grooming, it is necessary to record pertinent information on a client card. These particulars include owner's name, address, home and business phone numbers, dog's name, its vital statistics (age, sex, breed, color, etc.), inoculation dates (dog and cat owners should show proof of current immunizations) and medical history, the veterinarian's name and phone number. The reverse side should contain spaces to record the grooming work to be done, the price(s) charged, the date the dog is groomed and the name of the groomer. Klip Kards™, preprinted forms on which you can record this information, may be ordered from Barkleigh Productions (see Appendix). Barkleigh Productions, publishers of *Groomer-to-Groomer* magazine, sells many kinds of printed forms, releases and reminder cards for groomers. You also could design your own. It's a good idea to note the color and type of collar and leash the dog wears into your shop, so that no mistakes can be made at the end of the day. You should also design a filing system that enables you to locate clients' cards easily and quickly.

As soon as the owner arrives in your shop, examine the dog's coat immediately. If it is badly matted, infested with parasites, or if there is any other condition present that would be difficult to handle, tell the client at that point, that the grooming may take longer than normal and may be more expensive than usual.

As soon as the owner leaves, take the dog into your grooming room, put it inside a cage, and slip the work card into the holder or clip it to the cage door so there will be no misidentification of the dog during the day or confusion about the work to be done. Remove the dog's collar and leash and fasten them onto the cage also. Unless the dog is on the grooming table being trimmed, in the tub being shampooed, being dried or being exercised, it should remain in its cage at all times for safety's sake. Remember: fights often happen when animals are allowed to mix. When you have your business cards printed, add the following notation on the reverse: "Your next appointment is on ____ at ____ A.M. Please telephone at least 24 hours in advance for cancellation." What better time to make the next grooming appointment as each owner leaves with his or her freshly bathed and trimmed dog? And what better way to get your regular customers on a fixed grooming routine? Several days before each standing appointment, call the owner or send a reminder card that it's time for grooming.

When the owners of dogs that were dematted arrive to collect them, take the time to find out what kind of brush or comb they are using, if any, then show them correct type and sell it to them if necessary to help make your job easier in the future.

Special Care for the Older Dog

Like humans, dogs are living longer at the present and older dogs comprise a considerable percentage of a groomer's business. Be aware of the special handling older dogs require while they are in your care. In addition to recording the dog's history, be sure to check with the owner about any unusual conditions that may exist or special instructions from the veterinarian. As dogs grow older, they become fixed in their habits and less adaptable to change. If they have become accustomed to certain

Figure 26-14. Mobile vans can offer all the services of a grounded grooming salon and more, including free delivery of pet food and supplies when dogs and cats are being groomed. Grooming conversion companies, such as Wag'n Tails Mobile Conversions (Keemah, TX), Ultimate Groomobiles (Kennesaw, GA) and Odyssey Automotive (Wharton, NJ), can help you design and build the custom mobile salon of your dreams. (Photo courtesy of Wag'n Tails)

routines and being handled by specific individuals, it is important to change or disturb these routines as little as possible. For instance, if an old dog has a good relationship with a certain groomer, make every effort to see that it is handled and groomed by that person each time it visits your shop.

Some older dogs do not adjust well to changes in their environment; such animals should not have to spend long hours in a grooming salon. Schedule them on quieter days of the week, not when you will be busy or have many noisy or fussy dogs to groom. An older dog should not be confined to a cage for a long time, especially when it must endure the barking or potentially unsettling behavior of other dogs in your shop.

If the dog has been neglected, or its coat is a mass of tangles, either clip the hair short or suggest to the owner that the untangling or complicated grooming be done in several short sessions over a period of days, rather than subject the dog to one painful or exhausting

experience. Encourage owners of old dogs to select an easily maintained hair style.

When an older dog is in your care, it should never be left standing unsupervised on a grooming table or in a tub. If the dog cannot see well, it could fall and be seriously injured. Never force an old dog to stand or sit in uncomfortable positions for long periods of time. If the dog tires while standing, give it a rest period. If an old dog suddenly becomes irritable or tries to bite, remember that it could be suffering from arthritis and has no other way to let you know that it is in pain. And one last thought: no matter how difficult any dog is, young or old, no attempt must *ever* be made to sedate it.

A Grooming Shop on Wheels

Suppose you live in an area where suitable space for your salon is impossible to find at a rent you can afford, or you want to expand your existing salon to service

customers who are unable to come to you. Why not go mobile and take your grooming salon on the road? Mobile grooming gives you the opportunity to reach many more customers than might be possible in a permanent location (especially senior citizens or the handicapped, who may not have transportation), and gives you the opportunity of providing convenience and individual attention.

The advantages of being a mobile groomer are substantial: you own your "shop," even if you are financing it, and, aside from routine equipment maintenance, repair or replacement, your only operating costs are gasoline and conventional automotive expenses. You can establish your own routing schedule, reserving certain days of the week for specific locations.

All you need to establish a mobile grooming business is a fully outfitted van. Vans for mobile grooming come in all sizes and models, from converted RVs to custom-built units, containing cellular phones to receive customer calls, carpeting, cages, a hydraulic grooming table, bathing tub, hair dryers and storage units for towels, grooming products and other supplies. Many companies that sell mobile grooming vans exhibit their vehicles at grooming shows throughout the United States. Most also have Web sites; you can search for them on the Internet.

appendix

For more information about the grooming profession and about Poodles, consult the magazines presented here. Note that the addresses listed are correct as of this book's publication date; however, businesses do move. If you find that an address is out of date, check the Internet for the current one.

The internet is also an excellent resource for further information. Just search using the key words "poodle grooming" and "poodles."

MAGAZINES FOR PROFESSIONAL GROOMERS

Groom and Board

H. H. Backer Associates
200 S. Michigan Ave., Suite 840
Chicago, IL 60604
e-mail: groomboard@aol.com

Groomer to Groomer

Barkleigh Productions, Inc.
6 State Rd., #113
Mechanicsburg, PA 17055
e-mail: barkleigh@aol.com

The Pet Stylist

2702 Covington Dr.
Garland, TX 75040

Groomers Europe

(in Dutch)
Stichting Kynorama
Annapaulownastraat 62
2518 BG Den Haag,
The Netherlands
e-mail: jetty@worldonline.nl

La Revue du Toiletteur

(in French)
Les Editions Anima Press
Chazelette – BP 10
63390 St. Gervais d'Auvergne,
France
e-mail: toiletteur@aol.com

Le Toilette Canino

(in Spanish)
Avenue Evita Perón 5492
1439 Capital Federal
Buenos Aires, Argentina

La Rivista del Toeletatore

(in Italian)
Associazione Toelettatori Italiani
Via Valclava, 20
20052 Monza, Italy

Symetria

(in Spanish)
Asociación Española de
Estilistas Caninos
c/o Mestre Francesc Civil, 5
17005 Girona, Spain

Northern Groomers

(in English)
c/o Canine Cuts
20 Bridge Rd., Colinton
Edinburgh EH13 0LQ, Scotland

MAGAZINES FOR POODLE FANCIERS

Poodle Variety

P.O. Box 30430
Santa Barbara, CA 93130
e-mail: info@dogsinreview.com

Poodle Review

Hoflin Publishing Inc.
4401 Zephyr Street
Wheat Ridge, CO 80333
e-mail: donh@hoflin.com

The Scandinavian Poodle Magazine

(in English)
c/o Karin Lilljha
Amfeltsgatan 8
S-115 84 Stockholm, Sweden
e-mail: karin.lilljha@telia.com

EuroPudel

(in German with some English)
Attention: Sigrid Kalina
Alter Weg 3
57520 Niederdreisbach, Germany

Unsere Pudel

(in German)
Publication of the Deutscher
Pudel-Klub, e.V.
Am Dock 1
26789 Leer, Germany